MACRO MODELS FOR
DEVELOPING COUNTRIES

Economics Handbook Series

MACRO MODELS FOR DEVELOPING COUNTRIES

Lance Taylor

Massachusetts Institute of Technology

McGraw-Hill Book Company

New York St. Louis San Francisco Auckland Bogotá Düsseldorf
Johannesburg London Madrid Mexico Montreal New Delhi
Panama Paris São Paulo Singapore Sydney Tokyo Toronto

This book was set in Times Roman by Automated Composition Service, Inc.
The editors were Rose Ciofalo and Nancy Moore;
the production supervisor was Donna Piligra.
The drawings were done by Automated Composition Service, Inc.
Fairfield Graphics was printer and binder.

MACRO MODELS FOR DEVELOPING COUNTRIES

234567890 FGRFGR 7832109

Library of Congress Cataloging in Publication Data

Taylor, Lance.
   Macro models for developing countries.

   (Economics handbook series)
   Includes bibliographies and index.
   1. Underdeveloped areas. 2. Economic development—
Mathematical models. 3. Macroeconomics—Mathematical
models. I. Title. II. Series: Economics handbook
series (New York)
HC59.7.T37   339.5′09172′4   78-23412
ISBN 0-07-063135-2

CONTENTS

FOREWORD

In this volume Lance Taylor provides a synthesis of the major theoretical approaches to the analysis of developing countries. In the course of demonstrating the uses and limitations of two- and three-sector models, he clarifies the assumptions made in alternative formulations and brings out the differences in their policy implications. Although not all aspects of development theory can be encompassed in a macro framework, there are few major topics that are not treated to some degree.[1]

A major strength of Taylor's analysis is its grounding in the accounting identities and typical empirical relations that characterize developing countries. From this starting point, he is led to focus on issues of policy significance and to avoid the more sterile theoretical controversies. Although most of the analytical tools demonstrated here have been applied to developed countries, a substantial effort has been made to reformulate them to fit less developed economies. In so doing, Taylor emphasizes important structural features, such as surplus labor, the distinction between tradable and nontradable goods, the terms of trade between rural and urban sectors, and the changing distribution of income among different socioeconomic groups.

One of the valuable innovations of this book is its integrated treatment of short-run and longer-term analysis. Instead of assuming a world in which prices change slowly and inflation can be ignored, Taylor deals explicitly with more typical Latin American conditions in which inflation has a major effect on both resource allocation and income distribution. Although there is still much to be learned about the mechanics of inflation in open economies, its systematic introduction into a treatise on development theory and policy is most welcome.

While some readers may find the formal presentation of economic theory rather demanding, the author is quite successful in keeping the mathematical requirements of the main text to an elementary level and in providing verbal expo-

---

[1] The scope of the volume is complementary to the author's contributions to C. R. Blitzer, P. B. Clark, and L. Taylor (eds.), *Economy-Wide Models and Development Planning*, Oxford University Press, New York and London, 1975.

sitions of the principal results. The possibilities for using the models are extensively illustrated by case studies of Brazil, Egypt, and Portugal. All in all, this volume demonstrates that development theory has acquired most of the characteristics of an established branch of economics.

Hollis Chenery
The World Bank

PREFACE

This book is about macroeconomic models designed to deal with the difficulties faced by developing countries. The problems and possible solutions covered differ substantially from those that would apply to the North Atlantic nations, precisely because economic (and political) realities *are* different in the Third World. The most salient examples are listed in Chapter 1.

Formal macro models for developing countries are a fairly recent development—a glance at the source readings cited at the end of each chapter will show that most publications have appeared only within the last decade. The material has not yet been organized into an orthodoxy or paradigm; in fact, this book attempts to encourage that process. One thing that stands out for a sympathetic outsider (like the author, perhaps) on visiting a poor country is that its academic economists and policy makers are short on algebraic or numerical tools that might help them to deal with their own severe problems as well as those posed by visiting emissaries plenipotentiary from, for example, the International Monetary Fund. Even in dealing with misled but formalized arguments from the international agencies, Third World economists are at a disadvantage because they cannot put their own accurate economic perceptions into algebra and take advantage of the quantitative insights that such translation brings. As a few people (some from poor countries) have demonstrated, it is possible to be an excellent economist without making use of any formal or mathematical models. Unfortunately, most of us—being less gifted—have to take advantage of the help that algebra and a body of formal theory can provide. This book draws together much of the existing theory and may perhaps spur the development of this theory into a more complete structure of thought.

Perhaps even more than most academic productions, this book is based on others' ideas; Americans certainly cannot claim to speak with authority about the economic problems of poor countries unless they have learned most of what they know from economists in those very countries. During the 5 years or so that the material offered here was being put together, I benefited immensely from conversations with and the published work of friends from all over the world, particularly Edmar Bacha and Eliana Cardoso (who coauthored much of the material appearing in Chapters 6, 7, 9, and 10 and corrected my errors in the rest), Sergio Bitar, Michael Bruno, Teodora Cardoso, Graciela Chichilnisky, Carlos Diaz-Alejandro, Alejandro Foxley, Khalid Ikram, Leif Johansen, Paul Krugman (coauthor of part of Chapter 4), Amr Mohie-el-Din, Essam Montasser, and Jose da Silva-Lopes. My M.I.T. colleagues Richard Eckaus and Jagdish Bhagwati have always been quick to offer encouragement and suggestions. The same is true of Hollis Chenery, who has taught me a great deal over the 10 years or so since he started advising me on my Ph.D. dissertation. Rudi Dornbusch and Bruce Herrick read the entire first draft of the manuscript, and their suggestions have helped me greatly; the same debt is due Clive Bell for his perceptive comments on Chapters 10 and 11. Irene Ferriabaugh and Feroline Whitehead did an outstanding job of typing and organizing the manuscript. Finally, my family (including the pets) viewed my involvement in the "work in progress" with the appropriate degree of amused detachment. There *are* other things to life besides writing books, and I'm grateful to them for pointing this out.

Lance Taylor

MACRO MODELS FOR
DEVELOPING COUNTRIES

ONE

INTRODUCTION AND SUMMARY

This book is about macro models designed for planning and thinking about economic problems in developing countries. The "macro" qualifier means that the models are aggregated (with only one or at most a few sectors) and focus on interactions among major groups of actors in the economy. A great deal of vitally important detail about things like choice of technology, peasant behavior, and the causes of bad health and malnutrition among the poor in Third World countries has to be suppressed in macroeconomics; on the other hand, one gains by being able to ponder the economy in broad outline, as a whole. Many of the problems faced by economists in the underdeveloped world are essentially macro in nature—obvious examples are the balance of payments, employment and income distribution, and the historically important relationships between agriculture and industry—and they should be viewed as such. The models herein should make this view from an algebraic, quantifiable angle a bit easier to understand.

1-1 THE STYLIZED FACTS

Although macro problems have always existed in poor countries, most of the analysis described in this book is quite new—the product of the last decade or less. This situation contrasts sharply with the accepted, aggregate economic canon in the developed world, which has built up fairly steadily since Keynes wrote over forty years ago. There are reasons for the lag in elaboration of models for underdeveloped countries, which may serve to introduce the problems we want to discuss.

First, there is a simple matter of idiom. Macroeconomics has been pursued in the developing world, but its practitioners have often expressed themselves verbally rather than in algebra, and they have not followed arguments through according to the rules

1

of formal Anglo-American discourse. Many of the models presented here are translations and extensions of work done by Third World economists. The "translation" is largely from words and arithmetical examples into symbols, and the "extension" takes the form of working some of their ideas out a bit more fully. That task is undertaken without apology. Economists long ago learned that mathematical formulations of their problems help clear away logical and metaphysical cobwebs. There is no reason not to apply these tools to models for poor as well as rich countries.

Second, it is certainly true that many rich-country models have been applied indiscriminately in the Third World, where their implicit institutional and political assumptions are simply not appropriate. All practicing economists in poor countries know students who return home from universities in Europe or North America and try to apply their professors' pet ideas where they are irrelevant. After a while, the students learn better and try to think about the reality they face; but the whole detour seems unnecessary. One major goal of this book is to show that one can think, in formal terms, directly about the problems of poor countries, without a long detour through North Atlantic macro institutions and thought.

In the context of model building, it is useful to think of the broad characteristics (or "stylized facts") of the economy that one wants to discuss. Some of the important aspects of underdevelopment that models should capture follow:

1. There is a series of sectoral distinctions which become of crucial importance when specific problems are discussed. Two or three sectors are often required to describe problems of underdevelopment in a sensible way, whereas macroeconomists concerned with developed countries often seem to get away with one. An important distinction (which has just recently entered advanced-country balance-of-payments papers) is that between the traded- and home-goods production sectors, with the twist that both may be highly dependent on intermediate imports not produced within the country. The emphasis on the two sectors and the dependence on imports are key to many of the models here.

   A second major distinction is that between agriculture and industry, on grounds both of technology and of widely different patterns of consumer demand. Agricultural (or more generally traditional) sectors often do not depend heavily on physical capital, and they generate much employment. Demand for their products may be quite price- and income-inelastic, and prices vary rapidly and by large amounts to clear the market. Industrial sectors may have markup oligopolistic pricing which follows completely different rules. Both sectors are important in underdeveloped countries, and their interaction is the source of many policy puzzles.

   Finally, in some circumstances, one may want to distinguish sectors producing capital and consumer goods, especially for purposes of investment planning. This disaggregation is discussed only sporadically at best in the advanced-country literature.

2. Next, there is the question, not completely resolved, of the role of money and other assets. The key stylized fact here is that, in most poor countries, money is the only domestic financial asset that anyone wants to hold in substantial

quantity. There are a number of partial substitutes which are more or less difficult to obtain: gold, durable goods, foreign currency, or bank deposits. But for most purposes, the "bonds" which enter as an alternative interest-bearing asset in advanced-country models simply are not there. Their absence makes the distinction between monetary and fiscal policy obscure, since all increases in government debt effectively have to be financed by "printing" money. Portfolio choice ceases to be the appropriate theory of money demand, and the fact that governments sometimes resort to inflationary finance means that one has to fall back on hoary theories of price increase under excess growth in money supply and commodity demand. Finally, the availability of credit enters as a constraint on business decisions much more sharply than when there are flexible markets for borrowing and lending. An adequate synthesis of all these inflexibilities has yet to be achieved, but a number of models described here seem to point the right way.

3. Distributional processes are of much greater importance in the Third World than in rich countries, where there is less class conflict and the threat of loss of subsistence is less acute. Shifts in real incomes of different economic groups—resulting from price changes against which they cannot protect themselves—become of key importance, and a number of our models focus on them. In particular, achievement of macro savings-investment equality—through inflation-induced "forced saving" on the part of some group(s)—seems to occur frequently in the Third World; it is brought into the discussion consistently here. Examples include the effect of currency devaluation or inflationary finance in shifting the income distribution against wages and toward high-saving government and capitalist classes, or the way the government must accommodate its own levels of saving or dissaving to exogenous balance-of-payments shocks. Such redistributions strongly affect the characteristics of macro equilibrium in a way ignored by the conventional literature.

4. Finally, one's style of data handling and parameter specification must be attuned to the kinds of numbers that can be obtained readily from the overworked, undercomputerized statistical services of developing countries. Time-series data fit for the estimation of econometric models usually do not exist, nor would they be relevant when structural change and political/economic disequilibriums are ever present. For these reasons, one has to build up cross-sectional representations of the economy and rely on accounting identities, stylized facts, and intuition rather than two-stage least squares in deriving parameters. A number of examples of the approach are presented to help initiate the econometrically biased reader.

1-2 SUMMARY OF THE CHAPTERS

The book is organized into one introductory and 12 substantive chapters, which are followed by seven technical appendices devoted to more complex manipulations. An effort has been made to keep the chapter presentations as readable as the subject matter allows; at worst, they demand a knowledge of elementary calculus and linear algebra. The gist of the models should come through in the chapters, but in some cases the reader will have to consult one or another appendix in order to master the models' mechanics. In particular, since such material is hard to come by elsewhere, the appendices give relatively self-contained presentations on how to use complete systems of consumer-demand equations and production functions in setting up models.

Chapter 2 begins the story with a review of national accounts methodology. The accounting system actually used stresses the role of noncompetitive imports of intermediate and capital goods in constraining macro policy choice: for that reason it is a slightly nonstandard system. Extensions of the accounts to several sectors by means of a "social-accounting matrix" are also considered, and data problems are discussed. Finally, the chapter outlines the monetary accounts, which are closely linked to the national accounts because, as already noted, the government in a poor country can often finance its own deficits only by borrowing from the Central Bank. The importance of credit availability to a full understanding of the monetary situation is also stressed.

Chapter 3 shows how the accounting framework has been (and can be) applied in two practical situations. First, a consistent fiscal and monetary package for 1976 is developed from Portuguese data actually available in late 1975. At the time, Portugal faced a severe balance-of-payments deficit; the question arose of how to manage fiscal policy (especially the government deficit) to maintain employment while designing instruments to attack the fundamental payments problem. Since not much data were available, the national accounting identities provided a natural vehicle for organizing ideas about possible policy options. This technique is stressed in the chapter. Also described is its possible extension to the monetary side, taking advantage of stylized facts about money demand and the link between fiscal and monetary accounts.

After the Portuguese example, the discussion in Chap. 3 turns to a similar exercise for Egypt, where, given data from 1975, a three-sector accounting framework was used to draw up an economic balance for 1976. Because of the sectoral disaggregation, techniques of input-output analysis had to be used. These are presented in the chapter.

Although both the Portuguese and Egyptian examples demonstrate that one can use accounting plus common sense to say a great deal about policy options in the short run, more explicit model formulations are required to answer certain questions. One vexing problem that arises frequently in poor countries is currency devaluation—how will the economy respond to changes in the internal price of foreign exchange, and what will be the balance-of-payments, distributional, and macroeconomic effects of such changes? The first part of Chap. 4 is devoted to a simple model based on the Portuguese data to show that devaluation in that country might be expected to be contractionary. That is, devaluation would drive up the internal price level against a temporarily fixed money wage, shifting the income distribution toward capitalists, the government, and foreign savers. The resultant potential increase in savings would tend to force down the level of real economic activity. Since, like many poor countries, Portugal requires a substantial level of noncompetitive intermediate imports, the output contraction would improve the balance of payments, but perhaps at high social cost.

Like devaluation, subsidies on staple food consumption have become an increasingly important policy issue, especially in food-importing poor countries hit by the commodity price increases during the early 1970s. Egypt is a case in point and, in the latter sections of Chap. 4, a three-sector extension of the Portuguese model is used to discuss the impact of possible modifications of food subsidies. Subsidy reductions are shown to be contractionary and to have potentially damaging effects on the nutritional status of the poor. This type of result depends in part on the price- and income-inelasticity of staple food demand. One system of expenditure functions through which this stylized description of consumer behavior can be incorporated into models is discussed in detail in Appendix B. Appendix A deals with some technical manipulations in the Portugal model.

Both the Egyptian and Portuguese models assume markup pricing in certain sectors. That is, the sector's output price is assumed to be based on variable costs of production (mainly for wages and raw materials) multiplied by a markup factor which takes manufacturers' profits into account. Such pricing rules are characteristic of modern, oligopolistically organized firms. For agricultural and other primary or traditional products, by contrast, prices are often determined as they vary to equilibrate supply and demand in the traditional fashion.

Chapter 5 explores some of the macroeconomic and distributional consequences of these two different pricing rules. To fix ideas about markup pricing, a simple one-sector model in which the markup rate rises with the level of economic activity is first set out. The model is then extended to an important policy problem in many countries—the interactions of price inflation and indexing of wages to protect the real purchasing power of the employed. It is shown that as wages approach being fully indexed (in the sense that 100 percent of the previous period's price inflation is made good at wage readjustments undertaken at fixed intervals), then increasing the frequency of adjustment will substantially accelerate inflation under markup pricing. Issues of worker-capitalist bargaining power clearly underlie the discussion, as do domestic-foreign relationships when the analogous policy of "crawling peg" exchange rate adjustments is considered.

As a final application of markup models, the chapter closes with a discussion of agriculture-industry relationships in a model where food prices are determined by supply and demand while there is excess capacity in the industrial sector. Distributional and aggregate demand responses to tax and subsidy tools and agricultural supply fluctuations are shown to be extensive in this case, and the difficulties of managing price policy are underlined.

The models in Chaps. 2 through 5 are "short run" in nature, designed for comparative static analysis of how the economy might be expected to respond to policy changes within a period of a year or less. In Chap. 6, we take up models designed to deal with economic growth and inflation over the medium and long run. The chapter begins with a review of growth-rate accounting, based on the identity system already developed in Chap. 2. As with the short-run models based on that system, additional behavioral assumptions must be added to the identities to obtain a determinate model. Three of the simplest approaches—the Harrod-Domar, neoclassical, and Cambridge growth models—are developed from various closure rules in the chapter. The possible uses of the models in medium-term planning are stressed.

Chapter 7 takes up an applied growth analysis and forecasting exercise for Brazil.

The chapter begins with a review of two well-known closures for growth models—the neoclassical and the Cambridge sets of assumptions—and the way in which these lead, in a simple theoretical context, to rather different predictions of how various policies might affect the growth path of the economy. Thereafter, a more complex model is developed for Brazil, with details appearing in Appendices C, D, and E. Numerical simulations show that the neoclassical variant does not adequately track Brazilian experience in the 1960s, whereas the Cambridge version of the model does. The reason is that in neoclassical growth models, investment is determined by available savings, which, in turn, is the result of economywide patterns of "productivity and thrift." With plausible parameter values, the neoclassical specification simply cannot generate the levels of investment achieved in Brazil. In other words, the growth rates indicated by this model are substantially lower than those actually observed. By contrast, investment is exogenous (or determined by "animal spirits") in Cambridge models, and the income distribution adjusts through forced saving to meet the levels of capital formation imposed on the system. With an exogenous investment demand, the Cambridge model tracks observed growth *and* income distribution patterns rather well.

Forecasts of Brazilian growth in the 1970s based on the two models are also described.[1] A potentially large balance-of-payments deficit is foreseen as a serious problem in the Cambridge specification, while the problem is much less ominous in the neoclassical version. Under "plausible" assumptions about production and demand-substitution responses to changing prices, the neoclassical variant predicts that the large payments deficit can be eliminated by a steady devaluation of the exchange rate. Since both forecasts were made in 1973, they did not take the later, unanticipated boom in coffee prices into account; hence ex post facto checking of the forecasts is not possible. However, current Brazilian developments suggest that the Cambridge pessimism is closer to the mark.

The models in Chaps. 6 and 7 involve endogenous determination of both price and quantity variables and implicitly assume that prices can adjust to close any potential disequilibriums in the macroeconomic system. Especially in underdeveloped countries, this sort of assumption is very suspect; it is useful at times to think only of quantity models while assuming prices to be fixed. With this fixed-price approach, one is forced to worry explicitly about situations of disequilibrium. Chapter 8 outlines two models that have been used widely in practice. The first is due largely to the Soviet economist Feldman and the Indian Mahalanobis. It focuses on the problems created by nonshift-ability of fixed capital, once it is installed, between sectors producing consumption and investment goods respectively. The planning problem thus becomes one of decid-ing how many "machines to use in making machines," or what fraction of investment-goods output should be assigned to capital formation within that sector. The growth paths resulting from various investment policies are analyzed, and it is shown that early concentration on capital formation within the investment-goods sector will

---

[1]Unfortunately, the data base differs from that of the 1960s simulations, since there was a break in Brazilian national accounting methodology. Extremely short time series are a perennial problem to the economists of developing countries.

lead to higher levels of output in the long run. However, in the short run, it becomes necessary to squeeze consumption in order to implement such a policy. This trade-off is emphasized, and various empirical problems that arise when one attempts to apply the model in practice are pointed out.

A somewhat similar set of options appears in the two-gap model, also discussed in Chap. 8. Here the focus is on long-term inflows of foreign exchange (either from borrowing or from foreign aid) which can be used both to complement government and private savings generated within the country and to pay for needed noncompetitive imports. In disequilibrium, there is a potential "savings gap" between the national supply of savings and investment demand and a "trade gap" between available foreign exchange receipts and import demand. Under a planned growth rate (or exogenous investment demand), one or the other of these gaps will be larger and is said to be "dominant." The economy's feasible growth paths will be determined by the dominant gap, and some residual equilibrating mechanism is implicitly assumed to operate to close the "gap between the gaps" so that they will be equal (as they must be) in the national accounts data ex post facto.

The issues posed in the short run by two-gap models appear in the balance-of-payments literature under the rubric of achieving "internal and external balance," and various adjustment mechanisms are discussed there. The real interest in the model, however, lies in what it says about the medium and long run. The main implication is that early investment in the capacity to generate foreign exchange through either exports or import substitution will yield a substantial long-run payoff. The similarity to the trade-offs in the Feldman-Mahalanobis model is clear. Both approaches emphasize that present sacrifice is required to achieve long-term wealth, and both provide alternative methodologies for quantifying the costs involved.

Despite the substantial insights that either flexible- or fixed-price growth models bring, they sidestep the role of inflation in conditioning economic change. Chapter 9 presents three models dealing with aspects of inflation in poor countries, though a general treatment is not attempted (nor is it possible, given the present state of the art). In the first part of the chapter, the relationships between credit availability and the growth in the economy are stressed. Industry's need for working capital is shown to generate a demand for credit that, in turn, depends positively on the levels of output and prices. With an underdeveloped financial market, demand for credit translates into demand for money, and the usual form of that macro relationship results. By squeezing working capital, a reduction in available credit from the banking system will immediately affect output. The implications of this reaction for policy formation are stressed.

With this "derivation" of the money-demand relationship as background, the discussion then turns to a set of three monetary and real growth relationships that are often used for purposes of "financial programming." The three equations (all in growth-rate form) are the money-demand function, a markup pricing rule, and the growth of money supply. Potential incompatibilities between the rate of inflation resulting from money-market equilibrium on the one hand and markup pricing on the other are discussed, together with their implications for the economy's real side. Overzealous application of monetary restraint is shown to be complementary to repressive policies designed to hold down money wages and likely to lead to output contraction. The similarity to contractionary effects of other orthodox policies (as noted in Chaps. 3 and 4) is, of course, pointed out.

Chapter 9 closes with a model describing how inflationary finance through the "printing" of money (or borrowing from the Central Bank) can be expected to work. Extra real spending by the government can lead to higher output growth in two ways. First, some part of the increase in government purchases can be used for investment. Second, the increased aggregate demand will accelerate the rate of inflation. If money wages lag behind the price increase, the income distribution will shift toward profit recipients. If, as usual, the saving propensity from profits exceeds that from wages, savings and investment will rise. Both processes depend ultimately on the government's creation of money to finance its deficit. Anti-inflationist economists have long pointed out that this "inflation tax" is self-limiting, since, as people observe that prices increase steadily, they will hold less money (the velocity of circulation will become greater). That increasingly compromises the state's ability to generate more investment through more spending (the point stressed in the anti-inflationary literature), but it does not necessarily inhibit forced saving through wage repression. With more repression, in fact, both less inflation and more growth follow from an equal parcel of deficit finance. Formalization of this complementarity between repression and fiscal ortho-doxy is the purpose of the model presented in Sec. 9-3.

Somewhat similar issues are taken up in Chap. 10, describing "Ricardian" models of long-term economic change. The key assumption is that the labor supply to the part of the economy which is being considered is elastic at some fixed "subsistence" wage. Over 150 years ago, Ricardo himself constructed a model in which subsistence was defined by the cost of reproducing the labor. That is, if the level of living rose, population growth would accelerate, pressure on fixed resources such as land would increase enough to reduce incomes per head, and average incomes would fall back to the subsistence floor. The same basic idea has since been taken up by other econo-mists, including Marx, who postulated that the balance of power between capitalists and workers is such that some part of the latter class is maintained as a "reserve army of labor" at the subsistence level. The main recent variant is due to Arthur Lewis, who thinks that labor in underdeveloped countries is available to a modern (or industrial) sector at a fixed cost from a traditional (or agricultural) sector. Lewis draws a number of useful policy conclusions from this observation.

Surplus labor assumptions have strong implications for the behavior of models; if the models describe poor countries at all well, there are, ipso facto, sharp limitations on the policy choices these countries can make. The first major corollary of a fixed real wage is that, in models in which "capital" and "labor" are the only production inputs, neither relative prices nor choice of technique can change. The result is somewhat formal and depends ultimately on the assumption that cost determines price in each sector, with nominal cost being a function of the nominal wage and profit rates. Fixing the real wage imposes a relationship between nominal wage and nominal price and finally a choice of numeraire defines the scale of values in the system. All prices are determined by these assumptions, and choice of the capital-labor ratio (if it can vary) follows as well.

The economic import of the result is that subsitution responses to price changes are not likely to be very important in a surplus labor system—"getting the prices right" will have little impact on the allocation of resources. As a stylized description of price responsiveness in a poor country, this assumption is probably not so bad.

A second corollary is that employment of labor in fixed real-wage models is determined from the side of demand. That is, labor supply is elastic, prices and choice of technique are fixed, and the amount of employment varies with aggregate economic activity. Employment fluctuations play a major role in determining aggregate income distribution, as the models in Chap. 10 show.

The chapter begins with a comparison of the basic Ricardo and Lewis models of economic growth, stressing the underlying assumptions of each. A growth-rate equation for the modern sector is derived in the Lewis model, and it is shown that the accumulation of fixed capital is the main impetus for economic change. The "more important" surplus labor is, the more likely it is that the result will actually come about. Some quantification of these relationships is taken up in Chap. 11.

The next topic in Chap. 10 is the effect of labor-saving technical progress. In the short run, an increase in productivity reduces labor demand and shifts the income distribution toward profits. Employment increases in the long run if a sufficiently large fraction of the extra profits is used for capital accumulation. The chapter presents a formal growth model designed to assess the likelihood of the long-run favorable result and the severity of the short-term employment losses that technical change (perhaps imported from rich countries) can provoke.

The discussion then turns to a three-sector model in which low-wage and high-wage workers have demand patterns biased respectively toward staple and luxury goods. The third sector produces capital goods, and investment demand is assumed to respond to growth in demand for luxuries. If low-wage (or unskilled) workers are in elastic supply and upgrading from the low- to high-wage class is fairly easy, it is shown that growth in the economy can lead to a deteriorating income distribution, with a small class of high-wage workers getting most of the benefits while the rest of the population is left behind. The model is too abstract and simplified for real empirical testing, but it does suggest mechanisms through which increasing income inequality coupled with a rapid growth of output can arise. A number of real underdeveloped countries are, of course, plagued by just this syndrome.

Chapter 10 closes with another, meliorist income distribution model in which "rich" and "poor" classes receive income from both wage income and profits. Savings propensities, initial capital endowments, and rates of profit on capital held can all differ between the classes; but it is shown that there are very long-run tendencies toward income equalization if the unequalizing elements in the system (such as differential profit rates) are not too extreme. The income distribution will, of course, improve more rapidly if asset transfers are effected between rich and poor. This model underlies a number of recent proposals—for example, from the World Bank—regarding policies to improve income equity in the Third World. Its empirical and political relevance is assayed as the chapter ends.

Long-term relationships between agriculture and industry are discussed from another point of view in Chap. 11. In a comparative static model with the two sectors explicitly treated, it is first shown that—*if* the terms of trade between the sectors remain fixed—the supply of labor to industry is likely to be highly (though not infinitely) elastic as long as the agricultural sector is "large." Also, the share of profit incomes is likely to be rising until the amount of labor employed in agriculture is quite small, maybe 40 percent of the total or less. Though industry may expand and create jobs, "trickle down" of the benefits to workers may be long delayed in this strict representation of the Lewis economic world.

A key assumption underlying the foregoing results is the fixed intersectoral terms of trade (perhaps imposed on the economy from the outside by fixed world prices). If the relative price of agricultural goods (or "food") is determined endogenously, then the demand inelasticities underlying Engel's law can lead to large price changes (already discussed with regard to the short run in Chaps. 4 and 5). Complicating factors—such as technical change and increasing demand by agriculture for industrial products (e.g., fertilizer)—make simple stories harder to tell, but Lewis-style assumptions may still be approximately true.

Finally, the chapter takes up the effect of movements in food prices and real wages on the "marketed surplus," or the portion of agricultural output that is actually sold to capitalists and workers in industry. Various strategies the state can use to increase surplus are discussed; these range from taxes to "dekulakization" (forced formation of collective farms) along the lines of the Soviet model of the 1930s. The relevance of the two-sector model to thinking about these major issues in a manner that is at least economically consistent is stressed.

Input-output analysis provides the natural basis for the extension of macro models from one or two sectors to several. Chapter 12 describes applications of the basic interindustry (or Leontief-Sraffa) model which are of interest for current policy issues in the Third World. The treatment is not exhaustive; rather, it emphasizes essential quantity-side relationships and the role of the interindustry system in determining both prices and the distribution of income.

Drawing on the material in Chaps. 2 and 3, the discussion begins with price and quantity relationships in the "open" Leontief system, in which the circular loop of income flows from production to factor payments to consumption to output demand is *not* taken into account. The major planning uses and problems of the open system are described, in particular how the cost equations implicit in the Leontief system can be used to gauge the efficiency of investment projects or existing sectors. The discussion then turns to the "closed" model, which treats the flows of incomes in full detail. Several recent income distribution studies in poor countries have been based on the closed model; their severe reliability problems are pointed out.

Another classic distributional issue refers to the sharing of "output" between profits and wages. In a multisectoral system, the problem of how to measure total output and real income is a vexing one, since prices shift in complex ways as wages and markup rates change. One device is the use of a "standard commodity" suggested by Sraffa, which would be produced if the markup rate over raw-material costs (assumed equal across sectors) were at its maximum value. The labor share in the Sraffa system is shown to be equal to the proportional distance of the actual markup rate from the maximum, a neat decomposition of distributional strife.

The "dynamic" Leontief model—which takes into account the accumulation of investment into capital stock—is next taken up, and characteristics of the growth paths it generates are described. Growth in the dynamic model is often unstable; various stratagems to circumvent this problem in actual planning exercises are outlined. Finally, the characteristics of the balanced growth solution are analyzed and the corresponding system of dual prices is presented. The composition of the commodity basket stays fixed under balanced growth; it shares many of the characteristics of Sraffa's standard commodity. The corresponding dual prices are shown to be potentially useful in the evaluation of long-run investment projects.

Chapter 13, the last in the book, also analyzes project criteria; it includes models of optimal growth to calculate shadow discount and wage rates that have been suggested for use in investment choice. The mechanics are largely presented in Appendix G, but the key results for the widely publicized Little-Mirrlees and UNIDO (or Dasgupta-Marglin-Sen) criteria appear in the chapter. There is also a discussion of various methods for calculating the shadow exchange rate, and observations are made on the applicability of the whole project-analysis canon to the messy real world.

1-3 FINAL HOPES

As the foregoing summary amply shows, many issues arise from economic change, ranging from the "trickle down" of income to forced saving, government-induced price inflation to the strictures of the IMF, and the problem of how to handle surplus labor resulting from a large agricultural sector or from the Soviet collectivization experiment of the 1930s. To capture all these problems with one macroeconomic approach or model is impossible at the moment and probably always will be. There is simply too much diversity in underdevelopment to fit under one conceptual roof.

Despite the fact that "the" model of economic change is not likely ever to emerge, a few key themes and techniques still underlie this book's discussion. For example, accounting identities are important as a device for structuring thought about economic problems; they offer a technique that can be put to many uses. Also, forced savings and income redistribution as prices change constitute the process that makes many of the models work. These and a few other ideas (agriculture versus industry or market-clearing versus markup price distinctions, the limitations of orthodox neoclassical or monetarist approaches, and the strengths of a Ricardian or strictly Keynesian analysis) are at the heart of all the models presented here. The author's own view is that these few ideas, artfully employed, yield substantial insights into both short-term policy choices and long-term economic prospects of poor countries. There is no doubt that not all the issues have been treated here. What *is* treated is basically an approach to these problems. After finishing this book, readers should be able to employ this approach to make useful new analyses of their countries' problems. We are, in short, offering a beginning step toward relevant macro models of underdevelopment. The book will serve its purpose well only by becoming obsolete within a very few years.

TWO

NUMBERS FOR NATIONAL PLANNING

The people charged with making short-term economic policy in most underdeveloped countries operate under severe data constraints; national accounts, the monetary and foreign trade statistics, and a smattering of wage and price indexes may constitute virtually their whole provision of quantitative lore. With so little hard knowledge, the policy team inevitably has to rely on intuition and "feel" for the economy in deciding what to do. However, even intuitive assessments are more coherent when they are organized into an analytical scheme. One such is the system of identities underlying national income and monetary accounts. Accordingly, the use of accounting-cum-intuition for the formulation of policy is the subject of this and the following chapter.

Basically, accounting schemes allow one to organize estimates of the level of economic activity from disparate sources into a coherent pattern. The fact that various subtotals in the accounts have to be equal when calculated in different ways (e.g., savings and investment, gross national income and expenditure, etc.) permits a variety of checks on the mutual consistency of the partial indicators underlying them. The same observation, of course, applies to projections of the future: if you are fairly sure about how some macro variables will change, the identities in the accounts tell you how the rest of the system will have to evolve along with them.

Some examples on the forecasting side include:

1. Plausible levels for the fiscal surplus or deficit can be estimated, given some notion of the probable size of the balance-of-payments deficit and total investment. The estimate of the fiscal deficit, in turn, is required to evaluate the macro impacts of transfer, tax, and expenditure policies.
2. The deficit enters with the balance of payments into determination of changes in the money supply, which may feed back into demand pressure on the price level.
3. Prices are also subject to cost pressures. Therefore the national accounts break-

down of production cost into wages, intermediate imports, and profits provides a natural basis for forecasting price increases from anticipated changes in the average level of wages or the cost of imports (from changing world prices or currency depreciation). Such "cost-price" estimates are naturally compared with monetary projections of demand inflation, as noted above.

4. At least at the macro level, the national accounts provide a basis for asking how the functional income distribution might change in response to pressures for more (or less) national saving. Simple sectoral disaggregation makes it possible to analyze the effects of shocks to the system—such as a short crop for the staple food—on prices and overall consumption.

Examples of this type are worked out in detail in the following chapters, after an accounting scheme is set up and described. We now turn to that task, beginning with a simple one-sector system in Secs. 2-1 and 2-2. Sections 2-3 and 2-4 take up a multisectoral extension, based on a social-accounting matrix (SAM) as a device for analysis and presentation. Section 2-5 contains comments on the data sources which may typically be used to construct the accounts in a poor country, Sec. 2-6 summarizes the salient aspects of monetary accounts, and Sec. 2-7 concludes the chapter with observations about other possible sources of data.

2-1 THE ANALYTICAL BASIS OF NATIONAL ACCOUNTS

The starting point for all systems of national accounts is a dual decomposition of the value of output into its uses on the one hand and costs on the other. We begin by describing the identities summarizing these two sides of the ledger within the accounting framework used throughout this book. Our categories and emphasis differ somewhat from those in the "standard" accounts because of the detail accorded here to noncompetitive imports of various types. Experience has shown that full disaggregation of imports is essential to planning in the Third World.

The breakdown of the uses of total supply takes the form

$$\text{Total supply} = \text{total demand}$$

where total supply = national output (including costs of noncompetitive intermediate imports) and competitive imports

total demand = private consumption, government consumption, exports, gross capital formation, and stock changes

In an obvious set of algebraic symbols, this statement is compressed to

$$PX + PM^C = PC + PG + PE + PI + P\Delta S \tag{2-1}$$

where P is the overall price level. The quantity variables (really index numbers summing up the relevant detailed commodity flows using price weights of some base year) are

X = output
M^C = competitive imports

C = private consumption

G = government consumption

E = exports

I = gross fixed capital formation (creation of new capital stock plus that part of investment going to make up for "depreciation" of the existing stock)

ΔS = stock or inventory changes (positive or negative)

The analytical fiction underlying this identity is that national output and competitive imports are sufficiently plastic to be useful for all ends: private consumption, exports, support of government activity, building construction, etc. The one-commodity assumption means that we have to consider only one price (P in the above equation) and not worry about economists' hoary trade-offs between guns and butter (or—more relevant in the Third World—starving children and big cars for the local bourgeoisie). A multisectoral generalization of Eq. (2-1) will be presented later in this chapter. For the moment, however, we maintain the single-product fiction for exposition. Later chapters will show that this assumption is often a convenient one as long as the details it omits are not terribly important in the problem to which it is being applied.

As mentioned, the left side of Eq. (2-1) is the value of total supply, calculated in practice as the value of all commodities produced nationally for final sale plus the value of imports similar enough to national products to be called *competitive*. For example, wheat imports into a country growing that crop are classified as competitive; jet aircraft imports into almost any country but the United States are not and are therefore labeled *noncompetitive* or *complementary*. Competitive imports are treated as being the "same thing" as nationally produced output, which is why they add to supply in Eq. (2-1).

The right side of Eq. (2-1) lists total *final* demands, i.e., purchases of goods which are *not* used directly as current inputs into the production of other goods. The breakdown by uses is fairly standard; we will discuss the data base underlying it shortly. Once again, the one-good assumption means that we value all these demand aggregates by the same price index P.

The second identity underlying the accounts takes the form

Total value of output = total value of inputs

where total value of inputs = wage and salary payments, payments to proprietors, payments to capital, indirect taxes, and intermediate noncompetitive imports

In symbols, it is

$$PX = wL + vN + rK + T^{\text{Ind}} + P_0 M^{NC} \qquad (2\text{-}2)$$

The classes of payments separated on the right side of Eq. (2-2) are standard but still bear some explanation. The total *wage bill* is wL, broken down into some average wage (or salary), w, times total employment of wage recipients, L. In the next term, vN is in practice estimated as the total return to nonincorporated enterprise, v being the average return of proprietors (or proprietorial families). As a share of PX, vN may be quite large in underdeveloped countries: consider the overwhelming economic importance of peasant farmers and small independent tradespeople in many corners of the world. Payments to proprietors are lumped with either the wage bill or profits in many presentations of national accounts. Such aggregation may or may not be analytically useful; if one wants to stress the economically different functions of unincorporated and incorporated enterprise, it is not.

The payments-to-capital term, rK, sums up rent, interest payments, dividends, and retained earnings of incorporated enterprise. If one has some notion of the total available capital stock (the credibility of such a piece of information will be discussed below), then the profit rate, r, can be calculated from capital payments. Note that this is profit per *physical* unit of capital, assumed to be some sort of congealed store of the single plastic good in the economy. If the capital store is valued at the price-of-everything-else, P, then it is sometimes convenient to decompose the overall profit rate as

$$r = (\rho + \delta)P$$

Here, both ρ and δ have a dimension of $1/\text{time}$. The parameter δ is interpreted as the rate at which physical capital depreciates per unit time, and ρ is the net of depreciation value return on holding capital, again per unit time. We will make use of this split of the total rental on capital into profit and depreciation components in some of the models below.

Indirect taxes (T^{Ind}) in Eq. (2-2) are the sum of sales and value-added taxes, import tariffs, and so on. In general, such taxes impinge on the production or distribution process in some way, and not on income flows. Indirect taxes (especially tariffs) are likely to be the single most important revenue source for an underdeveloped country's government, since they are easy to levy on specific commodities and do not require much auditing of books.

The final term, $P_0 M^{NC}$, is the value of noncompetitive imports used for production purposes (e.g., lubricating oil in an economy that does not produce it). As usual, we work with a volume index of such imports, M^{NC}, and an index of their cost to producers, P_0. A more complete system of accounts will also include noncompetitive imports for consumption, investment, and other uses, but we forego such complication for the moment. The main thing to remember about *all* such imports is that they are commodities *not* produced in the economy; therefore they have to be treated separately in both price and quantity accounts. They bear emphasis because they are often critically important in keeping an underdeveloped economy that is starved for foreign exchange in some sort of working order.

Finally, note that the usual aggregations of national product and income differ slightly from those outlined above, taking the forms

$$\text{GDP} = PC + PG + PE + PI + P\Delta S - (PM^C + P_0 M^{NC}) \tag{2-1'}$$

and

$$\text{GDP} = wL + vN + rK + T^{\text{Ind}} = Y + T^{\text{Ind}} \tag{2-2'}$$

Gross domestic product (GDP) is the sum of all final demands by domestic residents less *total* imports in Eq. (2-1'), a measure of the value of commodities entering the home market from home production. Its cost breakdown in Eq. (2-2') cannot therefore include noncompetitive imports. A new term in Eq. (2-2') is Y, standing for *value added at factor cost*. It is just the sum of payments to participants in the production process residing within the economy. Subtraction of depreciation allowances on capital stock from Y gives another frequently used concept, *national income* (again at factor cost).

2-2 SAVINGS AND INVESTMENT RELATIONSHIPS

So far, we have described the economy from a purely technical point of view; there are certain aggregate breakdowns of the use of product and of costs, summarized in Eqs. (2-1) and (2-2). What the economic actors who receive production payments in Eq. (2-2) do to determine the uses of product in Eq. (2-1) has been left obscure. In this section, some accounting relationships which shed light on the determination of expenditure from income (and vice versa) are set out and analyzed.

First to be considered are payments in the form of wages, proprietors' incomes and profits, or value added at factor cost. After two important items are subtracted away, value added becomes personal *disposable income*, viz

$$Y^{\text{Disp}} = Y - T^{\text{Dir}} - S^{\text{Corp}} \qquad (2-3)$$

The first term subtracted in Eq. (2-3) stands for net *direct taxes*—i.e., the sum of payments such as income taxes, corporate profit taxes, and so on—from persons or corporations to the government. A complete accounting system would also split out payments from the government to persons (social security payments, government interest, etc.), but for simplicity we assume that these are netted out of T^{Dir}. The other term, S^{Corp}, stands for corporate retained earnings *and* depreciation allowances, or "corporate savings." This source of savings is substantial in a rich country and negligible in a very poor one; its importance will vary in underdeveloped countries between these two extremes. Its measurement is complicated by the fact that some corporate saving may be credited to the public sector in countries where state corporations account for a substantial share of economic activity.

Disposable income accrues to persons and is used by them either to purchase goods for their own consumption or for savings. The relevant breakdown is

$$PC + S^{\text{Priv}} = Y^{\text{Disp}} = Y - T^{\text{Dir}} - S^{\text{Corp}} \qquad (2-4)$$

As written, Eq. (2-4) is just an accounting relationship saying that the sum of private consumption and savings is equal to disposable income. However, it can be turned into a hypothesis about behavior by making PC (or S^{Priv}) depend in some functional way on Y^{Disp}. This consumption function, in one form or another, is an integral element in the short-term policy models considered in subsequent chapters.

Besides corporations and persons, the other economic actors starring in most systems of national accounts are foreigners (who buy exports from and sell imports to the economy being studied) and the government. If imports into an underdeveloped country exceed its exports (the usual case), then in foreign-exchange terms it is spending more than it receives and the rest of the world is making up the difference. Presumably foreigners cover the country's current account exchange deficit by direct investment, commercial lending, and foreign aid. All such payments contribute to the potential flow of savings within the economy, and for this reason it is convenient to write

$$S^{\text{For}} = PM^C + P_0 M^{NC} - PE \tag{2-5}$$

where S^{For} is defined as foreign savings.

Turning to the government, we note that its receipts come from direct and indirect taxes, while its purchases take the form of government consumption. If it takes in more than it pays out, then there is government saving, or

$$S^{\text{Gov}} = T^{\text{Ind}} + T^{\text{Dir}} - PG \tag{2-6}$$

Note that S^{Gov} is saving only from the government's *fiscal* operations. Often, the state will intervene directly in the production process through corporate ownership or control, but for national accounts purposes this portion of state activity (tax and subsidy payments aside) is considered to take place in the business sector. Any profits the state makes should, of course, be considered a receipt in Eq. (2-6); its (perhaps more likely) losses are an expenditure.

In national accounts systems, there is an identity stating that savings equals investment. This rule holds in the system being considered here, but it is important to recognize that it can be *derived* from the equations already presented as an overall condition of macroeconomic balance (in economic theory, called Walras's law).

The derivation is algebraically trivial. From Eqs. (2-4) through (2-6) we have

$$S^{\text{Priv}} + S^{\text{Corp}} + S^{\text{For}} + S^{\text{Gov}} = (Y - T^{\text{Dir}} - PC) + (PM^C + P_0 M^{NC} - PE)$$

$$+ (T^{\text{Ind}} + T^{\text{Dir}} - PG)$$

$$= (Y + T^{\text{Ind}} + P_0 M^{NC}) + PM^C - PC - PE - PG$$

$$= PX + PM^C - PC - PE - PG$$

$$= PI + P \Delta S$$

where Eqs. (2-2) and (2-1) are substituted in the last two lines. All sources of saving are just exhausted by gross capital formation plus stock changes, or total investment.

The savings-investment identity

$$S^{\text{Priv}} + S^{\text{Corp}} + S^{\text{For}} + S^{\text{Gov}} = PI + P \Delta S \tag{2-7}$$

will be relied on as an essential tool in understanding how most of the models in this book function. Even without models, it can be used to explain a great deal about poor economies. For example, in the short run, a poor country's balance-of-payments deficit at something approaching full employment may well be "structural"; that is, obvious policy fixes such as devaluation, export subsidies, and import tariffs will do little toward eliminating it. Investment may also be limited by such factors as lack of managerial skill, delays in construction and production of capital goods, and limited technical expertise in operating modern plants. Development economists sum these up under the rubric *absorptive capacity constraint.* In that case, an important corollary about fiscal policy follows: To sustain economic activity, the government may be forced to run a fiscal deficit precisely because investment is low and S^{For} is so large. The deficit, of course, stimulates aggregate demand and keeps employment high. A negative value of S^{Gov} under such circumstances is far from being the "inflationary finance" it is so often called. Rather, it supports demand for domestic production against unavoidable losses of purchasing power through the trade gap.

2-3 NATIONAL ACCOUNTS FOR SEVERAL SECTORS

The analytical usefulness of the single-product accounts system has been pointed out, but it obviously cannot deal with all possible planning problems. In many cases, choices regarding allocations between producing sectors have to be made, and an appropriate data base is required. *Interindustry* or *input-output* accounting is the framework of choice.

The key assumption (still a fiction!) is that formulas like Eqs. (2-1) and (2-2) hold for each of a number of sectors i ($i = 1, 2, \ldots, N$), with the added complication that *intermediate sales* from one sector to another have to be accounted for explicitly. Examples are sales of wheat from the agricultural sector to the food-processing sector, where it is made into bread; sales of fertilizer from the chemical sector to the agricultural sector, where it is used to grow wheat; and so on. The key criterion is that the intermediate purchases are used as *current* production inputs by the buying sector. The sale of a new building from the construction sector to the textile sector is *not* a current input, since the building is a capital good that will be used for many years. Such transactions are included in gross capital formation, a category of final demand.

In input-output accounting, the analog of Eq. (2-1) for sector i is

$$P_i X_i + P_i M_i^C = \sum_{j=1}^{N} P_i X_{ij} + P_i C_i + P_i G_i + P_i E_i + P_i I_i + P_i \Delta S_i \qquad (2\text{-}8)$$

Note that all symbols are now indexed by sector and that a completely new term, X_{ij}, has been introduced to represent the *volume* of intermediate sales from sector i to sector j. In principle, each X_{ij} could be measured in a physical unit like tons or kilowatthours, but since input-output sectors are in practice quite aggregated, index numbers have to be used. Thus X_{ij} will be expressed in units like "billions of locals of 1975" or something similar ("locals" standing for "units of local currency").

A second observation is that all final sales are of product(s) of sector i, that is, stock changes of product i or sales of product i for export or investment. In the jargon, the last item is called *investment by origin.* It differs from a unit of *investment by destination*, which represents a whole package of purchases from several sectors (machine tools, construction, transportation and distribution, noncompetitive capital goods imports) tied up in single investment project in a purchasing sector. This distinction will prove vexing in the sequel.

Finally, in Eq. (2-8), sector i is both importing and exporting the "same" commodity. This surprising transaction occurs because of aggregation across goods (the steel sector exports flat roll and imports stainless), across time (agriculture exports potatoes in fall and imports them in spring), or across regions.

Just as Eq. (2-8) gives a breakdown of sales by sector i, there is also a breakdown of its costs. It is

$$P_i X_i = \sum_{j=1}^{N} P_j X_{ji} + w_i L_i + v_i N_i + r_i K_i + T_i^{\text{Ind}} + P_{0i} M_i^{NC}$$

$$= \sum_{j=1}^{N} P_j X_{ji} + Y_i + T_i^{\text{Ind}} + P_{0i} M_i^{NC} \tag{2-9}$$

In these equations, the first term on the right side sums up intermediate purchases of sector i from all other domestic sectors j. Note the distinction between the volume of purchases, X_{ji}, and their price, P_j. In effect, Eq. (2-9) says that a price change in one sector will have an impact on costs (and presumably prices) in sectors purchasing from it. In inflationary countries, such linkages have proved to be deadly to stabilization programs. Also, in the second line, value-added Y_i is revealed as the *addition* to cost in sector i after all its intermediate purchases and indirect tax payments are taken into account. Thus the origin of Y_i's name becomes readily apparent.

Input-output accounting can be extended in an obvious way to trace value-added payments back around to final purchases, as in Eqs. (2-3) through (2-7). We leave this exercise to the reader, in particular counseling that rederiving Eq. (2-7) for a multi-sector economy would be an instructive thing to do.

2-4 SOCIAL-ACCOUNTING MATRIX (SAM) FOR INTERINDUSTRY ACCOUNTS

The accounting in Eqs. (2-8) and (2-9)—with a few additional items thrown in—is reproduced in the form of a partial SAM in Table 2-1. The matrix is only partial because it does not account fully for all flows of product and income in the economy, such as those summarized in Eqs. (2-3) through (2-7). A full matrix is discussed in the next chapter.

Each row in the first panel of the table (labeled "Domestic products") is a supply-demand balance for some good produced within the economy, similar to Eq. (2-8). Total supply is given at the left; reading toward the right, each subsequent entry represents a source of demand for product i.

In the second panel reading down, inputs of value added, indirect taxes, and non-competitive imports into the production process are displayed in the columns headed "Production demands." Further to the right along these rows are the new elements in the SAM. In the value-added row appear C^Y and G^Y, respectively standing for (1) purchases by consumers of services of domestic servants and other helpers and (2) government wage and salary payments. The row labeled "Indirect taxes" includes T_C^{Ind}, sales taxes on final consumer goods. New types of noncompetitive imports in value terms are $P_{0C} M_C^{NC}$ (typically consumer purchases of luxury imports), $P_{0I} M_I^{NC}$

Table 2-1 Partial SAM for interindustry flows

	Total supply	Production demands	Private consumption	Government consumption	Export	Gross capital formation	Change in stocks
Domestic products	$P_1(X_1 + M_1^C)$ . . $P_N(X_N + M_N^C)$	$P_1 X_{11}\ \cdots\ P_1 X_{1N}$ . . $P_N X_{N1}\ \cdots\ P_N X_{NN}$	$P_1 C_1$ . . $P_N C_N$	$P_1 G_1$ . . $P_N G_N$	$P_1 E_1$ . . $P_N E_N$	$P_1 I_1$ . . $P_N I_N$	$P_1 \Delta S_1$ . . $P_N \Delta S_N$
Value added	$\sum_{i=1}^{N} Y_i + C^Y + G^Y$	$Y_1\ \cdots\ Y_N$	C^Y	G^Y			
Indirect taxes	$\sum_{i=1}^{N} T_i^{\text{Ind}} + T_C^{\text{Ind}}$	$T_1^{\text{Ind}}\ \cdots\ T_N^{\text{Ind}}$	T_C^{Ind}				
Noncompetitive imports	$\sum_{i=1}^{N} P_{0i}M_i^{NC} + P_{0C}M_C^{NC}$ $+ P_{0I}M_I^{NC} + P_{0S}M_S^{NC}$	$P_{01}M_1^{NC}\ \cdots\ P_{0N}M_N^{NC}$	$P_{0C}M_C^{NC}$			$P_{0I}M_I^{NC}$	$P_{0S}M_S^{NC}$
Total costs		$P_1 X_1\ \cdots\ P_N X_N$					

(imports of machinery and equipment items not produced within the country), and $P_{0S}M_S^{NC}$ (noncompetitive import stock changes).

Finally, note that, for each domestic sector, its total cost in a column under the heading "Production demands" is equal to its total sales net of competitive imports along the corresponding "Domestic products" row. This row-column identity represents both the basic accounting principle around which a SAM is built and a basic tool for analyzing our subsequent formal models.

2-5 DATA SOURCES FOR THE NATIONAL ACCOUNTS

National accounts in poor countries are often constructed along rather similar lines, summarized in this section. Of course, one or another country may actually do something completely different, and a potential user of accounts information in *any* economy ought to find out where the numbers are coming from before starting to work. Some guidance about the likely origins of the published numbers is all that can be provided here.

Referring back to Eqs. (2-1′) and (2-2′), note that GDP has a dual representation as the sum of total final demands or as total value added in the economy (with appropriate qualifications about the role of noncompetitive imports, indirect taxes, etc.). In principle, GDP estimates should be made from both equations independently, and both results should agree within an acceptable margin of error. Some attempt at dual estimation is made in most countries, but really independent results are usually not achieved. We will summarize the problems shortly, after first describing how value-added levels by sector are derived.

From the columns of Table 2-1, it is clear that each sector's Y_i could either be estimated directly or else indirectly as the quantity

$$Y_i = P_i X_i - \sum_{j=1}^{N} P_j X_{ji} - T_i^{\text{Ind}} - P_{0i}M_i^{NC} \qquad (2\text{-}10)$$

Equation (2-9) gives the direct estimation formula as

$$Y_i = w_i L_i + v_i N_i + r_i K_i \qquad (2\text{-}11)$$

In practice, both these approaches are used. In agriculture, for example, estimates of total outputs and prices of major products are usually constructed; these together give total sales. Subtraction of national purchases of intermediate inputs (many times based on some ancient agricultural census) gives value added. Similar procedures are often also applied to the construction sector, with building permits, cement sales, or something similar used as the output indicator.

In large-scale manufacturing, factor payment data may be more plentiful, since corporations are required to produce balance-sheet results for tax or regulatory purposes. Together with some guesswork about total payments generated in unincorporated manufacturing enterprises, the corporate data give value added from Eq. (2-11). Both approaches tend to break down for the tertiary sector, in which both corporate and unincorporated enterprise are less well regulated and obscurity prevails. Some countries go so far as to assume that tertiary activity grows "about as fast" as some average of agriculture and industry; they let their estimation procedure go at that.

Finally, note that estimates of real value added are often constructed from Eq. (2-10) by deflating both the terms $P_i X_i$ and $\Sigma_j P_j X_{ji}$ (respectively the current price values of output and intermediate inputs in sector j) by some appropriate price indexes. Sometimes this "double deflation" procedure gives *negative* estimates for real value added. This paradox is related to similar negative estimates of shadow prices in investment project analysis or negative effective rates of protection in foreign trade calculations; it is discussed in Chap. 12.

On the demand side of the accounts, Eq. (2-1$'$) shows that GDP is the sum (minus imports) of expenditures on personal consumption, government consumption, exports, gross capital formation, and stock changes. All these quantities should be estimated, including the entries C^Y, G^Y, etc., in the lower right-hand panel of Table 2-1.

The standard approach is to estimate final demands using the "flow of product" method, which amounts to monitoring sales of a large, representative sample of consumption and investment goods and extrapolating to get total demands. Such information can be supplemented by consumer expenditure and government budgetary information to get consumption estimates. Data on building permits and capital import licenses may help clarify the investment picture. Unfortunately, neither flows of products nor government licenses provide much information about small on-the-farm construction projects, e.g., terracing, land-leveling, maintenance and construction of irrigation canals, and so on. Given that the rural sector makes up one-half or more of the economic activity in many poor countries, one suspects a strong bias toward underestimation of total investment demands (and the corresponding savings flows).

The big trouble with the flow-of-product method is that such data are *not* routinely collected in underdeveloped countries, since they are of no direct use to tax or regulatory agencies. (National accountants are always stringing together their estimates on the basis of other people's data, even in the best of circumstances.) Typically, solid estimates of final sales of products come only out of industrial or agricultural censuses, which are taken infrequently (every 5 or 10 years, perhaps). Between these census baselines, crude extrapolation is often the only method that can be used to come up with flow-of-product information. For this reason, the demand side of the accounts is on far weaker empirical ground than value added.

This problem is often "solved" by assuming that investment, exports, imports, and government expenditure are better known than personal consumption, so that the latter is calculated as a residual, i.e., GDP from Eq. (2-2$'$) minus all the items on the right side of Eq. (2-1$'$) except *PC*. Naturally, this piles all the errors in the other estimates into consumption; it makes the use of consumption functions and similar constructs in short-term policy planning a hazardous business. The same caution applies to estimates of capital stock depreciation and stock changes. The former is often computed as some constant share of either gross investment or GDP, and the latter is a blowup of very partial and perhaps misleading indicators (e.g., the Brazilian accounts use only changes in *coffee* stocks and let inventories in the other 98 percent of the economy go by the board).

The uncertainty about consumption and some components of total investment naturally carries over into the savings-investment identity Eq. (2-7). For example, if one believes the available numbers about investment and the balance-of-payments deficit (more on the latter shortly), then national savings becomes a residual. Its size is reduced by independent computation of the consolidated fiscal surplus, or total government savings, and reduced further still by a guess at corporate saving. This latter will, of course, include depreciation allowances; in an inflationary setting, companies themselves may well be understating "true" depreciation because they are carrying their capital assets at original purchase prices ("book values") instead of current values. Similarly, they may be using first-in-first-out (FIFO) instead of last-in-first-out (LIFO) rules for valuing inventories. With inflation, the former underestimates the current value of stocks but has at times been required by law as an "anti-inflationary" device. It is not clear that forcing firms, for accounting purposes, to understate their requirements for working capital is a good way to hold down price increases.

The ultimate residual after all these subtractions is personal saving, for which very few direct checks exist in a semimonetized economy. (Recall the problems discussed above of measuring rural savings-investment activity.) Personal savings may or may not be a large share of the total flow of resources in a poor country, but it is bound to be one that is known very imperfectly.

The only valid observation that one can make a priori about the reliability of data on foreign trade is that they can be good, bad, or perfectly horrid. The two main sources of information—usually not consistent in either coverage or timing—are the customs service and the import and export licensing authorities. Only in-country experience can tell which, if either, is more reliable. And for any source of foreign trade data, three specific problems arise.

First, underinvoicing of imports, overinvoicing of exports, and other forms of *transfer pricing* may be rife in economies with foreign-exchange controls. It is very difficult to correct for such falsification (and for plain old smuggling as well), but the problem should at least be recognized.

Second, customs data often provide information only on imports by type (i.e., by origin), whereas, for planning purposes, one often wants imports grouped by different using sectors or economic activities (i.e., by destination, as in the "Noncompetitive imports" row of Table 2-1). Sometimes this problem can be circumvented with the help of special surveys or import license information.

Third, customs data are often organized by a different classification scheme than production data. Then a conceptually trivial but extremely tedious reclassification may be required to marry the two sources of data in an input-output accounting framework like that of Table 2-1.

A final word on national accounts is that we can not only estimate GDP from both value-added and demand sides but also check the two estimates against each other at a *disaggregated* level by using an input-output matrix, as in Table 2-1. To date, it is simply impossible to refine the national accounts numbers to such a degree with data from underdeveloped nations, but the hope always remains.

2-6 THE MONETARY ACCOUNTS

Most countries have a central bank, and it is in the nature of such institutions to keep records of the financial flows they regulate. Monetary data are often embarrassingly (and uselessly) abundant in poor countries, but they are collected fast and have their own built-in checks. For those reasons, such data serve as a useful supplement to the national accounts as a basis for short-run policy decisions. In this section, we first set out a framework for monetary accounts and then discuss its planning applications.

Table 2-2 represents a consolidated balance sheet for a banking system typical of a poor country. On the left are *assets* of the various entities, i.e., their claims on stores of value in the form of the various financial instruments listed. On the right are their *liabilities*, or the financial claims on them by somebody else.

Most economic actors have assets equaling claims against them as long as assets include net worth. However, in the monetary accounts, two entities often assume net deficit or surplus positions. First, the government is a net debtor to the rest of the system. The debt item D in its liability column is not offset by any monetary asset; this is a simple representation of the fact that faith in the government is the basis of any system of fiat money.

Table 2-2 Balance sheet for the monetary sector*

Rest of the world			
Net credit to private sector	Z	Net foreign-exchange deposits	F

Government			
		Outstanding government debt	D

Central Bank			
Net foreign reserves	F	Currency and coins	C
Credit to public sector	D	Reserves for demand deposits	q_1
Credit to private sector	S	Reserves for near money	q_2
Rediscount	R		

Commercial banks			
Reserves for demand deposits	q_1	Demand deposits	Q_1
Reserves for near money	q_2	Near money	Q_2
Lending to private sector	L	Rediscount	R

Private sector			
Currency and coins	C	Credit from Central Bank	S
Demand deposits	Q_1	Credit from commercial banks	L
Near money	Q_2	Credit from abroad	Z

*Total assets of monetary system = $F + D + S + L$
Total liabilities of monetary system = $C + Q_1 + Q_2$

Second, the rest of the world can easily be in a net debtor or creditor position with respect to "our" country—net claims worldwide must sum to zero, but such equilibrium is certainly not required of any single economy. Table 2-2 presupposes that foreigners have lent a total of Z to the private sector but that they owe the Central Bank a quantity of reserves, F, deposited abroad. There is no particular reason for $Z - F$ to equal zero.

For everyone else in the system, assets equal liabilities. For example, for the private sector we have

$$C + Q_1 + Q_2 = S + L + Z \tag{2-12}$$

Similar identities hold for the commercial banks,

$$q_1 + q_2 + L = Q_1 + Q_2 + R \tag{2-13}$$

and for the Central Bank,

$$F + D + S + R = C + q_1 + q_2 \tag{2-14}$$

For the monetary system as a whole, assets include foreign reserves and government debt, $F + D$, and outstanding credit to the private sector, $S + L$. The system's liabilities are made up of currency and coin, C; demand deposits, Q_1; and *near money* or various forms of time deposits, Q_2. The money supply itself is usually defined as either

$$H_1 = C + Q_1 \tag{2-15}$$

or

$$H_2 = C + Q_1 + Q_2 \tag{2-16}$$

There are two important stylized facts about the monetary systems of underdeveloped countries which are built into Table 2-2. First, the fiscal authorities are assumed to operate only through the Central Bank and do not issue obligations directly to the private sector; there is no market for government bonds. The major implication is that government deficits can be met only through Finance Ministry borrowing from the Central Bank; that is, there is a direct linkage between government saving or dissaving and changes in the Central Bank's holdings of government debt.

Similarly, a current account balance-of-payments deficit has to be "financed" by a rundown of the Central Bank's reserves, F, or else by an increase in foreign lending, Z, to the private sector (say in the form of supplier's credits on import purchases). Since foreign borrowing by the private sector or semipublic agencies is usually tightly controlled in poor countries, balance-of-payments movements also tend to be linked directly to changes in the Central Bank's asset position.

The easiest way to see how the money supply is determined is through analysis of the Central Bank's (monetary) liabilities, often called high-powered money or the *money base, B*:

$$B = C + q_1 + q_2 \tag{2-17}$$

For expositional purposes, let us blur the distinction between sight and time deposits and rewrite Eq. (2-17) as

$$B = C + q \qquad (2\text{-}18)$$

where q is the total of reserves deposited by commercial banks with the Central Bank. If Q is the total of public deposits at commercial banks, the money supply becomes

$$H = C + Q \qquad (2\text{-}19)$$

Finally, we may define two useful parameters as $c = C/Q$, the currency-deposit ratio, and $r = q/Q$, the reserve-deposit ratio.

We want to express total money supply, H, as a function of Central Bank liabilities, B. From Eqs. (2-18) and (2-19) we get

$$\frac{H}{B} = \frac{C + Q}{C + q}$$

If both sides of this equation are first multiplied by B and top and bottom on the right side are then divided by total deposits, Q, the result is

$$H = \frac{c + 1}{c + r} B = mB \qquad (2\text{-}20)$$

which expresses money supply as a multiple, m, of the base. Since $r < 1$ in a fractional reserve banking system, m exceeds unity and $H > B$. Total money supply exceeds the base because of credit creation by the commercial banks.

The total credit that banks provide to the private sector (L in Table 2-2) is seen to be equal to bank deposits less reserves (if we ignore the rediscount item for simplicity):

$$L = Q - q$$

Adding and subtracting currency on the right-hand side gives

$$L = (Q + C) - (q + C) = M - B \qquad (2\text{-}21)$$

so that commercial bank credit is equal to the money supply less the money base. Evidently, Eq. (2-20) can be rewritten as a credit-to-base multiplier formula,

$$L = \frac{1 - r}{c + r} B \qquad (2\text{-}22)$$

which shows that an expansion of money base will lead to larger (smaller) growth in credit to the private sector as the reserve ratio r is smaller (bigger). We take up in Chap. 9 the influence of available credit on the level of economic activity, based on the idea that much of total lending, L, goes for working capital in a poor country. Contraction of L can have rapid impacts on economic activity by directly affecting the ability of firms to finance their production process.

Equation (2-20) shows quite clearly that the Central Bank can influence the money supply (or available credit) either by changing its monetary liabilities, B, or by shifting the parameters of the multiplier m. There are several ways in which it can do this:

First, since the Central Bank's assets equal its liabilities, any change in its asset position will affect the money supply. For example, the Finance Ministry may sell bonds worth a billion locals to the Central Bank to finance an irrigation project. The money is paid to the project contracting company, which deposits the money with its commercial bank, which in turn deposits the billion locals with the Central Bank. Hence, both D and, say, q_1 in Table 2-2 increase by equal amounts. Further lending from its new deposits by the commercial bank and subsequent transactions increase the total money supply by something more, as in Eq. (2-20).

In practice, the Central Bank modifies its asset position by buying or selling government obligations or by expanding or contracting its credit to the private sector or the quantity of commercial bank paper it is willing to rediscount. The last two options are feasible in countries with underdeveloped capital markets—you can usually find some entrepreneur to lend to and can rediscount old laundry bills if necessary—but the first one is not if there is no functioning market for government bonds. The impossibility of *open market operations* in bonds is a severe constraint, emphasized throughout this volume, on Central Bank operations.

The other way the Central Bank can modify the money supply is through shifting the parameters underlying the multiplier m in Eq. (2-20). Reserve ratios q_1/Q_1 and q_2/Q_2 can be changed through regulations for commercial banks, and public taste about the form in which to hold money can be manipulated within limits by propaganda and persuasion. However, the limits are often very tight.

The key conclusion to be drawn from this discussion is how *little* control the Central Bank of Table 2-2 has over the money supply. The two biggest components of its portfolio are likely to be government debt and foreign reserves, and fluctuations in these holdings may be completely beyond its control. The Bank has to "print" money by absorbing government obligations if the Finance Minister orders it to do so, and it has no possibility of subsequently contracting the money supply by selling in the open market. Similarly, it has little influence on the current account deficit and resulting foreign currency movements. Shifts in reserve requirements are a rather clumsy tool; if public demand for loans is not high, rediscount may be ineffective. The total supply of credit in the economy is determined by agents other than the Central Bank, and the money supply along with it.

"Endogeneity" of the money supply arises because of its close linkages with the balance-of-payments and fiscal deficits characteristic of many poor countries. Such lack of flexibility makes monetary programming difficult, but it does help in the construction of monetary checks on price and quantity projections coming from other sources. For example, in the next chapter we will compare projections of base creation from the standpoint of money demand on the one hand and balance of payments and fiscal projections on the other. If the two projections turn out to be "badly" inconsistent, there is good reason to go back and think through the whole exercise one more time.

2-7 OTHER KINDS OF DATA

Besides national accounts and the monetary statistics, other sources of data can be extremely useful in planning. Sometimes they are even trustworthy. In this section, the types of numbers available in poor countries are summarized, along with warnings about their probable quality.

For medium-term planning, it is necessary to know something about the processes of capital accumulation and population growth. Estimates of these (and other) stocks can be built up by the *perpetual inventory* method—one begins with an estimate of the variable(s) of interest, say population by 1- or 5-year cohorts, in some base year. The estimate is then updated by adding new entrants into the cohort (through births, aging, or immigration) and subtracting leavers (through deaths, aging, or emigration). Capital-stock data can be updated in a similar way—by adding gross investment and subtracting depreciation to go from one year to the next—although the variable usually considered is the total stock as opposed to age cohorts of capital goods (or "vintages").

The major problem is getting a reliable estimate of the stock in the base year. For populations, a demographic census may provide enough information. For capital (leaving aside all index number and aggregation problems), a census of manufacturing or agriculture may be the basic source. Alternatively, standard economic growth models can be applied "in reverse" to come up with capital-stock estimates, as discussed in Chap. 5.

Both short- and medium-term planning also require labor-force data: unemployment, labor-force participation rates by relevant socioeconomic categories, "underemployment," and so on. Sample surveys are usually the data sources for such variables; there are the usual problems of assessing the reliability of interviews, trying to see whether the concepts (unemployment, participation, etc.) used in the survey are really useful for planning purposes, blowing up the survey results to draw inferences about the total population, and so on.

Much the same sorts of observations apply to short-run economic indicators such as cement sales, electricity use, railroad movements, and others. Aside from the monetary statistics, such numbers may constitute the only information on economic activity which is collected rapidly and regularly. It may *not* be collected reliably, but that is something which only firsthand experience within a given country can reveal.

SELECTED ADDITIONAL READINGS

Blitzer, Charles R., Peter B. Clark, and Lance Taylor: *Economy-Wide Models and Development Planning*, Oxford University Press, New York and London, 1975. (A collection of interrelated papers surveying the current state of the art in the design and use of multisectoral planning models. Among others, Chaps. 3 through 7 describe data problems in developing countries.)

Burger, Albert E.: *The Money Supply Process*, Wadsworth, Belmont, Calif., 1971. (An exhaustive treatment of the topic.)

Dornbusch, Rudiger, and Stanley Fischer: *Macroeconomics*, McGraw-Hill, New York, 1977. [A clear, modern text written from the viewpoint of an advanced country. Chaps. 2, 8, and 18 (on the national accounts, the money supply process, and balance-of-payments analysis, respectively) are helpful.]

Pyatt, Graham, and Erik Thorbecke: *Planning Techniques for a Better Future*, International Labor Office, Geneva, 1976. (Brief, illuminating introduction to the use of social accounting matrices in planning.)

Rosen, Sam: *National Income and Other Social Accounts*, Holt, Rinehart and Winston, New York, 1972. (A textbook on accounting techniques. Clear, but focused on the United States system.)

United Nations: *A System of National Accounts*, ST/STAT/SER.F/2/Rev.3 (Sales No.: E.69.XVIII.3), New York, 1968. (A manual for the currently recommended system of accounts for all countries.)

THREE

CONSISTENT SHORT-TERM PROJECTIONS USING RUDIMENTARY DATA

The only way to find out how the accounting schemes of the last chapter work is to try them out with real numbers. This chapter undertakes that task, from two angles. First, we work through two short-term planning exercises based on explicit schemes for national income and monetary accounts. The basic goal of both is to construct consistent short-term forecasts of the future, or "backcasts" of the recent past, using incomplete data but relying on the identity restrictions of the accounts to close the empirical gaps. Inevitably, guesses about behaviorial economic parameters are brought into the analysis as well, but their role should be clear.

The two exercises demonstrate that besides the identities, various tests of "reasonableness" have to be applied to the numbers. In any country, whether or not a bit of information can be judged reasonable depends on the economy's own history and how well the information fits generalizations from experience elsewhere. "Stylized facts" (or better, "stylized parameters") describing representative developing economies are an essential component in any planner's kit of tools. The chapter closes with a review of attempts at describing stylized parameters in "patterns of growth" studies, and the reference list gives sources.

The first example refers to a semi-industrial economy, Portugal, using numbers produced there in late 1975 as part of an assessment of that country's prospects for the following year.[1] The focus is on the design of a consistent monetary and fiscal policy package to cope with historically unprecedented balance-of-payments deficits. The second exercise is the construction of a set of national accounts for Egypt in

---

[1] The source for the data about Portugal, described below, is a report to the Bank of Portugal by Richard Eckaus, Rudiger Dornbusch, and Lance Taylor. Teodora Cardoso of the Bank of Portugal contributed at least as much as its authors to preparing the report.

1976, on the basis of similar numbers from 1975.[2] The 1976 projection is generated from a social accounting matrix and illustrates how to manipulate numbers in a SAM. Some description of the economic problems facing both countries, of course, enters the discussion, but primary emphasis will be on techniques.

3-1 PAYMENTS PRESSURES IN PORTUGAL

Table 3-1 presents a series of annual estimates of Portuguese national accounts. The numbers for 1973 and 1974 are "official" historical data, while 1975 estimates were built up from 1974 by methods similar to those described in the exercise for Egypt, discussed below. There are two sets of projections for 1976 (I and II, respectively), in turn derived from the estimates for 1975. All the aggregates are in billions of Portuguese escudos, or millions of "contos." In 1975, one conto equaled about 35 United States dollars.

Several important characteristics of the Portuguese economy can be read out of Table 3-1. First, there is a rapid deterioration in the balance of payments (for goods and services). Imports grow from $1\frac{1}{4}$ times exports in 1973 to more than double in one of the projections for 1976. This shift reflects the changes in world food and oil prices after 1973 and some loss of export markets after the Portuguese revolution of April 25, 1974. Along with many other small importing countries, Portugal suffered a virtually unavoidable collapse in its payments position in the mid-1970s.

Second, investment declined and real consumer expenditure grew substantially after 1973. The fall in capital formation reflects fear of revolutionary change by capitalists and entrepreneurs; the increase in consumption followed such income redistribution as the revolution did achieve. The direction of the consumption shift seems clear, but its magnitude is harder to judge. Consumption is estimated as a residual in Portuguese accounts and implicitly includes inventory changes as well.

---

[2]The 1975 accounts are the basic data source for a planning model of Egypt described in the next chapter.

Table 3-1 Portuguese national accounts*

	Consumption	Investment	Government	Exports	−Imports	Gross domestic product
1973 in 1973 prices	206.8	36.6	38.2	76.2	−94.7	283.1
1974 in 1974 prices	292.4	72.9	46.0	92.3	−146.6	357.0
1975 in 1974 prices	304.1	43.7	46.0	59.3	−105.1	347.0
1975 in 1975 prices	364.9	52.4	55.2	65.2	−116.7	421.0
1976-I in 1975 prices	375.8	92.8	60.0	66.3	−150.3	444.6
1976-II in 1975 prices	375.8	86.5	60.0	77.6	−147.7	452.2

*Units are millions of "contos," or billions of Portuguese escudos.

Third, the consumption increase did not offset the decline in investment completely, and GDP fell during 1975. The 1976 projections include some modest recuperation (which actually did occur), but overall growth is not large.

Table 3-2 summarizes the effect of these changes—in the form of a time series of savings-investment identities—on macroeconomic balance. The year 1973 was typical of the Portuguese ancien regime in that a substantial deficit in foreign trade of goods and services (18.5 million contos) was offset by 27 million contos of remittances from emigrant workers. There was a net surplus of 8.5 million on current account, or negative foreign savings. As a matter of the arithmetic summarized in Eq. (2-7), the sum of government and private savings had to be positive to support investment at home and abroad through the trade surplus. As it turned out, even the government ran a small surplus.

After 1974, the situation altered dramatically. The current account surplus evaporated as the terms of trade shifted against Portugal, the world recession set in, and emigrant remittances under the specter of revolution shrank. The current account shifted 35 million contos toward deficit between 1973 and 1975; in real terms, investment fell. Since private savings, at least, continued positive, the only free variable in the system was the fiscal deficit. To maintain aggregate demand, the government had no choice but to run deficits, which show up clearly in 1975 and in both projections for 1976. As already pointed out in Chap. 2, a budget deficit is the way of life in countries with chronic balance-of-payments difficulties and weak investment demand.

How could the government budget deficit be realized? Table 3-3 provides some information for 1975 and 1976. In 1975, the government supported a substantial burden of transfer payments, in effect by deficit finance. Transfers increased dramatically after the revolution, to the benefit of social welfare and aggregate demand but to the detriment of "sound" fiscal policy.

The two projections for 1976 differ mostly in their assumptions about foreign trade. In Projection I, exports were assumed to maintain their 1975 volume in real terms, while imports were to rise substantially because of bad harvests and a resurgence in investment demand. Like most small countries, Portugal is greatly dependent on capital goods from abroad. The stylized fact is that about half the country's investment spending goes for imports, so that the assumed 40-million-conto increase in investment demand translates automatically into 20 million more contos of trade deficit. Projec-

Table 3-2 Portuguese savings-investment balances, 1973–1976*

	1973	1974	1975	1976-I	1976-II
Private saving	57.5	50.9	44.5	50.0	50.0
Government saving	7.6	−4.1	−20.0	−17.6	−10.0
Current account deficit	−8.5	26.1	27.9	60.4	46.5
Imports less exports	18.5	54.3	51.5	84.0	70.1
Less remittances	−27.0	−28.2	−23.6	−23.6	−23.6
Total investment	56.6	72.9	52.4	92.8	86.5

*1973–1975 in millions of contos of each year. 1976 estimates in millions of 1975 contos.

tion II is more bullish on export recovery (alas, with a 40 percent import content also) but assumes that investment would not grow by quite so much as in Projection I.

A quick glance at Table 3-2 shows that the two projections have different implications for fiscal policy. The big balance-of-payments gap in Projection I requires a large government deficit to achieve macro consistency; less deficit finance is required in Projection II because foreign savings is assumed to be lower. The implication in Table 3-3 is that, with taxes and other expenditure items held at "reasonable" levels for 1976, transfers would have to fall substantially in Projection II. An increase in aggregate demand from sales abroad means that fewer people and enterprises have to be maintained on the dole. Correspondingly, the government cash deficit is 7.6 million contos less in Projection II than in I.

As already noted in Sec. 2-6, government cash deficits (i.e., current expenditure deficits plus investment finance) in countries with underdeveloped capital markets lead almost automatically to equal increases in the money base; foreign reserve losses do the opposite. To trace through the monetary implications of our two projections, it is useful to begin with a look at recent historical statistics. Table 3-4 provides the relevant numbers.

The first point to note in the table is the big increase in the share of currency in the money supply after the revolution; as a fraction of the base, currency went up by almost 45 percent between 1973 and 1975. Such a shift should be expected for at least two reasons—(1) all people prefer cash in hand to checking deposits in the bank in unruly situations and (2) poor people who benefit from income redistribution do not have deposits in the first place—but it does make monetary policy more difficult. The resulting decrease in money multipliers means that equal changes in base have less overall effect on the money supply. Moreover, any reversal or slowing down of these trends could cause fluctuations in the money multiplier that would be extremely difficult to predict, making policy formulation that much more uncertain.

Second, note how *money velocity*—the ratio of GDP to some money supply concept such as M_2—rose after the revolution. The increase can be interpreted as the outcome of several partially conflicting forces. On the one hand, money demand might be expected to go up (and velocity to fall) as a result of income redistribution.

Table 3-3 Portuguese government accounts, 1975–1976*

	1975	1976-I	1976-II
Transfers	57.7	53.1	45.5
Government consumption	55.2	60.0	60.0
Government investment	13.0	25.0	25.0
Total expenditure	125.9	138.1	130.5
Direct tax	45.0	46.5	46.5
Indirect tax	37.6	40.0	40.0
Miscellaneous revenues	10.3	9.0	9.0
Cash deficit	33.0	42.6	35.0

*Millions of 1975 contos.

Table 3-4 Portuguese monetary survey, 1973–1976*

	1973	1974	1975	1976-I	1976-II
Base	67	79	104	(134)	(137)
Currency	37	55	93		
M_1	141	165	198		
M_2	268	318	360	(464)	(472)
Currency/base	0.552	0.696	0.894		
M_1/base	2.104	2.089	1.904		
M_2/base	4.000	4.025	3.462	(3.45)	(3.45)
Gross domestic product	283.1	357.0	421.0	533.5	542.6
M_2 velocity	1.056	1.123	1.169	(1.15)	(1.15)

*Monetary aggregates are in millions of contos and are yearly averages. Twenty percent inflation is assumed for 1976.

Suppose that the relatively poor people benefiting from redistribution treat money as a "luxury"—i.e., have a higher income elasticity of demand for money than do the relatively well-to-do—because the latter have other assets such as real estate or consumer durables in which to hold their wealth. Then, as income is shifted from rich to poor, money demand might be expected to rise.[3]

On the other hand, money demand might be expected to fall (velocity to rise) as inflation accelerated in response to increased import costs and wage push. Most countries' experience would seem to show that if the rate of inflation jumps by X percent per year, money demand might fall by $0.1X$ or $0.2X$ percent. If the value of the money they hold starts to go down faster, most people prefer to retain less of the stuff.

On balance, redistribution was completed in 1975, but inflation rolled on. For simplicity, assume that the velocity in 1976 would stabilize at 1.15 and the money multiplier at 3.45 as the run to currency would peter out. The resulting estimates of the *demand* for money base (with 20 percent price increases forecast for 1976) appear in the top line of Table 3-4. *Supply* of money base would decline because of reserve losses (equal to the current account deficit from Table 3-2 less capital inflows in the form of suppliers' credits on investment-good imports), but it would increase because of the government cash deficit (Table 3-3). The residual item required to bring supply of base in line with projected demand is the change in other Central Bank assets, mainly rediscount. The required increases in rediscount for the two projections are calculated in Table 3-5.

[3]Assume a population made up of workers and capitalists. After redistribution, the income share of the former goes up from 45 to 65 percent. Also assume that before redistribution workers held 60 percent of M_2 and that their income elasticity of money demand is 1.0 while that of capitalists is 0.5. Note that money demand will increase by about 20 percent because of redistribution.

**Table 3-5 Projected sources of Portuguese
money creation, 1976***

	1976-I	1976-II
Change in base	30	33
Government		
cash deficit	51.1	42.0
Reserve loss	−52.8	−37.2
Current account	−72.5	−55.8
Capital inflow	19.7	18.6
Change in rediscount	(31.7)	(28.2)

*Assumes 20 percent inflation in 1976.

In projection I, reserve losses almost equal the fiscal cash deficit. Hence, rediscount plays the major role in increasing the money base. What this financial flow really represents is lending from the commercial banks to private firms with low demand and high postrevolution wage bills, subsequently ratified by the Central Bank. The banks support enterprise payrolls and income redistribution; ultimately money is created to permit them to do so. In the somewhat more normal situation of Projection II, demand for workers' services is created by an export recovery, and less overt printing of money is required to keep them on the payroll.

Both the real and the monetary accounts end up telling a consistent story. Aggregate demand is low and the balance of payments is a disaster; there is no policy recourse in the short run but to run a fiscal deficit and use the banking system to prevent firms from going bankrupt. The medium-term exit from this unpleasant situation is presumably export promotion and/or concessionary financing of trade deficits from abroad. Such solutions may prove quite costly in terms of restructuring the national mode of production or becoming too dependent on one's "friends." The economics of foreign-exchange scarcity as captured by simple accounting identities leaves Portugal and similar countries little leeway for policy choice.

3-2 A SAM FOR EGYPT

The overall macro situation in the mid-1970s in Egypt was not dissimilar to that in Portugal; in both instances there was a large external deficit due to food and intermediate imports and a corresponding government deficit inside the country. In this and the following two sections, we show in greater detail than for Portugal how changes in this sort of economy in 1976 might be foreseen from 1975. To do this, a SAM similar to the one in Table 2-1 is used.

A 19 × 18 SAM for Egypt in 1975 appears in Table 3-6. We first explain the significance of its entries, cell by cell, and then go on to update its numbers for 1976. The 1975 matrix itself was constructed using similar procedures, with data culled from a variety of Egyptian sources. For both 1975 and 1976, the accounting restrictions built into the SAM are the key to its numerical estimation.

Table 3-6 SAM–Egypt 1975 (all flows in billions of 1975 pounds)

	1	2	3	4	5	6	7	8
	Rural	Urban	Food	Σ(1 to 3)	House-hold	Govern-ment	Σ(5 and 6)	Foreign-exchange inflows
1. Rural sector	0.4137	0.077	0.450	0.9407	0.7124	0.011	0.7234	0.301
2. Urban sector	0.1708	1.742	0.042	1.9548	1.6831	1.162	2.8451	0.289
3. Food sector			0.026	0.026	1.184		1.184	
4. Σ(1 to 3)	0.5845	1.819	0.518	2.9215	3.5795	1.173	4.7525	0.590
5. Household	1.3739	2.217	0.068	3.6589		0.0564	0.0564	0.110
6. Government		0.316	0.055	0.371				0.421
7. Σ(5 and 6)	1.3739	2.533	0.123	4.0299		0.0564	0.0564	0.531
8. Foreign-exchange outflows	0.0954	0.658	0.569	1.3224	0.043		0.043	
9. Import tariffs and subsidies	−0.0889	0.329		0.2401	0.053		0.0889	0.1419
10. Indirect tax		0.436		0.436				
11. Σ(8 to 10)	0.0065	1.423	0.569	1.9985	0.096		0.0889	0.1849
12. Food subsidies					−0.4909	0.4909		
13. Direct tax					0.0172		0.0172	
14. Σ(12 and 13)					−0.4737	0.4909	0.0172	
15. S_{Priv}					0.6235		0.6235	
16. S_{Gov}						−0.143	−0.143	
17. S_{For}								0.4994
18. Σ(15 to 17)					0.6235	−0.143	0.4805	0.4994
19. ΣΣ	1.9649	5.775	1.21	8.95	3.8253	1.6662	5.4915	1.6204

In Table 3-6, all flows are in billions of 1975 Egyptian pounds. (A pound at the official exchange rate equaled $2.40 in United States currency. The symbol for Egyptian pounds is LE.) Rows 1 through 3 in the SAM show uses of the products of three sectors: "rural" (R), "urban" (U), and "food processing" (F). This disaggregation was chosen because subsidies on processed foods such as bread were a major fiscal expenditure item in Egypt and therefore figured in policy debate.

Reading across the first three rows, we see that each sector satisfies intermediate demands (columns 1 to 3), household consumption demands (column 5), government purchases (column 6), export demands (column 8), and capital formation and stock changes (columns 16 and 17). Along row 2, for example, total sales are summed at the far right-hand side of the SAM as LE 5.775 billion. This same total appears at the bottom of column 2 as total cost of production in the urban sector. As already pointed out in Chap. 2, this row-column equality is the basic accounting principle underlying a SAM. The breakdown of costs down columns 1 to 3 comprises intermediate nationally produced inputs (rows 1 to 3), wages and profits paid to households (row 5), profits from nationalized industries and company direct taxes paid to the government (row 6), imported intermediate inputs at their c.i.f. value (row 8), and their associated subsidies (column 1) or tariffs (column 2) in row 9. A final cost item in each sector is its indirect tax payment in row 10.

Table 3-6 SAM—Egypt 1975 (all flows in billions of 1975 pounds) (*Continued*)

9 Import tariffs and sub-sidies	10 Indirect tax	11 Σ(8 to 10)	12 Food sub-sidies	13 Direct tax	14 Σ(12 to 13)	15 Capital forma-tion	16 Stock changes	17 Σ(15 and 16)	18 ΣΣ
		0.301							1.965
		0.289				0.546	0.140	0.686	5.775
									1.21
		0.590				0.546	0.140	0.686	8.95
		0.110							3.8253
0.421	0.436	1.278		0.0172	0.0172				1.6662
0.421	0.436	1.388	0.0	0.0172	0.0172				5.4915
						0.255		0.255	1.6204
						0.039		0.039	0.421
									0.436
						0.294		0.294	2.4774
									0.0
									0.0172
									0.0172
									0.6235
									-0.143
		0.4994							0.4994
		0.4994							0.980
		2.4774	0.0	0.0172	0.0172	0.840	0.140	0.980	

Row 5 gives different sources of household income, beginning with payments received from participation in productive activity in columns 1 through 3. Remittances from emigrant workers (in the quantity LE 110 million at the official exchange rate) are assumed to flow to households in column 8. Since remittances in fact entered the country at a more favorable rate, there is a further implicit subsidy of LE 56.4 million from government to households in column 6. Total household income at the right end of row 5 is LE 3.8253 billion, which equals household uses of income at the bottom of column 5. The column shows that households purchase nationally produced goods (rows 1 to 3) and consumer imports c.i.f. (row 8); the associated tariffs appear in row 9. Household income is also used to pay direct taxes (row 13), and part is saved (row 15). Finally, the food subsidy of LE 490.9 million appears with a negative sign in row 12; this is the difference between household purchases of food at production cost (LE 1.184 billion in row 3, column 5) and what was actually paid. In a SAM, each payment received by one economic group must ultimately be an expenditure on the part of another. With respect to food subsidies, this convention is maintained by the government expenditure item in row 12, column 6.

Other entries in columns 6 show government expenditure going to commodity purchases (rows 1 and 2; wages paid government employees are also included here), support of the favorable exchange rate for remittances (row 5), the food subsidy (row 12), and negative savings or current account fiscal deficit (row 16). A final expenditure item is a subsidy of LE 88.9 million on the rural sector's imported intermediate inputs (mainly fertilizer) in row 9, column 6; this same payment is subtracted from the rural sector's production costs in column 1 of the same row. In row 6, fiscal revenues come from profits of nationalized enterprises and corporate taxes (columns 2 and 3), direct foreign currency payments or transfers from other governments and international agencies (column 8), tariff collections (column 9), indirect taxes (column 10), and direct taxes (column 13). Rows 9, 10, and 13 show the respective sources from which tariffs, indirect taxes, and direct taxes are collected. Note that the sum along each of these rows appears in the corresponding column in row 6, showing government income.

Outflows of foreign exchange at the official rate appear in row 8; the only item not already mentioned is imports of capital goods of LE 255 million in column 15. Foreign-exchange inflows in column 8 include exports in rows 1 and 2, emigrant remittances in row 5, and foreign government transfers in row 6. The balancing item which makes row 8 and column 8 sums the same is net foreign borrowing or "foreign saving" of LE 499.4 million in row 17, column 8.

Finally, sources of savings are accounted in rows 15 to 17, and expenditures on gross capital formation and stock accumulation appear in columns 15 and 16. As usual, total savings of LE 980 million equals investment.

3-3 INPUT-OUTPUT ALGEBRA IN A SAM

Suppose that the 1975 Egyptian SAM in Table 3-6 is taken as a reasonably accurate representation of economic activity in that year. How can it be updated to give a plausible projection for 1976? In the next section, we describe an updating procedure, going by rows down the SAM. But before we do that, it is useful to sketch the elements of the interindustry or input-output planning model, first set out in modern form by the Russian-American economist Wassily Leontief four decades or so ago. Input-output calculations will be used for many purposes throughout this volume; at the moment we want to apply them to take account of price and final demand changes in a SAM. As stressed in Chap. 2, the SAM's row-column identities hold only in current price (not "real") terms, and this accounting restriction must be respected.

The demand-supply balance for interindustry accounting has already been given as Eq. (2-8). We can restate it as

$$P_i X_i = \sum_{j=1}^{N} P_i X_{ij} + P_i F_i \tag{3-1}$$

where X_i is an index of total output in industry i in the prices of some base year, P_i is a price index for the sector, X_{ij} are its sales to sector j for intermediate uses, and F_i is the sum of sector i final demands less competitive imports.

In most applications of input-output analysis, it is assumed that intermediate purchases X_{ij} of commodity i by sector j are related to its output level X_j by a *fixed* coefficient a_{ij}. That is,

$$X_{ij} = a_{ij} X_j \qquad (3\text{-}2)$$

where a_{ij} is supposed not to vary in response to, say, price changes. Such an assumption may or may not make sense in practice; if, for example, it is easy to shift from coal to oil in an electricity station or from copper to aluminum in assembling the electrical system of cars, the fixed-coefficient hypothesis does not make sense for these production processes. However, these are rather special examples. In the short run, for fairly highly aggregated sectors, fixed a_{ij}'s may approximately be observed. In any case, their fixity has traditionally been postulated in planning exercises.

If the input-output coefficients are fixed but prices vary across sectors, it is convenient to rewrite Eqs. (3-1) and (3-2) as

$$P_i X_i = \sum_{j=1}^{N} (P_i a_{ij}/P_j) P_j X_j + P_i F_i \qquad (3\text{-}3)$$

Here, we are expressing sector output and final demand levels in current price terms and revaluing the input-output coefficients as $P_i a_{ij}/P_j$ to keep the accounting consistent. In a base year (like 1975 in the Egyptian SAM of Table 3-6), all prices are set to unity, so they cancel in Eq. (3-3). However, if prices shift over time relative to each other, they do not cancel, and the more complicated expression for input-output coefficients has to be used.

The next step is to express input-output algebra in matrix terms. In the base year when all prices are one and cancel out, we have the familiar material balance equations

$$\begin{bmatrix} X_1 \\ \cdot \\ \cdot \\ \cdot \\ X_N \end{bmatrix} = \begin{bmatrix} a_{11} & a_{12} & \cdots & a_{1N} \\ \cdot & & & \cdot \\ \cdot & & & \cdot \\ \cdot & & & \cdot \\ a_{N1} & & \cdots & a_{NN} \end{bmatrix} \begin{bmatrix} X_1 \\ \cdot \\ \cdot \\ \cdot \\ X_N \end{bmatrix} + \begin{bmatrix} F_1 \\ \cdot \\ \cdot \\ \cdot \\ F_N \end{bmatrix}$$

This expression can be restated in shorthand notation as

$$X = AX + F \qquad (3\text{-}4)$$

where X is a column vector of output levels, A is an $N \times N$ matrix of input-output coefficients, and F is a column vector of final demands. For realistic input-output matrices, it is possible to solve Eq. (3-4) as

$$X = (I - A)^{-1} F \qquad (3\text{-}5)$$

This standard formula permits the computation of gross output levels required to satisfy a vector of final demands F after intermediate input requirements are taken into account.

To generalize these equations for varying prices, the simplest procedure is to introduce the *diagonal* price matrices

$$\hat{P} = \begin{bmatrix} P_1 & 0 & \cdots & 0 \\ 0 & P_2 & \cdots & 0 \\ \cdot & \cdot & & \cdot \\ \cdot & \cdot & & \cdot \\ \cdot & \cdot & & \cdot \\ 0 & 0 & \cdots & P_N \end{bmatrix} \tag{3-6}$$

and

$$\hat{P}^{-1} = \begin{bmatrix} 1/P_1 & 0 & \cdots & 0 \\ 0 & 1/P_2 & \cdots & 0 \\ \cdot & \cdot & & \cdot \\ \cdot & \cdot & & \cdot \\ \cdot & \cdot & & \cdot \\ 0 & 0 & \cdots & 1/P_N \end{bmatrix} \tag{3-7}$$

Using these "hat" matrices, it is easy to rewrite Eq. (3-3) as

$$\hat{P}X = (\hat{P}A\hat{P}^{-1})\hat{P}X + \hat{P}F \tag{3-8}$$

and the flexible price analog to (3-5) becomes

$$\hat{P}X = [I - \hat{P}A\hat{P}^{-1}]^{-1}\hat{P}F \tag{3-9}$$

Equations (3-8) and (3-9) show how to make current price estimates of output levels required to support a vector of final demands $\hat{P}F$ when both prices and quantities demanded are changing. We turn to the details of such a calculation for Egypt.

3-4 UPDATING THE EGYPTIAN SAM

At the outset of the 1976 calculation, the reader might want to verify that the input-output coefficients underlying the interindustry flows in the top left-hand corner of Table 3-6 are

$$A = \begin{bmatrix} 0.21055 & 0.01333 & 0.37190 \\ 0.08693 & 0.30165 & 0.03471 \\ 0.0 & 0.0 & 0.02149 \end{bmatrix} \tag{3-10}$$

that is, $0.21055 = 0.4137/1.9649$, and so on.

For 1976, available Egyptian price indexes seemed to indicate 20 percent inflation in the rural sector, 25 percent for most urban products, and 10 percent for food. In 1976 prices but with unchanging a_{ij} coefficients, the input-output matrix becomes

$$\hat{P}A\hat{P}^{-1} = \begin{bmatrix} (1.20)(0.21055)/1.20 & (1.20)(0.01333)/1.25 & (1.20)(0.37190)/1.10 \\ (1.25)(0.08693)/1.20 & (1.25)(0.30165)/1.25 & (1.25)(0.03471)/1.10 \\ 0.0 & 0.0 & (1.10)(0.02149)/1.10 \end{bmatrix}$$

$$= \begin{bmatrix} 0.21055 & 0.12800 & 0.40571 \\ 0.09055 & 0.30165 & 0.03944 \\ 0.0 & 0.0 & 0.02149 \end{bmatrix} \tag{3-11}$$

The *Leontief inverse* matrix appearing in Eq. (3-9) is

$$[I - \hat{P}A\hat{P}^{-1}]^{-1} = \begin{bmatrix} 1.26937 & 0.02327 & 0.52723 \\ 0.16459 & 1.43496 & 0.12608 \\ 0.0 & 0.0 & 1.02196 \end{bmatrix} \tag{3-12}$$

With this matrix in hand, we can begin updating the 1975 SAM of Table 3-6, summarizing the results in Table 3-7. The first steps are to calculate 1976 levels of final demands along the first three rows of the table.

1. Begin with household consumption, assuming minimal real expenditure changes per capita but a 3 percent increase in total expenditure for all commodities because of population growth. These assumptions, together with the consumption levels in the first three rows of column 5 in Table 3-6, give the corresponding entries in Table 3-7, viz:

$$0.8805 = 0.7124(1.03)(1.2)$$
$$2.1670 = 1.9548(1.03)(1.25)$$
$$1.3415 = 1.184(1.03)(1.1)$$

2. If world prices for noncompetitive consumer imports rose by 15 percent, we similarly get the entries in rows 8 and 9A (the latter corresponding to row 9 in Table 3-6).
3. Assume that real government purchases grew by 1 percent. Then we get rows 1 and 2 of column 6 in Table 3-7 by including price increases as in step 1 above.
4. If volume exports grew by 1 percent in the R and U sectors, then the entries in rows 1 and 2 of column 8 are computed as

$$0.304 = 0.301(1.01)$$
$$0.292 = 0.289(1.01)$$

Note that these are foreign-exchange export receipts, converted to Egyptian pounds at an unchanging official exchange rate.

5. But domestic prices increased by 20 and 25 percent respectively in the R and U sectors. Hence implicit subsidies were paid to exporters so as to maintain receipts on foreign and domestic sales equal. These are shown in column 9B. In the rural

Table 3-7 SAM—Egypt 1976 (all flows in billions of 1976 pounds)

	1	2	3	4	5	6	7	8
	Rural	Urban	Food	Σ(1 to 3)	House-hold	Govern-ment	Σ(5 and 6)	Foreign-exchange inflows
1. Rural sector	0.5075	0.088	0.5562	1.1517	0.8805	0.0133	0.8938	0.304
2. Urban sector	0.2183	2.075	0.0541	2.3474	2.1670	1.467	3.634	0.292
3. Food sector			0.0295	0.0295	1.3415		1.3415	
4. Σ(1 to 3)	0.7258	2.163	0.6398	3.5286	4.389	1.4803	5.8693	0.596
5. Household	1.6778	2.8203	0.096	4.5941		0.0682	0.0682	0.133
6. Government		0.6853	0.2835	0.9688				0.235
7. Σ(5 and 6)	1.6778	3.5056	0.3795	5.5629		0.0682	0.0682	0.368
8. Foreign-exchange outflows	0.0683	0.4606	0.3517	0.8806	0.0509		0.0509	
9A. Import tariffs and subsidies	−0.0616	0.2303		0.1687	0.0628	0.0616	0.1244	
9B. Export price differential								
10. Indirect tax		0.5194		0.5194				
11. Σ(8 to 10)	0.0067	1.2103	0.3517	1.5687	0.1137	0.0616	0.1753	
12. Food subsidies					−0.45	0.45	0.0	
13. Direct tax					0.02		0.02	
14. Σ(12 and 13)					0.43	0.45	0.02	
15. S_{Priv}					0.6557		0.6557	
16. S_{Gov}						−0.0614	−0.0614	
17. S_{For}								0.1588
18. Σ(15 to 17)					0.6557	−0.0614	0.5943	0.1588
19. ΣΣ	2.4103	6.8789	1.371	10.6602	4.7284		6.7271	1.1228

sector, for example, the subsidy was

$$0.301\,(1.01)\,(1.2) - 0.301\,(1.01) = 0.0608$$

In rows 5 and 6 of column 9B, the total export subsidy is assumed to come half from household and half from government income flows.

6. If real capital formation stayed constant, we get $0.6825 = 0.546(1.25)$ in row 2, column 15.
7. Finally, there was strong evidence that stocks were run down in Egypt during 1976 due to tight import controls in the face of growing aggregate demand. A guess of −0.15 for inventory decreases seems reasonable.
8. Total final demands are 1.2586 in the R sector, 4.5315 in the U sector, and 1.3415 in the F sector. Using the Leontief inverse matrix in Eq. (3-12), sector outputs required to support these demands become

$$\begin{bmatrix} 2.4103 \\ 6.8789 \\ 1.3710 \end{bmatrix} = \begin{bmatrix} 1.26937 & 0.02327 & 0.52723 \\ 0.16459 & 1.43496 & 0.12608 \\ 0.0 & 0.0 & 1.02196 \end{bmatrix} \begin{bmatrix} 1.2586 \\ 4.5315 \\ 1.3415 \end{bmatrix} \quad (3\text{-}13)$$

Table 3-7 SAM–Egypt 1976 (all flows in billions of 1976 pounds) (*Continued*)

9A Import tariffs and subsidies	9B Export price differential	10 Indirect tax	11 Σ(8 to 10)	12 Food subsidies	13 Direct tax	14 Σ(12 and 13)	15 Capital formation	16 Stock changes	17 Σ(15 and 16)	18 ΣΣ
	0.0608		0.3648							2.4103
	0.073		0.365				0.6825	–0.15	0.5325	6.8789
										1.371
	0.1338		0.7298				0.6825	–0.15	0.5325	10.6602
	–0.0669		0.0661							4.7284
0.3224	–0.0669	0.5194	1.0099		0.02	0.02				1.9987
0.3224	–0.1338	0.5194	1.076		0.02	0.02				6.7271
							0.1913		0.1913	1.1228
							0.0293		0.0293	0.3224
										0.0
										0.5194
							0.2206		0.2206	1.9646
										0.0
										0.02
										0.02
										0.6557
										–0.0614
			0.1588							0.1588
			0.1588							0.7531
0.3224	0.0	0.5194	1.9646	0.0	0.02	0.02	0.9301	–0.15	0.7531	

Deflating by the sector price indexes, we get the following results:

	Output in 1976 prices	Output in 1975 prices	Real growth, %
R	2.4103	2.0085	2.22
U	6.8789	5.5031	–4.71
F	1.3710	1.2464	3.0

so economic activity was nearly stagnant overall, on our assumptions. Note also how sector outputs in 1976 prices have been estimated endogenously from final demands and the input-output matrix. That is why they are put in a box at the right end of rows 1 to 3 in Table 3-7.

9. Next we fill in columns 1 to 3, using the output totals as controls. The first step is to calculate the 3 × 3 interindustry flow matrix at the top left of Table 3-7, using the 1976 input-output coefficients displayed in Eq. (3-11).

For example, sales of the rural sector to itself are 0.5075 = (0.21055) (2.4103) from the corresponding coefficient and sector output level.

10. To calculate imports, begin by noting that the 1975 coefficient for fertilizer purchases (at world prices converted to pounds at the official exchange rate) is $0.04855 = 0.0954/1.9649$ from rows 8 and 19 in column 1 of Table 3-6. If physical use of fertilizer per unit of rural output stayed constant but fertilizer prices on the world market fell by 30 percent, then the import coefficient in 1976 prices is $0.02832 = (0.04855)(0.7)/1.2$ and imports are $0.0683 = (0.02832)(2.4103)$. In *domestic* price terms, the 1975 fertilizer input coefficient was, of course, less because of the subsidy of 0.0889 appearing in row 9, column 1 of Table 3-6. If the subsidized price stayed constant in 1976, the new input coefficient becomes

$$0.00276 = \frac{0.0954 - 0.0889}{1.9649} \; \frac{1}{1.2}$$

and in internal prices 1976 fertilizer use is $0.00665 = (0.00276)(2.4103)$. The 1976 subsidy (row 9A in Table 3-7) is $0.0616 = 0.0683 - 0.0067$.

11. Assume that the world price of intermediate imports into the urban sector stayed constant but that the volume fell by 30 percent because of quantitative restrictions imposed by the government. This gives rows 8 and 9A of column 2 in Table 3-7.

12. Food import prices in the world market fell about 40 percent in 1976. This gives a new input coefficient into the F sector:

$$0.2565 = \frac{0.569}{1.21} \; \frac{0.6}{1.1}$$

and the level of imports (row 8, column 3) is $0.3517 = (0.2565)(1.371)$. Assume also that food subsidies fell from 0.4909 in 1975 to 0.450 in 1976 (row 12, columns 5 and 6).

13. For the U sector, the indirect tax coefficient in 1975 (row 10, column 2) was $0.0755 = 0.436/5.775$. Applying this coefficient to urban sector output of 6.8789 in 1976 gives the entry at row 10, column 2 of Table 3-7.

14. Household incomes as shares of gross output in 1975 were

$$\text{U sector:} \quad 0.3839 = 2.217/5.775$$
$$\text{F sector:} \quad 0.0562 = 0.068/1.21$$

There may have been a slight increase in these shares in 1976, so we apply coefficients of 0.41 and 0.07 to 1976 output levels to get the entries in columns 2 and 3 of row 5.

15. Household income in the R sector and government surpluses in the U and F sectors now become residuals in Table 3-7, to make total sector costs (columns 1 to 3) equal receipts (rows 1 to 3). Again, these entries are boxed to indicate their endogeneity.

16. Only a few items remain to be calculated. Because of import restrictions, assume first that capital-goods imports and their tariffs fell by 25 percent (column 15, rows 8 and 9A), world prices holding constant.

17. Remittances were 0.133 (row 5, column 8), and the associated transfer to households through a favorable exchange rate becomes 0.0682 (row 5, column 6).

18. Transfers of foreign currency to the Egyptian government were estimated at 0.235 in 1976 (row 6, column 8).
19. As a boxed residual item, the current account foreign deficit becomes 0.1588 (row 17, column 8).
20. The sum of government and private saving must be 0.5943 = 0.7531 - 0.1588, where 0.5943 is total investment from the sums of columns 16 and 17.
21. Assume direct tax receipts of 0.02 in row 13, column 5. To make the sum of column 5 equal to household income of 4.7284 (row 5), household savings as a residual is 0.6557. Since total national savings is 0.5943, government savings becomes -0.0614. As a check on the overall calculation, this is also the difference between government receipts (sum of row 6), and the sum of the government expenditure items appearing in column 6.

Table 3-8 provides a set of summary statistics for the Egyptian exercise, on the expenditure side of the national accounts; the numbers in the first two columns can be read directly from Tables 3-6 and 3-7. The price increases postulated throughout this section were used to deflate the 1976 current price estimates to 1975 "real terms" in the last column. Note the very substantial decline of LE 240 million in real imports, which is more than offset by a drop of LE 330 million in real investment (mostly from stock decumulation). The net result is a small increase in real GDP (a growth rate of 1.2 percent is calculated in the lower part of Table 3-8). If the numbers are correct Egyptian policy in 1976 sustained modest output growth by mortgaging the future through stock decumulation and a cut in real capital formation.

Table 3-8 Summary estimates for Egypt (billions of pounds)*

	1975	1976	1976 in 1975 prices
Consumption	3.6745	4.5027	3.7858
Investment	0.98	0.7531	0.6466
Government	1.173	1.4803	1.1847
Exports†	0.7	0.729	0.729
−Imports	−1.6204	−1.1228	−1.38
Rural	0.0954	0.0683	0.0976
Urban	0.658	0.4606	0.4606
Food	0.569	0.3517	0.5862
Consumption	0.043	0.0509	0.0443
Capital goods	0.255	0.1913	0.1913
Gross domestic product	4.9071	6.3423	4.9661

$$*\text{Real GDP growth} = \frac{4.9661}{4.9071} - 1 = 1.2\%$$

$$\text{Inflation} = \frac{6.3423}{4.9661} - 1 = 27.7\%$$

†Exports include emigrant remittances.

The final point worth noting is that one can calculate a useful price index as the ratio of GDP in 1976 prices to its value in 1975 prices. For 1976, this *implicit deflator* is estimated in Table 3-8 at 27.7 percent, a nontrivial rate of inflation.

3-5 OTHER ESTIMATION TECHNIQUES, STYLIZED PARAMETERS, AND ECONOMETRICS

Recall from Sec. 2-5 that national accounts are typically estimated in two ways: from patterns of expenditure or from estimates of value-added levels by sector. The foregoing procedure for Egypt essentially follows the expenditure method, with various components of value added and saving treated as residuals. Evidently, one could also construct 1976 accounts from the value-added side or from some combination of the two standard approaches. The main point to be recognized is that the SAM framework provides a convenient basis for organizing incomplete and perhaps contradictory data to say something *fast* about what is going on in the economy. Even with extensions in the monetary direction as in the Portuguese example, a calculation like the one for Egypt can be done on a fairly serious basis in a week or so. At year end, when the final economic results are in and the Finance Minister has to make a budget presentation in 2 months, one could do much worse than apply the methods of this chapter to drawing up a preliminary economic assessment for the next fiscal period.

Besides SAMs, other sources of information can be brought into short- and medium-term projections. We have already had reason to mention stylized facts about money multipliers and velocities as well as import coefficients. This list can be extended virtually ad infinitum, at least to include capital-output ratios, savings proportions from various income streams, typical shares of government expediture and tax take in GDP, patterns of income distribution, and so on.

Alleged regularities in stylized parameters across countries have been discerned by some economists in so-called *patterns of growth* studies. For example, one might want to think about probable changes in shares-of-industry value-added levels in the total over the medium term. Letting V be a vector of a value added by sector, $\hat{v}$ a diagonal matrix of value-added coefficients, and assuming that prices do not shift from their base-year value of unity, one can rewrite Eq. (3-5) as

$$V = \hat{v}X = \hat{v}(I - A)^{-1}(C + G + I + E - M^C) \tag{3-14}$$

where the notation of the last chapter is used for the various components of final demand.

Now suppose that the following assertions are more or less true:

Sectoral consumption levels per capita are largely determined by per capita income.

Investment demands by origin met from national production will tend to rise as there is substitution of capital-goods imports. The degree of substitution completed goes up with per capita income and the national population (as a proxy for market size in a sector where economies of scale are important).

Government commodity purchases probably go up a bit more than proportionately to total income.

Primary exports as a share of the total probably go down with per capita income, while manufactured exports go up. The growth of the latter is probably faster in big countries, again for reasons of scale.

Substitution of competitive imports follows a similar process.

The "technical coefficients" a_{ij} and v_i change in a regular pattern as the economy becomes more complex with per capita income growth.

If these hypotheses make sense, one might expect the composition of the value-added basket in a country to respond in a fairly regular fashion to evolutionary changes in per capita income and population. A number of studies (listed at the end of the chapter) seem to indicate that this is so. Their attempted extensions to other numbers such as tax shares, capital-output ratios, income distribution, and savings propensities are perhaps on less secure theoretical ground, but there is some hint of regular behavior on the part of these parameters also. The cross-section regressions of most such variables describing the development process on per capita GDP, population, and a few other explanatory factors usually come in with fairly high values for R^2. For sure, such econometric success does *not* imply that one can use "patterns" regression results to "predict" what will happen in a given country as its income and population changes, but at least they put plausible boundary conditions on projections derived from other means.

In effect, patterns regressions boil down the experience of a number of countries into some sort of "average" pattern with which one can compare parameters for the economy of interest. With equal justice, comparisons can be drawn with "similar" neighboring or far-distant countries. Both approaches are simply an attempt to bring outside information to bear on a situation where within-country numbers are unreliable and scarce.

A final approach is to estimate parameters econometrically from the country's own past data. At the national level, this may prove to be an unrewarding exercise, given the many weaknesses, discussed in the last chapter, in the accounts of underdeveloped nations. Also, many poor economies fluctuate dramatically. Therefore the effort to average this experience statistically, from the past in order to try to say something about the future, may be completely off the mark. How well would the best of econometric models for Portugal function after even the mild revolution of April 25, 1974?

For these reasons, the planning procedures discussed in this book are not structured with econometric estimation in mind. Rather, more a priori (or ad hoc) specification of parameters is envisaged from whatever evidence may be available—experience of other countries, own-country econometric studies that seem to be reliable, or even guesswork. The essence of good planning is good quantitative intuition, which is, regrettably, a rather elusive thing.

SELECTED ADDITIONAL READINGS

Blitzer, Charles R., Peter B. Clark, and Lance Taylor: *Economy-Wide Models and Development Planning*, Oxford University Press, New York and London, 1975. (Chapter 3 provides a fairly thorough review of the input-output model as applied in poor-country planning.)

Chenery, Hollis B., and Paul G. Clark: *Interindustry Economics*, Wiley, New York, 1959. (A classic text on applied input-output planning.)

Chenery, Hollis B., and Moises Syrquin: *Patterns of Development, 1950-1970*, Oxford University Press, New York and London, 1975. (A recent compendium of cross-country regression results for a wide variety of stylized parameters.)

Kuznets, Simon S.: *Modern Economic Growth*, Yale University Press, New Haven, 1966. (A summary of the massive studies of quantitative aspects of economic development by the 1971 Nobel Laureate. Essential reading for anyone seriously interested in planning economic change.)

Taylor, Lance: "Development Patterns: A Simulation Study," *Quarterly Journal of Economics*, 83: 220-241, 1969. (An elaboration and quantification of the "patterns" model sketched in Sec. 3-5.)

FOUR

PRICE CHANGES, INCOME EFFECTS, AND POLICY SURPRISES IN THE SHORT RUN

Analyzing a country's economic prospects by doing numerical crossword puzzles in a SAM is all right as far as it goes, but the technique ignores important aspects of economic underdevelopment. One is the role of *income effects* in determining how the economy behaves in the short run. Movements in real incomes induced by price changes can affect economic activity in a variety of ways, some of which are developed in this chapter with simple models based on the last chapter's data for Egypt and Portugal.

The Portuguese model (described in Secs. 4-1 and 4-2) focuses on the effects of currency devaluation in a poor country. The ruling hypothesis is that noncompetitive intermediate imports make up a substantial share of firms' outlays for production. By driving up the cost of imports, devaluation can lead to an increase in the overall price level relative to other payments that are temporarily fixed in nominal terms. If one of these is the wage, the income distribution shifts in favor of profit recipients, the government, and foreign savings. Total expenditure may fall or switch toward nonwage commodities. The expenditure reduction is emphasized in the one-sector Portuguese model; in general, it leads to contraction in aggregate demand. Because import levels are tied to production activity, the balance of payments improves. However, the political costs associated with the reduction in output and employment may be too high to permit use of the devaluation tool. Portugal is not unique among developing countries in this respect.

Expenditure switching in response to policy changes is emphasized in the model for Egypt in Sec. 4-3. The switching policy considered is an increase in controlled consumer prices in an attempt to reduce total payments for food subsidies. In fact, this sort of policy is not likely to achieve its ends directly, since demand for food is price-inelastic. The increase in food prices will reduce real income by more than it reduces food consumption, leading to a reduction in demand for nonfood commodities as well. This initial fall in aggregate demand leads to further economic contraction through multiplier processes. The Egypt model is set up to quantify these intersectoral switches in macro expenditures and shows that their impacts on the level and composition of demand can be quite large.

4-1 CONTRACTIONARY IMPACTS OF DEVALUATION

A glance back at Table 3-2 reveals that during the mid-1970s Portugal came under extreme balance-of-payments pressure, with the current account shifting from an 8.5-million-conto surplus in 1973 to a deficit of 27.9 million in 1975. Under such circumstances, currency *devaluation* (increasing the price of foreign exchange in terms of the local money) has long been the drug of choice. There is historical evidence that devaluation does not always lead to economic recoveries (see monograph by Richard Cooper in the Selected Additional Readings), but faith in its properties remains. Perhaps that is because traditional devaluation models ignore precisely the income effects stressed here.

Devaluation is *supposed* to improve the trade balance and stimulate the level of internal activity by raising the price of traded goods relative to home goods. This relative price shift works by generating excess demand for home goods while also making exporting or import substitution more profitable. Models differ on how the system reacts, but—in general—home goods output, domestic prices, or both rise. Not usually considered is the possibility that price movements caused by devaluation will create enough losers in terms of real income to cause an initial excess *supply* of home goods.

In this section, we sketch a simple theoretical model to show that another outcome is possible: output can *fall* after devaluation, if it increases real income of those who are inclined to save (as compared with the income of those who are not so disposed). If high savers are rich and low savers poor, currency depreciation brings both output contraction and unfavorable income redistribution as side effects to a possible cure for balance-of-payments disease. The drug may be successful, even if it kills the patient for other reasons in the end.

Table 4-1 sets out the equations in the devaluation model. They are somewhat more complicated than necessary to get the theoretical results we want in this section, but the extra detail will prove useful in setting up an empirical specification for Portugal. The model itself follows received macroeconomic tradition and can be used to get multiplier-based predictions of the effects of movements in policy variables. However, its structure is nonstandard in that relative price movements are considered explicitly, precisely to allow analysis of income effects. This theoretical approach is

Table 4-1 Equations for the Portugal model

P_H	$= (a_{LH}w + a_{0H}P_0)\,(1+z)\,(1+v_H)$	(4-1)
P_E	$= e\,(1 - t_E)\,P_E^*$	(4-2)
P_0	$= e\,(1 + t_0)\,P_0^*$	(4-3)
Y_W	$= (a_{LH}X_H + a_{LE}X_E)\,w$	(4-4)
Y_Z	$= z\,(a_{LH}w + a_{0H}P_0)\,X_H + (P_E - a_{LE}w)\,X_E + e\,(\text{REM})$	(4-5)
D_W	$= \gamma_W(Y_W - T_W)$	(4-6)
D_Z	$= \gamma_Z(Y_Z - T_Z)$	(4-7)
C	$= (D_W + D_Z)/P_H$	(4-8)
X_H	$= C + I + G$	(4-9)
S^{Priv}	$= (1 - \gamma_W)\,(Y_W - T_W) + (1 - \gamma_Z)\,(Y_Z - T_Z)$	(4-10)
S^{Gov}	$= v_H P_H X_H/(1 + v_H) + et_E P_E^* X_E + et_0 P_0^* a_{0H}X_H + T_W + T_Z - P_H G$	(4-11)
S^{For}	$= eP_0^* a_{0H}X_H - eP_E^* X_E - e\,(\text{REM})$	(4-12)
$P_H I$	$= S^{\text{Priv}} + S^{\text{Gov}} + S^{\text{For}}$	(4-13)

closer to the tradition of Michael Kalecki and subsequent Cambridge (England) economists than to that of most followers of John Maynard Keynes.[1]

Equation (4-1) follows Kalecki in assuming that prices of home goods (subscript *H*) are cost-based, determined by a markup over *prime costs*. In the present model, these comprise labor costs, wa_{LH}, and costs of intermediate imports, $P_0 a_{0H}$, per unit of output. The parameters a_{0H} and a_{LH} are respectively input-output coefficients for imports and labor, of the type introduced in Sec. 3-3. For simplicity, we assume away differences in import content of different components of final demand. The imports are, of course, noncompetitive, as defined in Chap. 2.

Since P_0 and w are the costs firms pay per unit of imports and labor, the total cost of these inputs per unit of output is $a_{LH}w + a_{0H}P_0$. This prime cost is multiplied by 1 plus an entrepreneurial markup, $1 + z$ in Eq. (4-1), to get factor costs per unit. ["Profits" per unit are given by $z(a_{LH}w + a_{0H}P_0)$.] The total cost per unit of output is P_H, marked up from factor costs by the term $1 + v_H$, where v_H is the rate of the government's indirect tax.

Equations (4-2) and (4-3) show how prices of traded goods are determined. Exports are assumed to have a "world price," P_E^*; in practice, this in an index of the prices the country receives for exports in foreign currency "free on board" (f.o.b.) a ship or airplane as they depart. Exporters themselves get the foreign currency price in domestic money—that is, after it is multiplied by the exchange rate e and an export tax, t_E, is taken away. Similarly, importers pay an amount determined by the world price P_0^*,

---

[1] The essays collected in the book by Kalecki (cited at the end of this chapter) give the essentials of his thought. Subsequent "neo-Keynesian" literature is reviewed in the article by Eichner and Kregel, while the kindred (and much deeper) ideas of Latin American "structuralist" economists are summarized and extended by Diamand. Useful multiplier-based analyses of fiscal policy initiatives are given in the books by Dornbusch and Fischer and by Johansen.

including "cargo, insurance, and freight" (c.i.f.); the exchange rate; and an import tariff, t_0.

Equations (4-4) and (4-5) define labor and profit incomes, Y_W and Y_Z. Labor payments are the sum of unit labor costs in the home-goods and export industries multiplied by their respective output levels, X_H and X_E.

Y_Z is the sum of markups in the home-goods industry, the difference between internal export revenue and its labor component, and emigrant remittances in home currency, $e(\text{REM})$. The next two equations give consumption expenditures from the two income streams as $\gamma_i(Y_i - T_i)$, where γ_i is the share of income flow i devoted to consumption and T_i is a direct tax (negative if a net transfer). Equation (4-8) shows that the *value* of total consumption, $P_H C$, is equal to expenditures $D_W + D_Z$.

Equation (4-9) closes the model by setting home-goods output equal to the sum of consumption, investment, and government purchases. The next three equations define savings from the private sector, government, and foreigners.[2] The reader should show that the savings-investment identity of Eq. (4-13) follows from the rest of the equations in the model.

In the short run, it is perhaps reasonable to assume that the markup z, consumption propensities γ_W and γ_Z, and the input-output coefficients are constant. If all this is true, then we can determine consumption C as a function of home-goods output X_H and other variables by substituting Eqs. (4-4) through (4-7) in Eq. (4-8). A further insertion of the result into Eq. (4-9) means that we can solve for X_H as

$$X_H =$$

$$\left(\frac{1}{Q}\right)\left\{\left(\frac{X_E}{P_H}\right)[(\gamma_W - \gamma_Z)a_{LE}w + \gamma_Z P_E] + \left(\frac{1}{P_H}\right)[\gamma_Z e(\text{REM}) - (\gamma_W T_W + \gamma_Z T_Z)] + I + G\right\}$$

$$(4\text{-}14)$$

where

$$Q = 1 - \gamma_W a_{LH}\frac{w}{P_H} - \gamma_Z \frac{z}{(1+z)(1+v_H)} \qquad (4\text{-}15)$$

and $(1/Q)$ is the multiplier.

The denominator Q in the multiplier formula of Eq. (4-15) is a transformation of savings propensities from labor and profit incomes. It will normally be less than 1, so that unit increases in the terms in the bracketed expression in Eq. (4-14) will lead to more than unitary increases in demand for the home good, X_H. Demand will typically rise with higher export volume, X_E, remittances REM, investment I, and government purchases, G. Increases in direct taxes, T_W and T_Z, will reduce purchasing power in the economy and therefore aggregate demand.

---

[2] All terms in Eqs. (4-10) through (4-12) are straightforward except perhaps for the indirect tax take $v_H P_H X_H/(1 + v_H)$ in Eq. (4-11). Here, observe that

$$P_H X_H/(1 + v_H) = (a_{LH}w + a_{0H}P_0)(1 + z) X_H,$$

or total payments to domestic factors and imports. The tax take is just v_H times total payments.

Now consider devaluation. One of its effects is to drive up home-goods prices from Eq. (4-1). Another is to raise export receipts from Eq. (4-2) and to increase import costs in Eq. (4-3) by more than the increase in P_H. Since profitability in the export sector and relative costs of imports both go up, the usual story is that the trade balance "should" improve as exporters expand sales and importers find domestic substitutes.

Unfortunately, the remedy may not work in a poor country. The import coefficient, a_{0H}, may well be rigid as a result of a past history of substituting, for competitive imports, new domestic industries which *require* noncompetitive inputs to stay in operation. And similarly, exports may not respond to greater profit incentives if they are "traditional" in the sense of having limited markets and little technical flexibility. Under these circumstances, the main effect of raising the exchange rate e is to drive up the prices P_H, P_0, and P_E. These price movements, in turn, change real incomes of various economic actors. As they revise spending patterns in response, economic activity will follow.

One could, in principle, calculate the effect of changing e directly from Eqs. (4-14) and (4-15); but since P_H, P_0, and P_E enter these equations in fairly complex fashion, it is better to proceed piecemeal. Consider four special cases:

1. Suppose that there are no remittances (REM = 0) and that merchandise trade is initially in balance ($P_0^* a_{0H} X_H = P_E^* X_E$). Also assume away any fiscal activity ($v_H = t_E = t_0 = T_W = T_Z = G = 0$). Finally, suppose that the money wage w stays constant (or at least lags behind increases in the exchange rate) in the short run. Then the impact of devaluation is to raise all three prices—P_H, P_E, and P_0— and to redistribute income from wage to profit recipients for two reasons: (1) the real wage, w/P_H, falls and (2) exporters get a windfall income from increases in their profit margin $P_E - wa_{LE}$ (even with export volume, X_E, fixed or responding only slightly to devaluation). If the propensity to save from profits exceeds that from wages, the overall propensity to save in the economy goes up. At a given level of income, potential savings rise above investment and, in the usual Keynesian fashion, forces are set in motion to reduce savings and eliminate the discrepancy through reductions in income and aggregate demand. As a consequence, output of home goods falls.

   To express the negative relationship between output and the exchange rate formally, it is useful to introduce notation which will be used extensively in this book. Recall the definition of *elasticity* (i.e., the proportional change in a dependent variable caused by a similar change in the independent variable). In the case at hand, the elasticity of home-goods output with respect to the exchange rate is

$$\frac{dX_H}{de} \frac{e}{X_H} = \frac{dX_H/X_H}{de/e} = \frac{X_H'}{e'}$$

Here, the "prime" notation $e' = de/e$ denotes the proportional change of the variable e (sometimes called a "log change," since de/e is the differential of $\log e$). As the above formula shows, log changes fit naturally with elasticity definitions. We will see later that they are a useful tool for analyzing economic growth as well.

In Appendix A, Eqs. (4-1) through (4-9) in log-change form are used to derive the devaluation elasticity formula

$$X'_H = \frac{\gamma_Z - \gamma_W}{Q}(1+z)\frac{a_{0H}P_0 X_H}{P_H X_H}\frac{Y_W}{P_H X_H}e' \tag{4-16}$$

As long as the consumption share γ_Z from profit income is less than the share γ_W from wage income, the elasticity on the right side of Eq. (4-16) is negative, and output falls with devaluation. On our assumptions, so also do imports in physical terms, $a_{0H}X_H$, and the balance of payments improves. Imports in domestic currency, $P_0 a_{0H}X_H$, may or may not fall, since P_0 rises proportionately to e. We return to this point below.

2. Consider the effects of changing the exchange rate when trade is not initially in balance. Devaluation gives with one hand, by raising export prices, while taking away with the other, by raising import prices. If trade is balanced and the prices at which our "small country" can trade are fixed by the rest of the world, these price changes offset each other. But if imports exceed exports, the net result is reduction in real income within the country. Output contraction follows.

An algebraic expression can be derived if we assume no difference in consumption propensities ($\gamma_W = \gamma_Z = \gamma$), no remittances (REM = 0), and no fiscal activity as in case 1 above. Then the elasticity of output with respect to the exchange rate is

$$X'_H = K\frac{P_E X_E - P_0 a_{0H}X_0}{P_H X_H}e' \tag{4-17}$$

where the constant K is $(\gamma/Q)[1 - (P_0 a_{0H}X_H/P_H X_H)(1+z)]$. Output of home goods—and hence total output, employment, and imports—will fall or rise depending on whether trade is initially in deficit or surplus. The economics of this response is fairly clear, but for the record the reader should derive Eq. (4-17) formally as well.

3. As a third case, suppose there are ad valorem taxes on exports or imports. Then depreciation redistributes income from the private sector to the government, which is assumed not to spend (or to save) the additional tax receipts in the short run. Once again, the outcome is a reduction in aggregate demand as income shifts toward a high saver.

To illustrate how such fiscal effects can make a devaluation contractionary, consider only an export tax and let $t_0 = v_H = T_W = T_Z = \text{REM} = 0$. Further assume that both the trade account and the government budget are initially balanced, so that $P_0^* a_{0H}X_H = P_E^* X_E$ and $et_E P_E^* X_E = P_H G$. Then we can solve for the result,

$$X'_H = -\frac{t_E \gamma}{Q}\frac{P_0 a_{0H}X_H}{P_H X_H}e' \tag{4-18}$$

The devaluation elasticity is proportional to the tax rate on exports and the share of imports (or exports) in income. If the *marginal* export tax rate is high—as would be the case where the state acquires an export good such as a crop at fixed prices and then takes the profit from a higher exchange rate—the contractionary effect of the increased tax take resulting from devaluation is quite strong.

4. Finally, suppose that direct taxes or transfers are fixed in nominal terms in the short run. Devaluation increases the home-goods price, P_H, relative to the nominal payment and reduces the real income of its recipient. If the recipient is a relatively low saver, the effect is contractionary.

To work out the algebra, assume a common consumption function ($\gamma_Z = \gamma_W = \gamma$) and nominally fixed income tax levy $T = (T_W + T_Z)$. With balanced trade and government accounts, the devaluation elasticity equation is

$$X'_H = \frac{(1+z)\,\gamma}{Q} \frac{P_0 a_{0H} X_H}{P_H X_H} \frac{T}{P_H X_H} e' \qquad (4\text{-}19)$$

If the government is making net transfers ($T < 0$) to the private sector, devaluation is contractionary. The government's saving propensity is assumed to be 1. The private sector's is less, devaluation reduces the real value of payments from the high saver to the low saver, and contraction follows.

4-2 A NUMERICAL EXAMPLE FROM PORTUGAL

Other special cases could be developed, but the thrust of the reasoning seems clear. Any policy which shifts relative prices helps some groups of economic actors and hurts others. There can be macroeconomic repercussions if the savings (or consumption) patterns of the groups differ sufficiently.

The practical import of such income effects can be illustrated with a numerical example. Here, we work one out based on the Portuguese data of the last chapter, beginning with an explanation of how parameters for a model like the one in Table 4-1 can be constructed from national accounts information. We use the Portuguese accounts for 1975, rounding off decimals in some cases to ease calculation.

1. If 1975 prices P_H, P_E, and P_0 are set to unity, then the entries in the home-goods output balance Eq. (4-9) are $C = 364.9$, $I = 52.4$, $G = 55.2$, and $X_H = 472.5$, from Table 3-1.

2. On the fiscal side, assume no trade taxes ($t_0 = t_E = 0$). Also assume that the exchange rate, e, equals unity. Then exports and imports at world prices in escudo terms are valued at $P_0^* = P_E^* = 1$. It is also simplest to measure employment in units such that the wage rate $w = 1$.

3. The decomposition of total home-goods output cost is

$$P_H X_H = B_H (1+z) X_H + B_H (1+z) X_H v_H$$

where $B_H = (a_{LH} w + a_{0H} P_0)$, from Eq. (4-1). Total indirect taxes (including miscellaneous government revenues) are 47.5 (Table 3-3), so the above equation can be solved as

$$B_H (1+z) = \frac{472.5 - 47.5}{472.5} = 0.89947$$

Since $P_H = 1$, the indirect tax rate, v_H, is given by

$$v_H = (1/0.89947) - 1 = 0.11176$$

4. Assume total imports are 116.5 (Table 3-1). If all are used as intermediate inputs into home-goods production (for simplicity, this ignores imported inputs into export-goods production), then $a_{0H} = 116.5/472.5 = 0.24656$.
5. Value added at factor cost is 308.5—that is, value of production 472.5 less indirect taxes 47.5 and imports 116.5. A good guess at the 1975 labor share in Portugal is 65 percent, so $a_{LH} = (0.65) (308.5)/472.5 = 0.42439$. Home-goods wage income is 200.52428.
6. Equation (4-1)—a cost equation—now reduces to

$$P_H = 1 = (0.42439 + 0.24656) (1 + z) (1.11176)$$

which can be solved to get $z = 0.3406$. A profit mark-up of about 35 percent on input costs including taxes is a typical value for such a number. It indicates that the profits make up about a third of the total value of output including raw material imports—a normal fraction for a semi-industrialized country.
7. If export value, $P_E X_E$, is rounded to 65 (Table 3-1) and the export labor share is 60 percent, then wage income from exports is 39 and profits are 26. Total labor income, Y_W, is 239.52428. With remittances REM = 23.6, profit income, Y_Z, is 157.57833.
8. Direct taxes net of transfers are -13.0 (Table 3-3). It is reasonable to assume a tax of 17.0 on capital income ($T_Z = 17$) and a compensating net transfer to labor ($T_W = -30$). Disposable labor and profit incomes become 269.52428 and 140.57833 respectively.
9. The stylized fact is that the consumption share from labor incomes usually runs between 95 and 100 percent. If we set $\gamma_W = 0.98$, then consumption expenditure from wage income is $D_W = 264.13379$. Since the total value of consumption is 364.9, consumption from profit income, D_Z, is 100.76621 as a residual. The profit income consumption share is $\gamma_Z = 100.76621/140.57833 = 0.7168$. Since savings from profit income includes corporate saving, depreciation allowances, and remittances, this is a plausible estimate for γ_Z.
10. As a check on the calculations, one can compute savings levels from Eqs. (4-10) through (4-12). Rounded off, these turn out to be $S^{\text{Priv}} = 45.2$, $S^{\text{Gov}} = -20.7$, $S^{\text{For}} = 27.9$. The sum of these three sources of saving is 52.4, the value of investment $P_H I$.

The key parameter in solving the model is the inverse multiplier Q, defined in Eq. (4-15). With the numbers just developed, Q takes the value 0.42029, and the multiplier $1/Q$ is 2.3793. Using Eq. (4-14), one can derive the following increases in home-goods output which should result from unit increases in the variables listed below:

Real exports (X_E)	2.08
Remittances (REM)	1.71
Workers' transfers ($-T_W$)	2.33

Profit income taxes (T_Z) −1.71
Investment (I) 2.38
Government purchases (G) 2.38

As static multipliers go, these values are relatively low, but then it should be remembered that Portugal suffers from considerable leakages of purchasing power through its trade gap. Measures aimed at increasing aggregate demand also increase net imports, so a substantial part of their effect is diluted.

Now consider a 25 percent devaluation, with the exchange rate e changing its value from 1.0 to 1.25. Internal prices of exports and noncompetitive imports also take a value 1.25, and one can show from Eq. (4-1) that the home-goods price rises to 1.092 as a result of import cost pressures (with an unchanged mark-up rate z). The multiplier falls from 2.38 to 2.20 as devaluation reduces the power of expansionary fiscal policy.

Table 4-2 summarizes the effects of devaluation on aggregate economic indicators. Along with a 9.1 percent price inflation, there is substantial contraction. Real GDP and home-goods output fall, while the trade balance improves by 10.1 percent in real terms as imports drop along with output. Because of the price increases, however, nominal GDP goes up with devaluation, and the trade balance in domestic prices gets worse.

These results have several implications for policy. First, on the basis of the pre-devaluation value of the multiplier, the home-goods output reduction could be offset by an increase of 10.19 in export volume, X_E. The required elasticity of exports with respect to the exchange rate would be about 0.63. It is uncertain whether traditional exports would be so responsive to devaluation in the time it would take the multiplier effects of the contraction to work through the economy. On these grounds, a reduction of economic activity after currency depreciation is a real possibility.

Second, devaluation induces a larger fiscal deficit. If steps such as tax increases or expenditure reductions were taken to counter this "adverse" development, further contraction would follow. Normally, tight fiscal policy is recommended by orthodoxy as a concomitant to devaluation. In most underdeveloped economies, this is scarcely a sensible course to follow.

Table 4-2 Effects of a 25 percent devaluation

	$e = 1.0$	$e = 1.25$	Change, %
GDP at nominal factor cost	373.5	385.4	+3.19
GDP at predevaluation factor cost	373.5	359.7	−3.69
Price of home goods	1.0	1.091	+9.10
Output of home goods	472.5	451.3	−4.49
Nominal fiscal deficit	20.7	23.7	+14.49
Trade balance at international prices	−51.5	−46.3	+10.10
Trade balance in domestic prices	−51.5	−57.8	−12.23
Nominal current account (includes remittances)	−27.9	−28.3	−1.43
Increase in money base	−7.2	−4.6	+36.11

Finally, devaluation induces an increase of 2.6 in the sum of the fiscal deficit and the current account surplus, or the increment in money base. With other sources of new base (such as the increase in rediscount) held constant, this amounts to an increase of less than 10 percent over the amount of base that would "normally" have to be created in Portugal during 1976 (Table 3-5). On the other hand, devaluation would induce additional price inflation of 9 or 10 percent. The creation of new money would barely keep up with the extra price increases, and devaluation could prove contractionary on the monetary side as well.

The main economic points of this section can be summarized as follows:

1. In the short run in a country like Portugal, the balance-of-payments deficit is "structural"; that is, neither imports nor exports are very sensitive to price changes at a given level of domestic output.
2. As a consequence, any favorable short-term effects of devaluation on the trade balance come mostly through economic contraction rather than substitution.
3. Devaluation not only reduces output and employment but redistributes income from wages to profits.
4. Thus devaluation is a costly cure, and a cure strong enough to reduce the trade gap substantially in the short run may be unacceptable.

Structural problems can never be eliminated by palliative policies. To drive the point home, another example for Egypt is presented next section.

4-3 MACROECONOMICS OF EGYPTIAN FOOD SUBSIDIES

In Egypt as in other food-importing countries, subsidies on staple foodstuffs became macroeconomically important in the mid-1970s. Operations of the General Authority for Supply Commodities, which administers most cost-of-living subsidies in Egypt, amounted to LE 491 million in 1975, with LE 266 million going to maintain a low consumer price for bread and the balance of expenditures going mainly to other food items. In one revealing comparison, total cost-of-living subsidies in 1973 were only LE 89 million. In another comparison, consolidated current government expenditures in 1975 were about LE 1670 million. In terms both of growth over time and share in the government budget, the subsidies obviously came to play a major role in fiscal policy.

The expansion of subsidies was largely a response to escalating world grain prices. Egypt imports about 3 million tons of wheat per year, plus other staples. Because of these irreducible imports, the Egyptian balance of payments went rapidly into deficit after the 1972 to 1974 grain-price explosion. The policy response was to maintain domestic food prices at their precrisis levels, with a consequent escalation in government expenditure and a deficit in the government's current account. Inquiry into the political reasons underlying the decision to subsidize staple foods is beyond our scope, but there is little doubt that the policy was unavoidable. What is more unsettling from the orthodox point of view is that the subsidies were inevitable on macroeconomic grounds as well. Table 4-3, which sets out a more complex variant of the Portuguese

Table 4-3 Equations for the Egypt model

	I Input-output balances	

$$X_R = a_{RR}X_R + a_{RU}X_U + a_{RF}X_F + C_R + E_R + G_R \tag{4-20}$$

$$X_U = a_{UR}X_R + a_{UU}X_U + a_{UF}X_F + C_U + kI + \Delta S_U + E_U + G_U \tag{4-21}$$

$$X_F = a_{FF}X_F + C_F + \Delta S_F \tag{4-22}$$

	II Cost and price determination	

$$B_R = a_{RR}Q_R + a_{UR}Q_U + a_{0R}P_{0R} + a_{LR}w_R \tag{4-23}$$

$$B_U = a_{RU}P_{RU} + a_{UU}Q_U + a_{0U}P_{0U} + a_{LU}w_U \tag{4-24}$$

$$B_F = a_{RF}P_{RF} + a_{UF}Q_U + a_{FF}Q_F + a_{0F}P_{0F} + a_{LF}w_F \tag{4-25}$$

$$Q_R = B_R(1 + z_R) \tag{4-26}$$

$$Q_U = B_U(1 + z_U)(1 + v_U) \tag{4-27}$$

$$Q_F = B_F(1 + z_F) \tag{4-28}$$

	III Balance of payments (at official rate, in Egyptian pounds)	

$$e_0 P_I^*(1 - k)I + e_0 P_{0C}^* C_0 + e_0 P_{0R}^* a_{0R}X_R + e_0 P_{0U}^* a_{0U}X_U + e_0 P_{0F}^* a_{0F}X_F$$
$$- e_0 P_R^* E_R - e_0 P_U^* E_U - e_0(\text{REM}) - e_0(\text{TRANS}) = e_0(\text{DEF}) \tag{4-29}$$

	IV Income generation	

$$Y_R = w_R a_{LR}X_R + n z_R B_R X_R \tag{4-30}$$

$$Y_U = w_U a_{LU}X_U + w_F a_{LF}X_F + (1 - n) z_R B_R X_R + e_{\text{REM}}(\text{REM}) \tag{4-31}$$

$$Y_R^{\text{Disp}} = Y_R \tag{4-32}$$

$$Y_U^{\text{Disp}} = (1 - t_U) Y_U \tag{4-33}$$

$$D_R = \gamma_R Y_R^{\text{Disp}} \tag{4-34}$$

$$D_U = \gamma_U Y_U^{\text{Disp}} \tag{4-35}$$

	V Consumer spending	

$$F_j = Q_R \theta_{Rj} + Q_U \theta_{Uj} + P_F \theta_{Fj} + P_{0C}\theta_{0j} \quad j = R, U \tag{4-36 and 4-37}$$

$$C_{Rj} = \theta_{Rj} + (m_{Rj}/Q_R)(D_j - F_j) \quad j = R, U \tag{4-38 and 4-39}$$

$$C_{Uj} = \theta_{Uj} + (m_{Uj}/Q_U)(D_j - F_j) \quad j = R, U \tag{4-40 and 4-41}$$

$$C_{Fj} = \theta_{Fj} + (m_{Fj}/P_F)(D_j - F_j) \quad j = R, U \tag{4-42 and 4-43}$$

$$C_{0j} = \theta_{0j} + (m_{0j}/P_{0C})(D_j - F_j) \quad j = R, U \tag{4-44 and 4-45}$$

$$C_R = C_{RR} + C_{RU} \tag{4-46}$$

$$C_U = C_{UR} + C_{UU} \tag{4-47}$$

$$C_F = C_{FR} + C_{FU} \tag{4-48}$$

$$C_0 = C_{0R} + C_{0U} \tag{4-49}$$

	VI Determination of import prices by tariffs	

$$P_{0i} = e_{0i}(1 + t_{0i}) P_{0i}^* \quad i = C, U, F \tag{4-50 to 4-52}$$

Table 4-3 Equations for the Egypt model (*Continued*)

VII Government revenues

$$GR = B_U(1 + z_U)\, v_U X_U + t_U Y_U + B_{UZ} z_U X_U + B_{FZ} z_F X_F$$
$$+ e_{It} t_I P_I^*(1 - k)\, I + e_{0C} t_{0C} P_{0C}^* C_0 + e_{0U} t_{0U} P_0^* u^a_{0U} X_U$$
$$+ e_{0F} t_{0F} P_{0F}^* a_{0F} X_F + (e_R P_R^* - Q_R)\, E_R + (e_U P_U^* - Q_U)\, E_U$$
$$+ e_0\,(\text{TRANS}) + (e_I - e_0)\, P_I^*(1 - k)\, I + (e_{0C} - e_0)\, P_{0C}^* C_0$$
$$+ (e_{0R} - e_0)\, P_{0R}^* a_{0R} X_R + (e_{0U} - e_0)\, P_0^* u^a_{0U} X_U$$
$$+ (e_{0F} - e_0)\, P_{0F}^* a_{0F} X_F - (e_R - e_0)\, P_R^* E_R$$
$$- (e_U - e_0)\, P_U^* E_U - (e_{\text{REM}} - e_0)\,(\text{REM}) \tag{4-53}$$

VIII Government expenditures

$$GE = Q_R G_R + Q_U G_U + (e_{0R} P_{0R}^* - P_{0R})\, a_{0R} X_R + (Q_R - P_{RU})\, a_{RU} X_U$$
$$+ (Q_R - P_{RF})\, a_{RF} X_F + (Q_F - P_F)\, C_F \tag{4-54}$$

IX Savings-investment balance

$$Q_U k I + e_I (1 + t_I)\, P_I^*(1 - k)\, I + Q_U \Delta S_U + Q_F \Delta S_F = (1 - \gamma_R)\, Y_R$$
$$+ (1 - \gamma_U)(1 - t_U)\, Y_U$$
$$+ (GR - GE)$$
$$+ e_0(\text{DEF}) \tag{4-55}$$

model, can be used to work out the probable macro effects of subsidy cuts through administered food price increases. Not surprisingly, raising the price of a staple item that is consumed preferentially by poor people turns out to be contractionary.[3]

The Egyptian model comprises 36 equations grouped into nine blocks. It amounts to an extension of the model of Table 4-1 to three sectors and two consumer groups and has about three times as many equations. We will use it here only to quantify the impacts of reductions in food subsidies, so some of the detail is otiose. In particular, many exchange rates are included in the specification, since at the time the model was designed there was much discussion in Egypt about the implications of simplifying that nation's multiple rate system. We will not go into that here and would get much the same results about food subsidies with a simpler balance-of-payments description. The art of practical modeling is to come up with a parsimonious set of equations which still provides interesting results. At least as far as food-subsidy reductions are concerned, the model of Table 4-3 does not reach that goal.

Block I

Here are input-output balances of the usual sort for rural, subscript R, urban U, and food F sectors. The numbers fitting these material balances for 1975 appear in the

---

[3]Our analysis broadly follows that in a consultant report prepared for the World Bank by the author in 1976. The Bank is of course not responsible for any conclusions reached here.

SAM of Table 3-6. In the data, the rural sector is identified with agricultural production, the food sector with the food-processing industry coupled with government food price subsidies, and the urban sector with all other economic activities. The final demand categories for these sectors are quite standard except that the urban sector is assumed to supply only a fraction, $k(= 0.65)$, of investment demand, I, the rest coming from imports. As usual, the input-output coefficients a_{ij} are supposed to remain constant in volume terms, although a_{RF} and a_{0F} for rural and imported inputs into food production are to some extent policy variables. Their values are initially chosen to reflect the supply mix in 1975.

Block II

Here are cost-determination equations similar to Eq. (4-1). Basic, or prime, costs B_R, B_U, and B_F are defined in Eqs. (4-23) through (4-25). Note that in several cases intermediate input costs are assumed to be fixed by the government; that is P_{RU} in Eq. (4-24) is the cost of rural inputs into the urban sector, instead of rural per-unit production cost, Q_R. The reduction in urban input costs, $Q_R - P_{RU}$, is maintained by subsidy. Equations (4-26) through (4-28) show how prime costs are multiplied into total costs Q_R, Q_U, and Q_F by markup and tax rates.

Block III

Equation (4-29) gives the balance of payments in world prices multiplied by the official exchange rate. Elsewhere in the specification, exchange rates for specific classes of traded goods are introduced to capture the effects of Egypt's multiple rate system. Five types of imports are shown in Eq. (4-29): intermediate imports for the three production sectors (subscripts $0i; i = R, U, F$) and capital goods and consumer imports. Foreign-exchange inflows are from exports of rural and urban goods, net export of services (mainly emigrants' remittances REM), and unrequited transfers (TRANS) from foreign governments.

Block IV

Equations (4-30) and (4-31) define rural and urban incomes in a two-way disaggregation of row 5 of Table 3-6. Surpluses in the rural sector (land rents, in practice) are assumed to be split between rural and urban income recipients; in the data, the factor n fixing the rent distribution is given a value of one-half. Also, city dwellers receive emigrant remittances, REM, at a favorable exchange rate, e_{REM}. Equations (4-32) and (4-33) define disposable incomes, with urban citizens paying an income tax at rate t_U. Finally, Eqs. (4-34) and (4-35) resemble Eqs. (4-6) and (4-7) in the Portuguese model, determining consumer expenditures $D_i(i = R, U)$ from disposable incomes, Y_i^{Disp} and consumption shares, γ_i.

Block V

The Egyptian model was set up with several sectors to capture the effects of shifts in consumer demand among different commodities in response to food price changes.

Of course, this additional detail requires some equations to forecast just how consumers will behave. Largely because it makes such a model easy to solve, the so-called *linear expenditure system* (LES) was used. Equations (4-36) through (4-45) describe the LES in an economy with two consumer groups and four commodities (the three domestic sectors plus imports). Appendix B presents details and interpretation of the LES demand system. In its application to Egypt, consumer prices are taken to be production costs in the rural and urban sectors Q_R and Q_U, the subsidized food price, P_F, and the posttariff import price, P_{0C}. Equations (4-46) through (4-49) sum consumption levels by class to get the totals appearing in the balance equations [Eqs. (4-20) through (4-22)] and the balance-of-payments equation [Eq. (4-29)].

Block VI

The three equations here relate domestic prices of consumer, urban, and food intermediate imports to their corresponding world prices through tariffs and differentiated exchange rates e_{0C}, e_{0U}, and e_{0F}. The government implicitly subsidizes or taxes certain classes of exports and imports in a multiple exchange rate system. These imputed transactions show up in Eqs. (4-53) and (4-54) for government revenues and expenditures.

Block VII

Government revenue is defined here, including the usual direct and indirect taxes and tariff revenues. In addition, enterprise surpluses from the urban and food sectors in the largely nationalized Egyptian economy are assumed to go to the government, which also receives benefits of export exchange subsidies and the domestic equivalent of the foreign-exchange inflow item **TRANS** . Finally, the government makes exchange profits (on imports) or losses (on exports) from differentials inherent in the multiple rate system.

Block VIII

Here is government expenditure, going for current purchases from the rural and urban sectors, and subsidies on (1) intermediate imports into the rural sector (fertilizer and pesticides), (2) intermediate sales from agriculture to the urban sector (subsidy on cotton inputs to textile manufacturing), (3) intermediate sales from the rural sector to food processing (no subsidy assumed in the present data specification), and (4) the subsidy on final sales of the food industry to consumers.

Block IX

This shows the savings-investment balance, which the enterprising reader might wish to derive from the rest of the equations in the model. On the investment side are capital formation (broken down into domestic and foreign components by the fraction k) and stock changes in the urban and food processing sectors. Savings comes from persons (including accumulation by the social security system), the government, and the balance-of-payments deficit. As shown in Table 3-6, the trade deficit and (urban) personal savings are the main positive items in this accounting.

As stated, the model has 35 independent equations with 78 variables; 43 additional restrictions must be imposed. Many of the variables, of course, are "naturally" exogenous or fixed by government policy. These include

World prices of seven types of traded goods: $P_I^*, P_{0C}^*, P_{0R}^*, P_{0U}^*, P_{0F}^*, P_R^*$, and P_U^*.
Exchange rates for these commodities, remittances, and official transactions: e_I, e_{0C}, $e_{0R}, e_{0U}, e_{0F}, e_R, e_U, e_{REM}$, and e_0.
Tariffs on four types of imports: t_I, t_{0C}, t_{0U}, and t_{0F}.
Foreign-exchange inflows from remittances and government transfers: REM and TRANS.
Tax rates on production and urban income: v_U and t_U.
Prices maintained by government subsidy: P_{0R}, P_{RU}, P_{RF}, and P_F.
Government purchases, investment, stock changes and exports: $G_R, G_U, I, \Delta S_U, \Delta S_F$, E_R, E_U.
Investment and income distribution parameters: k, u.
Sector markup rates and money wages: z_R, z_U, z_F, w_R, w_U, and w_F.

With these 43 exogenous variables, the rest are determined endogenously. The equations are structured so that they could be solved with a hand calculator, though in practice it would save time to program a computer to do the work. A solution routine would begin with Block II, where—with fixed input-output coefficients—all costs are determined independently of the quantity solution to the model. Quantities can, in turn, be computed with a simple iterative scheme. First, the equations of Block IV make consumption expenditures D_R and D_U linear functions of initially guessed sector output levels X_R, X_U, and X_F, with factor prices and tax rates given. Next, the LES equations of Block V make sectoral consumption levels $C_i(i = R, U, F, 0)$ linear functions of D_R and D_U. Finally, the linear demand-supply balances in Block I provide a new estimate of the output vector. This completely linear iteration is easy to keep up until "new" values of outputs from the demand-supply balances Eqs. (4-20) through (4-22) are a close approximation to the "old" levels used to generate them. With Egyptian parameters estimated from Table 3-6 along the lines indicated last section, at most ten iterations of this type were required to reduce the relative errors in demand and supply to about 0.01 percent.[4]

With the output iteration complete, the current account foreign trade deficit follows from Block III and the government accounts from Blocks VII and VIII. Block

---

[4] As stated, the model is completely demand-determined, as it should be in the short run. However, supply limitations could easily be imposed. For example, if rural output X_R were fixed in the short run, then each solution of the type described above with a fixed markup z_R would determine a level of demand for rural products. For demand above (below) supply X_R, the markup could be increased (reduced) until the market cleared. A model taking into account limitations in agricultural supply is discussed in the next chapter.

IX then gives a savings-equals-investment check (in current prices) on the whole procedure.

The foregoing is a thoroughly Keynesian (or Kaleckian) calculation and could be described in terms of price-responsive multipliers. The main point is that prices are fixed by markup rates in the cost functions of Block II, so that the model can show what happens to both real and nominal incomes when things like subsidies or exchange rates are changed. These income effects dominate the solutions to the model, as will be demonstrated shortly.

Now consider food subsidies. If the cost of production in the food sector is normalized at 1.0, then the subsidy of LE 491 million in 1975 had the effect of reducing consumer food prices to 0.5854. The immediate impact of an attempt to reduce total subsidies by raising food prices would be to drive up the cost of living for all consumers, with the heaviest burden falling on poor people who devote a large share of their budgets to subsistence products. Since food demand is price-inelastic, the percentage decrease in actual consumption would be considerably less than the percentage price increase. However, both real food intake and imports would fall to a certain extent.

Because of the increase in living costs, real income of all consumers would, of course, fall. As just noted, the larger share of this decrease in real purchasing power would show up outside the market for food, leading to a decrease in demand for nonagricultural products. The resulting slump in economic activity would lead to further reductions in imports, private saving, and government revenues. In terms of the savings-investment balance, foreign savings (imports less exports) and private savings would decline, and government savings (revenues less expenditures) would compensate by going up. The overall effect on the economy would be contractionary, with the poor bearing the brunt of the real income loss.

Table 4-4 summarizes the model-calculated effects of a 29 percent increase in the food price, which would, in the absence of compensating adjustments, reduce subsidies by LE 200 million. Such a price increase would drive up the cost of living of rural and urban income recipients by about 2.2 and 8.2 percent, respectively. The second column of the table indicates that the ensuing decrease in aggregate demand would reduce real GDP by about LE 240 million. Food imports themselves would fall by no more than LE 60 million, although the balance of payments would improve by LE 114 million as a result of the overall contraction in the economy.

Evidently, a reduction of food subsidies in and of itself would be a misdirected policy; it would not reduce food imports by very much, but it *would* lead to a substantial decrease in economic activity as consumers cut back on purchases of other goods rather than do without the chief necessity of life. Could the contractionary impact of the reduction in subsidies be offset? Two devices present themselves.

First, there would surely be pressure for increased wages if food prices went up. The third column in Table 4-4 shows what happens when wages rise enough to offset the loss in real income caused by higher food prices. By assumption, wage increments would be passed on in further price increases; we are in fact describing the first round of a wage-price spiral which might be touched off by the reduced subsidies. The table shows that a price index weighted by initial value-added levels in the three sectors

Table 4-4 Economic effects of increasing the subsidized food price to reduce subsidies by LE 200 million ex ante*

	Base solution	Solution with price increase	Solution with price and wage increases	Solution with price, wage, and investment increases
GDP in base prices	4.4173	4.1801	4.2572	4.4177
Percent change in real GDP		−5.37	−3.62	0.01
Percent changes in costs				
Rural			2.73	2.73
Urban			5.56	5.56
Food			0.70	0.70
Total			4.52	4.52
Total imports	1.6204	1.5069	1.5416	1.6314
Food imports	0.5690	0.5103	0.5252	0.5333
Trade deficit	0.4994	0.3858	0.4206	0.5104
Government expenditure	1.7857	1.5495	1.6458	1.6526
Government expenditure on food subsidies	0.4909	0.2608	0.2761	0.2804
Government deficit	0.1429	0.0058	0.0402	−0.0159
Percent changes in cost of living				
Rural		2.17	5.99	5.99
Urban		8.23	11.66	11.66
Percent changes in real income				
Rural		−6.77	−7.19	−6.20
Urban		−13.98	−8.80	0.60

*Note: The consumer food price increases from 0.5854 to 0.75439 in the last three solutions. Wage increases in the last two are rural sector, 0.19213 to 0.19629; urban sector, 0.44652 to 0.48329; food sector, 0.53544 to 0.57953. In the last solution, gross capital formation increases from 0.840 to 1.002.

would go up by 4.5 percent, while the additional inflation for rural and urban consumers would be 3.8 and 3.4 percent, respectively. The wage increases would generate enough demand to make the reduction in real GDP only LE 160 million. Further rounds in the wage-price spiral would close the gap by more, but only at the cost of a significant burst of inflation.

A second way to offset the subsidy decrease would be to increase aggregate demand—say by an increase in investment. The last column of Table 4-4 shows that if gross capital formation rose by 19 percent, to LE 1.002 billion, the higher investment plus wage increases could restore the original level of GDP. But note that there are still significant distributional effects—the real income of rural consumers falls by 6.2 percent, while that of urban consumers goes up by 0.60 percent. Moreover, the overall trade deficit widens by about LE 10 million. Investment mainly creates demand for urban workers and imported goods.

Any summary assessment of the effects of reducing food subsidies would depend on the likelihood of the events inserted into the various model solutions; a push for high wages in response to higher food prices seems quite probable, an increase in real investment less so. But the important thing to note is that even if the food price increase is offset in macro terms by higher investment, there will still be a significant loss in incomes in rural areas. This, of course, could be offset by higher agricultural prices, which could be offset by higher subsidies or higher urban wages ... and the story begins again.

SELECTED ADDITIONAL READINGS

Abel, Andrew B., and Luis M. C. P. Beleza: "Input-Output Pricing in a Keynesian Model of the Portuguese Economy," *Journal of Development Economics* 5:125–38, 1978. (An extension of the Portuguese model to take into account problems of agricultural pricing and imports.)

Cooper, Richard N.: *Currency Devaluation in Developing Countries*, Essays in International Finance, No. 86, International Finance Section, Department of Economics, Princeton University, Princeton, N.J., 1971. (Reviews the theory of contractionary devaluations and the problematic success of this policy instrument in practice.)

Diamand, Marcelo: "Towards a Change in the Economic Paradigm through the Experience of Developing Countries," *Journal of Development Economics*, 5:19–53, 1978. (An interesting analytical survey of Latin American "structuralist" ideas about devaluation, inflation, contraction, and other problems.)

Dornbusch, Rudiger, and Stanley Fischer: *Macroeconomics*, McGraw-Hill, New York, 1977. (Chapter 3 reviews multiplier calculations.)

Eichner, Alfred S., and J. A. Kregel: "An Essay on Post-Keynesian Theory: A New Paradigm in Economics," *Journal of Economic Literature*, 8:1293–1314, 1975. (Reviews post-Kalecki theoretical developments. Good bibliography.)

Johansen, Leif: *Public Economics*, North-Holland, Amsterdam, 1965. (Chapter 3 presents an insightful review of Keynesian fiscal analysis.)

Kalecki, Michael: *Selected Essays on the Dynamics of the Capitalist Economy*, 1930–1970, Cambridge University Press, Cambridge, England, 1971. (A basic collection of papers reflecting Kalecki's ideas about capitalist development. Useful background for the models of this chapter.)

Krugman, Paul, and Lance Taylor: "Contractionary Effects of Devaluation," *Journal of International Economics* 8:445–56, 1978. (A theoretical development of the ideas underlying the Portugal model here. Gives some history of previous thought along the same lines.)

FIVE

MARKUP PRICING, INFLATIONARY PRICE SHIFTS, AND MACRO DISTRIBUTION IN THE SHORT RUN

In this chapter, using three successive models incorporating the markup pricing hypothesis introduced in Chap. 4, we conclude our discussion of relatively short-run changes in macro equilibrium. Markup pricing is usually assumed to exist in industries organized along oligopolistic lines, where changes in variable cost are simply passed along to purchasers through the markup and supply varies to take up fluctuations in demand. The markup rate itself may be assumed constant or else an increasing function of the level of economic activity. Competitive "supply and demand" forces do not determine price behavior under markup assumptions. In nonoligopolistic markets—in much of agriculture, for example—the supply-and-demand analysis fits much better.

The three models discussed in this chapter are designed with inflationary situations in mind. The general environment is one in which "most" prices are increasing steadily, and we are worried about relative movements around trend. Another implicit assumption is that the monetary authorities are pursuing an accommodating policy or (nearly the same thing) that they cannot control the money supply at all, and liquidity is just materializing as required to meet demand. Explicit incorporation of monetary processes into models of inflation is postponed until more analytical tools can be brought to bear in Chap. 9.

In Sec. 5-1, we set out the rules by which equilibrium is determined in a one-sector economy with markup pricing and a fixed money wage. This sets the stage for the model of Sec. 5-2, in which it is assumed that the wage is fully indexed, with a certain lag, to previous rates of price inflation. The question asked is whether shortening the lag will accelerate inflation, and the answer turns out to be yes. Conflicts about income distribution implicit in the model are pointed out, as well as its possible applicability to other indexing policies, such as a "crawling peg" for the exchange rate.

Finally, in Secs. 5-3 through 5-5, we introduce another sector ("food" or "agriculture") in which supply-demand pricing applies. Impacts on both output and prices of such exogenous shocks as crop shortfalls are investigated, and the limitations on policy formation imposed by Engel's law and other rigidities in the system are pointed out.

5-1 THE SIMPLEST MODEL OF MARKUP PRICING

Consider a one-sector economy where the material balance takes the form

$$X = C + I \tag{5-1}$$

where, as usual, X is output (best considered as measured relative to trend), C is consumption, and I is investment. Prices are formed according to the rule

$$P = (1 + z) w a_{LX} \tag{5-2}$$

where P is the price level, z is the markup rate, w is the money wage, and a_{LX} is the labor-output ratio. This is the pricing theory introduced in the devaluation model of Sec. 4-1; the reader might want to compare the results there with those about to follow.

Let s_W and s_Z be the savings propensities from labor income wL and markup income zwL. Then the savings-investment balance takes the form

$$PI = (1 + z) w a_{LX} I$$

$$= s_W wL + s_Z zwL$$

$$= s_W w a_{LX} X + s_Z zw a_{LX} X \tag{5-3}$$

Many terms can be canceled here; after a bit more manipulation, one solves for the markup rate in equilibrium as

$$z = \frac{(I/X) - s_W}{s_Z - (I/X)} \tag{5-4}$$

where z will be positive as long as there is a (positive) difference between the savings propensities s_Z and s_W. With $s_Z > s_W$, the investment share I/X has to be somewhere in between if macro equilibrium is going to exist at all.

The interpretation of Eq. (5-4) is that z rises along with the investment share. With I/X going up, more savings is required, and this is obtained by increased markups and shifts in the income distribution toward profit receivers. The curves labeled I_1 and I_2 in Fig. 5-1 illustrate what is going on. With investment fixed at level I_1, the markup rate, z, required for savings-investment equilibrium is a decreasing function of output, X. The curve shifts out as investment rises to I_2. In effect, Eq. (5-4) defines an aggregate demand curve, for as long as the money wage and productivity stay constant, we could put the output price measured in wage units P/w on the vertical axis in place of z.

The rising line in Fig. 5-1 is a supply curve showing the markup rate

$$z = f(X) \tag{5-5}$$

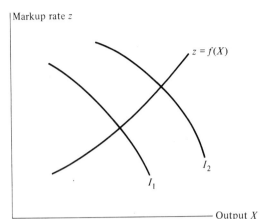

Markup rate z

$z = f(X)$

I_2

I_1

Output X

Figure 5-1 Macro equilibrium in an economy with markup pricing.

Such a relationship can be justified in various ways. One story in terms of monopoly power and decreasing returns appears in Sec. 9-1; another follows less formally from standard theories of oligopoly. In any case, when they are estimated econometrically, relationships like Eq. (5-5) tend to do pretty well. The relevant elasticity might range around $\frac{1}{2}$ or 1.

As Fig. 5-1 demonstrates, Eqs. (5-4) and (5-5) together define mutually consistent levels of output and the markup rate. Inflation can get started, at least, from an increment in investment, which will lead to both output and price increases on forced-saving lines. Further spins on the inflationary spiral require other mechanisms, but demand pressure can get things under way.

To fix ideas about magnitudes, note from Eq. (5-4) that the elasticity of the aggregate demand curve is

$$z' = \lambda(I' - X')$$

where

$$\lambda = \frac{s_Z - s_W}{[(I/X) - s_W][s_Z - (I/X)]}(I/X)$$

Furthermore,

$$z' = \phi X'$$

from Eq. (5-5), so that we can solve for X' as

$$X' = \frac{\lambda}{\lambda + \phi}I'$$

For savings shares of 0.05 from wage income and 0.425 from profits and an overall investment share of 0.2, the coefficient λ becomes 2.22222. If the elasticity of z with respect to X is 0.5, then $\lambda/(\lambda + \phi) = 0.81633$, or a 10 percent increase in investment leads to an 8.16 percent increase in real output. It also increases the markup rate by 4.08 percent and the price level (relative to the money wage) by 1.63 percent. More rapacious capitalists would enforce a higher markup elasticity, ϕ, making the price response to an increase in investment demand stronger. Workers' wage demands, on the other hand, would drive up the price with an elasticity of 1. Some implications of this observation when there are lags in worker and capitalist response to price changes are the subject of the following section.

5-2 WAGE INDEXING AND INFLATION

Throughout much of this book, we say very little about lags in response and the detailed dynamics of growth and inflation. In most underdeveloped countries, it costs little in terms of economic insight to ignore lags, since the numbers are available only infrequently and often late. Worrying seriously about quarterly or monthly behavior makes sense only when the relevant indicators are at hand.

In some circumstances, however, lag distributions are central in the determination of economic response. Then one has to guess their nature as best one can. The rather extreme example of 100 percent wage indexing is used in this section to illustrate the point.[1]

As before, assume markup pricing, but with an adjustment lag. The simplest formulation would replace Eq. (5-2) with an equation of the form

$$P_t = h(1 + z) w_t a_{LX} + (1 - h) P_{t-1} \tag{5-6}$$

where h is an adjustment coefficient which, on an annual basis, might take a value of $\frac{1}{2}$ or more. In words, Eq. (5-6) says that the price, P_t, at time t is some average of the markup on *current* labor costs, $w_t a_{LX}$, and the price last year, P_{t-1}. As before, we suppose that the markup rate z depends on the current output level, X,

$$z = f(X) \tag{5-7}$$

Wages typically lag behind price increases because of fixed-term contracts, management pressure, and perhaps a bit of money illusion on the part of workers. Very militant and well-organized workers might seek to maintain a real wage, say R; but, at best, they would try to do so through contracts with a *lagged* wage escalator tied to price increases.

If the money wage adjustments take place annually, they would be

$$w_t = RP_{t-1} \tag{5-8}$$

With substitution of Eq. (5-8) into Eq. (5-6), modest manipulations show that the annual rate of inflation would be

$$\frac{P_t - P_{t-1}}{P_{t-1}} = h[(1 + z) Ra_{LX} - 1] = hF \tag{5-9}$$

---

[1]The model of this section follows the paper by Modigliani and Padoa-Schioppa cited in the Selected Additional Readings.

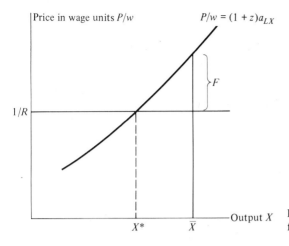

Figure 5-2 Markup inflation with a fully indexed wage.

As long as the term in brackets exceeds 0, there will be inflation. Figure 5-2 illustrates what is going on.

As in Fig. 5-1, the assumed positive relationship of Eq. (5-7) between the markup rate and output level generates a rising aggregate supply curve, representing the real price P/w which firms demand in return for a given volume of production, X. Workers, on the other hand, demand that the real wage w/P equal R, or that $P/w = 1/R$. This horizontal line replaces the downward-sloping aggregate demand curve of Fig. 5-1, which was based on forced saving by workers. They reject that in the present model, and stable prices are possible only at the output level, X^*. If, through aggregate demand policy, the government maintains an output level, $\overline{X}$, then there will be inflation proportional to the gap labeled F.

The distributional impacts of the inflation can be clarified if we observe that the real price of output at time t can be written as

$$P_t/w_t = (1/R) \, [Rh(1 + z) \, a_{LX} + (1 - h)] \qquad (5\text{-}10)$$

If the coefficient h in Eq. (5-6) increases so that capitalists' reaction to wage pressures is speeded up, then P_t/w_t rises in proportion to the inflationary gap term, F, of Eq. (5-9),

$$d(P_t/w_t)/dh = F/R \qquad (5\text{-}11)$$

and the income distribution shifts against labor. On the other hand, workers can, in effect, force a reduction in h and improve their position if they can increase the frequency of their wage readjustments. More frequent adjustment brings the real wage nearer to R on average, but only by accelerating the rate of inflation.

To study the effects of more frequent indexing, assume that instead of one readjustment per year, the rules of the game are changed to permit N of them. Firms will presumably still follow a pricing rule like that of Eq. (5-6), but because of the shorter time between readjustments, their response coefficient *per adjustment period* will be less than h. Let h_N be the coefficient corresponding to N adjustments per year. Then one can show that

$$h_N = 1 - (1 - h)^{1/N} \tag{5-12}$$

where h, as before, is the *annual* rate of price responsiveness by firms.[2] In what follows, we assume that firms maintain their annual rate of price adjustment (which is conservative), so that the rate per period when there are N adjustment periods in a year is given by Eq. (5-12).

By analogy to Eq. (5-9), the inflation rate per period is now

$$\frac{P_t - P_{t-1}}{P_{t-1}} = h_N F$$

and the annual rate becomes

$$\frac{P_N - P_0}{P_0} = (1 + h_N F)^N - 1$$

$$= [1 + (1 - (1 - h)^{1/N}) F]^N - 1 \tag{5-13}$$

For $F = 0.3$, one finds the following annual inflation rates, as a function of the number of adjustment periods, by applying Eq. (5-13):

Number of annual wage readjustments	$h = 0.50$	$h = 0.80$
1	0.150	0.240
2	0.183	0.359
3	0.197	0.422
4	0.205	0.461
5	0.209	0.487

[2] To derive Eq. (5-12), observe that at the end of the successive adjustment periods $1, 2, \cdots, N$ within the year, the price level will be

$$P_1 = h_N G + (1 - h_N) P_0$$

$$P_2 = h_N G + (1 - h_N) P_1 = h_N G[1 + (1 - h_N)] + (1 - h_N)^2 P_0$$

$$\cdots\cdots\cdots\cdots\cdots\cdots\cdots$$

$$P_N = h_N G[1 + (1 - h_N) + (1 - h_N)^2 + \cdots + (1 - h_N)^{N-1}] + (1 - h_N)^N P_0$$

$$= [1 - (1 - h_N)^N] G + (1 - h_N)^N P_0$$

where the term G represents $(1 + z) w_t a_{LX}$ in Eq. (5-6), and the second equation for P_N follows from the first after application of the high-school formula for the partial sum of a geometric series.

With N readjustments per year, P_N is the same as P_1 from Eq. (5-6). Hence, the annual adjustment coefficient is given by

$$h = 1 - (1 - h_N)^N$$

and Eq. (5-12) is a simple rearrangement of this equation.

More frequent readjustments obviously increase the rate of inflation. Moreover, since from Eq. (5-12), h_N is less than h, on a period-for-period basis the real wage rises and the real output price, P_t/w_t, falls from Eq. (5-11). As the above numbers show, the resulting real wage/inflation trade-off through more rapid indexing can be quite acute. Much the same observation would apply to attempts to tie increases in exchange rate to domestic rates of price inflation in a "crawling peg." If intermediate imports make up a substantial item of cost, more frequent adjustments in the exchange rate would both accelerate inflation and raise the real cost of imports, by direct analogy to the results for wages derived here.

This indexing model strongly suggests that one factor underlying the political economy of inflation is precisely the struggle over the level of the real wage. As Fig. 5-2 clearly reveals, conflict between capitalists and workers—coupled with government attempts to maintain high aggregate demand—go together to produce inflation. It is not clear how the political process could allow imposition of any of the three possible remedies for the inflationary gap: reduction of aggregate demand, reduction of workers' claims for a real wage, R, or reduction of capitalists' demand for markup income at a given level of output, X. Inflation is the broom that market economies often choose to try to sweep irreconcilable political conflicts under the rug.

5-3 PRICE POLICY AND THE FOOD THAT PEOPLE CONSUME

Another area of potential conflict centers around the price of "food"; the politically potent urban poor want it to be low; the farmers want it high; and the Finance Minister, who has limited resources for subsidies, is often caught in between. In this and the following sections, we work out a simple model to illustrate some of the problems that can arise. Many of the ideas have already appeared in the Egypt model of Chap. 4; the reader may wish to compare the two approaches. More basically, they stem from Latin American structuralist writings that appeared during the 1950s about the impact of lagging agricultural supply on inflation. References and discussion appear in the works by Seers and Wachter cited at the end of the chapter. A version of the same basic model, more oriented toward the North Atlantic nations, is in the paper by Okun.

The story is told in terms of two sectors—one for food or agriculture (which would represent an aggregate of staple crop production) and the other for the rest of the economy. The stylized facts underlying the formal specification include the following:

1. Staple food consumption is a large proportion of the total, say one-third or more. Food production and processing generate a similar share of total income. The market for food clears rapidly through a changing price, and neither demand nor supply respond much to price movements in the short to medium run. Food demand is also income-inelastic, which means that changes in real income induced by changes in food prices spill over into demand shifts for other sectors.
2. The nonfood sectors have fairly rigid prices, determined by an oligopolistic markup over variable costs of labor and other inputs. There is excess capacity in nonfood products, so supply and employment fluctuate up and down in response to aggre-

gate demand. Part of the demand comes from sales of fertilizer and other manufactured products to farmers.

3. The government intervenes extensively in food-related markets. It subsidizes the use of fertilizer by farmers and the price that consumers pay for food after it has been processed by workers off the farm. Food imports also enter the system in quantities regulated by quota or a government monopoly trading company. Because of the quota, there is no linkage between world and internal prices of food; especially after the "food crisis" of the early 1970s, almost all governments are very careful to insulate their farmers and consumers from the price fluctuations arising in world grain trade.

There are class differences among workers, profit recipients, and farmers in the proportions of income that they save (although for simplicity we assume that their consumer demand patterns are the same). Investment, exports, and government expenditures are—in standard Keynesian fashion—assumed to be exogenous and fixed in real terms in the short run.

The formal model equations appear in Table 5-1. The variables X_F and X_{NF}, respectively, represent output of agricultural products for use as food and inputs such as fertilizer from nonfood, subscript N, sectors into food production, subscript F. Equation (5-14) shows that food output responds to nonfood inputs with an elasticity b (which is given the empirically plausible value of 0.16 in our numerical examples below). Let P_F and P_N be the prices that producers of food and nonfood products receive and s the government subsidy rate on nonfood inputs into food production. Then if, for simplicity, we assume that farmers maximize their profits $P_F X_F - P_N(1 - s)X_{NF}$, their demand function for X_{NF} can be derived using Eq. (5-14). This

Table 5-1 Model equations

$X_F = K(X_{NF})^b$	(5-14)
$X_{NF} = [KbP_F/P_N(1 - s)]^{1/(1-b)}$	(5-15)
$M_F + X_F = C_F$	(5-16)
$P_N = (1 + z)wa_{LN}$	(5-17)
$X_N = X_{NF} + C_N + A_N$	(5-18)
$Y_F = P_F X_F - P_N(1 - s)X_{NF}$	(5-19)
$Y_W = w(a_{LN}X_N + a_{LF}C_F)$	(5-20)
$Y_Z = zwa_{LN}X_N$	(5-21)
$D = \gamma_F Y_F + \gamma_W Y_W + \gamma_Z Y_Z$	(5-22)
$Q_F = (P_F + wa_{LF})(1 - t)$	(5-23)
$E = \theta_F Q_F + \theta_N P_N$	(5-24)
$C_F = \theta_F + (m_F/Q_F)(D - E)$	(5-25)
$C_N = \theta_N + (m_N/P_N)(D - E)$	(5-26)

takes the form of Eq. (5-15)–the demand elasticity is $1/(1 - b)$, which will be a bit greater than 1. Finally, food imports, M_F, add to domestic supply, X_F, in meeting consumption demands, C_F, in Eq. (5-16).

In the nonfood sector, variable cost per unit output is just wa_{LN}, where w is the wage rate and a_{LN} the labor/output ratio in the sector. The output price, P_N, is given in Eq. (5-17), where, for simplicity, z (the rate of producers' markups over costs) is assumed constant. Nonfood output, X_N, goes to satisfy agriculture's input demand, X_{NF} and consumer and autonomous demands C_N and A_N in Eq. (5-18). The autonomous demand comprises investment, exports, and government purchases; it is assumed fixed in the short run.

Equations (5-18) through (5-20) define income flows. Farmers' income, Y_F, is the value of their sales less fertilizer purchases at the subsidized price $P_N(1 - s)$. Workers receive income, Y_W, from nonfood production $wa_{LN}X_N$ and also from processing of agricultural output and imports into consumable form. If total food consumption is C_F and the labor input coefficient into processing it is a_{LF}, then the income generated is $wa_{LF}C_F$. Equation (5-21) gives the income flow, Y_Z, from markups.

In Eq. (5-22), total consumer spending, D, is determined by consumption coefficients γ_F, γ_W, and γ_Z from the three income flows. Farmers and workers have fairly high consumption shares (assumed in the numerical examples to be 0.85 and 0.95, respectively) while the capitalists' share, γ_Z, will be lower (it is given a value of 0.301). Equation (5-23) shows that consumer price of food is the agricultural price plus processing costs $(p_F + wa_{LF})$ multiplied by a subsidy term $1 - t$. When the subsidy rate t is greater than 0, consumers will be acquiring processed food at less than its cost.

Equations (5-24) through (5-26) apply the linear expenditure system of Appendix B to the two-sector model at hand. The cost E of acquiring the base consumption levels of food and nonfood products (θ_F and θ_N, respectively) is defined in Eq. (5-24). The increment in expenditure above the base level, $D - E$, is split between the two commodities according to marginal budget shares m_F and m_N in Eqs. (5-25) and (5-26). The fact that food demand is relatively insensitive to both income and price means that its marginal budget share m_F will be small, while the fixed consumption level, θ_F, will be large in comparison to current purchases. The opposite observations apply to nonfood products.[3]

5-4 HOW THE MODEL WORKS

Policy changes can be traced through this equation system in at least two ways. The first is to confine the discussion only to the market for food. On the supply side, if

---

[3] In the numerical example of Sec. 5-5, the overall food budget share is 0.375; an empirically plausible value of 0.4 for the income elasticity of food demand makes the marginal budget share for food, m_F, equal to 0.15 (for more detail on the relationships among these parameters, see Appendix B). This value for m_F means that consumers allocate 15 cents out of each additional dollar expenditure to food and the rest to nonfood products.

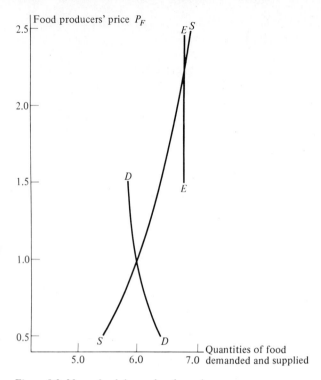

Figure 5-3 Macro food demand and supply curves.

the money wage, w, and markup rate, z, are fixed in the short run, then the nonfood producers' price, P_N, is determined in Eq. (5-17). Given the fertilizer subsidy rates, fertilizer demand, X_{NF}, comes from Eq. (5-15) and food output, X_F, in turn, from Eq. (5-14). Note that the scale of production is determined by the constant K, which stands for land, capital, and other fixed assets used in agriculture. For a given value of K, a supply schedule for X_F can be traced out as the price, P_F, varies. Supply rises as the price goes up, but for an empirically plausible value of the output elasticity b, the response will not be strong. The rising curve SS in Fig. 5-3 illustrates supply response (with a constant level of food imports, M_F, added to domestic production).

To trace the determination of food demand, we have to follow the whole circular flow of incomes in the economy. Begin by noting that agricultural income, Y_F, is essentially determined by the prices P_F and P_N through the supply equations [Eqs. (5-14) and (5-15)] and the definitional equation [Eq. (5-19)]. Both wage income, Y_W, and markup income, Y_Z, depend on nonfood output, X_N, which in turn depends on nonfood consumption, C_N, from Eq. (5-18). This consumption itself is affected by the income flows Y_F, Y_W, and Y_Z, in standard Keynesian fashion. If we let B denote the total consumer spending generated by a unit of output X_N,

$$B = (\gamma_W + \gamma_Z a) w a_{LN}$$

then we can solve for total spending, D, in a multiplier equation,

$$D = \frac{1}{1 - B\,(m_N/P_N)}$$
$$\times \{B[\theta_N + A_N - (m_N/P_N)E] + (\gamma_F P_F + \gamma_W w a_{LF}) X_F + \gamma_W w a_{LF} M_F$$
$$+ [B - \gamma_F P_N (1 - s)] X_{NF}\} \qquad (5\text{-}27)$$

The term outside the braces in Eq. (5-27) is the multiplier—the inverse of the fraction of income generated by X_N *not* spent on itself. The terms inside the braces are the spending on X_N generated, respectively, by autonomous demand, A_N, and the constants in the consumption Eq. (5-26); by food production and imports, X_F and M_F; and by fertilizer sales, X_{NF}. In effect, Eq. (5-27) shows how, for example, food production generates income, taking into account the spending by farmers on nonfood consumer goods and the further incomes that this creates.

With expenditure D determined from Eq. (5-27) plus the prices, it is easy to calculate total food consumption C_F from Eq. (5-25). By varying P_F, we can then trace out the pattern of food demand, as shown by the falling curve DD in Fig. 5-3. Note that this curve is very steep, so that food price changes do not strongly affect consumption demand. Any shifts in the supply curve with demand unchanged would therefore mostly affect prices and leave the consumption level nearly the same, as can be seen by imagining various intersection points of SS and DD as the former curve moves. This acute responsiveness of food prices to supply shifts is, of course, well known and is a key reason why governments intervene in food markets to try to hold prices stable.

Another response pattern is shown by the shifted demand curve EE, which illustrates an increase in the food subsidy rate t in Eq. (5-22). Increasing the subsidy leads to greater real purchasing power for consumers, most of which is *not* directed to food. However, the resulting rise in demand for nonfood products drives up worker and markup incomes in multiplier fashion from Eq. (5-27), and part of the increase does spill over into an upward shift of the food demand curve to EE. But here, the inelasticity of supply leads to a sharp price increase. This is another reason for governments to be wary about intervening in the market for food.

A second way of analyzing equilibrium in this economy is through the responses of saving and investment to changing prices for food. At an equilibrium point (such as the intersection of the SS and DD curves in Fig. 1), the savings-equals-investment identity will be

$$(1 - \gamma_F)\, Y_F + (1 - \gamma_W)\, Y_W + (1 - \gamma_Z)\, Y_Z + P_F M_F = P_N A_N + s P_N X_{NF} + t Q_F C_F$$
$$(5\text{-}28)$$

In terms of Eq. (5-28), the adjustment story can be told by assuming an initial disequilibrium—for example, if investment demand and other expenditures on the right side exceed savings plus imports on the left. A sudden increase in autonomous expenditure, A_N, from an established equilibrium would have this effect. The added demand would make markets tighten up and create more employment in industry.

The resulting increases in labor and markup incomes Y_W and Y_Z would add to savings on the left of Eq. (5-28), but by less than the increase in A_N, since part of the income increment would be consumed. Some of the consumption demand would be directed to food, the price of which would rise. Again, on the left of Eq. (5-28), the higher prices would stimulate savings from agricultural incomes $(1 - \gamma_F)Y_F$. On the right, the total expenditure on the food subsidy, tP_FC_F, would rise. In a stable economy, the farmers' savings response to higher food prices would ultimately outweigh the increased cost of subsidies, and equilibrium would be reestablished with a new, higher value of P_F. Because of the steepness of the supply curve SS illustrated in Fig. 5-3, this food price increase could be substantial. And, of course, the price rise would redistribute income toward the farm sector and away from the cities. This could cause political problems for the government as well.

5-5 SOME NUMERICAL EXAMPLES

The foregoing discussion suggests that macro responses of both prices and income distribution to dislocations of the market for staple foods are likely to be large. Presumably, the same statement would also apply to food (and calorie) consumption levels by different segments of the population. To drive these points home, we discuss in this section some numerical illustrations of how the model of Table 5-1 might respond to policy and other changes.

The numerical specification selected for the model appears in Table 5-2. Note that food consumption makes up $\frac{3}{8}$ of the total, while agriculture generates about 20 percent of total incomes. Another 7 percent of income (counted in Y_W) is generated by food processing. The income elasticity of food demand is 0.4. The price elasticity from the linear expenditure system Eq. (5-25) turns out to be -0.32. All these numbers are quite plausible in the aggregate for a low- to middle-income developing economy. Results from a number of policy experiments with the model appear in Table 5-3.[4] The rows give information about various aggregates: GDP in real (base-year prices) and current price terms and changes in real output and price indexes. Next come shares of the three income recipient classes in total income and their respective levels of food consumption. Percent changes in food consumption are also presented so as to provide a convenient summary indicator of the impact on both purchasing power and nutritional status by income class of the policies considered. Finally, the shares in GNP of total food and fertilizer subsidy payments appear in order to illustrate the relative importance of these fiscal interventions.

Increasing Food Subsidies

The initial percentage food subsidy is 20 percent, so that while the cost of consumed food is 1.25 (equals $P_F + wa_{LF}$), its consumer price is only $0.8 \times 1.25 = 1.0$. Suppose

[4]The model was solved numerically, along the lines of Fig. 1, by varying the food price P_F until food supply was equal to demand. Equation (5-28) was used as an additional check on the accuracy of the calculation.

Table 5-2 Model initial values and parameters

X_F	Food production	5.0
M_F	Food imports	1.0
C_F	Food consumption	6.0
X_{NF}	Nonfood inputs into food production	1.0
X_N	Nonfood production	15.0
C_N	Nonfood consumption	10.0
A_N	Nonfood autonomous demand	4.0
P_F, P_N	Prices received by producers	1.0
Q_F	Consumer food price	1.0
w	Wage	1.0
z	Nonfood producers' markup rate	0.5
Y_F	Income of food producers	4.2
Y_W	Income of wage recipients	11.5
Y_Z	Income of markup recipients	5.0
s	Subsidy rate on X_{NF}	0.2
t	Subsidy rate on C_F	0.2
b	Food output elasticity with respect to X_{NF}	0.16
K	Constant in food production function	5.0
a_{LF}	Labor input coefficient into food processing	0.25
a_{LN}	Labor input coefficient into nonfood production	0.66667
$\gamma_F, \gamma_W, \gamma_Z$	Consumption shares of income	0.85, 0.95, 0.301
θ_F, θ_N	Base consumption levels	4.8, 3.2
m_F, m_N	Marginal consumption shares	0.15, 0.85

that the subsidy rate is doubled from 20 to 40 percent to reduce the consumer price initially to 0.75. What will be the effects on the macro economy?

The second column shows that the impact would be profound. As already discussed in connection with Fig. 5-3, the subsidy would increase spending power directed to both food and nonfood products. Because of their asymmetric supply responses, the two sectors would react in completely opposite form. Since there is assumed to be excess industrial capacity, output of nonfood products would rise in response to the increased demand, generating higher incomes for workers and capitalists in the process. Most of the increase in food demand, however, would drive up prices and farmers' incomes without calling forth much additional supply. The table shows a solid 34 percent increase in real GNP, while the farm share of total income goes up 37 percent from 0.203 to 0.279. Food consumption for all classes increases, but mostly for the farmers. And instead of just doubling, the share of the food subsidy in GNP goes up almost three times because of the spiraling prices.

Clearly, food subsidies can have strong impacts on income distribution, prices, and aggregate demand. Instead of the increase considered here, a subsidy *decrease* (or an increased staple food tax) would substantially reduce real spending and food intake levels. For the poorer segment of the population in both urban and rural areas, the consequent reduction in food intake could lead to a visible increase in clinically

Table 5-3 Economic effects of policy changes

	Base solution	Raise food subsidy rate from 0.2 to 0.4	Raise fertilizer subsidy rate from 0.2 to 0.4	Farm yield decreases by 5%	Food imports increase 1.0 to 1.25	Labor productivity in food processing doubles	Autonomous expenditure increases by 25%
Real GNP	19.0	25.4	20.3	18.5	18.5	18.6	22.6
Percent change		33.9	6.8	-2.6	-2.7	-2.2	18.8
Nominal GNP	19.0	34.7	20.1	19.1	17.9	18.2	23.4
Food producers' price	1.0	2.35	0.95	1.15	0.85	1.02	1.20
Implicit GNP deflator	1.0	1.37	0.99	1.01	0.97	0.98	1.04
Income shares							
Farm	0.203	0.279	0.189	0.223	0.178	0.220	0.206
Worker	0.556	0.495	0.564	0.541	0.574	0.533	0.550
Markup	0.241	0.226	0.247	0.236	0.248	0.247	0.244
Food consumption levels							
Farmer	1.34	2.10	1.30	1.43	1.20	1.46	1.41
Worker	4.10	4.17	4.34	3.86	4.31	3.97	4.20
Markup	0.56	0.61	0.60	0.53	0.59	0.58	0.59
Percent change, in food consumption							
Farmer		57.1	-2.9	6.4	-10.7	9.3	4.9
Worker		1.8	6.0	-5.7	5.2	-3.0	2.5
Markup		7.3	6.7	-5.5	4.4	3.5	5.0
Food subsidy/GNP	0.079	0.206	0.075	0.085	0.075	0.076	0.077
Fertilizer subsidy/GNP	0.011	0.016	0.026	0.012	0.009	0.011	0.011

detectable malnutrition and morbidity, since the nutritional status of the poor is likely to be precarious in any case.

Increasing Fertilizer Subsidies

As discussed in connection with Eqs. (5-14) and (5-15), raising the fertilizer subsidy rate s should lead to a modest increase in overall food supply. Since it reduces agricultural costs, the increased subsidy would also lead to a drop in farm-gate food prices unless the government intervened to store or export some of the additional crop. The third column of Table 5-3 illustrates a case in which such intervention does not occur, and the producer price of food falls from 1.0 to 0.95 (in response to a doubling of the subsidy rate from 0.2 to 0.4). Food production rises from 5.0 to 5.24, or about 5 percent.

Observe that both workers and capitalists benefit from the supply increase, expanding their food consumption by about 6 percent each. However, the farmers' share of income drops, and their food intake falls. Whether or not they would accept such an income reduction in political terms is unclear; if they did, it would surely be the rural poor who would bear the brunt of the real decrease in food consumption. The solution illustrates quite clearly that policies aimed to increase food production alone are not sufficient to direct more calories to some of the people who need them most. Something has to be done to increase their real purchasing power as well.

A Reduction in Agricultural Yields

In both rich and poor countries, of course, agricultural productivity is anything but stable. We can capture the effects of bad weather and similar mishaps in the model by adjusting the constant K appearing in Eqs. (5-14) and (5-15). The fourth column of Table 5-3 shows what happens when K is reduced from 5.0 to 4.75, leading to a 5 percent shortfall in output before any price and subsequent production responses are taken into account.

As is often the case, when farm production falls, the effect is to drive up food prices (by 15 percent in this case) and shift the income distribution toward agriculture. Demand for nonfood products falls because the food price increase reduces real spending power, leading to a drop in output from 15.0 to 14.8. The decrease in food supply is borne mostly by urban workers and capitalists; because of their higher incomes, farmers actually eat more. The government could, of course, offset the price inflation and income redistribution by more food imports, but the foreign-exchange cost could be high. The options a government faces when crop yields decline are all very unpleasant.

Increased Food Imports

If a crop shortfall increases agricultural incomes, then more imports are bound to decrease them. The fifth column of Table 5-3 shows the consequences of an increase in imports, M_F, from 1.0 to 1.25. The farm-gate food price falls from 1.0 to 0.85, and the agricultural income share drops by over 12 percent. Real GNP also falls, since increased imports add to potential savings capacity on the left side of Eq. (5-28); with fixed exogenous expenditure, the economy contracts in response. Farmers suffer substantial food consumption losses, while the other groups gain. Overall food consumption actually increases slightly (from 6.0 to 6.09), so that imports add to total supply even after their negative impact on production is taken into account. However, the rural poor could be hard hit in the short run by a freer food import policy.[5]

Increased Labor Productivity in Food Processing

Like more imports, an increase in labor productivity in the "middleman" sector of food processing should be beneficial, since it potentially adds to aggregate supply. However, employment would drop because of the productivity increases unless the government took steps to create jobs elsewhere. The next-to-last column in Table 5-3 indicates that the drop in purchasing power resulting from an (unlikely) doubling of productivity would be enough to reduce real GNP by 2.2 percent, with some increase in the price farmers receive for food. If successful, attempts to reduce costs of food processing could adversely affect workers' income unless the government otherwise intervened. Absorbing technical advances or efficiency increases in the macro economy is not always as easy task. The results may prove beneficial in the long run (as we will see in Sec. 10-2 below), but the short-run adjustment costs can be heavy politically.

Increased Autonomous Demand

The last column of the table shows how an increase in autonomous spending from 4.0 to 5.0 would drive up aggregate demand. Real GNP goes up 18 percent in response to the 25 percent spending increase (implying an output multiplier of 3.6) and the food price goes up 20 percent. All classes gain in terms of real income and food intake, but the price increase is substantial. Together with productivity increases or increased import supply, increased expenditure can stimulate real output and help maintain the system in balance. However, by itself, more spending benefits farmers and capitalists more than wage recipients, and the food price increases it induces can be especially harmful to the poor.

The best way to summarize these experiments is to observe that, like many macro interventions, changes in food price policy cut with more than one edge. The numerical examples just presented show that plausible changes in tax and subsidy policies, import controls, and aspects of the overall economic environment will almost certainly have noticeable repercussions on income distribution, the level of economic activity, and

---

[5]There is an extensive literature on the deleterious effect on producer incentives of increased food imports in poor countries; see the papers by Schultz and Fisher in the readings. Our results show that this literature may be overly optimistic *if* the government does not tinker with prices and subsidies to offset the macro price and income responses to food imports demonstrated here. The government *will*, in fact, usually limit imports or else pursue offsetting policies, especially if agriculture is politically strong. However, the choices involved do not make the Finance Minister's life any easier.

patterns of food consumption. In general, some income classes are helped and others harmed by the policies considered, and no clear guidelines can be laid down. A fortiori, the same is true of the effects of these policies on the nutritional status of different groups in the population, insofar as that status is affected by changing intake levels of food.

This conclusion is somewhat negative, but it does point to an important corollary: attempts to "get the prices right" may indeed have positive effects on output or economic efficiency, but their negative distributional consequences for some groups in the population may be large. Contrariwise, "wrong" or taxed and subsidized prices may help the welfare of some segments of the poor. In any case, the inelasticities of food supply and demand mean that governments will always be present in the market to try to offset the effects of potentially large price fluctuations on some group of economic losers. A plausible case for nonintervention cannot be made, but the problem of choosing price manipulations with the least unfavorable side effects and the most benefits is and will remain a serious one.

SELECTED ADDITIONAL READINGS

Modigliani, Franco, and Tommaso Padoa-Schioppa: "The Economy with '100% plus' Wage Indexation," Massachusetts Institute of Technology, Cambridge, Mass., 1978 (mimeo). (Presents the wage/markup inflation model of Sec. 5-2, plus standard IS/LM themes and variations.)

Okun, Arthur: "Inflation—Mechanisms and Welfare Costs," *Brookings Papers on Economic Activity* No. 2, 1975, pp. 373–382. (The cited pages state a two-sector model of inflation somewhat similar to the one in Secs. 5-3 through 5-5.)

Schultz, T. W.: "Value of U.S. Farm Surpluses to Underdeveloped Countries," *Journal of Farm Economics*, 42:1019-1030, 1960; and Fisher, Franklin M.: "A Theoretical Analysis of the Impact of Food Surplus Disposal on Agricultural Production in Recipient Countries," *Journal of Farm Economics*, 45:863–875, 1963. (Both papers present models to analyze the impact of increased food imports through foreign aid. They are partial equilibrium models, omitting the macro effects stressed here.)

Seers, Dudley: "A Theory of Inflation and Growth in Under-Developed Economies Based on the Experience of Latin America," *Oxford Economic Papers*, 14:173-195, 1962. (Probably the canonical paper in English on Latin American structuralist economic thought, especially as regards the problems raised in the food model here. Good references to the source literature.)

Wachter, Susan M.: *Latin American Inflation*, Heath, Lexington, Mass., 1976. (Restatement and econometric testing of structuralist theories. Good references.)

SIX

SIMPLE MODELS FOR MEDIUM-TERM PLANS

In most planning offices, a great deal of effort is put into making medium- and long-term projections of economic change. The complexity of the models underlying these plans can range from simple trend extrapolation through many-equation computerized input-output forecasting programs. Nonetheless, almost all published country plans rest in the final analysis on a macro projection of investment and output flows over the next few years, combined with specific information on how major investment projects (a big fertilizer plant or steel mill, 100,000 hectares of newly irrigated land, and so on) are likely to shift the production and foreign trade scene. In this and the following two chapters, we concentrate on methods by which the macro projection exercise can be carried out. The fact that aggregate models are emphasized stems finally from the orientation of this book—there is no implication that dialogue between macro planners and sectoral experts does not matter enormously in setting up a plan. Another, deeper volume should be written from the investment project side.

The techniques used to make consistent projections of economic growth follow directly from the accounting identities spelled out in Chap. 2. One basically wants to restate these rules in growth-rate terms and ask how certain endogenous variables such as employment, the price level, or output are likely to grow in response to increases in variables like the stock of capital or labor productivity. New parameters such as the capital-output ratio and the "rate of technical progress" (or, more aptly, the "residual") enter these calculations and are introduced at appropriate points during the discussion. Most of the models we derive will result from a joint procedure of specializing the growth-rate accounting identities and adding behavioral assumptions. The macro planning literature is built around different hypotheses about how economic actors respond while satisfying the savings-investment balance in the aggregate, and these are emphasized throughout.

In the next section, we set out the basics of growth accounting; in Sec. 6-2, we go on to derive the well-known Harrod-Domar model from the material balance identity, restated in growth-rate form. Other demand-based models are taken up in Sec. 6-3, especially the Cambridge growth model, emphasizing the difference in savings propensities from labor and profit incomes. Supply-based forecasts and the "sources of growth" literature are described in Sec. 6-4, and their natural extension to the neoclassical growth model appears in Sec. 6-5. The discussion of medium-term planning techniques continues in Chap. 7, where applied Cambridge and neoclassical projection models for Brazil are contrasted; and in Chap. 8, where two disequilibrium quantity-side forecasting models are derived.

6-1 GROWTH AND INFLATION ACCOUNTING

Recall identity Eqs. (2-1) and (2-2) for supply-demand equilibrium and decomposition of costs in a one-sector model. If we omit consideration of fiscal activity and foreign trade for the moment, these can be rewritten as

$$PX = PC + PI \qquad (6\text{-}1)$$

and

$$PX = wL + rK \qquad (6\text{-}2)$$

where, as before, X is an index of total output like GDP, P is the price level, C is consumption, I is investment, w is the wage, L is employment, r is gross return to capital,[1] and K is capital stock. Since intermediate inputs are netted out, Eqs. (6-1) and (6-2), strictly speaking, apply only to national aggregates, though at times they are applied to sectors as well.

For medium-term planning, it is convenient to think in terms of growth rates. Reinterpreting the "prime" notation introduced in Chap. 4, we can express the *growth rate* of output as

$$X' = \frac{dX/dt}{X} \qquad (6\text{-}3)$$

so that 5 percent growth means that the relative change in X per unit time period (usually a year) is 0.05.

In differential form, Eq. (6-2) can be rewritten as

$$X(dP/dt) + P(dX/dt) = w(dL/dt) + L(dw/dt) + r(dK/dt) + K(dr/dt)$$

and transforming to growth rates gives

$$PX(X' + P') = wL(L' + w') + rK(r' + K') \qquad (6\text{-}4)$$

---

[1] Calling r the "gross" return means that it includes profit taxes and depreciation. Forgetting about taxes, we will later write $r = \rho + \delta$, where δ is the rate of depreciation, and the net return ρ is what is left over from r after depreciation is made good. For further discussion of different profit concepts, refer back to Chap. 2.

Now define $\alpha_L = wL/PX$ and $\alpha_K = rK/PX$ as the *factor shares* of labor and capital in total output. Evidently, $\alpha_L + \alpha_K = 1$. Using these definitions, Eq. (6-4) becomes

$$X' - \alpha_L L' - \alpha_K K' - \epsilon = \alpha_L w' + \alpha_K r' - P' - \epsilon \qquad (6\text{-}5)$$

where the extra term ϵ can be taken away from both sides of the equation without upsetting their equality.

So far, we have just been manipulating accepted accounting identities so as to put them in growth-rate form. But now we add the additional, restrictive hypothesis that *both* sides of Eq. (6-5) are equal to 0, and we derive the dual decompositions of output and price growth as follows:

$$X' = \alpha_L L' + \alpha_K K' + \epsilon \qquad (6\text{-}6)$$

and

$$P' = \alpha_L w' + \alpha_K r' - \epsilon \qquad (6\text{-}7)$$

The justification for the separate Eq. (6-6) and (6-7) is twofold. First, they make sense a priori as decompositions of output growth X' and price inflation P' in terms of relevant quantity- and price-side variables. Output growth depends on increases in the "factors of production" K' and L' as well as on the "residual" or "technical progress" term ϵ. Similarly, inflation is decomposed into labor and capital cost increases w' and r' *minus* the term ϵ, reflecting productivity gains.

To this apparent plausibility of Eqs. (6-6) and (6-7) one can add the observation that, taken separately, they seem to fit aggregate data well. That is, the national accounts often prove to be consistent in both output and price dimensions when tested by the two equations. One might as well take advantage of this empirical regularity in forecasting, with the provisos that growth rates of employment and use of capital stock can be accurately foretold and that the residual ϵ will take future values similar to those that show up when Eq. (6-6) is applied to data from the past. Such hypotheses may be justified from economic theory (as in Sec. 6-4) or just imposed ad hoc. In either case, they are operationally useful, which is why they were invented in the first place.

Besides these decompositions of output and price growth rates, a couple of other identity-type equations are required for medium-term planning. Evidently, output growth is exhausted by the expansion of different components of final demand. For the simplified material balance Eq. (6-1), the growth rate expression is

$$X' = (C/X)C' + (I/X)I' \qquad (6\text{-}8)$$

where the right-hand-side weights (C/X) and (I/X) in general shift over time [like α_L and α_K in Eqs. (6-6) and (6-7)].

Finally, it is customary to assume that investment I cumulates nicely to generate capital growth after due allowance for physical depreciation of the existing stock at a (constant) rate δ:

$$I = (dK/dt) + \delta K \qquad (6\text{-}9)$$

This widely used equation is built on a whole series of assumptions, most of them questionable. A simple economywide index of capital stock like K probably does not exist, for all kinds of reasons pointed out during a series of debates about capital theory during the 1960s that have come to be known as the "Cambridge controversies" (see the book by Harcourt and other items in the Selected Additional Readings for a summary). Even if a sensible capital-stock index could be constructed, technical change might well be built into each new "vintage" of investment goods, so simply summing up net investment over the years to build up a stock figure makes no sense. And a fraction δ of the capital stock might not choose to fall apart dutifully each and every year, as Eq. (6-9) implies. Despite all these problems, we persist in using Eq. (6-9), if only because it provides about the only available means to say something concrete regarding how much productive capacity investment is likely to add to the economy as it grows.

6-2 DEMAND-BASED FORECASTS: THE HARROD-DOMAR MODEL

The tried-and-true recipe for guessing medium-term output growth rates is based on the demand decomposition Eq. (6-8) plus another couple of assumptions, and is usually called the *Harrod-Domar equation*. Whether the equation fairly represents what Sir Roy Harrod and Evsey Domar meant to say when they wrote their famous analyses of the problems associated with capitalist economic growth (see readings) is something we shall take up soon.

The first Harrod-Domar assumption was already used in Chap. 4. It states that consumption is a constant fraction γ of output, $C = \gamma X$. If we limit the uses of output to consumption and investment only, as in Eq. (6-1), then $I = (1 - \gamma)X$. Such convenient proportionality means that $C' = I' = X'$; using Eq. (6-9), we can cancel X' and rewrite Eq. (6-8) as

$$1 = \gamma + \frac{(dK/dt) + \delta K}{X} \tag{6-10}$$

The second assumption is equally traditional—that the amount of capital required per unit output is given by a *capital-output ratio* a_{KX}

$$K = a_{KX} X \tag{6-11}$$

The similarity to the input-output notation of Chap. 3 is purposeful. Like intermediate input coefficients in the Leontief model, a_{KX} is usually assumed to be constant, at least over the relevant planning horizon. The stylized fact is that a_{KX} ought to take a value between 2.5 and 3.5 in the aggregate, though—as the readings at the end of Chap. 3 testify—this is not always so.

In any case, noting that now $K' = X'$ also, we can substitute Eq. (6-11) into Eq. (6-10) to derive

$$X' = \frac{1 - \gamma}{a_{KX}} - \delta = \frac{s}{a_{KX}} - \delta \tag{6-12}$$

where the aggregate savings share s is just $1 - \gamma$.

Even an equation as simple as Eq. (6-12) cannot be applied to run out a growth projection if one has no data. The national accounts are the most convenient source of numbers to estimate the parameters γ (or s), a_{KX} and δ. The savings share may come from comparisons of gross saving (perhaps from different sources) and GDP. Historically stable ratios may justify forward extrapolation, at least of the techniques the national income accountants use to estimate savings. The capital-output ratio may come from comparison of net investment (gross investment less depreciation) to increments in output in the following year. Finally, multiplying the ratio of depreciation allowances to GDP in the accounts by the capital-output ratio will provide an estimate of δ. If these calculations gave rise to the following values (which may be fairly typical)

$$s = 0.175$$

$$a_{KX} = 2.5$$

$$\delta = 0.03$$

then the growth rate would be 0.04, which is not awe-inspiring. At the very least, we learn from Harrod-Domar models that high savings rates and low capital-output ratios may have something to do with economic growth.

Naturally, the model has other uses as well. For example, capital-stock estimates are usually built up from the discrete-time version of Eq. (6-9):

$$K_{t+1} = K_t + I_t - \delta K_t \qquad (6\text{-}13)$$

The notation here is essentially the same as before except that the subscripts denote annual observations on capital and investment, since this is the way the data usually come. The equation provides a simple way to estimate capital if one knows yearly investment levels, the depreciation parameter, *and* initial capital stock, K_0. Finding this last quantity may be difficult, although some sort of number can be produced by using Eq. (6-12). Suppose that economic activity is expanding steadily at some rate, g. Then

$$g = X' = \frac{sX}{a_{KX}X} - \delta = \frac{I}{K} - \delta$$

By a simple rearrangement, we get

$$K = I/(g + \delta) \qquad (6\text{-}14)$$

If the economy grew at a fairly constant rate over some period in the past, then the ratio of the "average" level of investment over this period to the sum of the depreciation rate and the rate of growth can give a base level of capital K_0 for use in Eq. (6-13). Again, δ may be estimated from the national accounts or from capital life tables, depreciation guidelines, etc. Comparison of total depreciation δK_t from Eq. (6-13) with the national accounts estimates in years subsequent to the steady growth period can provide a check on the consistency of the whole procedure.[2]

Another application is the comparison of the growth rate resulting from Eq. (6-12)—Harrod called it the *warranted rate*—with the rate of growth of the labor force.

---

[2] The use of Eq. (6-14) to guess a base-period level of capital stock was proposed by Harberger. See the paper listed in the readings.

If total population grows at the rate n and labor-force participation rates do not change, then the rate of growth of employable labor L will be n as well, $L' = n$. For balanced, full-employment growth, the following equality must therefore hold,

$$n + \delta = s/a_{KX} \qquad (6\text{-}15)$$

If n is on the order of 0.03 or so and there is, in addition, some growth rate of labor productivity [which should be added to n on the left side of Eq. (6-15)], then this equation may well foretell severe problems in labor absorption in the medium run. The real policy problems begin there.

These employment bottlenecks can, of course, be avoided if the economy is sufficiently flexible. Usually such is not the case in developing countries, but it is still useful to consider how things *might* vary to guarantee equality in Eq. (6-15). Or, to put things more pessimistically, let us consider under two headings economic forces which might make the equilibrium of Eq. (6-15) impossible to sustain.

First there is the problem that institutional responses in the economy might make equilibrium unstable. This possible source of capitalist breakdown was really what Harrod was after. For example, suppose that for some reason investors—perhaps animated by hormones or a burst of animal spirits at some point in time—overspend. Then the capital growth rate will exceed the warranted rate and the rate of growth of output will be even higher because of the multiplier effects of additional investment expenditures. In symbols, the ratio (I/X) will rise from its steady growth value and (K/X) will fall. The effects of the multiplier are seen in an increase in the ratio $s/(K/X)$ and, from Eq. (6-12), an increase in X'. Faster growth in aggregate demand may, in turn, call forth still more investment from enthusiastic entrepreneurs, so that (I/X) takes another upward lurch and the economy spins off to super full employment and crisis.

Presumably, intelligent policy makers who have read their Keynes can avoid this kind of overspending crisis—and its mirror image on the stagnation side. At least, few advanced capitalist economies have been drowned in or starved of investable surplus in the years since World War II. It remains to be seen whether rapidly growing, developing countries (such as South Korea or Brazil) can be so fortunate.[3]

The second problem is that even if these Harrodian difficulties do not arise, parameters may be insufficiently flexible to permit Eq. (6-15) to hold with equality. In developing countries, for example, it is likely that

$$(s/a_{KX}) - \delta < n$$

so that investment-induced aggregate demand increases are too small to absorb the growing labor force.

Such inflexibilities will be avoided if *something* can change sufficiently. One can make up a catalog of varying parameters, as follows:

1. The growth rate of the labor force n can vary, putting population dynamics into the growth model. For medium-term planning, this is not a very interesting exten-

---

[3] Of course, overexpansion in poor countries may be choked off early by shortages of foreign exchange. Problems related to the "trade gap" are taken up in Chaps. 7 and 8.

sion, since the people who will be entering the labor force over the next 5 years or so were already born 10 years ago. However, "classical" income distribution models of the type developed by Malthus, Ricardo, and Marx are of interest in the context of long-term developmental change, as we will see in Chap. 10.

2. The capital-output ratio a_{KX} can vary. This is the basic assumption of the neo-classical growth model, discussed in Sec. 6-5.

3. The proportions saved from different income streams can differ, as in the short-term models of Chaps. 4 and 5. Different savings propensities allow aggregate savings to adjust to investment through changes in the income distribution, as outlined in the following section.

6-3 DEMAND-BASED FORECASTS: THE CAMBRIDGE GROWTH MODEL

Suppose recipients of income are split into two groups. It is traditional to call them capitalists and workers, but as far as the analysis here is concerned, they could be nonagriculturalists and agriculturalists, foreigners and nationals, the elect and the damned, or any other convenient two-way partition of class.

Sticking to the traditional names, let capitalists' income be Y_Z and workers' income Y_W. Then the accounting identity becomes

$$Y_Z + Y_W = PX \tag{6-16}$$

At the same time, savings must sum to investment, or

$$s_Z Y_Z + s_W Y_W = PI \tag{6-17}$$

where s_Z and s_W are the savings shares of the two classes. These two equations can be put together to give

$$(s_Z - s_W)(Y_Z/PX) + s_W = PI/PX \tag{6-18}$$

Using Eq. (6-12) and assuming that the economy will be growing at rate g, it is easy to get the relationship

$$a_{KX}(g + \delta) = PI/PX \tag{6-19}$$

Eliminating PI/PX between Eqs. (6-18) and (6-19) finally gives the *Kaldor equation*:

$$a_{KX}(g + \delta) = (s_Z - s_W)(Y_Z/PX) + s_W \tag{6-20}$$

This result has a number of piquant implications, such as that (1) the profit share Y_Z/PX and the rate of growth vary directly, given the savings parameters, and (2) for a given rate of growth, the profit share and the capitalists' saving propensity vary inversely, i.e., the less capitalists save the higher is their share of product. In his paper on income distribution (see the reading at the end of the chapter), Kaldor called the second result a *widow's cruse* distribution theory, after a somewhat obscure passage in Keynes's *Treatise on Money*. It could come about through a forced saving mechanism of the type discussed in previous chapters. For example, if real investment stays constant and the economy is more or less at full capacity, then an attempt by capitalists to save less or consume more will drive up prices from the demand side. If money wages lag behind the price increase, the real wage will fall and the income distribution will shift in favor of profits. More riotous living by the leisure classes works to their benefit, at least until the workers catch on.

How seriously one wants to take such a story is not clear, but it certainly is true that equations like Eq. (6-20) put an important restriction on macro accounting. Even if there are N sources of saving, one of them ultimately has to be determined as a residual, because of the savings-investment identity. We will see in the next chapter how a Kaldor-style savings restriction works out in an applied planning model.

For the moment, we can satisfy ourselves by showing how Eq. (6-20) provides a check on savings estimates when it is convenient to divide economic actors into just two groups. For example, suppose that the growth-rate target is 4 percent, the capital-output ratio is 3, the rate of depreciation of capital is 3 percent, and the profits share is $\frac{1}{2}$. Then Eq. (6-20) reduces to

$$0.42 = s_Z + s_W$$

If capitalists (or the urban sector, or whatever) save 30 percent of their income, then workers (or the agricultural sector) must save 12 percent of theirs. The 4 percent growth target may not be feasible, since a 12 percent savings rate is likely to be beyond the means of poor wage earners.

6-4 SUPPLY-BASED FORECASTS OR SOURCES OF GROWTH

In accounting terms, the Harrod-Domar and Kaldor equations are based on the material balance equation [Eq. (6-8)] and the accumulation equation [Eq. (6-9)]. Both describe demand relationships, for so far nothing has been said about supply. We now take up supply-based medium-term forecasting, using the dual production and cost decomposition of Eqs. (6-6) and (6-7).

To begin, let us be very neoclassical and rederive Eq. (6-6) from standard production theory. Assume that there is no technical change and the price level stays fixed at 1. Then total differentiation of an aggregate production function $X = F(K, L)$ would give

$$dX = (\partial F/\partial K)\, dK + (\partial F/\partial L)\, dL$$

or, in log-change form,

$$X' = \frac{\partial F}{\partial K} \frac{K}{X} K' + \frac{\partial F}{\partial L} \frac{L}{X} L'$$

$$= \frac{(\rho + \delta)K}{X} K' + \frac{wL}{X} L'$$

$$= \alpha_K K' + \alpha_L L' \tag{6-21}$$

In this chain of equalities, the wage w is equated to the marginal product of labor, and the gross return to capital ($\rho + \delta$) to the marginal product of that factor.[4] In the third line, factor shares are computed, as in Eq. (6-6). The incantation about marginal products "justifies" the output decomposition in Eq. (6-21) in a way different from the appeal to identities in Eq. (6-6).

As already noted, Eq. (6-21) as written does not fit the data very well. The weighted sum of growth rates of capital and labor on the right side usually turns out to be less than the output growth rate X'. The difference is made up by the "residual" ϵ in Eq. (6-6), which is sometimes taken as representing technical change. Note from Eq. (6-7) that either the wage w or the gross profit rate r should be growing relative to the price level if ϵ is positive. The price check on a quantity-side estimate of ϵ should, if possible, be applied in practice.

An example will help illustrate what is going on. Suppose that the observed rate of growth of the labor force over the past 5 years has been 0.03 and that the labor share in GDP at factor cost is 0.5. If the gross investment share of this measure of output is 0.16 and the depreciation share is 0.06, then one infers that dK/K is equal to 0.10. Dividing by a capital-output ratio of 2.5 makes dK/K equal to 0.04. At the same time, the second and third lines of Eq. (6-21) imply that

$$\rho(K/X) + \delta(K/X) = 2.5\,\rho + 0.06 = 0.50 = \alpha_K$$

so that the implied estimate of ρ is $0.44/2.5 \simeq 0.18$, which is credible. Accepting the consistency of the data, we conclude that the growth of factor inputs has been

$$\alpha_L L' + \alpha_K K' = (0.5)(0.03) + (0.5)(0.04) = 0.035$$

If the rate of growth of output has been 0.05, then the value of the residual is 0.015, or 1.5 percentage points of the 5 percent observed growth is "explained" by technical progress. In making forecasts of output growth in the future, this value can be combined with projections of employment increases and investment to project the evolution of the economy in the medium run.

The numerical values used in the foregoing example are more or less typical of semi-industrialized countries and "demonstrate" that growth of the traditional factors of production falls well short of explaining growth in supply. In more advanced countries, with slower labor-force growth and (perhaps) a higher depreciation share in gross investment, the contribution of the residual to growth must be even higher. Advocacy of capital accumulation as an engine of growth begins to look overdone.

Naturally, a counterattack has been launched against such skepticism. It has taken many forms; we review here only a few points relevant to underdeveloped countries.

1. The sources-of-growth methodology has been criticized theoretically, even by neoclassicists. Most simply, results may reflect aggregation errors, so that the analysis should be applied on the sector level taking into account input-output

---

[4] Here and elsewhere, the physical depreciation rate δ is assumed to be the same as the financial rate capitalists use in calculating depreciation reserves. As pointed out in Sec. 2-5, this identity of two conceptually distinct rates is not always observed, especially under inflation.

relationships. A more fundamental criticism has been that the price and quantity indexes underlying the usual GNP estimates are inadequate. Also, it is clear from Eq. (6-6) that the growth rates of factor inputs ought to be added together with current-price, *time-varying* shares in total costs. Jorgenson and Griliches (see their paper in the readings) recomputed variable-weight ("Divisia") indexes of this type for the United States and succeeded in reducing the residual to almost nil. After some sparring with critics, they finally settled on a technical progress contribution of about 1 percent to the historical $3\frac{1}{2}$ percent United States growth rate.

2. Somewhat earlier, Robert Solow—who gave the whole debate enormous impetus in 1957 with a celebrated article (also in the readings)—tried to recreate a role for capital accumulation by assuming that technical progress could not take place without investment: it must be "embodied" some way in new machinery and buildings. This is an intuitively appealing argument, especially welcome a few years later in the Kennedy administration, when people in and near the United States government wanted to get things moving. On embodiment grounds, a spurt of investment might bring enough technical progress with it to give an extra percent or two of growth over the medium run. As it turns out, data seem to show that the age distribution of the capital stock has not changed enough historically in the United States to justify macroeconomic embodiment (i.e., growth spurts have not been associated with a reduction in average capital age). Embodiment might be more important in analyzing growth in developing countries, but there have been few if any studies.

3. On the other hand, the standard methodology of Eq. (6-6) has been applied very widely. The results are diverse and difficult to summarize. If anything, they seem to indicate that factor shares and rates of growth in the developing world are such that capital accumulation is a more important source of growth there than in rich countries. This conclusion becomes sharper the poorer the country, and it tends to support surplus-labor models of the type discussed in Chap. 11. It also justifies the use of simple Harrod-Domar models for planning.

4. Educational contributions to growth have been the focus of much effort. If the labor force is broken down by education classes, then the right side of Eq. (6-6) can be extended in an obvious way to take into account the changing education levels of the workers. The stylized fact is that the wages of better-educated people fall *less* than their share of the labor force increases over time. Consequently, the estimated "contribution" of education to output growth is substantial. As usual, one can ask whether causation or just simple correlation is involved.

5. There have been some attempts to modify the sources-of-growth methodology to fit disequilibrium situations. For example, Michael Bruno observed some years ago that wage and employment data from Israel seemed to be related linearly when plotted on a scatter diagram. From that, he hypothesized that the demand relationship for labor was

$$\partial X/\partial L = aw + b$$

instead of the normal assumption that (in his notation) b is 0 and a is 1. Testing with the Israeli data seemed to indicate that, in practice, b was negative while a

was approximately unity. Thus the marginal product of labor was less than the wage, while the marginal product of capital exceeded its factor cost. Sources-of-growth analysis with "true" marginal products showed a substantial capital contribution to growth.

Just where one strikes a balance among all this is not clear; for example, if Bruno is correct, then studies which suggest that education contributes greatly to growth (measured at market wages) are misleading. About the only sure conclusion is that accumulation processes have something to do with increasing the growth rate. One planner's problem is to choose a model to show how the growth rate will respond to different policy instruments. In smoothly working economies with some labor-market tightness, the methods of this section may have their uses. Readers can draw their own conclusions after Chap. 7, where a detailed example is presented for Brazil.

6-5 THE NEOCLASSICAL MODEL OF ECONOMIC GROWTH

All the models discussed so far have been and can be used to make applied, quantitative growth projections. The same cannot be said of the model developed in this section, which is supposed to describe in a general way how capitalist economies behave in the medium and long run. We will not have many subsequent applications for either the model or its usual interpretation, but it is useful to have in one's mind as background for some of the growth models of developing countries discussed later on.

The neoclassical model as developed by Solow and Swan is supposed to answer Harrod's two questions about capitalist growth, as posed in Sec. 6-2. Really it answers just one, regarding which parameters can shift to allow the two sides of Eq. (6-15) to be equal. In a neoclassical world, the capital-output ratio adjusts to give full employment, and we will discuss how this comes about. But it bears emphasizing that the neoclassical model does *not* respond to Harrod's first question about how savings responds to a spurt in investment demand and what happens to the economy thereafter. The neoclassical model just makes investment equal to ex ante savings and sweeps all problems of adjustment between the two variables under the rug.

The formal version of the savings-investment hypothesis is

$$dK/dt = sX - \delta K \tag{6-22}$$

where the notation is as above and the output price is set to 1. If output is produced according to a constant-returns aggregate-production function, $X = F(K, L)$, we can write

$$x = \frac{X}{L} = F\left(\frac{K}{L}, 1\right) = f(k) \tag{6-23}$$

where the constant-returns property allows us to divide L "through" the production function F. The new variable k is the capital-labor ratio, with growth given by

$$k' = K' - L' = K' - n \tag{6-24}$$

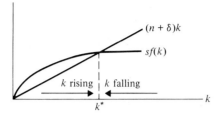

Figure 6-1 Stability of the neoclassical growth model.

These three equations can be put together to give

$$k' = \frac{sLf(k) - \delta K}{K} - n$$

$$= \frac{sf(k)}{K/L} - (n + \delta)$$

or, multiplying through by k, we get the *Solow equation*,

$$dk/dt = sf(k) - (n + \delta)k \tag{6-25}$$

For a steady-state solution with a constant capital-labor ratio k^*, we want $dk/dt = 0$, or

$$sf(k^*) = (n + \delta)k^* \tag{6-26}$$

This result is a twist on the Harrod-Domar equation and states that savings per capita $sf(k^*)$ is just enough to finance the increase in total capital per head required by population growth (nk^*) plus depreciation. The steady-state capital-output ratio $k^*/f(k^*)$ is determined by the other parameters. As is well known, the neoclassical growth model is stable in the sense that if the capital-labor ratio exceeds the equilibrium value k^* determined by Eq. (6-26), it falls, because then $(n + \delta)k$ exceeds $sf(k)$. A similar argument applies when k is below its equilibrium level. Figure 6-1 illustrates these easy corollaries of Eq. (6-25). The neoclassical production function $f(k)$ is conveniently concave, and this guarantees stability in the long run.

Just how *long* this process takes to converge to k^* is a question we do not pursue here, since computer simulations carried out by Atkinson (see Selected Additional Readings) and others indicate that with sufficiently "bad" parameters, it may require decades. Even if they accept the neoclassical model's benign optimism about gradual economic change, the value of k^* is of little interest to planners. The same can be said of attempts to select an "optimal" k^*, as in the so-called Golden Rule of Accumulation, an extension of the neoclassical model of growth. However, as a kind of dessert, we can review the Golden Rule briefly. It has some slight relevance to the optimal growth models used to derive investment shadow prices in the last part of this volume.

Suppose that the savings rate s in Eq. (6-26) can be controlled. The labor-force growth rate n and depreciation parameter δ are fixed, so the steady-state capital-labor ratio k^* has to respond. What level of k^* will give maximum sustainable consumption per head? The question is easily answered if we note that total consumption in the economy is

$$C(t) = [f(k) - (n + \delta)k] L(t)$$

and consumption per head is

$$c = \frac{C(t)}{L(t)} = f(k) - (n + \delta)k$$

Differentiating the right side of this equation with respect to k, we find that the maximum condition is

$$\frac{df}{dk} - \delta = \frac{\partial F(K, L)}{\partial K} - \delta = n \tag{6-27}$$

Thus consumption per head is maximized along a steady growth path when the rate of growth of population and product n equals the net marginal product of capital. The condition of Eq. (6-27) can be rewritten as

$$\frac{\partial F}{\partial K} \frac{K}{X} = \frac{(n + \delta)K}{X} = s \tag{6-28}$$

using Eq. (6-26). For maximum consumption per head, the capital share (the elasticity of output with respect to capital under constant returns and pure competition) must equal the share of savings in income.

Neither the condition of Eq. (6-27) nor that of Eq. (6-28) is observed in practice, since rates of return to capital considerably exceed the growth rate and savings rates fall far short of the capital share. Such empirical discrepancies make the Golden Rule profoundly uninteresting to people with practical minds, at least until they set up a consumption-maximizing planning model and find that it wants to make the savings rate equal to the share of capital in value added at factor cost. Then they will thank the theorists for having explained what is going on and try not to get tied up in something as silly as optimization the next time around.

SELECTED ADDITIONAL READINGS

Atkinson, A. B.: "The Timescale of Economic Models: How Long Is the Long Run?" *Review of Economic Studies*, **36**:137–152, 1969. (Numerical simulations of the neoclassical growth model and other economic systems. Convergence times to steady states are shown to be over a century.)

Bruno, Michael: "Estimation of Factor Contribution to Growth under Structural Disequilibrium," *International Economic Review*, **9**:42–62, 1968. (A sources of growth study assuming labor-market disequilibrium: assigns a high growth contribution to capital.)

Dixit, Avinash K.: *The Theory of Equilibrium Growth*, Oxford University Press, London and New York, 1976. (An accessible growth theory text, though written from an unswervingly neoclassical point of view.)

Domar, Evsey: "Capital Expansion, Rate of Growth and Unemployment," *Econometrica*, **14**:137–147, 1946, reprinted in the readings by Sen listed below. (An early statement of equilibrium requirements for steady growth.)

Dornbusch, Rudiger, and Stanley Fischer: *Macroeconomics,* McGraw-Hill, New York, 1977. (Chap. 17 is a succinct review of neoclassical growth theory—elegant variations on a discordant theme.)

Harberger, Arnold C.: "On Estimating the Rate of Return to Capital in Colombia," *Project Evaluation: Selected Papers,* Markham, Chicago, 1974. [Detailed exegesis and application of Eq. (6-14).]

Harcourt, G. C.: *Some Cambridge Controversies in the Theory of Capital,* Cambridge University Press, Cambridge, England, 1972. (Reviews the capital controversies from the English side. Moderately amusing.)

—— and N. F. Laing (eds.): *Capital and Growth,* Penguin Books, London and New York, 1971. (A useful collection of papers on the capital controversies.)

Harrod, Roy F.: "An Essay in Dynamic Theory," *Economic Journal,* **49**:14-33, 1939, reprinted in the readings by Sen listed below. (The initial probing of problems of stability and instability in economic growth.)

Jorgenson, Dale W., and Zvi Griliches: "The Explanation of Productivity Change," *Review of Economic Studies,* **34**:249-283, 1967, reprinted with a criticism by E. F. Denison in the readings by Sen listed below. (Elegant derivation and application of sources-of-growth methodology to United States data—neoclassical to the fingertips.)

Kaldor, Nicholas: "Alternative Theories of Distribution," *Review of Economic Studies,* **23**:83-100, 1955, reprinted in part, with some changes, in the readings by Sen listed below. (Original statement of the functional income distribution theory described in Sec. 6-3.)

Sen, Amartya K. (ed.): *Growth Economics,* Penguin Books, London and New York, 1971. (Good collection of readings in growth theory, with a very helpful introduction by the editor.)

Solow, Robert M.: "A Contribution to the Theory of Economic Growth," *Quarterly Journal of Economics,* **70**:65-94, 1956, reprinted in readings by Sen. (Original statement of the neoclassical one-sector growth model.)

——: "Technical Change and the Aggregate Production Function," *Review of Economics and Statistics,* **39**:312-320, 1957. [Pioneering application of the sources-of-growth equation; see Eq. (6-6).]

——: "Investment and Technical Progress," in K. J. Arrow, S. Karlin, and P. Suppes (eds.): *Mathematical Methods in the Social Sciences,* Stanford University Press, Stanford, Calif., 1960. (Early statement of the "vintage" capital model mentioned in Sec. 6-4.)

——: *Growth Theory,* Oxford University Press, New York and London, 1970. (Lucid introduction to the neoclassical theory.)

Swan, Trevor W.: "Economic Growth and Capital Accumulation," *Economic Record,* **32**:334-361, 1956. (Early statement of the neoclassical model.)

SEVEN

TWO FLEXIBLE-PRICE PLANNING MODELS IN ACTION

Most medium-term plans are based either on the Harrod-Domar model (or its two-gap extension) or on some variant of the sources-of-growth decomposition of Eq. (6-6). Such projections refer only to production and say nothing about price changes. The quantity forecasting equation has to be embedded in a bigger model if one wants to deal with income redistribution or inflation as well as growth.

In this chapter, two price-endogenous one-sector planning models are built around the sources-of-growth equation, since it fits GDP accounting conventions better than Harrod-Domar. Thereafter, more elaborate variants of the theoretical models are applied with data from Brazil. As long as one sticks with a single sector, the growth-rate identities developed in Chap. 6 give *almost* enough restrictions to determine a forecast of economic change, once the obvious exogenous variables are cranked in. But even with one sector, additional assumptions to give a completely closed model are required.

The first, theoretical part of this chapter discusses two alternative closure rules—one based on the Cambridge growth model discussed in Sec. 6-3 and another based on neoclassical production theory. A profits tax is introduced into the system to illustrate how the two models respond to changes in a typical policy variable; their reactions to a tax change turn out to be almost diametrically opposed. Thereafter, more complicated models (described in detail in Appendices C, D, and E) are set up for Brazil, and the divergent response to policy of the two closures is shown to persist. As it turns out, the Cambridge version appears to fit past Brazilian experience better than the neoclassical model, but whether that means one should make future plans Cambridge-style is something that we leave to the reader to decide. What we want to

Table 7-1a Symbols in the accounting equations

X	= Output
C	= Consumption
I	= Investment
G	= Real government expenditure
L	= Employment
K	= Capital stock
P	= Price level
w	= Wage
r	= Rate of profit after taxes
t	= Profit tax rate
dH/dt	= Change in the money base (= government deficit)
α_L	= Labor share
α_K	= Capital share
ξ_C, ξ_I, ξ_G	= Shares of consumption, investment, and government in total spending
γ_L, γ_K	= Shares of labor and capital income which are consumed
g	= Growth rate of the capital stock
ϵ	= Rate of technical progress in Hicks neutral form

do here is lay out blueprints and probable performance characteristics of both types of models, so that interested practitioners can apply them as they see fit.[1]

7-1 SOME PRELIMINARY ALGEBRA

We start out by analyzing a slightly more complicated version of the growth accounting identities already developed in Sec. 6-1. Table 7-1b gives the level form of the accounting system, and the equations are restated in growth rates in Table 7-1c. Notation is explained in Table 7-1a.

The first two equations in Table 7-1b are the usual national accounts identities for expenditure and incomes. Prices are included explicitly in Eqs. (7-1) and (7-2) to provide a basis for forecasting rates of inflation. The latter equation implies that windfall capital gains on the existing stock accrue to recipients of profit incomes; i.e., after-tax

[1] The results reported in this chapter draw heavily on joint research undertaken by the author and Eliana Cardoso of the University of Brasilia and M.I.T.

Table 7-1b Level form of the accounting equations

$PX = PC + PI + PG$	(7-1)
$PX = wL + rPK/(1 - t)$	(7-2)
$\alpha_L = wL/PX$	(7-3)
$\alpha_K = rPK/[(1 - t)PX]$	(7-4)
$PC = \gamma_L wL + \gamma_K rPK$	(7-5)
$PG = dH/dt + trPK/(1 - t)$	(7-6)
$I = gK$	(7-7)

Table 7-1c Growth-rate form of the accounting equations

$$X' = \xi_C C' + \xi_I I' + \xi_G G' \tag{7-1'}$$

$$X' = \alpha_L L' + \alpha_K K' + \epsilon \tag{7-2p'}$$

$$P' = \alpha_L w' + \alpha_K \left(r' + P' + \frac{t}{1-t} t' \right) - \epsilon \tag{7-2c'}$$

$$L' = \alpha_L' + P' + X' - w' \tag{7-3'}$$

$$K' = \alpha_K' + X' + P' - \left(r' + P' + \frac{t}{1-t} t' \right) \tag{7-4'}$$

$$P' + C' = (1/\xi_C) \left[\gamma_L \alpha_L (w' + L') + \gamma_K \alpha_K (1-t)(r' + P' + K') \right] \tag{7-5'}$$

$$P' + G' = \frac{trPK/(1-t)}{PG} \left[t'/(1-t) + r' + P' + K' \right] + \frac{dH/dt}{PG}(dH/dt)' \tag{7-6'}$$

$$I' = g' + K' \tag{7-7'}$$

profits are rPK, and these increase with the price level P, even when the after-tax profit rate r and capital stock K are constant. In this illustrative model, the corporate profit tax is the only fiscal instrument. Its rate t is calculated as a so-called *inside* tax, which is based on profits (income less wage payments) in the usual way; that is,

$$(PX - wL)(1 - t) = \alpha_K PX(1 - t) = rPK$$

and Eq. (7-2) follows directly. In the discussion below of implications of different ways of closing the model, we give examples by varying t and observing how other variables respond.

Equations (7-3) and (7-4) respectively define labor and capital shares in income and will prove useful in setting up neoclassical production relationships below. Equation (7-6) states that the government deficit is equal to dH/dt, the change in the money base (recall the discussion in Sec. 2-6 of money supply). For the moment, we assume that the interest rate varies enough to permit these monetary emissions to be absorbed. More explicit consideration of feedbacks from the money supply to the rest of the economy is deferred to the Brazilian model, described later in this chapter.

Finally, observe that the capital-stock growth rate g defined in Eq. (7-7) is determined by I and K at any point in time; but as the I/K ratio shifts in response to variations in either investors' anticipations or available savings, g will shift as well. Behavioral assumptions about the forces changing g are crucial to closing the model and are discussed in some detail below.[2]

If one eliminates PX from Eqs. (7-1) and (7-2) and applies Eqs. (7-5) and (7-6), it follows that

$$PI + dH/dt = (1 - \gamma_L) wL + (1 - \gamma_K) rPK \tag{7-8}$$

[2] Planners often call variables like g *stock-flow conversion factors* (see the paper by Manne in the Selected Additional Readings) and assume that they are fixed technologically. We prefer to treat the macroeconomic g as behavioral, determined by available savings in neoclassical models and by investors' enthusiasm in the Cambridge specification.

so that private savings (on the right-hand side) equals investment minus government savings, which is equal to $-dH/dt$. This savings-investment identity will, as usual, provide a skeleton key to understanding many of the empirical results of the model.

The growth-rate equations in Table 7-1c all follow from the Table 7-1b level forms by the methods of Chap. 6. Equation (7-1$'$) is a straightforward restatement of Eq. (7-1). The dual decompositions of production and cost growth rates [Eqs. (7-2p$'$) and (7-2c$'$), respectively] were already derived as Eqs. (6-6) and (6-7). The new term involving t' in Eq. (7-2c$'$) shows that an increase in the profit tax rate will drive up costs with an elasticity $\alpha_K t/(1-t)$. The rest of the equations follow readily from their level-form versions, including Eq. (7-5$'$), when one observes that

$$\frac{wL}{PC} = \frac{wL/PX}{PC/PX} = \alpha_L/\xi_C$$

and similarly for the profit recipients' share in total consumption.

The system in Table 7-1c comprises eight independent linear equations in 15 growth rates. In principle, seven additional restrictions are required to close the system, either through specification of exogenous variables or incorporation of extra equations. In addition, the model structure itself limits the possible ways it can be closed. For example, with exogenous specification of the residual ϵ, Eq. (7-2p$'$) shows that only two of the model's three quantity-side log changes L', K', and X' can be fixed independently.[3] A like observation holds regarding cost and price changes in Eq. (7-2c$'$). Finally, factor-share shifts must sum to 0, or, in growth-rate language:

$$\alpha_L(\alpha_L)' + \alpha_K(\alpha_k)' = 0 \qquad (7\text{-}9')$$

As we will see, neoclassical factor-demand equations automatically require factor-share changes to satisfy Eq. (7-9$'$).

To illustrate further characteristics of the model, we must introduce more detail. The following section is devoted to this task, using log changes in the profit tax rate t' to drive the model under our two sets of rules for closing it.

7-2 CLOSING THE GROWTH-RATE EQUATIONS

Assume that the level of investment I is fixed at any point in time. Then, with the historically given level of capital stock and our assumption of full-capacity utilization, the capital growth rate K' is predetermined by definition $(K' = I/K)$. For simplicity in medium-term forecasting, we also assume that the rate of growth of employment L' and the technical progress rate ϵ are fixed exogenously (although, if desired, the approach could easily be extended to include endogenous determination of these growth rates by appropriate supply functions). From Eq. (7-2p$'$) the output growth rate X' becomes an endogenous variable. To save symbols in the manipulations which

---

[3]There is an implicit assumption that neither unintended stock accumulation nor changes in capacity are important. For medium-term forecasts, this approach is traditional and justified by the nature of the problem at hand.

follow, we set ϵ equal to 0 for the moment and normalize prices by making P' equal to 0 as well.

To close the model, three additional restrictions are required. The most natural Cambridge assumptions would set two of the three policy variables—G', t', and $(dH/dt)'$—and the log change in the capital-stock growth rate g' exogenously. These hypotheses boil down to stating that the government respects its budget constraint, as in Eq. (7-6'), and that at any moment entrepreneurs (or the planners) are modifying the rate at which they accumulate capital in line with changes in expectations and "animal spirits." Together with the predetermined value of K', specification of g' makes the growth rate of investment I' endogenous from Eq. (7-7'). Also, if we let $(dH/dt)'$ be endogenous, we can insert Eq. (7-5') for the consumption growth rate C' into Eq. (7-1)', use the production function Eq. (7-2p'), and come up with an equation in which the "factor price" growth rates w' and r' depend on the already determined variables I', G', L', and K'. The log-differential cost function of Eq. (7-2c') gives another equation for the same two variables. Solving for r' and substituting the result into Eq. (7-4') finally gives

$$(\alpha_K)' = \frac{1}{\alpha_K [\gamma_L - (1 - t)\gamma_K]}$$
$$\times \{\xi_I I' + \xi_G G' - \gamma_K \alpha_K t t' - [1 - \gamma_L \alpha_L - \gamma_K \alpha_K (1 - t)] X'\}$$

This equation shows that an increase in the investment growth rate I' is associated with growth in the profit rate and capital share. Growth in the profits tax rate t' reduces these variables. However, if the immediate tax proceeds are respent by the government (so that $dG = \alpha_k PXtt'$), then the capital share will *increase* with this sort of balanced-budget expansion of government activity.

These are standard results for a "widow's cruse" specification in which wage recipients save less than those who receive profits, so that the denominator of the fraction outside the braces in the above equation is positive. With the investment growth rate predetermined, even if a tax increase takes income away from capitalists initially, the profit rate has to rise ex post facto to keep savings up. By the same sort of reasoning, the capital share falls if the output growth rate X' is higher; with more total output becoming available, a smaller share has to be diverted to high savers through high incomes for them.

Returning to fiscal effects, note that profits do fall if dG is enough smaller than dt. Contrary to many Cambridge-style models, this can occur because, from Eq. (7-6), decreases in monetary emissions dH/dt must accompany increases in tax revenue if government spending does not change. This government saving (or decrease in growth of private money stocks) can, in principle, support investment as effectively as private saving. How it is made available to investors is a financial market question, which we do not go into here.

The alternative way of closing the model is to adopt the neoclassical specification, in which factor shares are supposed to change in regular, predictable fashion as factor prices shift. Postponing until Appendix D the details about how technical change affects derived demands for labor and capital, assume—as in cost-minimizing textbook production theory—that the labor-output ratio, for example, depends only on the real wage, $L/X = f(w/P)$. In addition, if there is smooth substitution between capital and labor at a predictable ratio σ^X, this function in log changes becomes $L' - X' = -\sigma^X(w' - p')$. The trade-off parameter σ^X can be interpreted as the elasticity of factor substitution, defined in the usual way. If $w' - P'$ is added to both sides, this expression becomes

$$\alpha'_L = (1 - \sigma^X)(w' - P') \tag{7-10'}$$

The corresponding equation for the capital share is

$$\alpha'_K = (1 - \sigma^X)\left(r' + \frac{t}{1-t}t'\right) \tag{7-11'}$$

Adding Eqs. (7-10′) and (7-11′) to the equations of Table 7-1c gives a fully neoclassical model. To save algebra, we adopt the often-applied special case in which $\sigma^X = 1$ and factor shares stay constant; we are saying *either* that there is an aggregate Cobb-Douglas production function *or* that we do not expect factor shares to shift "significantly" in any case.

In the Cobb-Douglas (or any other neoclassical) case, it is easy to verify from Eqs. (7-10′) and (7-11′) that factor-share growth rates satisfy the adding-up condition of Eq. (7-9′). Hence, only one of the two factor-demand growth-rate equations is really independent. This additional restriction forces one exogenous variable from the Cambridge closure to become endogenous—the usual candidate is the log change of the growth rate of capital g'.

Now we can examine the impact of raising the profits tax, so set $t' > 0$. Equation (7-4′) and the Cobb-Douglas assumptions show immediately that the profit rate r *falls* as the tax rate increases, regardless of whether the government respends the revenue or not. The balanced-budget theory of an increasing profit share does not hold when the model is closed neoclassically.

The reason this theory does not hold is that factor payments (and therefore consumption) are fixed by marginal productivity assumptions and investment is endogenous. A tax increase raises government savings, leading in part to an *increase* in investment and in part to a fall in "required" private savings and the profit rate.

The increment in investment is surprising and bears close study. In the Cobb-Douglas specification, substitution of wage and profit growth rates from Eqs. (7-3′) and (7-4′) into Eq. (7-5′) gives

$$C' = (1/\xi_C)\{-\gamma_K\alpha_K tt' + [\gamma_L\alpha_L + \gamma_K\alpha_K(1 - t)]X'\}$$

so that consumption growth *declines* as the tax rate increases. Since output growth X' has been determined from Eq. (7-2p′), the growth rate of investment I' must *increase* from Eq. (7-1′). An increase in the profits tax leads to a decrease in consumption, and, paradoxically, to higher investment. Such a perverse investment response is no less disquieting than the widow's cruse in Cambridge models. It is a standard feature of full-employment neoclassical models (see A. K. Sen's paper in the Suggested Additional Readings) and illustrates once again how important are hidden implications of seemingly innocuous model-closing assumptions.

Finally, note that in both forms of the model discussed so far, output growth X' is fixed in the short run by predetermined variables in Eq. (7-2p'). However, the log change of capital-stock growth g' is exogenous in the Cambridge version but endogenous (determined by "productivity and thrift") in the neoclassical model. Over time, therefore, growth in output can differ between the two models because they determine rates of capital accumulation in different ways. As we will see in the Brazilian projections, this potential divergence in medium-term output growth rates can be highly significant in practice.

7-3 CALCULATION OF A NEW LEVEL-FORM SOLUTION

To get to medium-term projections, the log-differential equations discussed thus far must be integrated over time. In practice, this can be done by using the growth rates to make projections of the levels of all variables in some year subsequent to the base year and then using these projections as the initial guesses for an algorithm to solve fully the level form of the model. This solution then becomes the base for a further step forward in time. In our algorithms, we took the growth-rate-based projections of exogenous variables as exact, with the endogenous variables being determined by the identities and other equations of the models.

In a neoclassical closure, a solution algorithm can be based on iteration around the exhaustion-of-product identity of Eq. (7-2). An initial guess at the wage w determines the output level and profit rate from the level-form version of Eq. (7-10'), which can be written down for any well-behaved production function (we used the constant elasticity of substitution functions of Appendix D in the Brazilian simulations). A test based on Eq. (7-2) then shows how the guess at w should be modified to get closer to equilibrium. For the neoclassical version of the Brazil model discussed in the next section, only a few iterations of this type were required, since projections of all variables based on growth rates over 3 years satisfied exhaustion of product in the forecast year to within about 1 percent.

In a Cambridge model, price and quantity projections are not tied together by marginal productivity conditions, giving rise to potential inconsistency when both Eqs. (7-2p') and (7-2c') are applied with arbitrary finite changes of exogenous variables but with factor shares unchanged from their base-year values.[4] One way to finesse this problem is to treat either the price projection from Eq. (7-2c') or the output projection from Eq. (7-2p') as exact, calculating the other variable from identities holding in the forecast year. We chose the latter course, getting a forecast

---

[4]That is, the factor shares turn out to be weights in a first-order approximation to changes in the exhaustion-of-product identity Eq. (7-2). For finite changes of prices and quantities, this approximation will, of course, be in error, as the factor shares themselves will vary. One major difference between the Cambridge and neoclassical closures is that the latter restricts price and quantity changes in such a way as to make factor-share changes vanish to second order in equations like Eqs. (7-2p') and (7-2c'). (For a clear demonstration, see the paper by Jones in the readings.) This greater stability of neoclassical production responses goes far toward explaining the difference in accuracy of forecasts over 3 years in the two growth-rate specifications, as discussed in Appendix C.

of X from integration of Eq. (7-2p$'$) over time with constant factor shares. Iteration around the demand-supply balance of Eq. (7-1) then determined the other endogenous variables. For the Brazil exercise, ten or so iterations were usually required, since 3-year projections of prices from the log-differential model were usually 10 to 20 percent different from their final values in the level-form solutions.

7-4 THE MODELS AND BRAZILIAN DATA FOR THE 1960s

Our main purpose in this chapter is to contrast implications of the two closure rules in a practical model. This section is devoted to asking how well Cambridge and neoclassical specifications can be made to track Brazilian data for the 1960s; in the following two sections, some forecasting exercises for the 1970s are described. Unfortunately, there are distinct, incompatible national accounts series for Brazil in the two decades, so that numerical results cannot be considered jointly. However, the ways in which the two models work can be compared, and that is our chief interest.

The Brazil model appears in level form in Table C-1 of Appendix C. It has a strong family resemblance to the model of Table 7-1b but is more detailed and algebraically complex. The main extensions are

1. Incorporation of a balance-of-payments equation—with intermediate, consumption, and capital goods imports—and a trade gap acting as a savings source.
2. Treating production as requiring inputs from labor, nationally produced capital, imported capital, and intermediate imports. The trade-offs among these variables are described formally by the constant elasticity of substitution (CES) production functions of Appendix D.
3. Consumption expenditures are assumed to be directed to both national and imported goods, according to the direct addilog formulation of Appendix E. Total consumption expenditure is determined by income, wealth effects, and the interest rate. The last two variables respond to conditions in the market for (high-powered) money.
4. Government net savings is endogenous, and its level varies in response to fluctuations in a full array of tax and expenditure variables. Along with the balance-of-payments deficit, government savings can accommodate to permit savings-investment balance in ways not usually considered in simple widow's cruse specifications.
5. The government can finance its deficit either by borrowing from the Central Bank and thus creating money base or by selling inflation-indexed bonds to the public. Open-market operations are thus treated as a viable option in Brazil. The fact that the bonds are indexed, however, makes their servicing a large potential drain on fiscal resources.

Before analyzing the model results for the 1960s, it is worthwhile to recall that the rate of growth of the Brazilian economy fluctuated violently over the decade. There was an initial period of fairly rapid growth in the late 1950s and early 1960s, then a period of stagnation around the "revolution" of 1964, followed by rapid growth beginning about 1967 or 1968. The stagnation was prolonged by severe wage repression and demand constraint, which had profound distributional implications.[5]

Our chosen simulation period of 3 years cuts across some of this chronology. To trace it as faithfully as possible, employment growth was assumed to be nil in the first two periods considered (1960 to 1963 and 1963 to 1966) and 4.5 percent per year during 1966 to 1969. Because of variations in excess capacity and other factors, the residual ϵ was given different values for the three periods: 0.02 in 1960 to 1963, 0.005 in 1963 to 1966, and 0.012 in 1966 to 1969. The growth rates of national and imported capital were respectively 0.079 and 0.024, 0.068 and 0.024, and 0.068 and 0.024 in the three periods for the Cambridge model. As we will see shortly, the growth rates in the neoclassical specification were less.

Tables 7-2 and 7-3 present a series of comparisons between the model solutions and national accounts averages over the decade. In a crude sense, both models reproduce the official series well, but a number of contrasts still appear. First, output growth is slower in the neoclassical model. Since, in a Cambridge specification, one controls directly all the growth rates appearing in the sources-of-growth Eq. (D-20) shown in Appendix D, output growth can be tracked well. However, in the neoclassical model, only labor-force growth and the residual are exogenous—capital accumulation and imports are determined endogenously. As it turns out, the neoclassical specification generates less savings, investment, and growth; for that reason, it replicates Brazilian experience less accurately.[6]

The main cause of the slower neoclassical growth appears in lines 4 and 5 of Table 7-3, showing shares of saving in the value of output, PX. Note that both private and government saving shares are consistently higher in the Cambridge results. Private saving is higher because of a higher profit rate and lower labor share (more forced saving) than in the neoclassical simulations. The labor share stays fairly constant in the neoclassical columns of Table 7-3 but drops steadily from 54 percent to 47.6 percent in the Cambridge solutions. Although no thorough studies are available, partial evidence corroborates the private savings and distributional shifts displayed by the Cambridge results. (See the paper by Cardoso for more details.)

The difference in government savings shares stems from lower government revenues in the neoclassical model (Table 7-2). The most important tax in Brazil is on value added; in the models, this has the value of total output as its base. Lower prices or real output cut fiscal receipts and, with real government expenditures held constant by assumption, real government savings and total investment must be lower in the neoclassical specification. Both the private and public savings shortfalls cumulate, so that by 1969 real output is 4.2 percent less than in the Cambridge results. Since the

---

[5] Useful reviews of this period of Brazilian economic history are provided in the papers by Bacha and Fishlow cited at the end of this chapter.

[6] The behavior of the neoclassical model is sensitive to the capital-labor elasticity of substitution σ^X. As it varies from 0.3 to 1.8, the value of output in 1969 goes from 121.5 to 130.5, all other parameters and growth rates remaining the same. The official output estimate of about 130 billion cruzeiros is much better approximated when the elasticity of substitution is high, even though econometric estimates in Brazil and elsewhere usually make it less than 1.

Table 7-2 Comparison of observed macro variables and results from the Cambridge and neoclassical models—Brazil in the 1960s*

Macro variables	1963 Observed value	1963 Cambridge	1963 Neoclassical	1966 Observed value	1966 Cambridge	1966 Neoclassical	1969 Observed value	1969 Cambridge	1969 Neoclassical
1. Output growth rate (X')	0.050	0.040	0.040	0.034	0.034	0.023	0.070	0.065	0.060
2. Inflation rate (P')	0.434	0.443	0.420	0.470	0.442	0.447	0.230	0.296	0.300
3. GDP $[PX - P_0M + w(1 + t_L)L_G]$	11.929	11.269	10.547	53.724	48.344	46.898	133.100	141.665	130.537
4. Private consumption (D)	8.154	8.108	7.830	38.837	33.216	32.129	95.600	94.691	91.326
5. Private gross fixed capital formation $[P(I_X + \delta_X K_X) + P_{0K}(I_0 + \delta_0 K_0)]$	1.611	1.763	1.144	6.059	6.516	4.300	14.517	21.228	13.467
6. Government capital formation (PI_G)	0.488	0.510	0.475	2.140	2.094	1.975	7.432	8.759	8.370
7. Government consumption $[PC_G + w(1 + t_L)L_G]$	1.592	1.626	1.535	6.251	6.814	6.741	15.468	20.293	19.549
8. Government interest payments (PB)		0.408	0.379	0.148	1.781	2.056	4.149	4.881	7.146
9. Transfer payments (Q)	0.534	0.534	0.534	3.417	3.417	3.417	11.418	11.418	11.418
10. Government tax revenue (GR)	2.147	2.311	2.152	12.960	11.158	10.325	37.197	37.127	34.252
11. Direct taxes ($T_L + T_K$)	0.260	0.339	0.309	1.339	1.598	1.463	3.598	5.182	4.711
12. Exchange rate (e)	0.577	0.573	0.417	2.216	2.209	1.845	4.071	4.062	4.181
13. Exports in dollars ($P_E^* E$)	1.525	1.697	1.697	1.868	2.058	2.058	2.522	2.735	2.735
14. Imports in dollars $[P_0^* M + P_{0C}^* C_0 + P_{0K}^*(I_0 + \delta_0 K_0)]$	1.567	1.796	1.767	1.699	2.040	2.060	2.526	3.091	2.730

*Value figures (both dollars and cruzeiros) are in billions.

Table 7-3 Further comparisons between Cambridge and neoclassical simulations—Brazil in the 1960s

	1960		1963		1966		1969	
	Cambridge	Neoclassical	Cambridge	Neoclassical	Cambridge	Neoclassical	Cambridge	Neoclassical
1. Output (X)	2.675	2.676	3.016	3.023	3.343	3.256	4.063	3.892
2. Profit rate (ρ)	0.175	0.175	0.165	0.163	0.153	0.151	0.160	0.151
3. Labor share (α_L)	0.540	0.540	0.489	0.524	0.473	0.514	0.476	0.521
4. Private saving share	0.104	0.104	0.121	0.113	0.125	0.120	0.136	0.132
5. Government saving share	-0.037	-0.037	-0.046	-0.070	-0.031	-0.062	-0.049	-0.078
6. Capital inflow (F)	0.328	0.327	0.107	0.073	-0.017	0.0	0.362	0.0
7. Capital inflow/export value	0.225	0.224	0.063	0.043	-0.008	0.0	0.143	0.0
8. Interest rate (i)	0.060	0.060	0.113	0.106	0.147	0.136	0.141	0.131

latter had factor-input growth rates chosen to trace real output accurately, the neo-classical performance is deficient.

With regard to both growth and distributional variables, the Cambridge model seems to fit Brazilian experience better. Both sets of simulations leave something to be desired, but if we insist on forcing Brazilian experience of the 1960s in one or another Procrustean bed of economic theory, the one designed from blueprints provided by Kalecki and Kaldor is far less deforming. Now we ask a similar question about how the models perform in making conditional projections about the future.

7-5 CONDITIONAL FORECASTS FOR BRAZIL

In 1973 and 1974, when the results of this and the following sections were worked out, two aspects of the growth process were at the forefront of Brazilian policy debate: (1) the adjustments the economy would have to make to radically changed world prices for its imports and exports and (2) the impacts which alleviation of the rigid money wage controls of the 1960s might have on distribution and growth.[7]

To establish a reference point, "base" projections for the 1970s from both models are set out in Table 7-4 (based on the new Brazilian national accounts commencing in 1970). These solutions are, of course, not meant to be definitive forecasts; rather, they just define plausible growth paths around which policy variations can be rung to say a little bit about relevant trade-offs in the real economy.

The top panel in Table 7-4 contains results from a Cambridge model in which employment growth is set at 3 percent per year, hence the label A (0.03) attached to the solution. The residual ϵ is set to 0.02 after 1973, and the annual growth rates of domestic and foreign capital are respectively 9.1 and 9.6 percent throughout the forecast period. The elasticity of noncompetitive imports with respect to output is 1.5, and money wages grow at 23 percent. The second line shows that these assumptions generate output growth rates of about 9 percent per year from 1973, within the range usually discussed in Brazil. The inflation rate drops off gradually from 20 to 16 percent, so the real wage increases.

The fourth and fifth lines demonstrate a falling profit rate (ρ) and a rising labor share (α_L) over the 1973 to 1982 period. The cause of these developments shows up in the next line as a steady decrease in the proportion of private savings (not including depreciation) to the value of domestic output. Movements in private savings are mediated in Cambridge models by shifts in the functional income distribution. Here, profits fall because less private saving overall—and thus mainly from capital—is required.

A projected falling profit rate in Brazil is dubious; that is one reason why the Table 7-4 forecasts are not definitive. What is *not* dubious is that, like many oil importers, the nation will almost certainly face balance-of-payments deficits in the medium term. Since trade deficits represent foreign savings, national savings must

---

[7]The paper by Bacha in the readings gives a reliable summary of the policy issues of this period.

Table 7-4 Values of key variables in base solutions—3 percent annual employment growth

	1970	1973	1976	1979	1982
		Cambridge model, solution A (0.03)			
1. Output (X)	204.1	279.7	363.4	474.7	619.0
2. Growth rate (X')		0.105	0.087	0.089	0.088
3. Inflation rate (P')		0.208	0.191	0.164	0.160
4. Profit rate (ρ)	0.184	0.217	0.215	0.196	0.171
5. Labor share (α_L)	0.507	0.432	0.409	0.418	0.437
6. Private saving share	0.149	0.169	0.148	0.123	0.093
7. Government saving share	−0.023	−0.041	−0.024	−0.004	0.020
8. Foreign saving share	0.004	0.005	0.017	0.026	0.039
9. Capital inflows (F)	0.189	0.407	2.411	6.106	13.974
10. Exchange rate (e)	4.59	6.12	8.26	11.16	15.06
11. Capital inflow/export value	0.069	0.062	0.203	0.283	0.355
12. Interest rate (i)	0.240	0.262	0.235	0.226	0.225
13. Government interest (PB)	8.8	42.2	84.3	123.1	112.9
		Neoclassical model ($\sigma^X = 1/3$), solution α (0.03)			
1. Output (X)	204.1	276.4	345.3	417.3	499.7
2. Growth rate (X')		0.105	0.074	0.063	0.060
3. Inflation rate (P')		0.171	0.179	0.211	0.223
4. Profit rate (ρ)	0.184	0.196	0.193	0.211	0.240
5. Labor share (α_L)	0.507	0.489	0.499	0.479	0.446
6. Private saving share	0.149	0.153	0.127	0.131	0.146
7. Government saving share	−0.023	−0.059	−0.081	−0.109	−0.154
8. Foreign saving share	0.004	0.005	0.014	0.020	0.026
9. Capital inflows (F)	0.189	0.405	2.399	6.081	13.919
10. Exchange rate (e)	4.59	5.45	5.86	7.54	9.88
11. Capital inflow/export value	0.069	0.062	0.202	0.282	0.354
12. Interest rate (i)	0.240	0.232	0.196	0.205	0.235
13. Government interest (PB)	8.8	37.8	81.1	208.4	645.5
		Neoclassical model ($\sigma^X = 2/3$)			
1. Output (X)	204.1	277.1	343.6	414.5	490.4
2. Growth rate (X')		0.105	0.072	0.062	0.056
3. Inflation rate (P')		0.161	0.187	0.201	0.211
4. Profit rate (ρ)	0.184	0.191	0.192	0.204	0.224
5. Labor share (α_L)	0.507	0.503	0.504	0.499	0.489
6. Private saving share	0.149	0.148	0.126	0.124	0.133
7. Government saving share	−0.023	−0.062	−0.085	−0.119	−0.180
8. Foreign saving share	0.004	0.005	0.014	0.021	0.027
9. Capital inflows (F)	0.189	0.405	2.399	6.081	13.919
10. Exchange rate (e)	4.59	5.27	5.83	7.27	9.13
11. Capital inflow/export value	0.069	0.062	0.202	0.282	0.354
12. Interest rate (i)	0.240	0.226	0.194	0.197	0.216
13. Government interest (PB)	8.8	36.7	81.9	206.8	631.8

decline as a share of output, unless investment grows very rapidly. The magnitude of this shift in sources of savings is documented by lines 8 and 11. The latter indicates that foreign savings may rise from 7 to 35 percent of export value in world prices.[8]

National savings can adjust to an increased payments deficit through decreases in either private or government savings. We have just seen that the former leads to decreased profit rates and an improved labor share. The evolution of government savings is determined by tax revenue and public expenditure shifts over time. On the revenue side, taxes divided by the value of output PX rise from 0.245 in 1970 to 0.260 in 1982, largely because in Eqs. (C-15) and (C-16) the direct tax elasticities S_{TL} and S_{TK} are each set to 1.15 and generate rapidly rising receipts.

An increasing tax share is probably realistic, but our assumed growth rates of government activity are not quite sufficient to offset it, so that the government shifts from dissaving to saving over the period. Again, this can only be accommodated by a reduction in private saving.

Money emissions dH/dt grow at 20 percent per year, maintaining the interest rate stable (line 12). Throughout the period, the government ends up buying bonds to such an extent that even its nominal payments to bondholders decline (line 13). We will see shortly that such avoidance of debt on the part of government is difficult in the neoclassical model, with correspondingly unfavorable effects on its savings and overall growth.

The decrease in public debt in the Cambridge specification is a response to increasing government surpluses and the foreign trade deficit. Levels of bond sales could be modified by changes in expenditure policy, money emissions, or the exchange rate. For the period 1973 to 1982, the latter is assumed to increase at 10 percent per year. This trend represents real devaluation (that is, e rises substantially faster than the difference between world and domestic prices) and makes capital inflows an even more important source of savings than their dollar valuations would indicate.

As in the simulations for the 1960s, the neoclassical forecasts in the lower part of Table 7-4 are much less buoyant. Two sets of results are presented for values of the elasticity of substitution σ^X, which probably bracket the "true" parameter, assuming that it exists.

The key to understanding results again lies in the lower saving effort implicit in the marginalist specification. To repeat the chain of causality, growth in labor, capital, and productivity in the neoclassical model generates not only output increases, but also the configuration of relative prices and factor shares. Savings decisions and the availability of goods then determine investment. If savings under given production and institutional conditions is low, then the economy invests little and grows slowly. That is roughly what happens in the neoclassical simulations of Table 7-4. The stagnation relative to the Cambridge model is more striking than in the 1960s because overall employment and productivity growth are assumed to be higher in the current set of projections.

---

[8] The A (0.03) solution presupposes that export volume grows at 10 percent per year after 1973, with world prices increasing at the same rate. Import prices are assumed to increase at 10 percent from 1973 but at 12 percent in the 3 years preceding.

The details of the differences between the two sets of forecasts are similar to those already pointed out for the 1960s data set. Begin by observing that in 1973, both output and price level are lower in the neoclassical version, even though wage increases and growth of inputs from 1970 are the same in both models. The difference in inflation rates can be traced to the different price theories in the two closures; the growth rate of investment sharply drives up prices in the Cambridge theory. The neo-classical model has lower output growth because the marginal productivity of inputs declines as they substitute for one another in the level-form CES production function used to generate the Table 7-4 solutions. In the Cambridge forecasts, the log-change production function (D-20) is simply integrated with constant input productivities over time.

These differences assure that 1973 savings is less in the neoclassical simulations. Private savings is lower because the profit rate and labor share cannot move as freely in a marginalist world. The government's savings is lower because the yield on the value-added tax—still its major revenue source—depends on the product of real output and the price level. These shortfalls translate into lower real investment and increased reliance on bond sales by the public sector to cover its deficit.

Over time, these processes cumulate, so that growth is slower in the neoclassical models; real output in 1982 is one-sixth lower than in the Cambridge specification. Also, government savings is increasingly negative as the burden of meeting payments on its indexed bonds increases; the last lines in each panel show how this expenditure item grows.

With appropriate massage of policy, the neoclassical performance could be improved; reduction of the public deficit through heavy taxes on low-saving poor people is one way to increase growth in a world driven by productivity and thrift. Nonetheless, such tricks are only palliative; savings responses in neoclassical models *are* less flexible than in their Cambridge competitors. When marginal productivity relationships bind, the functional income distribution cannot change without limit. Therefore, savings shortfalls get translated in part into reductions in investment and growth, in part into increases in the profit rate. To explore these issues a bit further in the following section, we use the solution of Table 7-4 with the elasticity of substitution σ^X set to one-third as our reference, since its results are slightly more optimistic. This solution is labeled α (0.03), for comparison with the A (0.03) solution of the Cambridge model.

7-6 WAGES, INFLATION, DISTRIBUTION, AND THE TRADE GAP

Since the military and its political friends took over Brazil in 1964, an important aspect of economic policy has been the relationship between the apparent success of anti-inflationary efforts and wage repression, based on liquidation of labor unions with consequent cancellation of the power of workers as a class to fight for higher wages. The present model is well equipped to analyze shifts in the profit versus wage distribution, under different hypotheses about how the overall wage level might evolve. In particular, one might ask what would be the effects of a less draconian wage policy on distribution and growth. Table 7-5 provides some answers by comparing the base solutions of the model to growth paths in which nominal wage growth is increased from 23 to 30 percent per year.

The immediate impact of the wage increases is inflationary, as can be verified from the fourth line of the table's Cambridge panel. [Compare the columns headed "$A(0.03)$" and "Constant tariffs." We discuss the "Shifted tariffs" columns shortly.] However, inflation decreases over time and the real wage and real labor income (lines 5 and 9) grow noticeably. In the Cambridge specification, more rapid money wage growth clearly shifts the functional distribution toward labor. The costs associated with this benefit are higher inflation and a lower profit share. One wonders which weighs more heavily in official Brazilian calculations.

A troublesome aspect of more rapid wage growth is the increase in the foreign deficit it generates (line 9). This can be traced to a shift in consumer demand as prices of domestic goods accelerate, so that consumption of imports increases from the base solution (line 10). We countered this demand response in the "shifted tariffs" solution by increasing tariffs on consumer imports at rates of 37 percent per year for 1973 to 1976, 13.7 percent for 1976 to 1979, and 11 percent for 1979 to 1982. These changes brought capital inflows down to levels comparable to those of the A (0.03) solution.

Since output growth is maintained nearly constant across Cambridge solutions, the main impact of wage changes is on distribution. Line 7 of the neoclassical panel shows that the labor share also increases in the marginalist model, but the more interesting result in lines 1 and 2 is that output growth accelerates. If one takes the results of this fixed-employment model seriously, wage repression in Brazil may have slowed the growth rate, a major policy target! In the simple world of the model, it is easy to see how a wage inflation generates more rapid growth. In the first instance, government dissaving decreases because the price multiplied by the quantity base of the value-added tax increases with higher prices. The increased saving gets translated into higher real output and incomes, which generate more private savings and still more output. Whether such processes would cumulate in the real Brazilian economy as opposed to the model is another question but one that deserves further investigation.[9]

Both versions of the model arrive at broadly similar results when wage inflation is considered: the overall rate of inflation will increase, the labor share will rise, and there may even be some favorable output effects. Such agreement is less apparent when the two specifications are applied to another problem of interest in Brazil—the probable evolution of the balance of payments. In this context, we investigate how aggregate commercial policy—devaluation, import substitution, export promotion, etc.—affects forecasts from the two versions.

One potentially important trade-off is between the trade gap and output or employment growth. At least in a Cambridge specification, prospects are not very

---

[9]To understand how the models operate, the reader might want to think through a case in which the labor tax rate is reduced—another policy change which "ought to" benefit workers. As we have verified in other solutions, the result in a Cambridge model is a reduction in the labor share (because government savings fall as the tax decreases, and savings from capital must take up the slack). In a neoclassical version, both the labor share and output growth decrease, with the exact combination of evils depending on parameters, notably the elasticity of substitution σ^X.

Table 7-5 Model responses to different wage growth rates

	1976			1979			1982		
	A (0.03)	Constant tariffs	Shifted tariffs	A (0.03)	Constant tariffs	Shifted tariffs	A (0.03)	Constant tariffs	Shifted tariffs
Wage growth rate (w')	0.23	0.30	0.30	0.23	0.30	0.30	0.23	0.30	0.30
			Cambridge model						
1. Output (X)	363.4	363.4	363.4	474.7	470.9	470.8	619.0	604.7	604.4
2. Output growth rate (X')	0.087	0.087	0.087	0.089	0.086	0.086	0.088	0.083	0.083
3. Price level (P)	3.311	3.740	3.733	5.417	7.106	7.083	8.649	13.478	13.428
4. Inflation rate (P')	0.191	0.232	0.231	0.164	0.214	0.213	0.160	0.213	0.213
5. Real wage (w/P)	3.481	3.802	3.810	4.233	4.922	4.938	5.298	6.383	6.407
6. Profit rate (ρ)	0.215	0.204	0.204	0.196	0.179	0.178	0.171	0.149	0.147
7. Labor share (α_L)	0.409	0.447	0.448	0.418	0.489	0.490	0.437	0.540	0.542
8. Real labor income (Y_L/P)	123.9	135.3	135.6	165.2	191.7	192.3	225.7	272.0	273.0
9. Capital inflow (F)	2.411	2.929	2.016	6.106	8.227	5.051	13.974	20.271	11.151
10. Import consumption (C_0)	8.9	10.1	8.0	13.2	17.0	11.7	18.8	27.6	16.4
11. Private saving share	0.148	0.145	0.145	0.123	0.119	0.119	0.093	0.092	0.091
12. Government saving share	-0.024	-0.025	-0.019	-0.004	-0.005	0.006	0.020	0.018	0.036
13. Foreign saving share	0.016	0.018	0.012	0.026	0.027	0.017	0.039	0.037	0.021

Table 7-5 **Model responses to different wage growth rates** (*Continued*)

	Neoclassical model								
1. Output (X)	345.3	345.4	345.4	417.3	429.7	430.1	499.7	537.6	538.3
2. Output growth rate (X')	0.074	0.074	0.074	0.063	0.073	0.073	0.060	0.075	0.075
3. Price level (P)	2.854	3.523	3.523	5.375	7.492	7.475	10.501	15.612	15.519
4. Inflation rate (P')	0.179	0.249	0.249	0.211	0.252	0.251	0.223	0.245	0.244
5. Real wage (w/P)	4.036	4.037	4.037	4.278	4.669	4.679	4.363	5.511	5.544
6. Profit rate (ρ)	0.193	0.193	0.193	0.211	0.192	0.191	0.240	0.185	0.184
7. Labor share (α_L)	0.499	0.499	0.499	0.479	0.508	0.509	0.466	0.524	0.526
8. Real labor income (Y_L/P)	143.7	143.7	143.7	166.5	181.8	182.2	185.9	234.8	236.2
9. Capital inflow (F)	2.399	2.929	2.016	6.081	8.226	5.049	13.919	20.270	11.148
10. Import consumption (C_0)	11.6	11.0	8.7	18.5	18.1	12.5	29.6	29.9	17.9
11. Private saving share	0.127	0.137	0.137	0.131	0.134	0.133	0.146	0.129	0.128
12. Government saving share	-0.081	-0.059	-0.053	-0.109	-0.060	-0.048	-0.154	-0.062	-0.043
13. Foreign saving share	0.014	0.017	0.012	0.020	0.026	0.016	0.026	0.035	0.019

favorable. The upper panel of Table 7-6 provides some information on this score. The *A* solutions assume no import substitution—the elasticity of intermediate imports with respect to output is set to 1.5, tariffs are not changed, and historical growth rates of nationally produced and imported capital stocks are maintained at 9.6 and 9.1 percent respectively. On these assumptions, the growth in the trade gap is staggering and probably not feasible in reality. At 3 percent employment growth in the *A* (0.03) solution, the trade deficit rises to almost $14 billion in 1982. Another solution with 2 percent employment growth (more than 3 million less jobs in 1982) leaves the deficit at almost $13 billion. Clearly, more favorable alternatives must be sought.

The *B* solutions are based on the gamut of import substitution policies; beginning

Table 7-6 Model responses to enforced import substitution—3 percent annual employment growth

	1976		1979		1982	
Cambridge model	$A(0.03)$	$B(0.03)$	$A(0.03)$	$B(0.03)$	$A(0.03)$	$B(0.03)$
1. Output (X)	363.4	361.7	474.7	474.7	619.0	631.4
2. Price level (P)	3.311	3.564	5.417	6.382	8.649	11.036
3. Profit rate (ρ)	0.215	0.233	0.196	0.238	0.171	0.238
4. Labor share (α_L)	0.409	0.382	0.418	0.355	0.437	0.336
5. Private saving share	0.148	0.161	0.123	0.155	0.093	0.145
6. Government saving share	−0.024	−0.023	−0.004	−0.001	0.020	0.028
7. Foreign saving share	0.017	0.006	0.026	0.003	0.039	0.001
8. Capital inflows (F)	2.411	0.916	6.106	0.869	13.974	0.550
9. Exchange rate (e)	8.26	8.26	11.16	11.16	15.06	15.06
10. National investment (I_X)	44.2	47.7	59.2	70.4	79.3	105.9
11. Imported investment (I_0)	5.7	4.2	7.5	3.8	9.8	3.3
12. Intermediate imports (M)	16.4	14.3	24.5	18.8	36.5	25.0
13. Consumer goods imports (C_0)	8.9	8.9	13.2	13.4	18.8	19.7

	1976		1979		1982	
Neoclassical model	$\alpha(0.03)$	$\beta(0.03)$	$\alpha(0.03)$	$\beta(0.03)$	$\alpha(0.03)$	$\beta(0.03)$
1. Output (X)	345.3	345.3	417.3	413.9	499.7	490.5
2. Price level (P)	2.854	2.859	5.372	5.506	10.501	11.154
3. Profit rate (ρ)	0.193	0.193	0.211	0.214	0.240	0.247
4. Labor share (α_L)	0.499	0.499	0.479	0.471	0.446	0.428
5. Private saving share	0.127	0.127	0.131	0.135	0.146	0.159
6. Government saving share	−0.081	−0.080	−0.109	−0.105	−0.154	−0.152
7. Foreign saving share	0.014	0.005	0.020	0.003	0.026	0.001
8. Capital inflows (F)	2.399	0.910	6.081	0.863	13.919	0.547
9. Exchange rate (e)	5.863	5.873	7.544	8.216	9.877	11.908
10. National investment (I_X)	13.7	13.8	7.9	8.0	−2.5	−3.3
11. Imported investment (I_0)	7.7	4.9	11.2	6.2	15.1	8.4
12. Intermediate imports (M)	10.4	10.4	12.9	12.5	16.0	15.0
13. Consumer goods imports (C_0)	11.6	11.1	18.5	15.8	29.6	22.2

Note: *A* and α solutions are without import substitution; *B* and β solutions have substitution.

in 1973, the elasticity of intermediate imports with respect to output is set to unity (instead of 1.5), domestically produced capital goods are assumed to substitute for imports at approximately a 1 : 1 ratio (with volumes measured in 1970 cruzeiros), and consumer imports are held more or less at their A-solution levels by tariff increases of 9.5 percent per year in 1973 to 1976, 7.9 percent in 1976 to 1979, and 6.7 percent in 1979 to 1982. On these hypotheses, the trade gap is driven down to $0.5 billion in 1982, when employment grows at 3 percent. Again, 2 percent employment growth gives a balance-of-payments improvement of only $0.5 billion.

Now in the "real" future, the alternatives would probably lie somewhere between these two cases. The assumption of proportionality between intermediate imports and output is a traditional one, but it is unrealistic when the extreme dependence of the Brazilian economy on imported energy is taken into account. Similarly, national capital goods cannot trade off at even terms with imported ones—the step from simple lathes to 1000-megawatt steam turbines is not trivial. The B projections tend to be fatuous in many ways.[10]

We conclude that under the favorable conditions in which the nation can find finance for $3 billion to $7 billion per year in foreign exchange, the denouement will lie somewhere between cases A and B. An imposed smaller trade gap would lead to enough economic disruption to imperil the regime. A larger gap probably could not be financed. One still has to ask what the distributional implications of a middle course would be. From the extremes of high and low import substitution at 3 percent employment growth, Table 7-6 sheds some light on this question. Its main implications are the following:

1. In the Cambridge results, import substitution cuts foreign savings, increases required private saving, and causes the profit rate to rise and the labor share to fall (all as usual). The major policy question is how far α_L can drop before political disruption ensues; in such terms, the labor share of 0.336 in 1982 under an import substitution policy seems very low indeed. Of course, a $14 billion trade deficit with no import substitution but a decent labor share may not be feasible either. We observe the approaching horns of a gigantic policy dilemma.

2. Within its altogether more drab projection of the future, the neoclassical model reacts less violently to the trade crisis. A decrease in foreign savings comparable to that in the Cambridge model with import substitution is accommodated in the marginalist version through accelerated exchange-rate devaluation, reducing imports uniformly and making remaining foreign saving more valuable domestically. Exact estimates of the "required" devaluation of the cruzeiro would again be sensitive to parameters, but in the solutions here they are moderate. Without import substitution, the exchange rate rises in 1976 to 1979 and 1979 to 1982 respectively, 8.3 and 9.0 percent per year. These rates increase to 11.2 and 12.3 percent in the $\beta(0.03)$ solution with import substitution.

[10]But in other ways they do not. From the point of view of 1977, the main drawback of Table 7-6 (as generated in 1973) is that it did not take into account the tremendous rise in coffee prices in 1976. But what rational, moderately pessimistic planner could have foreseen that? Like most other countries, Brazil still finds a major part of its destiny in the hands of the gods.

3. Income distribution gets slightly worse in the neoclassical runs as more private savings are generated. And as usual, reduced foreign savings also force down the rate of growth. The effect is fairly small, however, since foreign savings are initially a small share of the total. The reduction in output in 1982 would be only a bit more than 1 percent, which is acceptable.

In effect, we arrive at two views of how the economy might adjust to its future trade problems. The Cambridge model stresses limited adjustment possibilities and their resulting unfavorable impacts on employment and the functional distribution of income. The marginalist model points to the conclusion that import substitution is possible (through some appropriate policy of devaluation of the cruzeiro) and, in fact, will lead to only modest reduction in the growth of real output. Our own opinion is that—coffee booms aside—the Cambridge forecasts give a more realistic view of what is in store for Brazil; but we could be wrong. We hope so, else export-led economic miracles may be in for very serious trials indeed.

SELECTED ADDITIONAL READINGS

Bacha, Edmar L.: "Issues and Evidence on Recent Brazilian Economic Growth," *World Development*, 5 (1 and 2):47–67, 1977. (Perceptive review of Brazilian development policy and its results.)

Cardoso, Eliana A.: "Brazilian Growth and Distribution in the 1960s: An Identity-based Post-mortem" in L. Taylor, et al.: *Models of Growth and Distribution for Brazil* (to appear). (The source of Sec. 7-4, here. Further results and analysis are presented.)

Fishlow, Albert: "Some Reflections on Post-1964 Brazilian Economic Policy," in A. Stepan (ed.): *Authoritarian Brazil*, Yale University Press, New Haven, 1973. (Review of Brazilian stabilization through wage repression and other policies.)

Jones, Ronald W.: "The Structure of Simple General Equilibrium Models," *Journal of Political Economy*, 73:557–572, 1965. [Elegant presentation of the neoclassical cost-minimization equations; see Eqs. (7-10') and (7-11').]

Manne, Alan S.: "Key Sectors of the Mexican Economy, 1960–70," in A. S. Manne and H. M. Markowitz (eds.): *Studies in Process Analysis*, Wiley, New York, 1963. [Uses variables like g of Eq. (7-7) in investment planning. See also the Chenery-Bruno article cited in Chap. 8 for something similar.]

Sen, Amartya K.: "The Money Rate of Interest in the Pure Theory of Growth," in F. H. Hahn and F. P. R. Brechling (eds.): *The Theory of Interest Rates*, Macmillan and St. Martin's Press, London, 1965. (Discusses paradoxical investment behavior in neoclassical growth models as well as other problems.)

EIGHT

TWO FIXED-PRICE DISEQUILIBRIUM MODELS

The models discussed in the preceding two chapters place great emphasis on price flexibility as a means to reduce potential economic disequilibrium—either by forced saving under inflation or by neoclassical substitution in production and demand. Models aside, however, there are enough rigidities in underdeveloped economies to prevent the price mechanism from smoothing things out every time. In this chapter, to show where the problems arise, we develop two lines of analysis that focus on situations in which price-mediated adjustment does not work. Section 8-1 reviews a model that has been important in Soviet and Indian planning, based on the hypothesis that capital cannot be shifted from the sector in which it is first installed. The key issue turns out to be choice between high investment in capital-goods production coupled with low consumption now, or lower growth rates of consumption later on. In Sec. 8-2, one variant of the well-known two-gap model is set out. Foreign exchange is the limiting factor, and the model emphasizes the usefulness of investment and foreign borrowing now to develop industries that will "produce" dollars for future use via export or import substitution. The story is really not different from the one in Sec. 8-1, since only the limiting factor changes. Both models stress that some resource is likely to be very scarce in a poor country, and there are hard decisions involved in using it well.

8-1 THE FELDMAN-MAHALANOBIS-DOMAR (FMD) MODEL

One of the most creative discussions of applied planning problems took place during the so-called Soviet industrialization debate of the mid-1920s. Dual-economy and surplus-labor models were introduced by the left opposition in the debates, as we will see in more detail in Chap. 11. Given the acute capital shortage the Soviet Union faced at the time, it is not surprising that there were models stressing that, too. One was introduced by the economist G. A. Feldman; much later, his paper was translated and introduced in an improved version to Anglo-Saxon economics by Evsey Domar, whose work we met in the context of the Harrod-Domar model as well.

After Independence in India, there was a similar preoccupation with capital shortage, and a model essentially equivalent to Feldman's was introduced by P. C. Mahalanobis, a statistician turned national planner, in 1953. The Mahalanobis variant was an elegant formalization of ideas current in India at the time, and it served as a sort of intellectual underpinning for the early 5-year plans (see the survey paper by Bhagwati and Chakravarty—cited in the Selected Additional Reading—for details).

The model is based on an accounting scheme with two sectors, producing capital and consumption goods. Intermediate product flows between the sectors are ignored (or somehow aggregated away), and there is no foreign trade. The key assumption is that capital *cannot* be shifted away from the sector in which it is first installed; that is, a steel mill cannot be turned into a shoe factory, and vice versa. In a poor country, where capital is scarce overall and the engineering skills which might be used to modify the final products emerging from a given machine do not exist, this is not an overly strong assumption. What *is* more questionable is whether aggregation into two sectors is possible, but we take that up below.

For planning purposes, the main question to be answered is what fraction of capital-goods production to assign to the capital-goods sector itself and how much to production of new consumer goods. The Soviet example suggests that if this fraction (call it λ) is large, the costs to consumers can be great. How large is large? To develop quantitative intuition, begin by noting that accumulation in the capital-goods sector is given by the equation,

$$dK_1/dt = (\lambda b_1 - \delta)K_1$$

or

$$K_1' = \lambda b_1 - \delta \tag{8-1}$$

where sector 1 produces capital goods, b_1 is its output-capital ratio [the inverse of a parameter like a_{KX} in Eq. (6-11)] and δ is the physical rate of capital depreciation. Total output of capital goods is $b_1 K_1$ (assuming full-capacity utilization), the fraction $\lambda b_1 K_1$ of this output is assigned to gross investment in sector 1, and net capital formation dK_1/dt is what is left over after depreciation δK_1 is made good.

Suppose that capital-goods production is not itself very capital-intensive (which appears to be the case in reality), so that $b_1 = 0.5$, or the capital-output ratio in the sector is 2.0. Let the depreciation rate be 0.04. Then, if $\lambda = 0.2$, capital-goods output in Eq. (8-1) will be growing at 6 percent per year. This shows already that the share of capital-goods output which must be reinvested to generate a "reasonable" growth rate in the sector is not very big.

The growth of capital stock in the consumption-goods sector is given by

$$dK_2/dt = (1 - \lambda) b_1 K_1 - \delta K_2 \tag{8-2}$$

Accumulation of the consumer-goods sector's capital stock ultimately depends on the

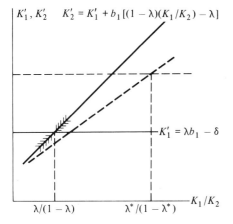

Figure 8-1 Solution of the FMD model.

output of (and previous accumulation in) the capital-goods sector. Investment in "machines to make machines" is the driving force in the model.

To see the key role of investment, rewrite Eq. (8-2) as

$$K'_2 = K'_1 + b_1 [(1 - \lambda)(K_1/K_2) - \lambda] \tag{8-3}$$

The relationship between Eq. (8-1) for K'_1 and Eq. (8-3) for K'_2 can be seen quite clearly in Fig. 8-1.[1] The horizontal line for K'_1 shows that the growth rate of the investment sector's capital stock is independent of the composition ratio K_1/K_2. On the other hand, the growth rate of the consumption sector's capital K'_2 does depend on K_1/K_2 and will only equal K'_1 when K_1/K_2 takes on the equilibrium value $\lambda/(1 - \lambda)$ shown in the figure. There will be convergence to this equilibrium, as can be seen by assuming that $K_1/K_2 > \lambda/(1 - \lambda)$, so that there is a relative excess of K_1. Then the term in brackets in Eq. (8-3) will be positive, and K_2 will grow faster than K_1 until equal growth rates are attained at the equilibrium composition of capital stocks.

Now suppose that the state adopts a more aggressive investment policy, beginning from an initial steady-state equilibrium. The resultant increase in λ to a new value of λ^* will shift the lines to the new (dashed) positions shown in Fig. 8-1. The growth rate of K_1 will rise to $\lambda^* b_1 - \delta$, and the line for K'_2 will be less steep. Ultimately, the growth rate of the consumption-sector capital stock will rise to the new level $\lambda^* b_1 - \delta$. For policy purposes however, it is essential to ask what will happen to consumption under the new investment plan in the short run. A rapid decline, for example, could involve either repression or impossible political pressure against the current regime. Most governments might prefer to avoid either alternative.

Graphically, this equation reduces to asking whether the new line for K'_2 lies above or below the old line for K'_1 at the initial capital stock ratio $\lambda/(1 - \lambda)$. If it lies below, there will be an initial fall in the growth rate of K_2, which could lead to shortages in the amount of consumer goods being produced. An analytical expression can be obtained if we observe that, just after the change in the value of λ, the growth rate of K_2

[1]Rudi Dornbusch suggested this neat graphical presentation.

will be given by

$$K_2' = b_1(1 - \lambda^*)\, \frac{\lambda}{1 - \lambda} - \delta \tag{8-4}$$

For high enough values of λ^*, the right side of Eq. (8-4) can be negative, meaning that the initial effect of the increased investment activity will be to make not only the growth rate but the *level* of consumption-goods output fall.

For example, with the parameters given above, we have $\lambda = 0.2$, $\lambda b_1 = (0.2)\,(0.5) = 0.1$, and $\delta = 0.04$. Then one can show from Eq. (8-4) that the growth rate of K_2 will decrease for any value of λ^* that exceeds 0.2, the initial value of λ. The growth rate will become negative if λ^* exceeds 0.68. Such a violent acceleration of investment is not likely, but a higher depreciation rate (δ) or lower output-capital ratio in the investment-goods sector (b_1) could make this situation reverse.

This type of trade-off between current consumption and investment growth rates is characteristic of planning models, which are usually set up to choose certain key variables—in this case the amount of investment which should be plowed back into capital-goods production. In the present example, the capital-goods reinvestment rate λ was set to the value 0.2 arbitrarily, to illustrate how FMD models work. However, there is no particular reason for λ to take that value or even to remain constant. In fact, it would be interesting to look at the growth implications of a time-varying λ, using a computer to simulate Eqs. (8-1) and (8-3) for sectoral growth rates forward through the planning period. This would give some feeling for the sensitivity of the growth path to variations in λ and *might* help in selecting an appropriate time path for it.

Many practitioners would be willing to stop with this type of simulation. However, others would go further and try to select a reinvestment rate on more fundamental grounds. One way of doing so is to maximize some sort of planner's preference function over time, subject to Eqs. (8-1) and (8-3). By tacit agreement in the literature, this maximand takes the form of the integral of discounted utility of consumption over the planning period, "utility" being measured by some simple function of consumption per capita. The whole exercise therefore becomes an "optimal savings" problem, of a type to be discussed later. In the present context, the "optimal" time path would probably involve assigning all capital-goods output to the capital-goods sector for the first part of the planning period and all to consumption goods thereafter. One would not want to tell the planning minister to follow this sort of strategy, but it does illustrate the kind of extreme specialization to which optimizing planning models are prone. In part, this explains why they are not used very much in practice.

More subtle planners would recognize that simple optimization of this type is irrelevant, because they would know that they could not, politically, force extreme investment specialization on the economy in any case. Therefore, they might look at the implications of politically feasible time paths for λ in the type of simulation outlined above, carrying in the back of their minds knowledge of the possible range of its variation (given control of import licensing, investments by government corporations, and so on). Or an optimization problem of the type discussed could be solved, but putting additional arbitrary restrictions on the range of λ, for example, $0.15 \leqslant \lambda \leqslant 0.37$. Another course would be to try to model how agents in the economy who decide about investment would respond to variation in the policy tools at hand, so that the capital reinvestment rate could be optimized subject to the capital-accumulation equations and these additional restrictions. In any case, some sort of choice would have to be made.

These are the main points that FMD models illustrate. Assuming that one is willing to worry about the value of λ, they also have some use in practical planning. However, their applicability is limited by the fact that it is extremely difficult to isolate capital- and consumption-goods sectors in the industrial statistics at any reasonable level of disaggregation. There are two reasons for this. First, the capital-consumption dichotomy completely ignores intermediate goods, yet these make up the bulk of manufacturing output even in semi-industrialized economies. Second, at the common "two-digit" or "three-digit" levels in the industrial classifications, most sectors produce at least two types of goods. For example, the motor-vehicle industry produces replacement parts (intermediate goods), trucks (capital goods), and cars (consumer goods). Trying to force this diversity into two little boxes called capital and consumption is unrewarding.

8-2 TWO-GAP MODELS

FMD models, in their concentration on technical rigidities in production, play down the importance of savings limitations on growth. Restrictions on both savings and production flexibility appear in another family of aggregate planning schemes, the two-gap models. One way to view the two-gap approach is as an extension of Harrod-Domar planning to economies with foreign trade, and it was so popularized in the early 1960s by Hollis Chenery and collaborators (see their papers cited at the end of the chapter). But more profoundly, two-gap models trace back to ideas about "external strangulation" of underdeveloped countries proposed by Latin American structuralist economists in the 1950s (for presentations in English, see the books by Furtado and Hirschman listed at the end of the chapter). Here, we just review the salient characteristics of one particular two-gap variant, leaving the student to pursue detailed applications in the literature (e.g., the paper on Israel by Chenery and Bruno).

Suppose that the economy produces two goods, the first for domestic consumption (and perhaps for export in an exogenously given quantity) and the second for export or substitution of imports at fixed world prices. Foreign-exchange revenues are used to pay for imports of intermediate goods which are current inputs into production and of capital goods which make up a certain share of investment. By hypothesis, both these types of imports are noncompetitive; for various technical reasons, they cannot be produced within the country. This is a particularly realistic assumption for small countries, which do not usually enter into production of a full range of capital equipment until they achieve quite high income levels.

Most of the foregoing can be rephrased in terms of a few simple algebraic constraints. For example, the balance-of-payments restriction becomes

$$a_{0I}(I_1 + I_2) + a_{0X}(X_1 + X_2) - F - X_2 \leqslant 0 \qquad (8\text{-}5)$$

In this inequality, X_1 is output of the home good and X_2 is the export good. Both are assumed to have an intermediate import component determined by the coefficient a_{0X} (which might take a value like 0.2 or 0.3 in practice). New capital formation in each sector (I_1 and I_2) has an import component a_{0I}, which might be as high as 0.5.[2]

Foreign-exchange receipts come from exports X_2 (we implicitly assume that both world and national prices of the export commodity are unity) and also from foreign lending F. The inequality of Eq. (8-5) therefore requires that total imports not exceed foreign-exchange receipts. If this first "gap" between foreign-exchange inflows and outflows is not 0, the devices by which it is closed (more imports, reserve accumulation, etc.) are not considered in the model. Its structure is much less tightly specified than (for example) the foreign-trade models discussed in Chap. 4. The type of output adjustment to initial trade imbalances that was considered there simply does not apply in the present context. Two-gap models are often criticized for their lack of realism or behavioral content on precisely these grounds.

Besides helping close the trade gap in Eq. (8-5), foreign lending also contributes a positive term to the national savings-investment identity. Written in inequality terms, this becomes

$$I_1 + I_2 - F - s(X_1 + X_2) \leqslant 0 \qquad (8\text{-}6)$$

where s is the overall national savings rate from whatever income aggregate the sum $X_1 + X_2$ represents. Again, there is no indication of what happens if investment differs from potential savings $F + s(X_1 + X_2)$ ex ante. Since the model, as far as Eq. (8-6) is concerned, is of Harrod-Domar form, one might expect some sort of Keynesian adjustment process. Alternatively, there could be increases in consumption and government expenditures rather than investment as F gets bigger. There has been debate about how strong this effect is—see the papers by Griffin and Enos, Marris, and Papanek cited at the end of the chapter—but it exists (as Cambridge growth theory suggests it should). In the formal model, it could be captured by multiplying F in Eq. (8-6) by a coefficient less than unity, so as to turn the inequality into a behavioral relationship instead of a thinly disguised identity.

We can complete the specification by assuming that there is some floor below total investment, perhaps from a projection of planned growth within the economy:

$$\underline{I} - (I_1 + I_2) \leqslant 0 \qquad (8\text{-}7)$$

Also, investment in any one year cannot be too large because of limitations in *absorptive capacity* (due to lack of skilled personnel, increasing costs due to rapid installation of capital goods, etc.) of the form

$$(I_1 + I_2) - \overline{I} \leqslant 0 \qquad (8\text{-}8)$$

---

[2] As written in Eq. (8-5), a_{0I} is the average import content in capital-goods production and a_{0X} is the import content in other sectors of the economy. This particular disaggregation is convenient for analytical exposition of the two-gap model, but it might be difficult to implement in practice. Readers should try their hands at alternative formulations, perhaps based on an average content for some measure of economic activity like GDP and marginal coefficients for imports to support production of exports or capital goods.

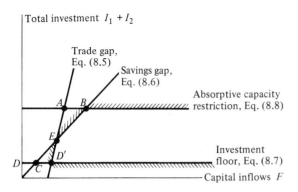

Figure 8-2 Two-gap model restrictions.

Both $\underline{I}$ and $\overline{I}$ in these restrictions should be related to current or immediately past income levels, but we ignore this for the sake of simplicity.[3]

The two-gap specification allows even more freedom of choice than the FMD model, as a glance at Fig. 8-2—where the feasible area within which the planner can operate is shown by cross-hatching—will reveal. Restrictions in Eqs. (8-8) and (8-7) are shown to bound investment $I_1 + I_2$ from above and below, while the two-gap constraints of Eqs. (8-5) and (8-6) put lower bounds on capital inflows F (assumed in the figure to be necessarily positive). The slope of the trade gap of Eq. (8-5) is steeper than the savings gap of Eq. (8-6) because the investment import coefficient a_{0I} is less than 1. If Eq. (8-5) actually binds the economy, extra foreign lending permits more than a dollar-for-dollar increase in investment, because capital formation comprises national components like building construction in its makeup as well as imports.

Suppose that the planning ministry is aiming for a high growth rate with minimal capital inflows (we discuss below the question of *which* sector should be growing). Then, as the figure is drawn, growth will be limited by the absorptive capacity constraint of Eq. (8-8) and capital inflows will be required to close the savings gap of Eq. (8-6). Since, ex post facto, something else must be going on to make both savings and trade gaps equal—the "gap between the gaps" AB cannot persist—there will be imports beyond those absolutely required for production and investment, or reserve accumulation.

In another case, assume that capital inflows are limited exogenously to the level DD'. Then the minimal growth constraint of Eq. (8-7) and the trade gap of Eq. (8-5) will be binding. There will be excess potential savings in the amount CD', which may be translated into excess capacity or unemployment. In more colorful language, the economy is drowning in surplus because of the shortage of essential imports.

Finally, at point E, the gap between the gaps does not exist, as ex ante demands for foreign exchange to supplement domestic savings and to close the trade gap are

---

[3]The paper by Marris cited in the readings gives a good review of the macro implications of absorptive capacity constraints. Their micro foundations are illustrated in the context of a linear programming planning model by Eckaus.

equal. There is no problem in utilizing capital inflows, although the absorptive capacity constraint would permit higher investment levels if planners opted for a high-growth policy.

All this should indicate that there are many decisions to be made regarding where the economy stands vis-à-vis Fig. 8-2. These can be made in various ways. The examples just discussed essentially rely on the planner's "feel" (or clairvoyance) about the binding constraints.[4] However, the fact that the model forces the practitioner to decide which gap is binding a priori is a drawback, but not an insuperable one; the extent of agreement on the matter among economists in any specific country is usually quite impressive.

An alternative approach to the decision problem is to set up some sort of dynamic optimizing model to explore which gap "should" be binding and also to decide about investment allocation between the two sectors. One possibility is to maximize, over the planning period, the integral of the difference between discounted consumption and foreign lending valued at some shadow price exceeding 1 (the "shadow price of foreign exchange"; see Chap. 13). An equivalent procedure would be to minimize the discounted sum of investment and foreign lending (valued at its shadow price) subject to constraints on consumption or output growth. In either case, the usual result is that there should be high capital inflows and investment at the beginning of the planning period followed by a gradual decrease of such efforts over time. Thus the optimal resource allocation runs from point B (savings gap binding) to E (no gap between the gaps) to D' (trade gap binding). During the initial period of the plan, there is also likely to be investment specialization in sector 2, which, as the structuralists said, is really a "quasi-capital goods sector." This result is entirely consistent with the early specialization in the capital-goods sector discussed above in connection with the FMD model; it pays to invest in capital-goods capacity early in the planning period, since this allows for the addition of more production possibilities over a longer time.

Regardless of the specific approach planners take to decision making, they can do worse than analyze their economy in two-gap terms. With a little bit of prying, the statistics can be forced to fit the model, and it does focus on issues that are, unpleasantly, relevant for most developing countries.

SELECTED ADDITIONAL READINGS

Bhagwati, Jagdish N., and Sukhamoy Chakravarty: "Contributions to Indian Economic Analysis: A Survey," *American Economic Review*, 59(4): part 2, 1969. (An illuminating survey of much research effort related to Indian planning.)

Chenery, Hollis B., and Michael Bruno: "Development Alternatives in an Open Economy: The Case of Israel," *Economic Journal*, 72:79–103, 1962. (An early and insightful application of the two-gap planning approach.)

[4]Note that one key conclusion which follows from the planner's assessment of the binding gap regards the importance of foreign aid. Additional aid will clearly permit a larger increment in investment and growth when the trade gap rather than the savings gap is binding. In Fig. 8-2, this can be seen by comparing the extra investment resulting from a move from D' to E to that from a move from E to B.

Chenery, Hollis B., and Arthur MacEwan: "Optimal Patterns of Growth and Aid: The Case of Pakistan," in I. Adelman and E. Thorbecke (eds.): *The Theory and Design of Economic Development*, The Johns Hopkins Press, Baltimore, 1966. (Linear programming model built around the two-gap specification. Follows the investment specialization phases discussed in Sec. 8-2.)

Domar, Evsey D.: "A Soviet Model of Growth," *Essays in the Theory of Economic Growth*, Oxford University Press, New York, 1957. (Presents the Feldman model discussed in Sec. 8-1.)

Eckaus, Richard S.: "Absorptive Capacity as a Constraint due to Maturation Processes," in J. N. Bhagwati and R. S. Eckaus (eds.): *Development and Planning: Essays in Honor of Paul Rosenstein-Rodan*, M.I.T. Press, Cambridge, Mass., 1973. (Discusses the absorptive capacity constraint from its micro foundations.)

Furtado, Celso: *Development and Underdevelopment*, University of California Press, Berkeley, Calif., 1964. (Chapter 5 presages the two-gap model very neatly.)

Griffin, Keith B., and John L. Enos: "Foreign Assistance: Objectives and Consequences," *Economic Development and Cultural Change*, 18:313-327, 1970. (Presents the case that increased capital inflows do not automatically lead to more investment internally.)

Hirschman, Albert O.: *The Strategy of Economic Development*, Yale University Press, New Haven, 1958. (Chapter 9 anticipates the two-gap model, growing from Latin American roots.)

Mahalanobis, P. C.: "Some Observations on the Process of Growth of National Income," *Sankhya*, 12:307-312, 1953. (Statement of the Indian variant of the FMD model.)

Marris, Robin: "Can We Measure the Need for Development Assistance?" *Economic Journal*, 80:650-668, 1970. (Useful critique of two-gap calculations of "aid requirements." Also reviews macro implications of the absorptive capacity constraint.)

McKinnon, Ronald I.: "Foreign Exchange Constraints in Economic Development and Efficient Aid Allocation," *Economic Journal*, 74:388-409, 1964. (A two-gap model with imported investment goods underlying the trade constraint. Conclusions in the manner of Harrod-Domar are derived.)

Papanek, Gustav F.: "The Effects of Aid and Other Resource Transfers on Savings and Growth in Less Developed Countries," *Economic Journal*, 82:934-950, 1972. (Argues the case that aid inflow leads to additional savings and not consumption.)

Taylor, Lance: "Investment Timing in Two-Gap Models," in H. B. Chenery, et al. (eds.), *Studies in Development Planning*, Harvard University Press, Cambridge, Mass., 1971. (Analyzes phasing of investment in a two-gap model similar to that in the Chenery-MacEwan article cited above, using optimal control theory.)

Weitzman, Martin L.: "Shiftable vs. Non-Shiftable Capital: A Synthesis," *Econometrica*, 39:511-530, 1971. (A neat extension of the FMD model in optimal control terms.)

NINE

THREE MODELS WITH MONEY AND CREDIT, INFLATION AND GROWTH

The trouble with the kind of economics preached and practiced in this book is that one begins to take the mathematics too seriously. Equations are precise, at times elegant, but they can fail utterly to reflect what is going on in the real economy. A protoplasmic blob with a bit of vaguely discernible structure is often a better metaphor than esthetically pleasing algebra.

Nowhere is the contrast between formal precision and amorphous reality more apparent than in the domain of money and finance, where plasticity and continual evolution within a complex institutional structure are the rule. For example, we will shortly justify dependence of the demand for credit on prices and the level of economic activity and then link credit availability to the supply of money. But credit can come from institutional sources ranging from the World Bank to the loan shark, and it can be substituted through inventory reductions or withholding workers' payments at the point of a gun. Similarly, the overall money supply can fluctuate unpredictably, despite tight government control over the money base and requirements for bank reserves. Under such circumstances, inventing simple equations to forecast economic activity from changes in the money base may conceal more than it tells.

Nonetheless we persist, since the formal treatment can at times clear away cobwebs and supplement more intuitive assessments of the financial situation; the "tone and feel of the City" tell something about the money market, but not necessarily all. Macro restrictions which can be both formalized and quantified help form the signals tickling the sensitive nerve endings of all sorts of financiers.

In this spirit, three topics are taken up in this chapter. First, we analyze the key determinants of demand for money and credit in an institutional setup close to that of many semi-industrialized countries; Sec. 9-1 should be read in connection with the discussion of money supply in Sec. 2-6. Thereafter, we take up a simple disequilibrium model, which can prove extremely useful in assessing the state of the macroeconomy from its monetary side. Finally, we discuss how printing money can drive a model of inflation, forced saving, and growth in Sec. 9-3.

9-1 THE DEMAND FOR MONEY AND CREDIT

Conventional treatments of the demand for money stem from Keynes and Hicks. The key institutional assumption is that a good capital market exists, so that it makes sense to talk about "the" interest rate on bonds as part of the cost of holding money. If expected price increases are another item of cost and the uses of money depend mostly on the volume of transactions in the economy, then the conventional equation for money demand in growth-rate form becomes

$$(H^d)' - P' = aX' - b[i' + (j')] \tag{9-1}$$

where H^d is the demand for money, P is the price level, X is output, i is the real interest rate on bonds, and j is the expected rate of inflation. Money demand relative to the price level rises with the volume of economic activity and falls with the costs (from either interest or inflation) of holding cash balances. Absence of *money illusion* implies that, in level form, the public desires to hold real balances (H^d/P), so that nominal money demand is unit-elastic with the current price level. This explains the $(H^d)' - P'$ term to the left of Eq. (9-1). The elasticities a and b on the right might hover around 1 and $\frac{1}{2}$ respectively.[1]

Underlying Eq. (9-1) is the general presumption that money is one of several assets making up the "public's" portfolio. If the volume of transactions PX goes up, for example, then one needs a bigger stock of money to finance them and shifts out of bonds or other security holdings in response. Similarly, if a bigger interest return on bonds can be obtained, one shifts out of money. All these responses are supposed to be smooth and rational and, with some naïveté, may be said to describe the monetary behavior of people in developing countries (recall the assumption that money in Portugal is a sort of necessity—with Engel elasticity less than 1—in Sec. 3-1).

Another approach, perhaps more realistic in poor countries with fragmented capital markets, focuses on the availability of *credit* as a constraint on the economy. Of course, credit from the organized banking system and the money supply are closely linked, and the two views are complementary. However, we stress credit here, since its role is often overlooked in monetarist/nonmonetarist controversy, probably to the detriment of arguments from both sides. The presentation generally follows recent work by Bruno and Cavallo (see Selected Additional Readings). It should be read in connection with Sec. 2-6 on the money-supply process. The Chap. 5 discussion of markup pricing is also relevant, since we will find something very close to a markup in

---

[1] Occasionally time trends are included in econometric versions of Eq. (9-1), to stand for population growth, increased monetization of the economy, and so on. The credibility of such specifications obviously depends on the circumstances in which they are used.

the following model of price and output responses in an economy with rising marginal costs in the short run.

Suppose that, in the modern sector, labor with cost w and intermediate imports with cost P_0 are the main variable inputs into production. If the rental cost r of fixed capital is also taken into account, then the results of Appendix D indicate that per-unit production costs Z will grow according to the rule

$$Z' = \alpha_K r' + \alpha_L w' + \alpha_0 P_0' \tag{9-2}$$

where α_K, α_L, and α_0 are respectively the shares of capital, labor, and intermediate imports in per-unit cost.

In the short run of enterprise decision making, the capital stock K is supposed to be fixed. The demand schedule for capital along the lines of Appendix D will take the form

$$K' - X' = -\sigma^X(r' - Z')$$

where σ^X is the elasticity of substitution and X the level of output. With $K' = 0$, this equation shows that an increase in demand for capital will bid up the rental rate. Substituting for r' into Eq. (9-2) and some simplification gives

$$Z' = \beta_X X' + \beta_L w' + \beta_0 P_0' \tag{9-3}$$

in which $\beta_X = \alpha_K/(1 - \alpha_K) \sigma^X$, $\beta_L = \alpha_L/(1 - \alpha_K)$, and $\beta_0 = \alpha_0/(1 - \alpha_K)$.

Equation (9-3) suggests that in the short run, output costs are likely to rise with money wages, import costs, and the level of output. The last effect arises because of decreasing returns to capital—the neoclassical analogy of the rising markup rate postulated in Sec. 5-1.

To bring credit into the picture, assume that firms purchase variable inputs at some time prior to the sale of their product. If they borrow to finance these payments at the rate of interest i, then interest-inclusive unit costs will be $Z(1 + i)$, growing at the rate

$$MC' = Z' + \frac{i}{1+i} i' \tag{9-4}$$

The new symbol MC denotes marginal cost, which will be proportional to average cost $Z(1 + i)$ as long as the parameters α_K and σ^X stay fixed (or, to an approximation, vary slightly) in the short run.

A simple description for the demand function of a firm "representative" of the modern part of the economy can be written as

$$X = D(P/P^e)^{-\lambda} \tag{9-5}$$

where the price elasticity λ exceeds 1. The sale price is P, while D and P^e are the expected level of demand and the expected general price level respectively. Standard manipulations from Eq. (9-5) show that the growth in marginal revenue (MR) will be:

$$MR' = P' = (P^e)' + (1/\lambda)(D' - X') \tag{9-6}$$

Equating Eqs. (9-6) and (9-4) on the assumption that the representative firm maximizes profits, we can substitute from the other equations to derive the following two expressions for price and output growth rates:

$$X' = (\lambda/\gamma)[(P^e)' + (1/\lambda)D' - \beta_L w' - \beta_0 P_0' - ii'/(1 + i)] \qquad (9\text{-}7)$$

and

$$P' = (1/\gamma)[\lambda\beta_X(P^e)' + \beta_X D' + \beta_L w' + \beta_0 P_0' + ii'/(1 + i)] \qquad (9\text{-}8)$$

where $\gamma = 1 + \lambda\beta_X$.

These equations have a number of interesting implications about cost increases, growth, and inflation. For example, increases in either input costs w and P_0 or the interest rate i will increase the inflation rate and reduce output growth. Increases in the expected inflation rate $(P^e)'$ and in demand drive both actual prices and output up. These predictions are in general correspondence with what one expects in a semi-industrialized economy.

To focus a bit more on the role of the interest rate and credit, let L denote *total* production cost, $L = ZX$. From Eq. (9-3), its growth rate is given by

$$L' = (1 + \beta_X)X' + \beta_L w' + \beta_0 P_0' \qquad (9\text{-}9)$$

Suppose that firms fail to finance an increment in L resulting from increased input costs. Then Eq. (9-9) implies that their production will have to be restricted.

Where would additional credit come from? The most descriptive adjective for credit markets in poor countries is "segmented." One source of finance is always the official banking system, perhaps with controlled interest rates and hidden costs such as requirements that borrowing firms keep minimum balances on deposit. Another source could be semiofficial *financieras* or other legal, high-cost lenders; a third source would be loan sharks or the curb. To try to reflect this picturesque complexity in algebra, suppose that firms can obtain a fixed ration of credit L_0 from organized financial entities at a pegged interest rate i_0 that does not clear the market. For the finance of $L - L_0$, their remaining variable costs, firms must go to a risky, poorly organized informal credit market, where the interest rate goes up with the volume of borrowing. Suppose that borrowing cost i is a constant elasticity function of the total credit demand to official supply:

$$i = i_0(L/L_0)^\phi$$

In growth-rate terms, this equation becomes

$$i' = i_0' + \phi(L' - L_0') \qquad (9\text{-}10)$$

The borrowing rate rises with the pegged interest rate i_0 and total credit demand L, but it falls with credit supply L_0.

We know from the discussion in Sec. 2-6 that the total of bank credit L_0 will be related to the money supply H. Combining Eqs. (2-21) and (2-22), in fact, shows that

$$L_0 = \frac{1 - r}{1 + c} H \qquad (9\text{-}11)$$

where r is the reserve-deposit ratio and c is the currency-deposit ratio. If reserve requirements and the public's desired balance between currency and deposits do not shift, then official credit will grow at the same rate as the money supply, $L_0' = H'$. Substituting this equality together with Eq. (9-9) into Eq. (9-10) gives a final expression for the marginal cost of borrowing:

$$i' = i_0' + \phi(1 + \beta_X) X' + \phi\beta_L w' + \phi\beta_0 P_0' - \phi H' \qquad (9\text{-}12)$$

Equation (9-12) closely resembles the conventional expression of Eq. (9-1) for the demand for money, but it is perhaps founded on grounds more appropriate for poor countries. It can be used, for example, to illustrate the monetary contraction effects of currency devaluation mentioned in Sec. 4-1. Suppose that the internal import price P_0 is determined by an equation like

$$P_0 = eP_0^*$$

where e is the exchange rate and P_0^* is the world price. Then devaluation leads to an increment in P_0 on the right side of Eq. (9-12). Also, the growth rate of the money base can be decomposed as

$$BB' = G - eF \qquad (9\text{-}13)$$

Where G is the government cash deficit and F is the balance-of-payments deficit in dollars. It is likely that after devaluation from an initial deficit, F will become smaller but eF larger in absolute terms (compare Table 4-2). Hence the money base will decline, and also the money supply in Eq. (9-12). The outcome will be an increase in the marginal cost of borrowing i. But from Eqs. (9-7) and (9-8), this increase in interest rate together with higher import costs will lead to higher inflation and slower growth in real output. "Stagflation" in the economy is the result of devaluation through the channel of credit restriction and higher interest costs.

More generally, _any_ policy restricting money-supply growth policy will _not_ be anti-inflationary, since, in fact, the increases in interest rate that it induces will drive prices up. Rather, the brunt of the resulting credit restriction falls on the output side. Short-run orthodoxy in a semi-industrialized economy may have effects precisely opposite to those usually assumed.[2]

9-2 MONETARY PROGRAMMING

Using the apparatus just developed, we can now outline a simple technique for testing the ex ante compatibility of different fiscal, balance-of-payments, and monetary

[2]To get some idea about the strength of the responses involved, suppose that the profit, labor, and import shares in production cost are respectively $\alpha_K = 0.4$, $\alpha_L = 0.4$, $\alpha_0 = 0.2$. The elasticity of substitution σ^X could be in the vicinity of $\frac{2}{3}$. The parameters appearing in Eq. (9-3) are then $\beta_X = 1.0$, $\beta_L = \frac{2}{3}$, and $\beta_0 = \frac{1}{3}$. The demand elasticity λ in Eq. (9-5) might take a value near 2; the same is true of the interest elasticity ϕ in Eq. (9-10). Suppose that the initial value of the interest rate i is 0.1. Then a decrease in the growth rate of the money supply by 5 percent (say from 15 to 10 percent) will make the interest rate increase by 10 percent. From Eq. (9-7), the output growth rate will drop by 0.6 percent (say from 3.0 to 2.4 percent). From Eq. (9-8), the inflation rate will go up by about 0.3 percent. The latter effect may not be terribly important in an already inflationary situation, but the loss in output growth is quite severe.

growth targets. The basic approach is due to Jorge Cauas (see the readings) and has been used in Chile and elsewhere. In what follows, the equations are tailored to a highly inflationary situation, but appropriate modifications for other circumstances should be apparent.

Begin from the money supply. Equation (9-13) already shows the main elements in the change in the money base in an economy where capital markets are under-developed and open-market operations not feasible. Let m be a money multiplier of the type developed in Sec. 2-6 and H the money supply. Then $H = mB$, and

$$H' = m' + B' = m' + (1/B)(G - eF) \qquad (9\text{-}14)$$

This equation amounts to a catalog of the tools of monetary policy. From the point of view of the monetary authorities, the multiplier m is a policy instrument, though not a terribly flexible one. It will be ignored from here on. The government cash deficit G and balance-of-payments deficit F are usually beyond monetary control, though some exceptions exist. For example, the Central Bank might encourage commercial banks or trading firms to acquire credits abroad. In monetary terms, such a buildup of foreign liabilities would represent a capital inflow and reduce the rate of decrease of the home country's reserves, leading to a smaller value of F in Eq. (9-14). Countries under balance-of-payments pressure frequently resort to such maneuvers, which *sterilize* reserve movements, at least for a time. The reader can no doubt think of other examples.

In a highly inflationary situation, growth in money demand will come mainly from current and expected inflation rates—output increases and interest costs will be quantitatively minor influences. The appropriate simplification of Eq. (9-1) or (9-12) is

$$(H^d)' = P' - b(P^e)' \qquad (9\text{-}15)$$

A third equation can be added to these two for cost pressures on the price level. If again we ignore growth of output and interest rate as being small in comparison to price changes, we drop terms from Eq. (9-3) to get

$$Z' = \beta_L w' + \beta_0 P_0' \qquad (9\text{-}16)$$

One can imagine applying Eqs. (9-14) through (9-16) ex ante to ask whether money creation and demand will be compatible with expected price increases. Used in this way, the equations resemble the inequalities of the two-gap model, since they impose boundaries on the range of possible economic disequilibriums. Two common examples appear in Fig. 9-1.

In the left-hand diagram is a case of excess growth in the money supply. Inserting cost-induced price increases from Eq. (9-16) into Eq. (9-15) indicates that demand for nominal balances should be increasing at the rate A. On the other hand, supply is increasing at the rate B. Excess money-supply growth in the amount AB is the mirror image of growing excess demand in the goods market, i.e., shortages, increased cost pressures as firms use up excess capacity, and ultimately balance-of-payments diffi-culties as requirements for noncompetitive intermediate imports increase sharply. The "solution" to such a problem is reduction in the rate of growth of nominal money, but often this is impossible if the government deficit cannot be cut (perhaps because of

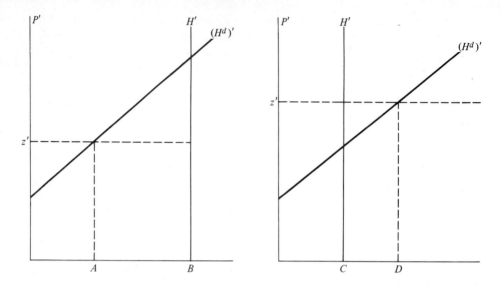

Figure 9-1 *Ex ante* disequilibrium positions in the money market (excess supply of money on the left, excess demand on the right).

militant public-sector employees' organizations) or international reserves cannot be defended further.

Under circumstances of rapid monetary growth and short reserves, the government is likely to be under great pressure from agencies like the International Monetary Fund to slow down the expansion of the nominal money supply. In fact, the IMF will be using a model very similar to the present one to calculate how much budget slashing or balance-of-payments improvement is required to reduce money supply growth from B to A in Fig. 9-1. As suits their purposes, the team of visiting experts will usually ignore all the contractionary impacts of their policy package discussed in the preceding section and Chap. 4. The present analysis plus the models developed earlier should at least enable a beleaguered planning team to fight the enemy on its own ground in an underdeveloped country.

Besides staging a recession, the monetary authorities may try to escape from demand inflation by trying to convince people that price increases are going to slow down for one reason or another. The public will presumably respond by shifting the $(H^d)'$ line to the right, reducing excess money growth (or growth in excess demand for goods). The Central Bank may not be the entity best equipped to carry through this sort of propaganda, but it may have to try. To paraphrase Dennis Robertson, the job of the Central Bank in a developing economy is to convince the public that the rate of inflation is soon going to be what it is not.[3]

---

[3]In a footnote, we may note that an alternative means of getting people to hold higher monetary balances is to increase the rate of interest they get on their deposits; presumably the relevant elasticity is the same b that appears in Eq. (9-15). This is a policy strongly recommended by McKinnon and Shaw (see the readings). The problem is that it is practically impossible to raise

The right side of Fig. 9-1 represents excess demand for money at the going rate of inflation, such as may result from a no-holds-barred stabilization program beginning from the situation in the left-hand graph. There is a corresponding excess supply in the goods market, i.e., slow growth and unemployment. The obvious policy measure is reflation through expansion of the rate of growth of the nominal money supply. Or a sufficiently puritanical monetary authority might hold off until unemployment forced workers to cut back their demands for nominal wage increases, reducing w' in Eq. (9-16) and therefore the cost inflation Z'. With a little help from their friends in the Army and the police, the monetary authorities may be able to make this sort of treatment for inflation work, but it can be a long and painful process. In Brazil, for example, between 1964 and 1967, it took almost 3 years of deflation, with a good deal of social unrest as a by-product.

Of course, the denouement need not be so dramatic as Brazil's. Most developing economies oscillate between the two graphs in Fig. 9-1; the monetary authorities, at best, may reduce the magnitude of the swings while striving to maintain acceptable output growth in the face of the restrictive effects of credit reduction discussed in Sec. 9-1. Their task is not easy and may be impossible, but models like the present one help place it in rational perspective.

9-3 MONETARY INFLATION FOR FORCED SAVING

At times, of course, finance ministers and Central Bank governors turn vice to virtue by printing money to force up the rate of economic growth (and, incidentally, the income share of capitalists, which class they might well represent). The dynamics of such a strategy are pursued in the present section; real-world experiments have been known at least since the time of *Faust*.[4] To set the stage, we note three major effects that inflationary finance can have on the economic situation:

1. If the government raises its own real investment, financing the expenditure by borrowing from the Central Bank, then both the real growth rate and the inflation rate will probably increase—the former from a higher rate of capital formation and the latter from the effect of more rapid monetary growth on prices.
2. If nominal wages lag behind the price increases, the income distribution will shift toward capital. If the windfall profit increases are invested, at least in part, they provide another source of more rapid output growth. An active policy of wage repression by the government will help this process along. This channel for inflationary finance has been stressed by structuralist writers. We base a formal analy-

---

the deposit rate in an inflationary situation where banks are making good money out of the spread between the inflation rate and the low nominal deposit rate. A strong monetary authority can escape the problems of Fig. 9-1 by doing this (just as a strong government can presumably escape from two-gap dilemmas by devaluing the currency sufficiently), but such a tour de force is beyond the reach of most policy-makers in developing countries.

[4]See Part II, Act I in Goethe's play for Mephistopheles's advice to the king about printing money, using his undiscovered treasures in the ground as the Treasury's corresponding asset.

sis on the institutional paper by Georgescu-Roegen noted in the readings. He tells the story very well.

3. As the public recognizes that the inflation rate has gone up, they will tend to hold less money; after all, its value is going down all the time. The resultant increase in velocity chokes off the effectiveness of printing money, especially if it only increases growth by permitting more government investment, as discussed above. Authors critical of inflationary finance emphasize the velocity increase; a good example is the cited book by Robert Mundell.

In the discussion that follows, these three consequences of inflationary finance are put into a formal model to evaluate their relative impacts on price increases and growth. The presentation closely follows pioneering work by Eliana Cardoso.

We begin with money supply and demand. If we work with an economy in which the balance-of-payments deficit or surplus is not large, growth in the money base B is described by the equation

$$dB/dt = PG \tag{9-17}$$

As usual, P denotes the price level; G represents the real government deficit (expenditures less tax revenues).

Let H be the money stock. If the money multiplier is m, then $H = mB$. The growth rate of the money supply is

$$H' = m(dB/dt)/H = mPG/H \tag{9-18}$$

The simplest way to describe money demand is with the traditional *quantity equation*

$$HV = PX \tag{9-19}$$

The right side of Eq. (9-19) represents total economic transactions, the price P times output X. With a behaviorally determined money velocity V, some quantity H of money is required to finance PX. If H changes and V stays constant, then either the price level or the level of output (usually the former) is assumed to adjust so that Eq. (9-19) is maintained as an equality.

If we represent the proportion of the real fiscal deficit in output as g,

$$g = G/X$$

then, using Eq. (9-19), we can rewrite Eq. (9-18) as

$$H' = mgV \tag{9-20}$$

This equation shows that the rate of growth of the money supply is in part controlled by the government (the multiplier m and the expenditure ratio g) and is in part influenced by the behavioral parameter V. Money supply is endogenous to the economic system insofar as V is concerned.

The effect of inflation on velocity can for practical purposes be modeled by the simple function

$$V = \overline{V} + \eta P' \tag{9-21}$$

Here, the 0 inflation velocity $\overline{V}$ might take a value around 2 or 3, and the coefficient η might be between 5 and 10 (see Mundell and Cardoso for these stylized facts).

To make use of Eq. (9-21) in a growth model, it is simplest to consider steady states in which the inflation rate P' is constant and V is not changing.[5] Then we have

$$P' = H' - X' \qquad\qquad \text{from Eq. (9-19)}$$
$$= mgV - X' \qquad\quad \text{from Eq. (9-20)}$$
$$= mg(\overline{V} + \eta P') - X' \quad \text{from Eq. (9-21)}$$

We can solve for the inflation rate as

$$P' = \frac{1}{1 - mg\eta}\,(mg\overline{V} - X') \tag{9-22}$$

The next step is determination of the output growth rate X'. Assume that the only source of private saving is from nonwage income (at rate s) and that some proportion ϕ of the government deficit is invested. The value of investment is

$$PI = s(PX - wL) + \phi PG$$

in which I is real investment, w is the nominal wage rate, L is employment, and the other symbols have been previously defined. This equation is easily rewritten as

$$I = s(X - qL) + \phi G \tag{9-23}$$

where $q = w/P$ is the real wage.

To keep the story as simple as possible, assume fixed factor-input coefficients in production,

$$X = aK \tag{9-24}$$

and

$$L = bX \tag{9-25}$$

Evidently, capital and output grow at the same rates $(X' = K')$ and straightforward manipulations transform Eq. (9-23) to the form

$$X' = sa(1 - qb) + \phi ag \tag{9-26}$$

---

[5] One could add formality if not a great deal of economic insight to the discussion by assuming that velocity depends on the expected inflation rate $(P^e)'$:

$$V = \overline{V} + \eta(P^e)'$$

Some sort of adaptive expectations might be postulated for $(P^e)'$, say

$$d(P^e)'/dt = \epsilon(P' - (P^e)')$$

Under stability conditions, which could be explored, these two equations would converge to something like Eq. (9-21), with velocity increasing gradually to its steady-state value as money holders recognize the effects of inflation on the value of their deposits and currency. The interested reader can consult the paper by Yarrow for the appropriate manipulations.

Back substitution into Eq. (9-22) gives our final expression for the inflation rate,

$$P' = \frac{1}{1 - mg\eta} \, [mg\overline{V} - a(s + g\phi) + sabq] \tag{9-27}$$

To understand this equation, it is useful to consider a couple of special cases. The first follows Mundell in assuming that s equals 0 and only the government invests,

$$P' = \frac{(m\overline{V} - a\phi)\,g}{1 - mg\eta} \tag{9-28}$$

A plausible set of parameters might take the values

$$m = 2 \quad \overline{V} = 4 \quad a = 0.4 \quad \phi = 1 \quad \eta = 5$$

Hence, the numerator in Eq. (9-28) will almost certainly be positive. However, since the product mn is in the vicinity of 10, a high share of the government deficit in total output (0.1 or more) could make the denominator negative and without meaning. Somewhat lower values of g would give rise to extremely high rates of inflation. Since the growth contribution of the fiscal deficit is only ϕag (say $0.4g$), the trade-off between inflation and growth is extremely sharp. This is the basis of Mundell's argument against inflationary finance.

The Georgescu-Roegen trade-off has a different set of arguments—growth and income distribution. In effect, he assumes that either because of government repression or because of money illusion, nominal wages lag behind price increases,

$$w' = \lambda P'$$

with $\lambda < 1.$[6] Growth in the real wage q then becomes

$$q' = (\lambda - 1)\,P' \tag{9-29}$$

If there is no government saving, the rate of inflation from Eq. (9-27) is

$$P' = \frac{1}{1 - mg\eta} \, [mg\overline{V} - sa(1 - bq)] \tag{9-30}$$

Suppose that the inflation rate is initially 0. Then an increase in the fiscal deficit g will immediately kick off price increases from Eq. (9-30). The nominal wage will follow with a lag, and the real wage will fall from Eq. (9-29). Even if there is no direct government investment ($\phi = 0$), output growth will increase from Eq. (9-26). Ultimately, this process will settle back down to a 0 inflation rate, but the real wage will be lower and the growth rate faster than before. The equilibrium real wage from Eq. (9-29) with $P' = 0$ is

$$q = \frac{sa - mg\overline{V}}{sab} \tag{9-31}$$

---

[6] Even when there is 100 percent wage indexation, a parameter like λ can be less than unity when lags are taken into account. Refer back to Sec. 5-2.

and the output growth rate from Eq. (9-26) is

$$X' = mg\overline{V}$$

Since the product $m\overline{V}$ is a rather large number (say, 8 or more), the impact of increased government expenditure on both the real wage and output growth is strong. So long as there are wage lags, substantial rates of real growth are possible at the (political) cost of a decreasing labor share in the Georgescu model.[7]

Following Cardoso, one can synthesize the Mundell and Georgescu models through a plausible set of assumptions about how the labor market functions. First note that the quantity $qb = (w/P)(L/X)$ is just the labor share. Bargaining and/or strife between capitalists and workers is often said to center on factor shares. Let us accept the hypothesis and assume that capitalists insist on some maximum labor share θ; below θ, they are willing to bargain. Under such rules of the game, the money wage would be set according to the formula

$$w' = \lambda P' + \gamma(\theta - bq)$$

where γ is a parameter representing the ability of wage earners to push the wage share back toward the level θ when it falls below. A simple transformation of this equation gives the growth rate of real wages as

$$q' = (\lambda - 1)P' + \gamma(\theta - bq) \tag{9-32}$$

this differs from Eq. (9-29) by taking the bargaining element into account.

If real wages are not changing ($q' = 0$), Eq. (9-32) defines an equilibrium relationship between q and the inflation rate P' as

$$P' = \frac{\gamma}{1 - \lambda}(\theta - bq) \tag{9-33}$$

Another equilibrium condition between the real wage and the inflation rate (holding velocity constant) is given by Eq. (9-27). Figure 9-2 shows how Eqs. (9-27) and (9-33) fit together. Both the inflation rate and the real wage will not change once they arrive at their respective equilibrium values $(P')^*$ and q^*. When λ is less than 1 in Eq. (9-33), it is easy to show that this equilibrium is stable.

The effect of shifts in the policy variables can easily be traced in Fig. 9-2. For example, an increase in g, the proportion in total output of the government deficits, shifts the intercept A of the "$V' = 0$" line to the left and increases its slope. The new equilibrium would involve a lower real wage and a higher growth rate than before. En route to the new equilibrium, the inflation rate would first accelerate and then drop off to its new and higher stable level.

In another story, one might imagine that the ability of workers to maintain nominal wage increases near the rate of inflation might be curtailed. The "$q' = 0$" line

---

[7]Of course, the transient inflation kicked off by an increase in government spending will be more severe as g approaches its Mundell bound of $1/mn$ from Eq. (9-27) or (9-30). Similarly, the real wage cannot fall below 0, requiring $g < sa/m\overline{V}$ from Eq. (9-31). Both these politically rather extreme bounds suggest that an absolute maximum value for g might lie well below 0.1.

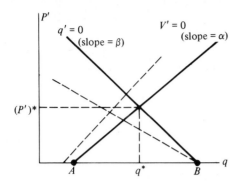

Figure 9-2 The consolidated model of inflationary finance. In the symbols of the text,

$$A = (g(a\phi - m\overline{V}) + as)/sab$$
$$\alpha = sab/(1 - mg\eta)$$
$$B = \theta/b$$
$$\beta = -\gamma b/(1 - \lambda)$$

would become flatter. In the new equilibrium, the output growth rate would be higher (and the real wage lower) in connection with a slower rate of inflation. In this sense, wage repression makes inflationary finance a much more attractive policy option.[8]

The story of a number of stabilization episodes might be told in terms of Fig. 9-2. For example, Cardoso shows that the Brazilian stabilization of 1964 represented a clear shift from a "$q' = 0$" curve that was nearly vertical to one lying much closer to the horizontal axis. Concurrently, the output growth rate increased, inflation fell, and the inflationary consequences of a given fiscal deficit proportion g became much less severe. The only people who lost were wage recipients.

In fact, the models of Secs. 9-2 and 9-3 both show that unfavorable shifts in income distribution appear to be part and parcel of orthodox attacks on inflation. Sections 9-1 and 9-2 add output contraction as another consequence. A degree of recession and wage compression may be inevitable under certain circumstances, but there is no use pretending, as monetarist economists often do, that reducing inflation does not entail severe political and social costs. One obvious extension of the models discussed here would be in the direction of asking how the burden of stabilization might be spread more evenly across all the economic classes. The answer would depend on institutional details about the specific country concerned, but it would be well worth searching out.

SELECTED ADDITIONAL READINGS

Bruno, Michael: "Stabilization and Stagflation in a Semi-Industrialized Economy," in Rudiger Dornbusch and Jacob A. Frenkel (eds.): *International Economic Policy: Theory and Evidence* (to appear). (Compact model presentation of stabilization problems—among other realistic items is the Sec. 9-1 model.)

[8]The Mundell special case discussed above is, in effect, based on the assumption that $\lambda = 1$, so that the "$q' = 0$" locus is vertical. An increase in the deficit g will mostly drive up inflation and not have much impact on growth under these circumstances. The Georgescu special case set $\lambda = 0$. The "$q' = 0$" locus corresponds to the horizontal axis in Fig. 9-2. An increase in g shifts the intercept A to the left, giving rise to faster growth and a lower labor share with a long-run inflation rate equal to 0.

Cardoso, Eliana A.: "Growth and Real Wages: Modelling the Brazilian Economic Miracle," M.I.T., Cambridge, Mass., 1977, mimeo. (Original version of the model of Sec. 9-3; contains an interesting empirical application for Brazil.)

——: "Deficit Financing and Real Wages: The Brazilian Experience in the 1960's," Department of Economics, University of Brasilia, 1978, mimeo.

Cauas, Jorge: "Short-Term Economic Policy," in Jagdish N. Bhagwati and Richard S. Eckaus (eds.): *Development and Planning: Essays in Honor of Paul Rosenstein-Rodan*, M.I.T. Press, Cambridge, Mass., 1973. (Compact statement of the model developed in Sec. 9-2.)

Cavallo, D. F.: "Stagflationary Effects of Monetarist Stabilization Policies," unpublished Ph.D. dissertation, Harvard University, Cambridge, Mass., 1977. (Presents a money-demand model like that of Sec. 9-1. Good discussion of policy implications.)

Dornbusch, Rudiger, and Stanley Fischer: *Macroeconomics*, McGraw-Hill, New York, 1977. (Chapter 7 gives a good presentation of received theory about the demand for money.)

Georgescu-Roegen, Nicholas: "Structural Inflation-Lock and Balanced Growth" *Economies et Societes*, 4:557–605, 1970. (A convincing "structuralist" and institutionalist interpretation of inflation along the lines of the model of Sec. 9-3.)

McKinnon, Ronald I.: *Money and Capital in Economic Development*, The Brookings Institution, Washington, D.C., 1973. (A plea for increased financial intermediation in underdeveloped countries, with the means not too well specified.)

Mundell, Robert A.: *Monetary Theory*, Goodyear Publishing Co., Pacific Palisades, Calif., 1971. (Presents the model described in Sec. 9-3, along with other work of interest.)

Shaw, Edward S.: *Financial Deepening in Economic Development*, Oxford University Press, New York, 1973. (Similar to McKinnon book, but the theoretical content is a bit more developed.)

Yarrow, G. K.: "The Demand for Money Function and the Stability of Monetary Equilibrium," *Economic Journal*, 87:114–123, 1977. [Gives stability conditions for inflation equations similar to Eq. (9-22), in which velocity depends on expected instead of actual inflation rates.]

TEN

CLASSICAL MODELS OF THE FUNCTIONAL INCOME DISTRIBUTION AND GROWTH

An enduring tradition in economics invests the labor market with social and political dimensions that are not apparent in the usual supply-demand cross. For example, many of the short-run models developed in previous chapters treat the *money wage* or the *labor share* as the object of labor-capitalist (or peasant-landlord) class conflict, with profits often getting the upper hand—for reasons discussed in Chap. 9 and elsewhere. In the long run, if workers at least demonstrate the ability to keep their wage demands in pace with capital accumulation and technical progress, a fixed *real wage* becomes the relevant abstraction. This chapter is devoted to models of distribution and growth in which the real wage is fixed either absolutely or as the convergent point of some politicoeconomic process.

Fixed real wages are closely associated with *classical* economic models—those of Ricardo and contemporaries over 150 years ago, Marx at one generation's remove, and W. Arthur Lewis in the post–World War II theory of economic development. The mechanisms these authors postulate to maintain a fixed (or target) real wage vary. For example, in the Ricardian system, short-run real wages may be assumed to be somewhat flexible, but total employment is finally determined by the amount of working capital that entrepreneurs have available—the wages fund. In the long run, the cost of reproduction of labor (the "subsistence" basket of consumption goods) fixes the real wage through population dynamics. If the wage lies above subsistence, fertility is supposed to rise or mortality to fall until population pressure drives the level of living back down. Marx maintained the idea of a fixed consumption basket by workers, but he relied on a reserve army of the unemployed—growing and shrinking in response to vagaries of worker-capitalist struggle—to keep the real wage stabilized. Lewis postulates that there is a large agricultural and traditional sector with nearly constant productivity per worker. The supply of labor from this sector to the rest of the economy is highly elastic at a wage level close to subsistence productivity.

In this chapter, we accept the macroeconomic assumptions of the fixed-real-wage school at face value and work out their implications for income distribution and growth. In Sec. 10-1, there is a brief summary of the Ricardo-Lewis model as an introduction. Section 10-2 is devoted to a model of the modern sector in a Lewis-style economy, in which there is labor-saving technical change that reduces employment in the short run but may increase total demand for labor through stimulating capital accumulation as time goes by. The relative strength of these two forces of technical advance and capitalists' thrift is assessed. Section 10-3 examines a more disaggregated modern-sector model, in which upper- and lower-income (or skilled and unskilled) workers have consumption patterns emphasizing luxury and wage goods respectively. If investment demand responds preferentially to growth in the consumption of luxury goods and if there is a difference in savings propensities between the two classes, rapid capital accumulation and growth accompanied by a deteriorating income distribution (through forced saving) is shown to occur. Section 10-4, the last in the chapter, switches gears somewhat to present a model of asset transfers between classes that has a politically more moderate ring than its predecessors. Throughout the chapter, the Lorenz curve as a summary description of the income distribution is mentioned from time to time. Its properties are briefly described in Appendix F.

10-1 RICARDO AND LEWIS

The hallmark of classical distribution models is the fixed subsistence wage. Other common assumptions are that most or all of savings comes from capitalists and that there are differences in consumption patterns between rich and poor. "The" classical model is, of course, Ricardo's. The accepted modern statement of his analysis—due to Nicholas Kaldor (see the Selected Additional Readings)—appears in Fig. 10-1. There is just one sector in the economy, producing "corn" with a 1-year production cycle, and

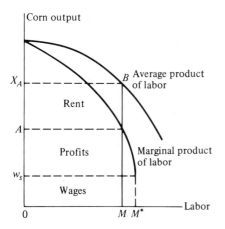

Figure 10-1 The Ricardian model.

the theory is about how the annual crop is distributed among three economic classes—workers, capitalists, and landlords.

It is assumed that capitalist farmer-entrepreneurs begin the crop year with a fixed wages fund of stored corn. Workers are in highly elastic supply at the subsistence wage w_s and are hired to the limit of the wages fund, producing employment M. We consider a long-run situation in which—by the demographic assumptions mentioned above—the wages fund and the total supply of labor at the subsistence wage are roughly in balance.

Given the average product-of-labor schedule shown in Fig. 10-1, employment M results in a total corn output of $OMBX_A$. Landlords receive as rent the difference between output and the marginal product of labor times the number of people employed. This imputation arises because, on the last bit of land brought into production by capitalists renting from landlords, rent must be driven to 0 by competition. The output from this land is divided between capitalists and workers only, with the latter receiving the subsistence wage w_s. Profits are determined as a residual, but competition among capitalists assures that the profit *rate* on marginal land (Aw_s/Ow_s) applies on more productive intramarginal land also. This yields the "profits" rectangle in Fig. 10-1. The surplus intramarginal output beyond wages and profits accrues to landlords as rent.

Some element of exploitation enters all classical models; it is clear in Fig. 10-1 because the M workers are deprived of much of the fruit of their toil, largely to the benefit of landlords who receive rents only because they happen to own the land. Capitalists are simply assumed to save their profits, add them to the wages fund, and hire more workers the next year. Eventually, the whole process will run down to the dreaded stationary state in which the profit rate Aw_s/Ow_s becomes so small that entrepreneurs will cease to function. In Fig. 10-1, if the profit rate actually fell all the way to 0, then the marginal product of labor would equal the subsistence wage and M^* workers would be employed.

Like mathematics when it is applied to real problems, economic analysis is much more interesting when it is applied to issues with political content. Ricardo's model is an almost unique blend of analytical elegance and political advocacy. He was opposed to landlords and used his model to argue that the Corn Laws, essentially restrictions on the import of wheat, should be repealed. Repeal would, in effect, shift out the agricultural production function, reduce the rent share, and stave off the arrival of the stationary state. Two-sector analysis pointed to the possibility that stagnation might be deferred forever, since many classical authors seemed to believe in increasing returns to scale (or perpetual technical advance) in manufacturing. A cheap source of food was all that was required. It was finally assured well after Ricardo's death by repeal of the Corn Laws in 1846, perhaps in part because of his writings.

The Lewis model builds on this industrializing theme of the classical economists. The basic premise is that the economy is divided into two spheres, one controlled by capitalists or state functionaries who hire labor, obtain profits or surplus from using fixed reproducible capital in production, and reinvest the surplus so that capital grows. Food for the workers may be obtained from international trade, capitalist production, or the subsistence sector in the economy. Implications of different model formulations vary, depending on whether or not the subsistence sector is supposed to provide food for industry as well as labor. In either case, the subsistence sector is usually assumed not to use reproducible capital. Its hired or self-employed workers live at consumption levels determined by a standard minimum accepted by society. If peasant farmers form a substantial portion of the subsistence population, the standard would be set by the average product per farm.

The grand theme of Lewis is that labor becomes available to capitalists at the subsistence wage, permitting the generation of surplus and investment; if the investment share of national output grows from 4 or 5 to 12 or 15 percent, the prerequisites for economic growth are satisfied. Naturally, there is a shift in the distribution of functional income to the benefit of high-saving capitalists—"people who think in terms of investing capital productively." Such forced saving is viewed as necessary to support economic growth. Luxury-loving landlords being absent in the Lewis formulation, the volume of saving is measured by the sections of Fig. 10-1 labeled "Rent" and "Profits." For a low subsistence wage, this surplus can be substantial.

The key assumptions underlying this story are that (1) capital is used only in the modern sector; (2) the subsistence wage is fixed in terms of food by labor productivity on the land; (3) limitations on absorptive capacity are not important in the long run; (4) there exists a saving function such that the savings share in income rises with the share of profits; (5) savings is automatically translated into investment and additional productive capacity.

Most criticism and emendation of Lewis has turned around assumption 2; the survey paper by Dixit listed in the readings is ample testimony to this obsession of the academics. Since—in macro terms—a fixed subsistence wage for most poor people is a perfectly reasonable approximation (see the following chapter for verification from even a neoclassical point of view), the sound and fury it has provoked looks almost pointless. For the planner, assumptions 3 and 5 are the critical ones; some of their implications are taken up below.

Before leaving the simple Lewis model, it is worthwhile to attempt some modest quantification: just how fast is output in the modern sector likely to grow if assumptions 1 through 5 really apply? To answer this sort of question, it is simplest to adopt the neoclassical production specification of Appendix D, in which the modern-sector output growth rate is given by

$$X_N' = \alpha_K K' + \alpha_L (L_N' + \epsilon_N) \tag{10-1}$$

where K and L_N are the amounts of capital and labor used in the nonsubsistence sector, α_K and α_L are the shares of capital and labor in nonsubsistence product X_N, and ϵ_N is the rate of labor-augmenting technical progress.

Assume that a fraction s of surplus is invested and that the rate of depreciation is δ. The growth of capital stock then becomes

$$K' = s\alpha_K X_N/K - \delta \tag{10-2}$$

Employment growth is determined by the standard labor-demand relationship

$$L_N' - X_N' = -\sigma^N(w' - P_N') - (1 - \sigma^N)\epsilon_N \tag{10-3}$$

in which w is the wage, P_N the price of X_N, and σ^N the elasticity of substitution in the nonsubsistence sector. By choice of numeraire, $P'_N = 0$, and $w' = 0$ from the surplus-labor assumption.

Putting these equations together shows that output growth is given by

$$X'_N = s\alpha_K X_N/K + (\alpha_L/\alpha_K)\,\sigma^N \epsilon_N - \delta \tag{10-4}$$

Equation (10-4) predicts that—for capital and labor shares of 0.6 and 0.4, respectively, a savings rate from capital income of 0.25, a capital-output ratio of 2.5, an elasticity of substitution of 0.67, technical progress at 3 percent annually, and a depreciation rate of 0.025—nonsubsistence output will grow at 4.83 percent annually, with most growth coming from capital accumulation. As long as a substantial proportion of profits is reinvested and workers for the modern sector are in elastic supply, this sector's growth can proceed quite briskly.

10-2 DISTRIBUTIONAL IMPACTS OF TECHNICAL CHANGE

Whether or not the nonsubsistence labor force will look with favor on technical change is another question. After all, classical economic analysis was developed at a time of severe labor unrest caused by the successive technical innovations we now call the industrial revolution. In the famous Chapter XXXI, "On Machinery," of his *Principles*, Ricardo was concerned with whether "such an application of machinery ... as should have the effect of saving labor" could be "injurious to the interests of the class of laborers." In counterpoint to the sanguine view of the output-increasing effects of technical change enshrined in Eq. (10-4), we now ask how productivity increases may influence the contest over wages and income distribution in the modern sector. The presentation follows the paper by Leif Johansen cited in the readings.

Johansen points out that a once-for-all labor-saving technical improvement has two consequences. It reduces modern-sector employment and labor income levels in the short run, but it may increase them in the long run because it increases the surplus of output over the wage bill, permitting more rapid accumulation of capital. *Continuous* technical change of the type discussed in the last section may then be unfavorable to labor even in the long run if the first, employment-reducing effect dominates. This reasoning sheds at least oblique light on the common observation that mechanization does little for either employment or distributional equity in poor countries.

Johansen's model is very similar to the one already developed in Sec. 9-3. Modern-sector output X_N is determined by the available capital stock K through a fixed output-capital ratio a,

$$X_N = aK \tag{10-5}$$

Since we assume that a stays constant, we can relate employment L to the capital stock (as opposed to the output level) by a coefficient b,

$$L = bK \tag{10-6}$$

The assumption of continuous labor-saving technical change means that the labor-capital ratio declines from time 0 at a rate ϵ_N,

$$b(t) = b_0 \exp(-\epsilon_N t) \tag{10-7}$$

We assume that unemployment in the modern sector is possible. Let the number of people looking for modern-sector jobs (the economically active population, according to statisticians) be E. The size of E can vary as people move back and forth between the subsistence and modern sectors. Most migration theory points to a differential equation such as

$$E' = \lambda(w - w_s) \tag{10-8}$$

for the growth of E, where w is the current industrial wage and w_s is the subsistence wage, set by the level of living in the countryside or the slums. For simplicity, the coefficient λ is assumed to be fixed, although this could be relaxed.

Momentary nonsubsistence labor supply is given by another relationship,

$$L/E = g(w) \tag{10-9}$$

which reflects the usual presumption that an increase in employment as a share of the economically active population bids up the wage.

As in both Ricardo and Lewis, capital accumulation is assumed to be determined by profits,

$$dK/dt = sY_K \tag{10-10}$$

where Y_K is profit income and s is the savings rate from it. Total profits are, of course, the residual after labor is paid,

$$Y_K = X_N - wL \tag{10-11}$$

Note that the profit *rate* ρ is given by $\rho = a - bw$. If ρ stays roughly constant, higher real wages in the long run are permitted only by a falling labor-capital ratio b. On the other hand, a decrease in b in the short run throws people out of jobs from Eq. (10-6) and reduces the wage from Eq. (10-9). We now take up the quantitative comparison of these two effects.

First, observe that the model is well behaved, running forward in time from initial values E_0 and K_0 for population and capital stock. To investigate its qualitative implications, we can reduce the whole system to a differential equation in w by the following steps:

1. Putting Eqs. (10-6) and (10-7) in growth-rate form, one easily gets

$$L' = K' + b' = K' - \epsilon_N$$

But from the rules for capital accumulation, it is also true that

$$K' = s(X_N - wL)/K = s(a - bw)$$

so that

$$L' = s(a - bw) - \epsilon_N \tag{10-12}$$

This equation determines the rate of growth of labor demand from capital accumulation and technical change.

2. Labor-supply growth is given by the log-change version of Eq. (10-9),

$$L' = E' + \gamma w'$$

where γ is the elasticity of the function $g(w)$. For simplicity, assume that γ is constant. Insertion from Eq. (10-8) into the above equation then gives

$$L' = \lambda(w - w_s) + \gamma w' \tag{10-13}$$

3. Now it is easy to eliminate L' between the demand and supply Eq. (10-12) and (10-13) to get the market-clearing growth rate of the wage w. It is

$$w' = (1/\gamma) [\beta - (\lambda + sb)w] \tag{10-14}$$

where $\beta = sa + \lambda w_s - \epsilon_N$

Differential equations of the form of Eq. (10-14) are usually named after the mathematicians Riccati or Bernoulli in the literature. They have the distinct advantage of permitting closed-form solutions. Evidently, one particular solution is $w = 0$; the rest of the solutions can be obtained by the transformation $w = 1/z$, which gives the linear equation

$$dz/dt = (1/\gamma) [-\beta z + \lambda + sb_0 \exp(-\epsilon_N t)] \tag{10-15}$$

Equation (10-15) can be solved with standard methods. When the inverse transformation back to $w(t)$ is completed, one finds that

$$w(t) = [z^* \exp(-\beta t/\gamma) + w_w(t)^{-1}]^{-1} \tag{10-16}$$

where z^* is a constant of integration and $w_w(t)$ is the wage "warranted" by the rate of technical progress and other parameters,

$$w_w(t) = w_s + \frac{\beta[s(a - bw_s) - \epsilon_N] + \gamma\epsilon_N(\epsilon_N - sa)}{\beta(\lambda + sb) - \gamma\lambda\epsilon_N} \tag{10-17}$$

To interpret these results, begin by noting that the constant β is almost certainly positive.[1] Therefore the term involving z^* in Eq. (10-16) will damp out, and the wage will approach $w_w(t)$. It is easy to see that the derivative of w_w with respect to the labor-capital ratio b is negative. Since b falls with technical progress, the warranted wage rises over time; in the long run, the actual wage must rise as well.[2]

Despite such long-term benefits from the technical progress, the situation in the short and medium run may be less pleasant. For example the warranted wage w_w may lie below subsistence, as can be seen by considering the second term in Eq. (10-17).

---

[1] That is, a will have a value such as 0.3 or 0.4, and s might be 0.25. The product sa will very likely exceed the rate of technical progress ϵ_N even without taking into account the additional positive term λw_s in β.

[2] When β is negative (i.e., when the savings rate and output-capital ratio are very low and the rate of technical change is very high), the wage tends to 0, or the other particular solution to Eq. (10-14).

Its denominator is almost surely positive (as the reader can verify), so the sign depends on the numerator. Here the term $\gamma \epsilon_N (\epsilon_N - sa)$ will be negative for the same reason that β is positive. Thus, $w_w(t)$ will lie below w_s if the quantity $s(a - bw_s) - \epsilon_N$ is also negative. From Eq. (10-12), this condition implies that labor demand is declining in the short run and is pulling wages down with it. Continuing technical progress will finally reduce the labor-capital ratio b and generate profits high enough to call forth positive employment growth; reduction in the subsistence wage w_s by policies such as the English enclosures or the Soviet farm collectivization campaign would do the same. However, the waiting time for these investment-stimulating policies to take effect might be substantial.

Finally, note from Eq. (10-16) that the constant of integration z^* is given by

$$z^* = w(0)^{-1} - w_w(0)^{-1}$$

where $w(0)$ is the wage just "before" technical progress begins and $w_w(0)$ is the wage warranted by the technical change at time 0. If the initial wage is relatively high, z^* can be negative. This means that $w(t)$ from Eq. (10-16) may fall for a time after technical change begins, until the exponential term $\exp(-\beta t/\gamma)$ damps out.

To summarize, we have found out that

1. In a surplus-labor model of the modern sector with labor-saving technical progress, the real wage can rise above subsistence in the long run. From the technical relations of Eqs. (10-5) and (10-6), the profit rate will be $\rho = a - bw$. With roughly constant ρ, only a long-term decrease in b will permit a secularly rising real wage w. *Total* employment will grow only with accelerated capital accumulation, which a falling labor-capital ratio b (or subsistence wage w_s) permits.
2. However, in the medium to long run, the real wage can fall below the subsistence level if capital accumulation is not fast enough to permit short-run creation of industrial jobs. This situation is most likely to occur when technical change is rapid or the share of profit income devoted to investment is small.
3. When a spurt of technical change begins, it can cause the real wage to fall absolutely in the short to medium run.

One concludes that rapid labor-saving innovation in the modern sector of a developing country may benefit few besides capitalists in the near future. The rewards to the poor from technical change come only in the long run. Who knows if they will be patient enough to wait?

10-3 LUXURY AS THE FRUIT OF MISERY IN THE MODERN SECTOR

Besides technical change, other aspects of modernization may harm the poor. In some countries, the contrast between rapidly growing wealth for a few in the face of continuing, miserable subsistence for the many is so striking that it begs to be explained. The present section develops a classical model of a fictional economy called Belindia in which the speeding up of capital accumulation is likely to lead to reduced modern-sector employment and a more unequal income distribution overall.[3] The name of the economy comes from its bifurcation into a small, rich industrial state like Belgium and a much larger subsistence sector of the type usually imagined to exist in parts of India. In the real world, Brazil might approximate Belindian conditions; there, Edmar Bacha and the author put together the following model.

The model focuses on the contrasting roles of upper-class, "skilled" workers and lower-class, "unskilled" workers in the modern sector. In production activities, the former receive a much higher wage than the latter, presumably because they are more productive. Moreover, cross-sectional econometric evidence seems to indicate that as the ratio of skilled (and executive) to nonskilled workers increases in an economy, the wage differential does not narrow very much. The neoclassical rationalization of this fact is that the elasticity of substitution between the two labor types is high. It serves the present purposes to let the elasticity go to infinity, so that, as shown in Appendix D, the production function for the "effective" labor force N is given by the linear function

$$N = w_L L + w_M M = L + wM \qquad (10\text{-}18)$$

where L is modern-sector employment of unskilled workers and M is employment of skilled. The coefficients w_L and w_M are measures of the productivity of the two types of labor, and the expression after the second equality is based on a normalization such that $w > 1$.

By our extreme surplus-labor assumptions, the wage q_L of unskilled workers is fixed in real terms by their productivity of a wage good (or "food") in the subsistence sector. A natural simplification is to treat the unskilled wage as the numeraire also: $q_L = 1$ always. If q_M is the wage of the skilled, then (following Appendix D) the cost function dual to the production function of Eq. (10-18) is

$$q_N = \min (1/1, q_M/w) = 1 \qquad (10\text{-}19)$$

where q_N is the cost of the labor aggregate. By choice of numeraire and assumptions regarding surplus labor, both the wage and productivity of unskilled workers are equal to 1. The wage of the skilled must then equal their productivity w for them to be employed at all.

The next step is to bring the other production relationships into the picture. Three goods are produced in the economy—one consumed mainly by unskilled workers, a second consumed mainly by the upper classes, and a third used only for capital accumulation. To sidestep a number of complications discussed more fully in Chap. 11, neither international trade nor the subsistence sector is assumed to provide the modern sector with a significant quantity of the wage good (as an import or a "marketed

---

[3] There is a famous conjecture made by Simon Kuznets in 1955 that the income distribution probably becomes more unequal during the first, surplus-labor stages of economic growth. He arrived at the idea by showing that, with reasonable aggregate numbers, population shifts from an egalitarian subsistence sector to a richer but more unequal modern sector will lead to a more unequal distribution for the economy as a whole. The Belindia story is consistent with Kuznets. The cross-section data appear to be so as well; see the paper by Ahluwalia in the readings.

surplus" of food). The subsistence sector in Belindia therefore acts only as a sponge for labor, taking back and yielding up unskilled workers as demand conditions dictate. Also, observe that our classification ignores the complications resulting from input-output connections among sectors; recall the warnings of Sec. 8-1 on that count!

For each of the three commodities, assume fixed-coefficient production functions of the type used in Secs. 9-3 and 10-2. Two rationalizations are possible, the first being simply that since technical capacity to explore capital-labor substitution possibilities in underdeveloped countries is limited, one might as well rule out the possibility altogether. The second, more subtle argument begins from the observation that if one fixes the real cost of labor w/P along a wage-rental frontier of neoclassical form as in Eq. (D-9), then the cost of capital r/P is determined as well. But then the labor-output and capital-output ratios follow also from factor-demand equations like Eq. (D-2). Hence, a classical assumption of fixed real wages determines both relative prices and choice of technique in the modern sector (under constant returns to scale). Ricardian-Marxian models all take analytical advantage of this convenient result.

In formal terms, the fixed-coefficient production functions can be written as

$$X_i = \min\,(N_i/a_i, K_i/b_i) \qquad i = 1, 2, 3 \tag{10-20}$$

where X_i is the output of the ith sector and N_i and K_i are the amounts of effective labor and capital that it uses. In contrast to the model of the last section, we relate capital and labor inputs to output and not capital stock, so as to make subsequent algebra somewhat simpler.

As the straight-line production function of Eq. (10-18) has a right-angle dual—Eq. (10-19)—so the right-angle isoquant of Eq. (10-20) has a straight-line wage-rental frontier. It is

$$P_i = a_i q_N + \rho P_3 b_i = a_i + \rho P_3 b_i \qquad i = 1, 2, 3 \tag{10-21}$$

in which P_i is the price of the ith good. As long as the capital stock has an infinite life (a notion that is not entirely farfetched in a developing economy), ρ can be identified with the rate of profit and ρP_3 with user cost (or rental rate) for capital. As usual in growth models, we assume that there is sufficient competition in the economy to guarantee that Eq. (10-21) holds at least in the medium run.

Recall the surplus-labor assumption that unskilled labor is in completely elastic supply to the modern sector at the subsistence real wage rate. Industry 1 produces wage goods and—again to simplify algebra and sharpen economics—assume that its product is only consumed by unskilled workers, one unit per worker (per unit time). Under these circumstances, the fixed unskilled real wage means the $P_1 = q_L$ or, given the numeraire,

$$P_1 = 1 \tag{10-22}$$

Equations (10-21) and (10-22) together number four. They also have four unknowns. Prices and the rate of profit comprise the solution to this subsystem, so that as long as changing demand conditions are anticipated well enough by producers as a group to maintain relations of Eq. (10-21) as equalities, then they play no direct role in the determination of prices (or choices of technique, if permitted). As in all equilibrium Ricardian-Marxian models, values are determined ultimately by technology and the subsistence consumption basket of the unskilled. This leaves demand free to determine employment and distribution patterns. Before going into detail on how this comes about, it is useful to record the explicit solutions for prices, the profit rate, and the user cost of capital from Eqs. (10-21) and (10-22). These are

$$P_i = a_i + \frac{b_i(1 - a_1)}{b_1} \quad i = 2, 3 \tag{10-23}$$

$$\rho = \frac{1 - a_1}{a_3 b_1 + b_3(1 - a_1)} \tag{10-24}$$

and

$$\rho P_3 = \frac{1 - a_1}{b_1} \tag{10-25}$$

Note that ρ is positive as long as a_1 is less than 1; that is, an additional unit of effective labor hired in sector 1 must give a positive profit or surplus after being paid the subsistence wage. Moreover Eq. (10-25) shows that the user cost of capital depends only on the technical parameters of the wage-goods sector. This again is characteristic of Ricardian models.

The next stylized fact about Belindia is that people's consumption and savings patterns shift markedly as they climb the status-income ladder. In terms of our model, skilled, middle-class citizens not only get higher pay but also move to the local version of Copacabana, diversify their consumption dramatically in the realm of luxury goods, and learn to save a bit (if only to keep up the payments on their new durables).

A shorthand, highly exaggerated version of this taste change has each skill class consuming only the good it favors. Under these conditions, demands for goods X_i^D are given by the equations

$$X_1^D = L \tag{10-26}$$

$$X_2^D = \gamma(w/P_2) M \tag{10-27}$$

$$X_3^D = \overline{X}_3 \tag{10-28}$$

The first of these equations states that unskilled workers spend all their income on the first good. Skilled workers devote a fraction γ (less than 1) of their income to the acquisition of the second, "luxury" good. Demand for the capital good is for the moment assumed to be exogenous at the level $\overline{X}_3$. On the other side of the ledger, these equations imply that a fraction $(1 - \gamma)$ of skilled-labor income and all of profits are devoted to saving, as we will see in more detail below.

These demand levels can, in principle, differ from supplies X_i; but in a tight economy, near-term supply shortfalls are likely to be wiped out by shifts in employment of the two skill classes. And since, on the other hand, generalized excess supply is improbable in a fast-growing, capital-short economy like Belindia's, we assume that the equilibrium conditions $X_i = X_i^D$ hold. Together with Eq. (10-18), these comprise four equations among six quantity variables: X_1, X_2, X_3, L, M, and N.

To close the system, we must add two equations. The first follows from the production functions and gives total demand for the labor aggregate,

$$N = a_1 X_1 + a_2 X_2 + a_3 X_3 \qquad (10\text{-}29)$$

Since we are not restricting labor supplies, this equation basically serves to link employment and demand patterns, as we will see shortly. The final equation *is* a demand-supply balance in the traditional sense and refers to scarce capital:

$$\overline{K} = b_1 X_1 + b_2 X_2 + b_3 X_3 \qquad (10\text{-}30)$$

Our general assumption that Belindia has a taut, capital-limited economy assures equality in this relationship.

Solving the model as stated is straightforward. Before we go into this, however, it is worth noting explicitly that the six quantity-side Eqs. (10-18) and (10-26) through (10-30) determine skilled employment M given investment demand $\overline{X}_3$, or vice versa. We *cannot* specify both variables exogenously (or through labor-supply and investment-demand functions); therefore different distribution theories can be constructed depending on which variable is considered to be the driving force in the economy.[4]

In Belindia, investment demand is probably more important in shaping economic growth than are limits to the supply of skilled labor. Although a more complete model would in some way take the two factors into consideration, we prefer to limit ourselves and assume that investment *determines* skilled employment, through institutional mechanisms to be discussed shortly. This seems closer to the reality of Belindia than the alternative hypothesis that savings by skilled workers and capitalists determines investment, as in the usual neoclassical specification.

The quantity-side equations just stated imply that

$$X_1 = L \qquad \text{from Eq. (10-26)}$$

$$= N - wM \qquad \text{from Eq. (10-18)}$$

$$= a_1 X_1 + a_2 X_2 + a_3 X_3 - wM \qquad \text{from Eq. (10-29)}$$

$$= a_1 X_1 + a_2 \gamma(w/P_2) M + a_3 \overline{X}_3 - wM \qquad \text{from Eqs. (10-27) and (10-28)}$$

Note already that as long as supply-demand equilibrium is maintained, an increase in skilled employment M is associated with a reduction in modern-sector unskilled employment L and therefore demand for X_1. There are two effects involved—the first appearing in the second equation which shows that when N is constant, an increase in M must be accompanied by a decrease in L through substitution along the isoquant for

---

[4]The paper by Amartya Sen cited in the references provides a clear analysis of how most income distribution models are overdetermined, in the sense that *both* investment-demand functions *and* all factor-supply functions can rarely be specified exogenously. Different theories emphasize demand or supply considerations to the extent of ignoring the other blade of the scissors. Our model clearly falls into the former category, largely because we think that such things as work-leisure choices and accumulation of human capital are quite unimportant in determining *who* gets upgraded to the middle classes.

"production" of N. Demand for modern-sector wage-good output X_1 declines pari passu.

Besides this effect, an increase in M creates demand for unskilled labor and therefore the wage good through the coefficient $a_2 \gamma (w/P_2)$ in the last equation. We can see the net impact of these substitution and income effects by solving explicitly for X_1:

$$X_1 = (1 - a_1)^{-1}(-\alpha w M + a_3 \overline{X}_3) \tag{10-31}$$

where

$$\alpha = 1 - a_2 \gamma / P_2$$

In the coefficient α, the income effect is represented by the second term. Since $\gamma < 1$ (skilled workers save) and $a_2 < P_2$ [costs of capital enter price determination, from Eq. (10-23)], the income effect is smaller in magnitude than the substitution effect of unity, so that L falls when M rises.

Since X_1 in Eq. (10-31) and X_2 in Eq. (10-27) are functions only of wM, we can insert these equations into Eq. (10-30) to determine wM as a function of the capital stock $\overline{K}$ and investment demand $\overline{X}_3$ alone. This gives

$$\left[\left(\frac{1}{\rho P_3} \right) \left(\frac{a_2 \gamma}{P_2} - 1 \right) + \frac{b_2 \gamma}{P_2} \right] wM + \left[b_3 + \frac{a_3 \gamma}{\rho P_3} \right] \overline{X}_3 = \overline{K} \tag{10-32}$$

where $(\rho P_3)^{-1}$ is substituted from Eq. (10-25) for terms of the form $b_1 /(1 - a_1)$. Multiplying through by ρP_3 and some further simplification based on the price equation [Eq. (10-23)] results in the formula

$$(1 - \gamma) wM = P_3 \overline{X} - \rho P_3 \overline{K} \tag{10-33}$$

This is a derived equilibrium condition, following directly from Eqs. (10-18) and (10-26) through (10-30) and/or other relationships in the model. It amounts to a savings-investment balance in Kalecki form, since $(1 - \gamma) wM$ is total savings from skilled-labor income which must, in equilibrium, equal the value of investment $P_3 \overline{X}_3$ less total (exclusively saved) profits $\rho P_3 \overline{K}$. Given the capital stock, skilled employment responds *positively* to a spurt in investment, with unskilled workers bearing the brunt of any overall employment cutbacks. Since the price system is completely determined by the surplus-labor assumption and the technical conditions of production, forced saving in Belindia appears in the guise of quantitative shifts in employment. It is reasonable to ask what sort of institutional arrangements will permit labor hiring rules to satisfy the savings-investment balance of Eq. (10-33). Two possibilities are the following:

1. The market itself may guarantee the result. Imagine that investment demand increases and is met, if necessary, by governmental diversion of resources to the production of capital goods (a frequent enough event in taut economies). Then the cost of capital to industries producing consumer goods will rise and the cost of labor will fall. But because unskilled workers have a stable real wage, the skilled wage will bear the brunt of the adjustment, with a consequent shift in the skill mix toward higher-wage employees. As a result, *more* skilled jobs will open up in

the substitution response to increased capital scarcity. In the Taylor-Bacha paper cited in the readings, it is shown that if the two skill types trade off at a high but not infinite elasticity of substitution, then this is the market response that will occur. Under these conditions, Eq. (10-33) is valid as an equilibrium relationship before and after an increase in $\overline{X}_3$. Naturally, the skilled wage w is higher *before* investment increases; but with a high elasticity of substitution, the wage reduction will be far outweighed by the increase in skilled employment (and decrease in unskilled employment). That is, the results from our infinite-substitution model will be largely correct.

2. The market response just sketched is abetted by a number of social institutions in countries like Belindia. Given a repressed, inactive labor movement and strong social desires for upward mobility, it is easier to cut back blue-collar than white-collar jobs in the short run, particularly if some blue-collar employment reductions really take the form of upgrading to middle-class positions. On the supply side, it is also true that increases in levels of production of both capital and luxury goods levels will be related, since both subsectors are in the "advanced" part of the economy and their entrepreneurs make investment decisions in the same expectational milieu. Once again, capital shortages will hold back expansion in more traditional wage-goods industries, and poor workers facing escalating relative prices or elongated queues are always welcome to disappear back into the subsistence sector. (In part because of labor mobility laws which favor permanence in upper-level jobs, the poor deploy much weaker defenses against downgrading than the middle classes.) Under conditions of potential excess supply of luxuries and increases in the costs of maintaining subsistence living conditions in the modern sector, the substitution effect again works to favor increases in skilled employment.

Assuming on these or similar grounds that the savings-investment balance does hold, we can substitute it back into Eqs. (10-31) and (10-27) to get final equations for X_1 and X_2 in terms of the exogenous variables. The equation for the latter is

$$X_2 = \frac{\gamma}{(1 - \gamma) P_2} (P_3 \overline{X}_3 - \rho P_3 \overline{K}) \tag{10-34}$$

a simple transformation of Eq. (10-33). After some manipulation, the equation for X_1 can be put in the form:

$$L = X_1 = \frac{1}{(1 - a_1)(1 - \gamma)} (-\beta P_3 \overline{X}_3 + \alpha \rho P_3 \overline{K}) \tag{10-35}$$

where α was defined in connection with Eq. (10-31) and

$$\beta = 1 - \frac{a_2 \gamma}{P_2} - \frac{a_3 (1 - \gamma)}{P_3}$$

In discussing Eq. (10-31) we saw that $\alpha > 0$, so that an increase in investment would lead to a decrease in unskilled employment, since—from Eq. (10-33)—it would be associated with an increase in wM. In the coefficient β, the latter terms represent income effects in demand for X_1 resulting directly and indirectly from increased

Table 10-1 Income distribution under different employment patterns

	Employment	Wage	Employment share, %	Income share, %	Cumulated employment share, %	Cumulated income share, %
A						
Subsistence	40	$\frac{1}{2}$	40.0	20.0	40.0	20.0
Unskilled	55	1	55.0	55.0	95.0	75.0
Skilled	5	5	5.0	25.0	100.0	100.0
B						
Subsistence	42	$\frac{1}{2}$	42.0	19.6	42.0	19.7
Unskilled	51	1	51.0	47.7	93.0	67.3
Skilled	7	5	7.0	32.7	100.0	100.0
C						
Subsistence	39	$\frac{1}{2}$	39.0	18.0	39.0	18.0
Unskilled	54	1	54.0	49.8	93.0	67.8
Skilled	7	5	7.0	32.2	100.0	100.0

demand for X_3. Their sum is a weighted average of fractions $[a_i < P_i$ from Eq. (10-23)] and so is less than 1. As in Eq. (10-31), the substitution between L and M outweighs income terms and X_1 responds negatively to increases in exogenous demand.

Most of the model's implications about short-run income distribution can be read from Eqs. (10-34) and (10-35). Because of the fixed wages, distribution depends on shifts of workers among the different skill groups. The equations show how these occur in response to changes in investment demand and availability of capital. For example, an increase in $\overline{X}_3$ leads to an increase in skilled employment from Eq. (10-34) and a decrease in unskilled employment from Eq. (10-35).

Perhaps the best way to get a feeling for the effect of such employment changes on distribution is from an arithmetical example. Imagine that initially there are 100 people in the working population: 40 in the subsistence-sector reserve army, 55 unskilled workers in the modern sector, and 5 skilled workers. Suppose further that the wages of these workers are $\frac{1}{2}$, 1, and 5 respectively. Then the overall distribution is as shown in panel A of Table 10-1.

Panel B shows an unfavorable shift in employment patterns from case A—two new skilled-job slots open up, but at the same time four unskilled slots disappear. Thus, two unskilled workers are promoted but two others are forced back into the subsistence sector. It is easy to see that the *Lorenz curve* for case B lies below that of case A up to approximately the 95th percentile of the population, above which point the two curves essentially coincide.[5]

Case C corresponds to the most favorable type of employment change the model permits. Two new skilled slots are opened up and one unskilled slot is lost; one can imagine two unskilled workers being promoted and one person entering unskilled

---

[5] The Lorenz curve is widely used to describe the inequality of income distributions. Its characteristics are summarized in Appendix F.

employment from subsistence. The Lorenz curve of panel C still lies below that of panel A up to the 95th percentile, but it is above the panel-B curve. Furthermore, the panel-C curve is above that of panel A for high income levels. Because the curves cross, one could conceivably claim a welfare gain—at least on the basis of a measure giving high weight to high incomes.

The example shows that short-run distribution will depend in a crucial way on the *total* employment impact of shifts in the exogenous variables. If unskilled employment falls by more than skilled employment rises when there is an increment in exogenous demand $\bar{X}_3$, then the reserve army grows and we are in a case-B situation; inequality measured by most standards will have increased. To check the likelihood of this, we can sum coefficients in Eqs. (10-33) and (10-35) to get the employment impact of an investment increase. This takes the form:

$$(M + L) = \frac{P_3}{(1 - a_1)(1 - \gamma)} \left[\frac{1 - a_1}{w} - \beta\right] \bar{X}_3$$

Using the definition of β, the term in brackets (which determines the sign of the employment response to $\bar{X}_3$) can be written as

$$\left[\frac{1 - a_1}{w} - 1\right] + \left[\frac{a_2}{P_2}\gamma + \frac{a_3}{P_3}(1 - \gamma)\right]$$

In the first bracket here, $1 - a_1$ is a fraction and w (the wage differential between unskilled and skilled) might have a value between 3 and 5. Hence the whole term might have an arithmetical value of -0.75 or less. The second bracket is a weighted average of labor shares in the luxury and capital-goods industries; it would be unlikely to exceed 0.5 or 0.6 in a developing country. Hence, with "reasonable" parameter values, the short-term effect of an increase in exogenous demand is similar to the shift from case A to case B in Table 10-1. There will very likely be a deterioration in the income distribution, which will be less serious to the extent that the skill differentials are low (small value of w) and labor shares in luxury and capital goods production are high (values of a_2/P_2 and a_3/P_3 near 1).

The next step is to extend these comparative static results to a growing economy. Most growth theory does not apply well to Belindia because it deals with steady states, whereas the topic of interest is a secular shift of production and employment patterns within the modern sector. As with the rest of the model, we only sketch out a formal analysis of such an evolution here in order to show that unequalizing growth is a real possibility in developing economies—one that merits further study.

The unequalizing Belindian income distribution spiral is closed by growth in investment, excited by continual expansion of demand for consumers' durables and other luxuries. The first round in the helix might take the form of an investment response to a fortuitous increase in demand (which could come from the government, middle classes who have been newly assured of stability by a military coup, or whatever). Through the mechanisms of Eq. (10-33), this will lead to further increases in middle-class employment and demand for luxury goods. If investment once again responds, the spiral becomes apparent in the next round of more skilled employees, their additional demands for high-status goods, and so on.

Putting all these dynamics into the form of a tractable differential equation is a daunting task. For present purposes, we assume that investors form expectations *only* on the basis of what is going on with luxury-goods demand. Moreoever, after capital is accumulated, it can be shifted easily among sectors, so that Feldman-Mahalanobis problems of the type discussed in Chap. 8 do not arise. New capital formation is related in accelerator fashion to the luxury-goods sector, as follows:

$$dK/dt = X_3 = X_2' \, (F_2 X_2/K)^\theta K \tag{10-36}$$

Here, X_2' is the current growth rate of luxury-goods production (and sales). Multiplied by a term $(F_2 X_2/K)^\theta$ which reflects entrepreneurial expectations, it becomes the investors' desired growth rate for capital stock. The constant F_2 in the expectations term—which may or may not be equal to the capital-output ratio b_2—essentially rescales luxury-goods output into capital terms. The exponent θ reflects the buoyancy of expectations; they are stronger as θ is higher.

Define λ as $\gamma P_3/(1 - \gamma) P_2$, the response of luxury-goods demand to an increase in investment from Eq. (10-34). Then one can use Eq. (10-34) in differentiated form to show that Eq. (10-36) is equivalent to

$$X_3' = \frac{[(X_3/K) - \rho]^{1-\theta}}{(\lambda F_2)} + \rho$$

This can be further simplified if we let k denote the rate of growth of capital stock (equaling X_3/K) and note that $k' = X_3' - k$. Making the appropriate substitutions gives a final equation for the change in the rate of growth,

$$k' = \frac{(k - \rho)^{1-\theta}}{(\lambda F_2)^\theta} - (k - \rho) \tag{10-37}$$

It is easy to verify that this equation has two stationary solutions. The first has k' equal to 0 when k equals ρ; this represents an initial steady-state growth path in which only wage and capital goods are produced and all profits are automatically reinvested. The other steady state has luxury-goods production; in it, the capital-stock growth rate is $k = \rho + (\lambda F_2)^{-1}$. This new equilibrium is reached after a transient stage of accelerated growth during which the economy adopts the new pattern of production and consumption. The time period involved in the transition will be shorter (with a correspondingly higher rate of growth) the larger the value of θ.[6]

---

[6] Once the transition begins, it will go through in this model, since the lower steady growth path is unstable. To see this, let $k = \rho + \epsilon$ and derive the equation

$$k' = \epsilon[(\lambda F_2)^\theta - 1]$$

For any positive θ, this gives $k' > 0$, with growth being more rapid as θ is greater. At the upper root, one sets $k = (\lambda F_2)^{-1} + \rho + \epsilon$ and finds

$$k' = (\lambda F_2)^{-1}[(1 + \lambda F_2 \epsilon)^{1-\theta} - (1 + \lambda F_2 \epsilon)]$$

$$\simeq (\lambda F_2)^{-1} [1 + (1 - \theta) \lambda F_2 \epsilon - (1 + \lambda F_2 \epsilon)]$$

$$= -\theta \epsilon$$

During the period preceding the luxury-goods growth phase, only unskilled workers are employed in the modern sector. Recognizing that investment along this initial steady-state path is given by $X_3 = \rho K$, we can substitute into Eq. (10-35) to express unskilled employment as

$$L = \frac{a_3}{1 - a_1} \rho K \tag{10-38}$$

The role of the unskilled declines after the luxury-goods industries get into operation; along the second steady-state path, their employment is given by

$$L = \frac{1}{1 - a_1} \left(a_3 \rho - \frac{P_2}{\gamma F_2} \beta \right) K \tag{10-39}$$

which follows from substituting $X_3 = [\rho + (\lambda F_2)^{-1}] K$ into Eq. (10-35). Similarly, steady-state skilled employment is

$$wM = (P_2 \gamma F_2) K$$

Combining this with Eq. (10-39) and simplifying shows that total modern-sector employment is

$$M + L = \frac{K}{1 - a_1} \left\{ a_3 \rho + (P_2/\gamma F_2) \left[\frac{1}{w} - 1 + \frac{a_2}{P_2} \gamma + \frac{a_3}{P_3} (1 - \gamma) \right] \right\}$$

This expression can be interpreted in the usual growth-theory manner by considering two island economies with equal capital stocks. In one which has not gone through the luxury-goods transition, total modern-sector employment is $a_3 \rho K/(1 - a_1)$ from Eq. (10-38). In the other, assumed to be on a steady-state path with luxury-goods production, modern-sector employment will be *lower* if the sum of the terms

$$\left[\frac{1}{w} - 1 \right] + \left[\frac{a_2}{P_2} \gamma + \frac{a_3}{P_3} (1 - \gamma) \right]$$

is negative. The discussion of the results in Table 10-1 suggests that this is likely to be the case; i.e., the economy with luxury-goods production will have a less equitable income distribution even in the long run. On the other hand, since the transition to the luxury-goods steady state will go through once it is begun (subject to threshold effects which cannot be analyzed properly here), an economy entering transition will observe a deteriorating income distribution over time—at least until such point as output growth overtakes population growth in the subsistence sector and all Lewis-style stories come to an end. The sobering point about Belindia is that even though all the Lewis predictions of increased saving and more rapid capital accumulation in the modern sector come true, nobody but the emergent "skilled worker" middle class benefits very much. The Lewis vision begins to turn a bit sour. An elastic supply of unskilled

---

This, of course, implies that the higher growth-rate path is stable. The event that actually starts the process going is not specified. But once the investment demand function of Eq. (10-36) and forced saving start to interact, they inevitably bring the economy up to the higher steady-state growth rate.

labor permits rapid growth, all right. The trouble is that the vast majority of the unskilled have scant hope of benefiting from the increased output it brings, even in the very long run.

10-4 A MELIORIST DEVELOPMENT MODEL

Of course, planners of reformist bent can always hope to design a strategy that will transfer some benefits to the poor in the foreseeable future. Such a quintessentially social-democratic vision of change finds elegant expression in a model proposed by James Meade. We first review his theory and then illustrate it with an example inspired by work from that most civilized of reformist organizations, The World Bank.

Suppose that there are two economic classes in the society, rich (subscript R) and poor (subscript P). The total income of each group is made up of labor earnings W_i and returns to capital $r_i K_i$. There is no particular reason to assume that capital quasi-rentals r_i will be the same for both groups, since in fact the rich can benefit from cheaper credit, economies of scale in investment, better information, and a host of other advantages which massive participation in a capital market brings to an investor.

If the savings share of group i is s_i, the rate of growth of its capital stock is

$$K_i' = \frac{s_i(W_i + r_i K_i)}{K_i} = s_i r_i \left(\frac{W_i}{r_i K_i} + 1 \right) \tag{10-40}$$

The difference in growth rates of the two capital stocks is therefore

$$K_P' - K_R' = r_P s_P \left(\frac{W_P}{r_P K_P} + 1 \right) - r_R s_R \left(\frac{W_R}{r_R K_R} + 1 \right)$$

Various cases can be developed from this equation. First, it will certainly be true that the ratio of labor to capital earnings $W_i/r_i K_i$ will be higher for the poor (the traditional widows and orphans living on small annuities excepted). Thus, if saving and profit rates do not differ greatly for the two groups, the capital stock of the poor should be growing more rapidly than that of the rich. In fact, one can show that if $s_P = s_R$ and $r_P = r_R$, then ultimately incomes *per group* will be equalized. Incomes *per member* will, of course, continue to diverge if the poor are more numerous than the rich or their population grows faster. Policy should be aimed at reducing differential returns to capital (perhaps through taxation), changing patterns of asset ownership (perhaps through land reform), and redirecting savings flows.

Table 10-2 shows typical numerical implications of the model. Note first that even when income and asset distributions are highly unequal and the saving rate of the poor is low, their capital stock can grow more rapidly than that of the rich (see line 8), for the reasons already discussed. On the other hand, the income share of the rich gets bigger after 5 years (line 12) because of the low base level of the poor group's capital stock. This increase in relative inequality can almost be offset by a transfer of 2 percent of total output from the savings of the rich to the savings of the poor (line 13). Over a period of 15 to 20 years, such a transfer might increase the share of the bottom

Table 10-2 **Effects of savings transfer**

	Rich	Poor
1. Income of group	70	30
2. Number of persons	1	4
3. Income per head	70	7.5
4. Capital owned	275	25
5. Capital income at 10 percent profit rate	27.5	2.5
6. Labor income	42.5	27.5
7. Savings rate	0.2	0.05
8. Rate of growth of capital	0.051	0.06
9. Rate of growth of capital when 2 percent of total output is transferred from group 1 to group 2 savings	0.044	0.14
10. Approximate income per head after 5 years, no transfer*	80.0	7.72
11. Approximate income per head after 5 years, with transfer*	76.7	8.13
12. Income share after 5 years, no transfer*	0.722	0.278
13. Income share after 5 years, with transfer*	0.702	0.298

*Forecasts made by simple extrapolation of initial growth rates.

80 percent of the population from 30 to 35 percent or so. As income distributions go, this is a fairly substantial shift.[7]

Of course, this shift comes from a meliorative, gradualist policy. Its implicit "people's capitalism" may be feasible in some underdeveloped countries but not in others. More profoundly, the whole idea of substantial capital accumulation by the poor may be absurd in the context of rural exploitation by landowners and money-lenders and urban exploitation in the slums. The more radical models in the classical tradition are much less optimistic about the chances of success of gradualist policies, as we have already seen. A planner's perception of the political realities in his or her country must ultimately determine the choice of models to be applied.

SELECTED ADDITIONAL READINGS

Ahluwalia, Montek S.: "Inequality, Poverty and Development," *Journal of Development Economics*, 3:307–342, 1976. (Useful review of cross-country evidence regarding the Kuznets income distribution conjecture.)

——, and Hollis B. Chenery: "A Model of Distribution and Growth," in Hollis B. Chenery, et al. (eds.): *Redistribution with Growth*, Oxford University Press, New York and London, 1974. (Applies the Meade model cited below to changes in income distribution in poor countries.)

Bowles, Samuel: *Planning Educational Systems for Economic Growth*, Harvard University Press, Cambridge, Mass., 1969. (Presents evidence, since widely replicated, on the high elasticity of substitution among types of labor skills.)

Dixit, Avinash: "Models of Dual Economies," in James A. Mirrlees and Nicholas H. Stern (eds.): *Models of Economic Growth*, Wiley, New York, 1973. (Useful review of agriculture-industry models of the type considered here and in the following chapter.)

[7]Ahluwalia and Chenery (see the readings) get results of this magnitude from simulations of a more carefully parameterized income distribution model of the Meade type.

Furtado, Celso: "The Post-1964 Brazilian 'Model' of Development," *Studies in Comparative International Development*, 8(2): 1973. (Institutional description of a model similar to that of Sec. 10-3.)

Johansen, Leif: "A Classical Model of Economic Growth," in C. H. Feinstein (ed.): *Socialism, Capitalism and Economic Growth: Essays Presented to Maurice Dobb*, Cambridge University Press, New York and London, 1967. (Original presentation of the model of Sec. 10-2. Gives a clear discussion of its economic implications.)

Kaldor, Nicholas: "Alternative Theories of Distribution," *Review of Economic Studies*, 23:83–100, 1955. (Presents the Ricardian distribution model sketched in Sec. 10-1.)

Kuznets, Simon S.: "Economic Growth and Income Inequality," *American Economic Review*, 45:1–28, 1955. (Contains the famous "Kuznets conjecture" that income inequality first worsens and then improves during the course of economic growth.)

Lewis, W. Arthur: "Economic Development with Unlimited Supplies of Labor," *The Manchester School of Economics and Social Studies*, 22:139–191, 1954; "Unlimited Labor: Further Notes," *The Manchester School of Economics and Social Studies*, 26:1–32, 1958. (The classic statement of the Ricardian model as applied to modern underdevelopment.)

Lluch, Constantino: "Theory of Development in Dual Economies: A Survey," Development Research Center, The World Bank, 1977, mimeo. (Clear statement and mathematical discussion of a number of dual economy theories.)

Meade, James E.: *Efficiency, Equality and the Ownership of Property*, George Allen & Unwin, London, 1964. (Elegant initial statement of the model of Sec. 10-4.)

Sen, Amartya K.: "Neo-classical and Neo-Keynesian Theories of Distribution," *Economic Record*, 39:53–64, 1963. (Discusses the problem of multiple possible closing rules in growth models.)

Taylor, Lance, and Edmar L. Bacha: "The Unequalizing Spiral: A First Growth Model for Belindia," *Quarterly Journal of Economics*, 90:197–218, 1976. (Variations on the theme of Sec. 10-3.)

ELEVEN

AGRICULTURE AND INDUSTRY

This chapter is about interactions between the agricultural and nonagricultural sectors that work themselves out in the medium to long run. The extended time period is key to the analysis, for it is assumed that agricultural supply is quite elastic. For periods up to a year or two, such an assumption is unrealistic, and we have seen some of the problems that short-run agricultural supply inelasticity creates in Chaps. 4 and 5. When people and resources have time to shift in and out of agriculture, supply rigidity disappears; one can then deal with longer-term issues of growth and income distribution as structural economic change proceeds.

Solely for reasons of mathematical convenience, most such stories are told here and elsewhere with comparative statics in a model of two sectors. This simple agriculture-industry dichotomy cannot capture all the details that structural transformation involves. Much economic activity takes place in service sectors, which do not clearly fit into either agriculture or industry; much of industry is organized along artisanal, "subsistence" lines, while agriculture may be highly capitalistic; connections among sectors through a *changing* input-output matrix make a neat production bifurcation impossible to sustain in the long run. For these and other reasons, this chapter's results from agriculture-industry models provide no final guides to policy formation. At best, they suggest points in the system at which policy problems are likely to arise.

Our first story is about how the wage rate is likely to evolve in an economy similar to that analyzed by Lewis. One sector uses labor and a nonreproducible asset such as land in its production process, and the other uses labor and reproducible capital. The sectors are also "dual" in the sense that the imputed labor share and the elasticity of substitution are assumed to be higher in agriculture than industry. Under these hypotheses, both employment and output are highly price-responsive in agriculture, and the sector can be a source of labor supply for industry at a wage that is nearly constant in terms of agricultural output, or "food." In Sec. 11-1, we follow Bell to show that if the price of food is, in turn, fixed relative to the price of the industrial product (say by government price policy abetted by stock changes and foreign aid, or else by price arbitrage under international trade), then the elasticity of the wage with respect to capital-stock growth and economic expansion in the modern sector is likely to be small. The Lewis approximation of a constant wage for labor in a growing modern economy turns out to be a good one. And precisely because Lewis is correct, the Kuznets hypothesis that the income distribution will worsen during the early stages of growth—mentioned in the last chapter—also makes sense.

In Sec. 11-2, however, complications appear when the food price and therefore the income distribution are determined from the world market through unregulated international trade. Under conditions of technological dualism and fairly income-elastic demand for food on the part of workers and farmers (as analyzed by Chichilnisky), an increase in the world food price can lead to a greater increase in food consumption than output *or* to a lower exportable surplus. The balance-of-payments complications that can arise from this "perverse" export price response are pointed out.

The key factor causing the downward-sloping export-supply curve relates to another appearing under the rubric of "forced saving" in Chaps. 4, 7, 9, and elsewhere. The mechanism there took the form of price shifts against nominally fixed payment flows that changed the income distribution in real terms. Something similar occurs in this chapter if we assume that the technological dualism between the two sectors is strong enough. A rise in the agricultural price can then shift the income distribution toward workers and farmers who intensively consume food and lead to the decrease in excess supply. In Sec. 11-3, we ask what happens in an economy closed to foreign trade, where exports cannot drop off as the food price goes up. It is shown that the potential disequilibrium is transferred to the labor market and may take the form of a downward-sloping labor-supply curve from agriculture to industry. In a closed economy without government intervention to hold relative prices stable, duality in demand can substantially modify the basic Lewis result.

Finally, in Sec. 11-4, we take up in less formal terms some of the policy problems implicit in attempts to capture both a "marketed surplus" of food and an adequate, cheap labor supply for urban industrialization. Historical and technological examples are presented to illustrate the fundamental issues that the agriculture-industry dialectic involves. In this as in other sections, most of the ideas come from others who have written in this field. On the first three sections respectively, the reader will find the cited papers by Clive Bell, Graciela Chichilnisky, and Avinash Dixit to be original and rewarding.

11-1 HOW LONG DOES SUBSISTENCE LAST?

Most theoretical models start out when a modern industrial sector just begins to form in an overwhelmingly subsistence economy; these models ask how the two sectors interact and develop over time. One common question is about labor movements and another is about the availability of food from the countryside for workers in the cities or for export. In this section, we take up the question of labor supply, on the initial assumption that relative prices of the two sectors—call them "agriculture" and "nonagriculture"—do not vary but that the wage *can* shift with respect to either price. Since we do not say anything about the balance between agricultural supply and demand, the implicit assumption is that any discrepancies are made up from stock changes, foreign trade, or aid. To keep the presentation simple, we do not go into the balance-of-payments or fiscal details of how these adjustments come about. As we will see shortly, they are likely to be unimportant, since Lewis-style technological assumptions will hold the wage quite stable indeed.

Throughout this chapter, we treat the nonagricultural good as the numeraire, with price equal to 1. Modern-sector output is X_N, and our usual log-change equations for output and employment can be written as

$$X_N' = \alpha_L L_N' + \alpha_K K' \tag{11-1}$$

$$L_N' - X_N' = -\sigma^N w' \tag{11-2}$$

and

$$K' - X_N' = -\sigma^N r' \tag{11-3}$$

in which α_L and α_K are, respectively, the labor and capital shares in the nonagricultural sector, L_N and K are employment levels of labor and capital, σ^N is the elasticity of substitution, and w and r are the wage and quasirent on capital, respectively.

In the agricultural sector, labor is the only variable factor, and the log-change production function takes the form

$$X_A' = \beta L_A' \tag{11-4}$$

in which β is the elasticity of agricultural output X_A with respect to labor L_A (and also the neoclassically imputed labor share). If there is some possibility of production substitution between agricultural labor and land and if farmers minimize costs in usual neoclassical fashion, then the demand for L_A takes the form

$$L_A' - X_A' = -\sigma^A (w' - P_A') \tag{11-5}$$

in which σ^A is the elasticity of substitution in agriculture and P_A' is the log change in the agricultural price (which we assume in this section to equal 0 from unchanging intersectoral terms of trade). The wage w is supposed to be equal in the two sectors (this ignores higher costs of urban living, etc.) and varies so that overall full employment is maintained.[1] In a comparative static model, full employment implies that differential changes in sectoral employment levels must be exactly offsetting or, in log-change form,

$$L_N L_N' + L_A L_A' = 0 \tag{11-6}$$

---

[1] In the literature, it is often assumed that the urban wage is equated to the average product in agriculture, so that $w = P_A X_A / L_A$. Of course, Eq. (11-5) is based on the assumption that the wage equals the *marginal* product of agricultural labor. Some details of the results of this chapter would change under the alternative assumption, but in general the analysis goes through.

Now we want to address the following question: How will the wage respond to capital accumulation in the modern sector? Equations (11-1) through (11-6) can be solved to get the elasticity θ of w with respect to the capital stock K ($w' = \theta K'$); then we can compute how θ changes in response to shifts in the relevant parameters. As a first step in the solution procedure, note from Eqs. (11-4) and (11-5) that

$$L'_A = \frac{-\sigma^A}{1 - \beta} (w' - P'_A) \tag{11-7}$$

Similar manipulations in Eqs. (11-1) and (11-2) give the expression

$$L'_N = K' - \frac{\sigma^N}{\alpha_K} w' \tag{11-8}$$

and we can substitute Eqs. (11-7) and (11-8) into Eq. (11-6) to show that the elasticity of the wage with respect to modern-sector capital stock is

$$\theta = \frac{L_N/L}{\lambda}$$

where

$$\lambda = \frac{L_A}{L} \frac{\sigma^A}{1 - \beta} + \frac{L_N}{L} \frac{\sigma^N}{\alpha_K} \tag{11-9}$$

The new parameter λ is a weighted average of the production parameters in the two sectors. It will be large (and θ small) when the agricultural share of the labor force L_A/L is near 1. In agriculture, the stylized fact is that the elasticity of substitution σ^A exceeds 1, so a labor-demand elasticity $\sigma^A/(1 - \beta)$ somewhere between 2 and 4 is plausible. Since the industry substitution elasticity is usually thought to be less than 1, a value of σ^N/α_K between 0.5 and 1 makes sense. Table 11-1 contains values of θ for various values of the parameters; it is clear that for the ranges just stated, θ is small

Table 11-1 Values of the wage-capital elasticity θ for different values of the labor-demand elasticities in the agricultural and nonagricultural sectors

		Share of labor force in agriculture		
$\sigma^A/(1 - \beta)$	σ^N/α_K	0.8	0.6	0.4
4	0.5	0.0606	0.1538	0.3158
2	0.5	0.1176	0.2857	0.5455
1	0.5	0.2222	0.5	0.8571
0	0.5	2.0	2.0	2.0
4	1.0	0.0588	0.1429	0.2727
2	1.0	0.1111	0.25	0.4286
1	1.0	0.2	0.4	0.6
0	1.0	1.0	1.0	1.0

until less than half the labor force is in agriculture. The simple Lewis story holds up quite well.

Table 11-1 can also be used to give an alternative explanation of the Kuznets conjecture mentioned in the last chapter. Kuznets's idea was that the income distribution is likely to worsen during the first phases of economic growth and possibly improve later on. In the simple model at hand, an appropriate distribution measure might be based on the importance of modern-sector capital income rK relative to income from agriculture $P_A X_A$ and from urban employment wL. In terms of income *equality*, the indicator

$$D = \frac{P_A X_A + wL}{rK} = \frac{\xi_A + \alpha_L \xi_N}{\alpha_K \xi_N} \qquad (11\text{-}10)$$

is easy to interpret. After the first equality in Eq. (11-10), D is defined as the ratio of agricultural plus urban labor income to urban capital income. After the second equality, the definition is restated in terms of modern-sector factor shares and the sectoral shares ξ_A and ξ_N in total income $P_A X_A + X_N$.[2]

After a certain amount of manipulation, one can show that

$$D' = \left[\frac{\alpha_L \theta}{\alpha_K \gamma} - 1 \right] K' \qquad (11\text{-}11)$$

in which the new symbol γ stands for $1 - \alpha_K \xi_N$, the share of all incomes except urban-sector quasirents in the total.

When the bulk of the labor force is in agriculture, θ is close to 0 from Table 11-1 and the relationship between income equality and modern-sector capital accumulation approximates $D' = -K'$, so that Kuznets's conjecture holds. As L_A/L approaches 0 and the modern-sector output share ξ_N approaches 1, the elasticity relationship becomes $D' = [(1 - \sigma^N)/\sigma^N] K'$, so that the income distribution will continue to worsen unless $\sigma^N < 1$.

Fortunately, this condition is likely to hold, so that there will be a *turning point* at which, as the agricultural share of the labor force falls, the income equality measure D will start to rise. This momentous change occurs just when $\theta = \alpha_K \gamma/\alpha_L > \alpha_K$ and the elasticity of D with respect to K is 0. From Table 11-1, it appears that θ is likely to become substantially larger than α_K only quite late in the growth process, when the share of the agricultural labor force, L_A/L, is 0.4 or less. "Trickle down" of income benefits from increased accumulation takes a very long time to appear in the Lewis world if the economic system is allowed to run along on its own without explicit policy interventions to prevent the relative income distribution from getting worse.

---

[2]The general view of the world underlying the use of the equality index D is that rent recipients and wage recipients in agriculture behave more or less alike; e.g., there is a large number of roughly similar peasant proprietors. Other distribution measures would have to be used if one wanted to distinguish, say, the role of landlords. See Bell's paper (listed in the Selected Additional Readings) for an equality measure based on relative labor and capital incomes alone. In an earlier paper, Bardhan presents a parallel analysis, within the agricultural sector only, of large and small farmers.

11-2 FOOD DEMAND AND THE BALANCE OF PAYMENTS

So far, we have been relying on government interventions and international trade to keep the prices of agricultural and industrial products fixed, while the wage can move against them. Now we want to change focus somewhat and make two new assumptions. The first is that the world price of food P_A varies and that the government does not intervene in trade, so that the internal price equals P_A as well. The underlying hypothesis is that if traders can buy and sell food in both internal and international markets, they will arbitrage their purchases until the two prices are equal. As discussed in Chap. 5, this is not a very good description of government behavior with respect to food markets in the short run, but it may not be so bad as a story about long-run policy response.

Our second assumption is that the wage will adjust to maintain full employment as P_A shifts. Prices and incomes within the country will thus be determined from outside—the standard assumption in the theory of international trade. We want to ask how long-run output and consumption of the agricultural product will vary in response to changes in the price P_A. We start on the supply side and then go on to consider income and price effects in demand. The change in *excess supply* (or supply minus demand) determines how agricultural exports and the balance of payments respond.

If we let P'_A be nonzero but hold modern sector capital stock constant ($K' = 0$) for simplicity, then we can solve Eqs. (11-6) through (11-8) to get the change in the wage that is required to assure full employment:

$$w' = \frac{1}{\lambda} \frac{L_A}{L} \frac{\sigma^A}{1 - \beta} P'_A \tag{11-12}$$

A glance back at Eq. (11-9) defining λ shows that the elasticity of w with respect to P_A in Eq. (11-12) will be positive and just slightly less than 1 as long as the share of the agricultural labor force, L_A/L, is close to unity. Even when full employment is maintained, as in Eq. (11-6), the wage in terms of food w/P_A will fall very little as P_A rises, from the assumptions we have made about duality of production parameters in the two sectors. From Eqs. (11-4) and (11-5), one can also show that agricultural supply will be price-responsive, the formal expression being

$$X'_A = \frac{\sigma^A}{\lambda} \frac{\beta}{1 - \beta} \frac{L_N}{L} \frac{\sigma^N}{\alpha_K} P'_A \tag{11-13}$$

Suppose that all income from capital in the modern sector is saved or spent on manufactured goods. Then demand for food will depend on wage income in the modern sector and total income from agriculture. Making the appropriate substitutions for income log changes, we can find the log change of demand for food C'_A from the Slutsky equation [Eq. (E-1) of Appendix E]:

$$C'_A = \eta_A [(1/\gamma)(\alpha_L \xi_N w' + \xi_A P'_A) - \phi_A P'_A] + \eta_{AA} P'_A \tag{11-14}$$

In this equation, η_A is the income elasticity of demand for food and η_{AA} the compensated own-price elasticity. In the bracketed expression multiplied by η_A, the first two terms show how the income of everyone but urban profit recipients responds to log changes in the wage w' and agricultural price P'_A. The term $\phi_A P'_A$ is the income effect in demand, capturing the decrease in real spending power that occurs as P_A goes up; the parameter ϕ_A is the initial budget share of food.

Now we want to ask how supply of food varies relative to demand when its price changes. If we consider the log change of the supply-demand ratio (X_A/C_A), then we can combine the equations of this section to get

$$X'_A - C'_A = \left[\frac{\sigma^A}{(1-\beta)\lambda} \left(\beta \frac{L_N}{L} \frac{\sigma^N}{\alpha_K} - \eta_A \frac{\alpha_L \xi_N}{\gamma} \frac{L_A}{L} \right) - \eta_A \xi_A/\gamma + (\eta_A \phi_A - \eta_{AA}) \right] P'_A$$

$$(11\text{-}15)$$

This equation is unpleasantly long, but it does summarize all the changes going on in the economy as the agricultural price shifts. The two terms in the expression in parentheses multiplied by $\sigma^A/[(1-\beta)\lambda]$ are, respectively, the agricultural supply response from Eq. (11-13) and the demand increase from increased urban labor income as the wage w increases with P_A from Eq. (11-12). The $\eta_A \xi_A/\gamma$ term represents the demand increase from increased rural incomes as P_A rises, and the last term in parentheses (which will be positive) shows how demand for food falls from income and substitution effects when its price goes up.

The elasticity of (X_A/C_A) with respect to P_A can be of either sign, depending on how the parameters work out. In one important case, however, it will be negative. Consider what happens when there is strong technological dualism (so that the ratio of elasticities of substitution σ^N/σ^A is near 0) and also concentration of the labor force in agriculture (so that L_A/L is near 1). Then, to a good approximation, Eq. (11-15) can be restated as

$$X'_A - C'_A = -[\eta_A(1 - \phi_A) + \eta_{AA}]P'_A \qquad (11\text{-}16)$$

This equation shows that under conditions of dualism, the sign of the response of excess supply to price changes depends on the balance between income changes and price effects in food demand. The income gain to workers and farmers from a high agricultural price leads to increased demand according to the Engel elasticity η_A, while income and substitution effects in demand cut consumption by $(-\phi_A \eta_A + \eta_{AA})$.

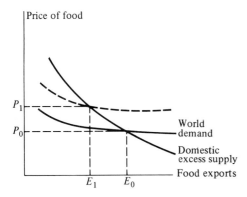

Figure 11-1 The export market for food with a negative elasticity of supply.

Since the nonfood budget share $(1 - \phi_A)$ will exceed 0, the nominal income gain is not offset completely by food price increases. A large Engel elasticity coupled with a near-zero compensated price elasticity η_{AA} can make the bracketed expression on the right side of Eq. (11-16) positive and give a negative sign to the elasticity of excess supply.[3] This means that demand for food goes up more rapidly than supply because of income effects when its price rises and supply to exports or other uses drops off.[4]

If the excess supply does go to exports, the situation is as shown in Fig. 11-1. An upward shift in world demand (even if the curve is quite elastic) will lead to a *decrease* in export volume along with a rise in price. Total foreign-exchange receipts (price times quantity exported) might well go down. A poor country exporting food (or, more generally, a collection of necessities that are heavily consumed by poor people who also produce them) may find its internal consumption standards helped but its balance of payments hurt by more active world demand for its products. The relevance of this possibility to the assertion by rich countries in the "North-South debate" that they have to grow fast to generate more export demand for the Third World would be interesting to explore, but it would take us too far afield. The reader should consult the paper by Chichilnisky.

11-3 THE LABOR MARKET IN CLOSED AND OPEN ECONOMIES

So far, we have seen that the Lewis story holds up reasonably well as long as the economy is open to international trade and income effects in food demand can be "exported" to the rest of the world. What happens, however, when food exports or imports are not large relative to the total size of the market and the economy must be considered autarchic or closed? In that case, real income changes (due to a changing food price) spill over into the internal market; in the absence of state intervention, these changes have to be worked out there. In this section, to add a bit of contrast to last section's focus on the market for food, we tell the story in terms of the supply and demand for labor in the modern sector.

---

[3]From Eq. (E-8) in Appendix E we have the approximation

$$\eta_{AA} = -\sigma^C \eta_A \, (1 - \phi_A \eta_A)$$

so that the bracketed expression in Eq. (11-16) becomes

$$\eta_A [1 - \phi_A - \sigma^C + \sigma^C \eta_A \phi_A]$$

For a poor population, the value of σ^C (which measures overall substitution responsiveness in demand) would be less than 0.5. The food budget share ϕ_A would be a bit more than 0.5, and the Engel elasticity would have a value of 0.5 or perhaps more. On balance, one might expect the above expression to be positive but fairly small and the elasticity of excess food supply to be less than 0.

[4]Other formal hypotheses can give similar results. For example, Chichilnisky assumes that capital is shiftable between the two sectors and that there is no choice of technique, but she drops full employment and postulates a high elasticity of labor supply with respect to the real wage (w/P_A). Both her specification and the one here capture part of the Lewis vision of the stylized facts.

Labor demand is already given by Eq. (11-8); with reasonable values of the parameters σ^N and α_K, it will not be highly elastic with respect to the wage.

To get modern-sector labor supply, we note that it must be equal to $L - L_A$, where L is the total labor force. By log differentiation and substitution from Eq. (11-7), we can write out the supply function in elasticity form as

$$L'_N = (L_A/L_N) \, [\sigma^A/(1 - \beta)] \, (w' - P'_A) \tag{11-17}$$

In the case from Sec. 11-1 where the intersectoral terms of trade do not change but the (real) wage can vary, we have $P'_A = 0$, and the elasticity of supply of L_N with respect to the wage will be large. This is the case shown by the supply curve S_I in Fig. 11-2. An outward shift in labor demand (from capital accumulation, for example) will substantially increase employment but have little effect on the wage or the real per capita income of workers and farmers.

In a closed economy, the story is a bit more complicated. To get an expression for the labor-supply change, first note that $L'_A = (1/\beta)X'_A$ from Eq. (11-4). The output log change X'_A, in turn, must be equal to the log change in food demand C'_A from Eq. (11-14). Substitution of Eq. (11-12)—linking wage and price changes—and a bit of manipulation finally give the modern-sector labor-supply function as

$$L'_N = -\frac{L_A}{L_N} \frac{1}{\beta} \left[\left(1 + \frac{L_N}{L_A} \frac{\sigma^N}{\sigma^A} \frac{1-\beta}{\alpha_K} \right) \left(\frac{\eta_A \xi_A}{\gamma} - \eta_A \phi_A + \eta_{AA} \right) + \frac{\eta_A \alpha_L \xi_N}{\gamma} \right] w'$$

Like Eq. (11-15), this expression is pretty obscure. It simplifies nicely, however, if we assume strong production and/or employment dualism, so that the ratios (σ^N/σ^A) and/or (L_N/L_A) go to 0. Then the labor-supply function reduces to

$$L'_N = -(L_A/L_N\beta) \, [\eta_A(1 - \phi_A) + \eta_{AA}] \, w' \tag{11-18}$$

This equation strongly resembles Eq. (11-16) and shows that, under conditions of dualism, the sign of the labor-supply response to a wage increase may be negative, as exemplified by the curve S_{II} in Fig. 11-2. An upward shift in the labor-demand curve will bid up the wage enough to *reduce* modern-sector employment. The perverse

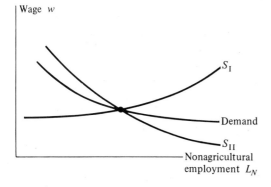

Wage w

S_I

Demand

S_{II}

Nonagricultural employment L_N

Figure 11-2 General equilibrium demand and supply curves for nonagricultural employment.

balance-of-payments behavior in Fig. 11-1 is mapped into the labor market when the economy is assumed to be closed to international trade.[5]

Results like this one underline the medium-run problems that highly dualistic economies face. However, before we write off completely the Lewis-Kuznets story about structural change, a few caveats are in order:

1. Even under extreme conditions of technological and employment dualism, the existence of negatively sloped export- or labor-supply curves [from Eqs. (11-16) and (11-18), respectively] depends on strong income and low substitution elasticities in food demand. How realistic this combination is empirically remains unclear. However, even when the demand parameters are such as to give the supply curves the "right" slope, they could still be quite inelastic, or steep. Manipulation of policy under inelastic export- and labor-supply conditions is not necessarily an easy task.

2. Whichever way the curves slope, the basic Lewis postulate that the wage will remain approximately constant *in terms of food* retains its validity from Eq. (11-12). What a negatively sloped or steep labor-supply curve implies is that, as labor demand goes up, there will be an increase in the price of food in terms of manufactures. As far as their own purchasing power goes, peasants and workers would benefit relatively little from this change in the terms of trade. Only capitalists would lose real spending power, and they would perhaps invest less.

3. Another option for modern-sector entrepreneurs would be to select capital-intensive techniques. This outcome of rising food prices in the modern sector goes under the name of the *marketed surplus problem* and has almost been drowned by economists' ink. There are a number of reasons, some taken up below, why the problem in theoretical models tends to be oversimplified. And even if food prices and money wages did rise, the government could offset the incipient inflation by appropriate policy measures. In fact, overcompensation has been less the exception than the rule; Eq. (11-18) should *not* be considered as a recommendation for wholesale subsidy of industry to make up for the rising cost of food. If food prices go up (taking wages along with them), the problem should be attacked at the source, either by imports or by measures to improve productivity.

4. Finally, even the conclusions of the agriculture-industry model in a more general context are not so clear cut. For one example (others appear below), suppose that labor-augmenting technical progress is added to the production specification along the lines of Appendix D. Then the formula for wage log changes (perhaps now better interpreted as growth rates) becomes

$$w' = \theta \left\{ K' + \frac{L}{L_N} \left[\frac{L_A}{L} \left(\frac{\sigma^A}{1 - \beta} - 1 \right) \epsilon_A + \frac{L_N}{L} \left(\frac{\sigma^N}{\alpha_K} - 1 \right) \epsilon_N \right] \right\} \quad (11\text{-}19)$$

---

[5] Note that as Fig. 11-2 is drawn, the labor market with supply curve S_{II} is stable; i.e., when the wage is high, there is excess labor supply and w could be expected to fall toward equilibrium. However, if the urban-sector labor-demand curve is inelastic or steep enough, it would cut the supply curve S_{II} from above and the market would be unstable or subject to ever-increasing wage oscillations, which would be extremely difficult to control.

in which ϵ_A and ϵ_N are, respectively, the rates of technical change in agriculture and industry. Probably the term in parentheses multiplying ϵ_A will be positive and that multiplying ϵ_N negative. If technical change in industry outpaces that in agriculture, the wage in terms of modern-sector products can fall, for many of the same reasons discussed in Sec. 10-2. It is not sure that such dislocating technical advance *will* occur, but—by the same token—one should be dubious of long-run conclusions from simple models in which it will not.

11-4 THE MARKETED SURPLUS

The linked problems of assuring supplies of labor and food to urban industry give rise to a number of policy suggestions. Three are reviewed briefly here, drawing on the formal model results of the preceding sections.

First, flows of both labor and food from the countryside depend on complicated factors of demand and supply. The results of Sec. 11-2 indicate that it is by no means obvious that the amount of food sold by farmers to the city (*the* marketed surplus) will go up with the food price. Econometric results are mixed. For example, following previous work by Bardhan and others, a recent study for India by Isher Ahluwalia shows a negative elasticity in the short to medium run. However, assume for the sake of discussion that the elasticity of marketed surplus S_A with respect to price is positive and call it μ $(S_A' = \mu P_A')$. Then it is reasonable to ask how prices ought to be manipulated to make crops flow toward the city.

The classic suggestion is due to the Soviet economist E. A. Preobrazhenski, who participated in the Soviet industrialization debate already mentioned in Chap. 8. He wanted to use the state's potential monopsony purchasing power to extract food from the countryside. To illustrate the argument, we may follow a suggestion by Hornby and assume that the government can get food either from rural areas in quantity S_A at price P_A or from imports in quantity S_M at a fixed world price P_M. Then its problem is to minimize the cost of acquisition $P_A S_A + P_M S_M$ subject to the nonagricultural food demand requirement $S_A + S_M = D_N$, where D_N is assumed to be given. The government is acting as a discriminating monopsonist purchasing food in two separated markets; naturally, it pays less to the sellers with less elastic supply

$$P_A(1 + 1/\mu) = P_M \tag{11-20}$$

As long as their supply elasticity μ is less than infinite, farmers should be subject to price discrimination. The recommendation is elegant and has a certain economic logic, but as N. I. Bukharin and other participants in the Soviet debate pointed out, farmers might just respond to lower prices by withholding their stocks in speculative fashion from the market; they might also cut back production of food and go into other products in the long run. Regrettably, economic policy is rarely as simple as Eq. (11-20). What the algebra and Preobrazhenski both imply is that it makes economic sense for an industrializing state to pay as little as possible to farmers—but that it may have to do so at the point of a gun. Such implications were not lost on those who took over the Soviet state after the participants in the industrialization debate were banished from the scene. That brings us to our second policy point.

Figure 11-2 reveals that an effective policy to lower urban labor costs is to shift the supply curve out (that is, increase the amount of labor available at a given wage) regardless of whether it takes a shape like S_I or S_{II}. Of course, if the supply curve is negatively sloped—as it might be in large, closed economies with strong food demand in the countryside—such policies become all the more appealing.

One way for the wage in terms of manufactures to drop is through labor-augmenting technical change in the modern sector, as we have already seen in connection with Eq. (11-19). Another route would be through capital accumulation or the reorganization of production in agriculture to use *less* labor in connection with other resources. The linked Soviet efforts at "dekulakization" and creation of the collective farms can be viewed as having this impact; some economic historians think that the enclosure movement in eighteenth-century England had similar results. In both cases, new modes of production were introduced to maintain agricultural output while rural employment fell. In the Soviet case, the collectives also provided an efficient device for funneling food flows toward urban consumption and export, in effect causing rural real income and food demand to shift down. Stalin's solution to Preobrazhenski's problem took a form that the nonviolent economist never thought to propose.[6]

Besides institutional and technical change in the countryside induced by the state from the outside, one final consideration bears on the marketed surplus problem—that of agricultural demand for industrial products. So far, we have been assuming that agriculture sells food to industry for its workers to consume. But in fact, in poor countries, agricultural products are the dominant intermediate inputs to urban manufacturing sectors such as food processing and textiles, so that the input-output matrix A is likely to take the *triangular* form

$$A = \begin{bmatrix} a_{AA} & a_{AN} \\ 0 & a_{NN} \end{bmatrix}$$

where the a_{ij} are input-output coefficients for the two sectors. In effect, we consolidated intermediate sales from agriculture to crop-processing industries in the demand equations used heretofore. The triangular input-output structure was a prerequisite for this manipulation.

With the modernization of agriculture, it begins to demand inputs from industry—fertilizers, pesticides, and capital equipment. The input-output table changes to take the form

$$A = \begin{bmatrix} a_{AA} & a_{AN} \\ a_{NA} & a_{NN} \end{bmatrix}$$

---

[6]In formal terms, the Stalinist solution might be modeled through the imposition of a stiff tax in kind on agricultural product, with the proceeds redistributed to urban industry for use in paying workers. Readers should probably work through the formal economics of the tax, using the model of Sec. 11-3. They will see that Stalin's device was effective, *and* he had the troops to make it work.

in which the industry-to-agriculture coefficient a_{NA} may grow to be substantially larger than a_{AN}. Under these circumstances, the purchasing power of value-added in agriculture relative to value-added in industry falls and the general-equilibrium labor-supply curves of Fig. 11-2 must shift outward.[7] Technical changes of a type which must be anticipated as agriculture modernizes make the marketed surplus problem less acute in the long run. It should be added that they may also change ownership patterns and supply response enough to make analysis on the basis of simplified two-sector models with fixed parameters completely beside the point.

To summarize, many factors intervene in determining how severe the marketed surplus problem in practice is likely to be—among them are possibilities for agricultural trade, technical change, and capital accumulation as they affect both labor productivity and use of intermediate inputs from industry on the farm. Another factor is the effectiveness of the state in coercing peasants on the one hand and the urban proletariat on the other. One of the grand themes in economic history describes the changing roles and power of lords and peasants, bourgeoisie and the working class. Models like those in this chapter can shed some light on the economic issues that arise, but the wise planner will recognize that, in dealing with the agrarian problem, he or she grapples with great historical forces, and that the course of history is always impossible to foretell.

SELECTED ADDITIONAL READINGS

Ahluwalia, Isher J.: "An Analysis of Price and Output Behavior in the Indian Economy, 1951–1973," *Journal of Development Economics* (to appear). (A macroeconomic model of India displaying, among other features, a negative elasticity of marketed surplus with respect to the food price.)

Bardhan, Pranab K.: "A Model of Growth of Capitalism in a Dual Agrarian Economy," in J. N. Bhagwati, and R. S. Eckaus (eds.): *Development and Planning: Essays in Honor of Paul Rosenstein-Rodan*, M.I.T. Press, Cambridge, Mass., 1973. (Discusses growth and distribution in a model with large and small farmers; the former usually win.)

Bell, Clive: "The Behavior of a Dual Economy under Different 'Closing Rules,'" *Journal of Development Economics* (to appear). (Original presentation of the comparative statics of the Lewis model in Sec. 11-1.)

Chichilnisky, Graciela: "Terms of Trade and Domestic Distribution: Export-Led Growth with Abundant Labor," Harvard Institute of International Development, discussion paper, 1978. (Derives the downward-sloping export-supply curve for "basic" goods of Fig. 11-1 in a Lewis-style economy and discusses its implications in the "North-South debate.")

Dixit, Avinash: "Models of Dual Economies," in James A. Mirrlees and Nicholas H. Stern (eds.): *Models of Economic Growth*, Wiley, New York, 1973. (Presents an agriculture-industry model with Engel curves like the one in Sec. 11-3.)

[7]In formal terms, agriculturalists receive a *net price*

$$V_A = P_A(1 - a_{AA}) - a_{NA}$$

for their output, of the type discussed in the next chapter. Using V'_A in place of P'_A in Eq. (11-5) gives the results asserted in the text.

Dobb, Maurice: *Soviet Economic Development Since 1917*, Routledge & Kegan Paul, London, 1966. (Clear review of the Soviet industrialization debate.)

Hornby, J. M.: "Investment and Trade Policy in the Dual Economy," *Economic Journal*, 78:96–107, 1968. (Probably the first of a series of papers suggesting price discrimination against the peasants along the Preobrazhenski lines of Sec. 11-4.)

Moore, Barrington H., Jr.: *Social Origins of Dictatorship and Democracy: Lord and Peasant in the Making of the Modern World*, Beacon Press, Boston, 1966. (Brilliant review of the political economy of the agriculture-industry transition.)

TWELVE

INPUT-OUTPUT QUANTITY AND PRICE CALCULATIONS

The truth that justifies input-output analysis is that sectors in the production process are linked, on both the price and quantity sides. The price in one industry depends on prices of all the others, because it uses inputs from them and they from it. Similarly, any single industry's output depends on levels of demand from the sectors to which it sells. Total demands for labor, capital, and intermediate imports also are determined by adding up both intermediate and final demands, and patterns of factor use in the economy as a whole are strongly influenced by its interindustry production structure.

In this chapter, some planning implications of these observations are worked out in algebraic detail. To keep the presentation tolerably compact, matrix notation will be used, unapologetically. Readers who are unfamiliar with this sort of manipulation should brush up, or get someone to translate the results for them. Also, one important and well-known theorem in linear algebra will be invoked, but its economic interpretation should become clear enough as we go along.

The outline of the chapter is as follows: We begin with a quick review of input-output quantity-side calculations, using the so-called *open Leontief model.* Much of the material has already been covered in Chaps. 2 through 4 but is restated for completeness here. The price relationships implicit in interindustry accounting are then analyzed, and their use is illustrated by calculations of *domestic resource costs* and *effective rates of protection* in economies open to foreign trade. Section 12-3 is devoted to the *closed Leontief model,* which takes the linkages between income flows and consumption into account. The usefulness of both the open and closed models in income distribution calculations is questioned from the point of view of the often simplistic assumptions about price theory that they contain. Section 12-4 runs through

177

a set of pricing exercises due to the Cambridge economist Piero Sraffa, to illustrate the measurement of labor exploitation and investment project selection in the input-output system. The so-called *dynamic Leontief model* is then put through its paces, and the chapter closes with an extension of Sraffa prices to the dynamic system. A number of other input-output planning applications—most notably computable planning models of linear programming or other variety—are not discussed here, since they are surveyed in the article by Manne and the book edited by Blitzer, Clark, and Taylor in the Selected Additional Readings. Also, more detailed presentations of what have become "standard" input-output manipulations are widely available, for example, in the classic text by Chenery and Clark.

12-1 THE OPEN LEONTIEF MODEL

Suppose that we possess volume indexes of the levels of output in a number of sectors X_1 through X_N. Then, as discussed in Sec. 3-3, the material-balance equation for each sector can be written as

$$X_i = \sum_{j=1}^{N} X_{ij} + F_i = \sum_{j=1}^{N} a_{ij} X_j + F_i \tag{12-1}$$

where X_{ij} is the volume of intermediate sales from sector i to sector j and F_i is the volume of final demands (net of competitive imports) for product i. In input-output planning it is usually assumed that intermediate purchases of each input by sector j are proportional to its volume of production ($X_{ij} = a_{ij}X_j$, for all inputs X_{ij}); this postulate is used in Eq. (12-1) after the second equality. If we let X be the column vector of the X_i, F the column vector of the F_i, and A the square $N \times N$ matrix made up of the input-output coefficients a_{ij}, then Eq. (12-1) can be rewritten in considerably more compact form as

$$X = AX + F \tag{12-2}$$

Formally, Eq. (12-2) can be solved as

$$X = (I - A)^{-1} F \tag{12-3}$$

where I is the $N \times N$ *identity matrix* with 1s along its main diagonal and 0s elsewhere, and $(I - A)^{-1}$ is the so-called *Leontief inverse*. In a two-sector model, the solution for X_1 is

$$X_1 = [(1 - a_{11})(1 - a_{22}) - a_{12}a_{21}]^{-1} [(1 - a_{22})F_1 + a_{12}F_2]$$

The term in the first bracket is the determinant $|I - A|$, a measure of the ability of the economic system to produce a surplus for final demand in excess of current intermediate input requirements. For a sensible system, $|I - A|$ should be positive, which is guaranteed if for example all the column sums in A are less than 1. The second bracket has to do with intermediate input requirements per unit of final demand. Simple consideration of coefficients shows that X_1 will exceed F_1, so the final demands are "expanded" or "multiplied" into the corresponding sectoral outputs by the inverse Leontief matrix.[1]

The most common use of the Leontief inverse is to calculate total resources required to support a unit of final demand. For example, suppose that the *value* of noncompetitive intermediate imports (at constant world prices and exchange rate) required per unit of output in sector i is given by

$$M_{0i} = a_{0i}X_i \qquad (12\text{-}4)$$

Evidently,

$$M_0 = \sum_{i=1}^{N} M_{0i} = \sum_{i=1}^{N} a_{0i}X_i \qquad (12\text{-}5)$$

is an expression which can be used to calculate total intermediate imports M_0. This formula can be put in matrix notation if we let Z denote the "summing vector" of 1s,

$$Z = \begin{bmatrix} 1 \\ 1 \\ \cdot \\ \cdot \\ \cdot \\ 1 \end{bmatrix}$$

and Z^T denote its transpose

$$Z^T = [1 \quad 1 \ldots 1]$$

Also let a_0^T be the vector of coefficients a_{0i}, written as a row, and M be the vector of the M_{0i}, written as a column. Using these definitions, Eq. (12-5) can be written as

$$M_0 = Z^T M = a_0^T X = a_0^T (I - A)^{-1} F \qquad (12\text{-}6)$$

which shows the total of intermediate imports required to support the final demand vector F. The row vector $a_0^T (I - A)^{-1}$ gives *direct and indirect* imports required per unit of final demand. That is, its ith entry shows how import-intensive is a final pur-

---

[1] The same observation follows in another way. Recall from high school that if a is a positive fraction, $0 < a < 1$, then the sum of the series $1 + a + a^2 + \ldots$ is just $1/(1 - a)$. Similarly, a well-behaved A matrix with all elements nonnegative and column sums less than one satisfies the series expansion

$$(I - A)^{-1} = I + A + A^2 + \ldots$$

Since all elements of A are nonnegative, so are all elements of $(I - A)^{-1}$. Moreover the elements on the diagonal of the Leontief inverse exceed unity, so that $X_i > F_i$, the "expansion" mentioned above. Empirically founded A matrices also have the property that all elements of $(I - A)^{-1}$ are strictly positive, so that each sector's final demand is supported by production from every sector in the economy, at least indirectly.

chase of product i, after all the intermediate inputs into its production are accounted for. Similar calculations are obviously possible for labor, capital, and other primary inputs. Direct and indirect input coefficients from vectors like $a_0^T(I - A)^{-1}$ are often considerably larger than the corresponding direct input coefficients a_{0i}.

Equations like Eq. (12-3) for sectoral outputs and Eq. (12-6) for factor uses are widely applied to provide at least partial answers to a number of questions that arise during the planning process. Examples follow.

1. Evaluation of investment projects: Expenditures on road construction, say, could be plugged in as components of the vector F in Eq. (12-6). The import total M_0 would then represent the foreign-exchange component of domestically produced commodities and services going into the road. Direct foreign-exchange costs of the project (e.g., speciality steels or construction equipment) would have to be added to get the total foreign exchange bill. Similar calculations are, of course, possible for employment, capital, or total value added. All such computations serve as an important complement to the more traditional project analysis methods discussed in the next chapter, since these are based on profit-and-loss assessments of the social worth of an investment that is small in comparison to the economy as a whole. When the investment package is "large," benefits from economies of scale, or even has many interindustry linkages with the rest of the economy, it is important to look at its macroeconomic ramifications. Input-output calculations provide the natural vehicle for doing so.

2. As already shown in Eq. (2-8), the final demand vector F is the sum of vectors of demand for personal consumption, government consumption, capital formation, stock changes, and exports net of competitive imports. Forecasts of these final demand components are almost routinely made—private consumption from projections of income growth in equations like Eq. (E-1) in Appendix E, with all the $P_i' = 0$, government consumption from the Ministry of Finance, investment from the Ministry of Industry, and exports and imports from specialists in foreign trade. If somebody is willing to throw all these projections into an intersectoral accounting scheme, then the input-output system can be used to test their internal consistency or lack of same at a degree of disaggregation more interesting than that of a purely macro forecast.

3. When all this computation is done, it will provide a basis for dialogue between central planners and specialists in the various sectors. Suppose, for example, that a target of 4 percent aggregate consumption growth is mandated by the central authorities. After Engel effects and interindustry linkages are duly quantified, this target might imply 2.5 percent growth for agricultural production. If agricultural supply is only likely to grow at 2 percent, there is an obvious need for plan revision. On the other hand, the *consistent* input-output forecast of growth in demand for chemicals (which go largely to intermediate uses) may be 6 percent. If chemical-sector experts are plumping for 10 percent growth without significant import substitution, interindustry calculations can serve as a valuable reality check on their enthusiasm.

12-2 PRICES IN THE INPUT-OUTPUT SYSTEM

Reading across a row in a matrix of interindustry flows gives the breakdown of the corresponding sector's sales; reading down a column gives its total costs. If instead of flows one uses a table of input-output coefficients, then the column would give the following decomposition of cost per unit output in sector i:

$$P_i = \sum_{j=1}^{N} a_{ji}P_j + a_{Li}w + a_{Ki}r + a_{0i}P_0 \tag{12-7}$$

Here, P_i is the cost-determined output price in sector i, and w, r, and P_0 are the respective costs of labor, capital, and noncompetitive imports (assumed for simplicity to be equal for all sectors). The a_{ji} are the domestic input-output coefficients introduced previously, while a_{Li}, a_{Ki}, and a_{0i} are coefficients for labor, capital, and imports. In the base year for which the input-output table is made, all prices are set to 1, and the accounting rule

$$\sum_{j=1}^{N} a_{ji} + a_{Li}w + a_{Ki}r + a_{0i}P_0 = 1 \tag{12-8}$$

should be satisfied. From Eq. (12-8), each column sum within the interindustry coefficient matrix will be less than unity, and the matrix will be well behaved.

Equation (12-7) can be restated in matrix form as

$$P^T(I - A) = wa_L^T + ra_K^T + P_0 a_0^T \tag{12-9}$$

in which P^T is a row vector of sectoral prices and a_L^T, a_K^T, and a_0^T are row vectors of labor, capital, and import coefficients. After a matrix inversion, Eq. (12-9) becomes

$$P^T = (wa_L^T + ra_K^T + P_0 a_0^T)(I - A)^{-1} \tag{12-10}$$

Each entry in the row vector $wa_L^T(I - A)^{-1}$ is the direct and indirect labor cost per unit of output in the corresponding sector. Since similar statements apply to the capital and import terms in Eq. (12-10), the whole equation states that each sector's output price will be the sum of direct and indirect primary factor costs in its production. Equations like Eq. (12-10) usually do a reliable job of forecasting sectoral inflation rates from wage, profit, and exchange rate changes in the medium term, as discussed, for example, in the paper by Watanabe and Shishido in the readings.

An extremely useful investment project evaluation criterion called *domestic resource cost* (DRC) follows almost directly from Eq. (12-10). Suppose that there is no protection on intermediate imports, so that their domestic cost is determined from foreign trade as

$$P_0 = eP_0^* \tag{12-11}$$

where e is the exchange rate and P_0^* is the world price of the imports. Also suppose that a new opportunity to export (or competitively import substitute) arises in sector i. This transaction will be profitable if the foreign-exchange return eP_i^* (where P_i^* is the world price of product i) exceeds the sector's production cost P_i. Such will be the case when

$$eP_i^* > (wa_L^T + ra_K^T + eP_0^* a_0^T) (I - A)^{-1} z_i$$

where z_i is the column vector with all elements equal to 0 except for the ith, which is equal to 1. In effect, z_i isolates the ith cost-determined sector price from Eq. (12-10), for comparison with eP_i^*. The above inequality can be rearranged to give

$$e > \frac{(wa_L^T + ra_K^T) (I - A)^{-1} z_i}{P_i^* - P_0^* a_0^T (I - A)^{-1} z_i} \tag{12-12}$$

so that the sale will be profitable if the direct and indirect *domestic* cost of producing product i, divided by the *net* foreign exchange gain from its export or import substitution, does not exceed the exchange rate.

For purposes of project evaluation, the DRC ratio can be applied to any new investment alternative, with its technology appended to the preexisting input-output matrix as an extra row and column. If the factor prices w, r, and e are *shadow prices* in the sense of being derived from some sort of social optimality conditions of the type discussed in Secs. 12-4 and 12-6 and Chap. 13, then Eq. (12-12) is the correct general equilibrium project criterion, since it measures social profits.[2]

Theoretical correctness is a strong argument for using criteria like DRC, but not an overwhelming one. However, the case in favor of DRCs can be further strengthened on practical grounds. In actual planning, social cost-benefit analysis and shadow prices are debaters' tools used in the discussion of an investment project along with regional political arguments; attempts to evaluate side benefits to a project like skill creation, backward and forward production linkages, and access to new technology; and appeals to national pride. If quantitative economists are going to be listened to at all in the skirmish, they have to put their arguments in a form that nontechnical bureaucrats and politicians can understand. As a measure of "our" costs to achieve certain foreign exchange returns, DRC is admirably suited to this end. Good economics *can* be put in comprehensible packages, as the DRC criterion amply demonstrates.

Although, strictly speaking, DRC is a profitability criterion (all sectors' domestic resource costs should be equal in an economy "optimally" run), it can be used in a crude fashion to gauge relative inefficiencies of different, actual industries. For example, if the domestic cost per net foreign exchange return in some industry is high or negative, then one has reason to doubt that its production should be allowed to go on. Typically, higher DRCs are observed in import-substituting than in export industries, and past policy decisions can be found which make this the case. It is usually not so hard to get tariff protection to start producing almost anything already imported and consumed in an industrializing country; and once it starts, everyone from the workers to the local tax collector wants to keep a price-inefficient factory rolling along. The fact that such factories sometimes roll along together and create major industrial

---

[2] See the papers in the readings by Bruno and Srinivasan and Bhagwati for further elucidation. Even after years of theoretical debate, the 1967 paper by Bruno remains the best introduction to investment project analysis in an economy open to foreign trade.

centers like São Paulo or Bombay ought to make the planner think twice before applying partial-equilibrium, undynamic cost calculations too rigorously, but there still are many projects which are so expensive or ill designed for the local market that they should be stopped.

Partial-equilibrium lore about comparative costs of industries can usefully be summarized by DRCs. Another catalog, similar though usually not identical, can be constructed by using the concept of *effective rate of protection* (ERP). ERPs are based by analogy on the use of tariffs to measure the degree of protection (or "inefficiency") in an economy without intermediate goods. In such a system, the internal price of a traded good P_i will be determined by the relationship

$$P_i = (1 + t_i) P_i^* \qquad (12\text{-}13)$$

where t_i is the ad valorem tariff on imports of commodity i and the exchange rate is set to 1. In effect, Eq. (12-13) states that a purchaser will be indifferent between purchasing the "same" commodity from a domestic producer at price P_i or the world market at $(1 + t_i) P_i^*$. Hence, the two prices must be the same.[3] From Eq. (12-13), it immediately follows that the extent of protection in sector i is measured by

$$t_i = (P_i - P_i^*)/P_i^* \qquad (12\text{-}14)$$

The higher t_i is, the stronger, presumably, is the case for limiting production in sector i. However, the partial-equilibrium nature of this assertion is clear in a perfectly competitive, trade-arbitraged model even without intermediate goods but with many sectors. If one tariff is raised, production in the sector will go up; but if two or more are varied, the results can be perverse—production may go down in a sector that is given more protection. Under such circumstances, the use of tariffs to gauge the extent of government favors granted to different sectors may not lead to much illumination.

Nonetheless, we can persist with an interindustry extension of Eq. (12-14). To do so, assume as usual that input-output coefficients are insensitive to price changes and define a sector's *net price* V_i as

$$V_i = P_i - \sum_{j=0}^{N} P_j a_{ji} \qquad (12\text{-}15)$$

The net price measures the revenue per unit of output that the entrepreneur in sector i receives after paying for all intermediate inputs required for production (including imports). In other words, V_i is just the sector's value added per unit output. Value added at world prices is defined as

$$V_i^* = P_i^* - \sum_{j=0}^{N} P_j^* a_{ji} \qquad (12\text{-}16)$$

By analogy to Eq. (12-14), the protection given value added in sector i can be calculated as

---

[3] But see the paper by Kravis and Lipsey for some reasons why such convenient trade arbitrage may not be observed in reality.

$$\text{ERP}_i = (V_i - V_i^*)/V_i^* \qquad (12\text{-}17)$$

i.e., the proportional change in value added induced by price shifts away from free trade for both commodity i and its intermediate inputs.

One can show that if there are fixed input-output coefficients, then a change in tariffs increasing ERP_i but leaving relative ERPs in other sectors unchanged will lead to an increase in output of product i. The impact of more complex tariff modifications is unpredictable a priori, and the situation becomes even more complex when price-responsiveness of the a_{ji} is allowed.

In practice, the conclusion has to be that if a sector has either a high DRC or a high ERP, then one should look at it with suspicion. Otherwise, these and other standard measures of "inefficiency" say very little about how the general equilibrium economy is likely to respond when tariffs and other protective devices are modified drastically.

12-3 THE CLOSED LEONTIEF MODEL AND INCOME REDISTRIBUTION

So far, our input-output calculations have ignored the accounting truism that, roughly speaking, you can spend only about as much as you earn. More precisely, we have been treating private consumption expenditures as part of the final demand vector F without asking whether enough value added is generated by production activities to pay for the consumption undertaken. The *closed Leontief model* extends the open model to deal with this income-consumption linkage.

For simplicity, we ignore intermediate imports and assume that all nonwage incomes are saved. Total wage income Y_W can be defined as

$$Y_W = wa_L^T X \qquad (12\text{-}18)$$

i.e., the sum of labor payments in all sectors. We also assume that prices are fixed and that workers devote a constant fraction ϕ_i of their income to consumption of the ith commodity. If workers consume all they earn, the sum of the ϕ_i will be 1. The vector C of final consumption demands is given by

$$C = \begin{bmatrix} C_1 \\ C_2 \\ \cdot \\ \cdot \\ \cdot \\ C_N \end{bmatrix} = \begin{bmatrix} \phi_1 \\ \phi_2 \\ \cdot \\ \cdot \\ \cdot \\ \phi_N \end{bmatrix} Y_W = \phi Y_W \qquad (12\text{-}19)$$

If the vector F now represents final demands besides consumption, Eqs. (12-18) and (12-19) can be combined with the material balance equation [Eq. (12-2)] to give the following partitioned matrix equations in X and Y_W:

$$\begin{bmatrix} X \\ Y_W \end{bmatrix} = \begin{bmatrix} A & \phi \\ wa_L^T & 0 \end{bmatrix} \begin{bmatrix} X \\ Y_W \end{bmatrix} + \begin{bmatrix} F \\ 0 \end{bmatrix}$$

or

$$\begin{bmatrix} I - A & -\phi \\ -wa_L^T & 1 \end{bmatrix} \begin{bmatrix} X \\ Y_W \end{bmatrix} = \begin{bmatrix} F \\ 0 \end{bmatrix} \tag{12-20}$$

The first "row" in Eq. (12-20) just represents the material balance expression $X = AX + \phi Y_W + F$, while the second row is Eq. (12-18). Using standard matrix manipulations the solution for X can be written as

$$X = (I - A - w\phi a_L^T)^{-1} F \tag{12-21}$$

This is similar to the open model solution of Eq. (12-3) except that each element of the A matrix is extended to the form $a_{ij} + w\phi_i a_{Lj}$, the sum of the technical intermediate input requirement plus the amount of sector-i product required for the consumption of workers employed per unit output in sector j. As long as there are positive profits in all sectors, the column sums in the extended matrix will be less than 1 and the solution to Eq. (12-21) will exist.

Models like Eq. (12-21) or the simpler Eq. (12-3) have recently been used extensively to try to measure the probable effects of income redistribution on consumption and growth. In the open model, for example, some income shift between "rich" and "poor" may be assumed to change the consumption component of the final demand vector F. In the closed model extended to include several classes of income recipients [several rows of income aggregates like Y_W and columns of ϕs in Eq. (12-20)], taxes and transfers may be assumed to shift income flows among them.

In either case, the calculated impacts of the hypothetical redistribution on sectoral growth and patterns of factor use may sometimes be substantial, sometimes not. Using the open model, for example, the Indian Planning Commission in 1973 estimated that an income redistribution which would bring the poorest third of the population up to their level of "basic needs" might change annual output growth rates in 22 of the 66 sectors considered by *more* than 1 percent; this would mark a substantial change in production priorities. On the other hand, Cline calculated that shifting the Brazilian income distribution to the British pattern would modify total employment and use of foreign exchange only slightly. Other studies have shown that improving the income distribution might reduce employment if the rich happen to consume a high proportion of labor-intensive services.

The results of such calculations thus depend on parameters, in particular *differences* in Engel elasticities and sectoral intensities of use of the different classes of income recipients in the model. And on the other hand, all the static models leave out cumulative processes like the investment response to increased luxury goods consumption in the Belindia model of Chap. 10. Under the circumstances, it is perhaps not surprising that closed input-output models are not very informative about the dynamics of income distribution. They do not ask the right questions.[4]

12-4 WAGE AND PROFIT SKIRMISHES IN THE OPEN INPUT-OUTPUT SYSTEM

Since input-output accounting seems to show that income inequality is not likely to go away, it becomes interesting to approach the problem from another angle and try to measure how exploitative current politicoeconomic arrangements really are. Such calculations are fully in the classical tradition of the models of Chap. 10; we work through one example here. It is based on the model used by the Cambridge economist Piero Sraffa in his book *Production of Commodities by Means of Commodities* which, when actually written in the 1920s and 1930s, foreshadowed Leontief and many of the conclusions of the capital controversies 30 years later on. The details of the presentation are from the paper by Bacha, Carneiro, and Taylor cited in the readings.

As in our discussion of the closed Leontief model, we treat labor as the only non-intermediate input into production, although this restriction is substantially weakened in Sec. 12-6 below. To bring income distribution into the picture, we also assume that production takes time—along the lines of Sec. 9-1, a rate of interest r must be paid on the use of intermediate working capital. The cost function for a producer in sector i thus becomes

$$P_i = (1 + r) \sum_{j=1}^{N} a_{ji}P_j + wa_{Li} \qquad (12\text{-}22)$$

so that the producer pays interest on the market value of the intermediate inputs, plus wage costs. The matrix version of Eq. (12-22) is

$$P^T = (1 + r) P^T A + wa_L^T \qquad (12\text{-}23)$$

which has the solution,

$$P^T = wa_L^T [I - (1 + r)A]^{-1} \qquad (12\text{-}24)$$

so that, after interest payments are taken into account, prices are determined by direct and indirect labor costs.

Assume that some output vector X is being produced. It is convenient to scale units so that total employment generated by this output is equal to 1,

$$a_L^T X = 1 \qquad (12\text{-}25)$$

---

[4]The same conclusion applies by and large to recent extensions of the closed model by Adelman and Robinson and Lysy and Taylor. These make the vectors a_L, a_K, and a_0 of Eq. (12-10) price-sensitive in neoclassical fashion, include several classes of income recipients, and make their consumption price-responsive along the lines of Appendixes B and E. Both sets of authors find their model's income distribution quite insensitive to plausible policy interventions. Using ideas similar to those in Chap. 7, the cited paper by Taylor and Lysy explains why.

Also note that the N sectoral cost functions of Eq. (12-23) are homogeneous of degree 0 in the N prices P_i and the wage w; hence we need a numeraire. For example, we can set

$$P^T(I - A)X = 1 \tag{12-26}$$

so that the value of total final sales of output, or GDP, is also equal to 1. Substituting Eq. (12-24) for P^T into Eq. (12-26) and going through some manipulation gives a *wage-interest frontier*,

$$wa_L^T[I - r(I - A)^{-1}A]^{-1}X = 1 \tag{12-27}$$

which is highly nonlinear in w and r. We must find a simpler version of Eq. (12-27) to say something definite about the struggle between workers and capitalists over functional income shares.

To do this, it is convenient to view the income distribution from an extreme angle, specifically the situation in which wages are equal to 0. In this case, the price equation [Eq. (12-23)] becomes $P^T = (1 + r)P^T A$, or

$$P^T\left[\frac{1}{1+r}I - A\right] = 0 \tag{12-28}$$

There are N equations in the homogeneous system (12-28), one for each sector in the model. They suffice to determine $N - 1$ relative prices and the rate of interest r. The mathematical justification for this assertion is a well-known theorem attributed variously to Frobenius and Perron.[5]

If a solution with the nonzero prices of Eq. (12-28) is to exist, the bracketed matrix must be singular, i.e., have a 0 determinant. The Perron theorem asserts that when all elements of A are nonnegative and such that each sector requires inputs from every other sector (at least indirectly), then the polynomial equation in terms of $1/(1 + r)$ associated with the 0 determinant will have a positive root (*eigenvalue*) larger in magnitude than any other eigenvalue. The corresponding value of r is the maximum possible profit rate in the economy. The eigenvalue $1/(1 + r)$ has associated with it a positive *left eigenvector* P^T which determines the price system up to the imposition of a numeraire, e.g., Eq. (12-26). Call the profit rate and price vector satisfying Eqs. (12-26) and (12-28) $\bar{r}$ and $\bar{P}^T$, respectively.

The prices in the zero wage system obviously satisfy the equations

$$\bar{P}_i / \Sigma \bar{P}_j a_{ji} = 1 + \bar{r} \tag{12-29}$$

i.e., the ratio of price to working capital expenditures is the same in all sectors. Similarly, one might imagine an output vector $\bar{X}$ for which the ratio of total output to intermediate sales was equalized for all sectors,

$$\bar{X}_i / \Sigma a_{ij} \bar{X}_j = 1 + \bar{r}$$

---

[5] Appendix A in the book by Arrow and Hahn listed in the readings gives a useful review of the various forms of Perron's theorem. We use the variant they state as Theorem 3. The book by Schwartz also provides a readable and iconoclastic view of general equilibrium mathematics.

For such a vector, the surplus of final output over intermediate sales would be the same for each commodity. One could then go on to wonder how this surplus is being distributed, without bothering about interindustry complications.

The matrix version of the equation defining the $\overline{X}_i$ is

$$\left[\frac{1}{1+r} I - A\right] X = 0 \tag{12-30}$$

which is similar to Eq. (12-28) except that X is a *right eigenvector* of the matrix A, dual to the left eigenvector P^T of the previous equation. By the Perron theorem, the same $\overline{r}$ will satisfy Eqs. (12-28) and (12-30), and the corresponding output vector—or what Sraffa calls the *standard commodity*—will be positive. We can scale employment as before, so that

$$a_L^T \overline{X} = 1 \tag{12-31}$$

Having constructed the zero-wage price and output vectors, we can now ask about income distribution when the wage is positive. Evaluating the standard commodity in terms of the actual prices using Eq. (12-23) gives

$$GDP = 1 = P^T (I - A) \overline{X} = rP^T A\overline{X} + wa_L^T \overline{X} = rP^T A\overline{X} + w$$

where the normalization rules of Eqs. (12-26) and (12-31) are used. Rearrangement of these equalities gives

$$r = (1 - w)/P^T A\overline{X} \tag{12-32}$$

On the other hand, from the solution to Eq. (12-30), we have

$$A\overline{X} = (1/\overline{r})(I - A)\overline{X}$$

the proportionality between intermediate and final sales of the each component of the standard commodity mentioned before. Multiplication of this equation by P^T and use of Eq. (12-26) shows that

$$P^T A\overline{X} = (1/\overline{r}) P^T (I - A) \overline{X} = 1/\overline{r}$$

Substitution into Eq. (12-32) finally provides

$$r/\overline{r} = 1 - w \tag{12-33}$$

as the wage-interest frontier in the Sraffa economy. With our normalizations, the wage w also represents the labor share; Eq. (12-33) shows that the labor share rises as the profit rate falls from its maximum $\overline{r}$. As shown in Fig. 12-1, the trade-off between wages and profits is linear and reasonably clear. What Sraffa does not address are the social mechanisms which pick out the wage and profit rate along the Fig. 12-1 frontier. We will ignore this question also, except to note that it lies at the core of determining the distribution of income in all classical models.

As a last exercise with the Sraffa model, we can ask what the distributional implications of technical change are. From Eq. (12-22), it is clear that any fall in a labor-input coefficient a_{Li} will increase profits in sector i and will be adopted. More

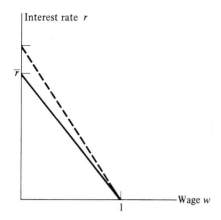

Figure 12-1 The wage-interest frontier in the Sraffa system.

complex are shifts in the interindustry coefficients a_{ij}. These will change relative prices, reducing profits in some industries and raising them in others. However, if the coefficient changes *increase* the maximum profit rate $\bar{r}$, then ultimately they will be accepted. Their impact is to shift up the wage-interest frontier as shown by the broken line in Fig. 12-1 and make a higher profit rate possible for a given wage.

How does one measure the effect of technical shifts on $\bar{r}$? The obvious measuring rod is the set of standard prices defined by Eq. (12-29). Suppose that a new technique vector $(\alpha_{1i}, \alpha_{2i}, \ldots, \alpha_{Ni})$ becomes available in sector i. Then if

$$\bar{P}_i > \sum_{j=1}^{N} \bar{P}_j \alpha_{ji} \tag{12-34}$$

the zero-wage profit rate in the sector can rise above its common value $\bar{r}$, and the new technique will be adopted. A new set of equilibrium prices will, of course, result, and the new $\bar{r}$ will be higher.

To summarize, the Sraffa prices $\bar{P}_i$ can be used as a device to select among possible techniques (or, loosely, investment projects) in the input-output model. If a new interindustry technology satisfies Eq. (12-34), it will be adopted. Pursuing the argument further, selection through Eq. (12-34) among a set of technologies for all sectors leads ultimately to highest possible $\bar{r}$ and a set of profit-maximizing techniques independent of the composition of final demand. This result is sometimes known as the *nonsubstitution theorem* in input-output analysis. A proof along the lines sketched here appears in the paper by Johansen cited in the readings.

12-5 THE DYNAMIC INPUT-OUTPUT MODEL

So far, we have been treating investment as a component of final demand but not as the means for accumulating capital and productive capacity. The dynamic Leontief model amounts to a formal recognition of the two-sided role of investment in growing economies, and we work out its characteristics here.

Let K_{ji} be the amount of the jth commodity used as a capital good in sector i and $b_{ji} = K_{ji}/X_i$ be the corresponding capital-output ratio. We will assume that the b_{ji} are constant in each using sector i; that is, there is no substitution among capital types. Also, for many producing sectors indexed by j, the b_{ji} will equal 0. In a realistic inter-industry classification, probably only about a third of the sectors will produce capital goods.

If the economy is working at full capacity, then any increment in production is going to have to be supported by new capital stocks in place next year (we work with discrete annual time periods for simplicity). That means the material balance equation for a sector producing capital goods must take the form

$$X_i(t) = \sum_{j=1}^{N} a_{ij} X_j(t) + \sum_{j=1}^{N} b_{ij}[X_j(t+1) - X_j(t)] + F_i(t) \qquad (12\text{-}35)$$

so that the sector's output must satisfy intermediate, capital accumulation, and other final demands on the right-hand side. The demands for new capital goods depend on the growth in each sector between this and next year; a degree of foresight missing in the static model is required for dynamic input-output planning.

If we let B represent the matrix of the b_{ij}, then Eq. (12-35) can be expressed in matrix notation as

$$X(t) = AX(t) + B[X(t+1) - X(t)] + F(t) \qquad (12\text{-}36)$$

which is a forward difference equation in $X(t)$. Working out formal solutions to Eq. (12-36) is a bit cumbersome, since B will usually have a number of 0 rows corresponding to sectors not producing capital goods, so that the N-variable equation system is not of full rank. Nevertheless, some key observations about the qualitative characteristics of solutions to Eq. (12-36) are readily available.

First, consider solutions to the *homogeneous equation* in which exogenous final demands $F(t)$ are set to 0. Since there is no consumption in the homogeneous system, it clearly describes the maximum growth possible in the economy; all surplus product is being invested. If all elements of the vector $X(t)$ settle down to grow at some constant rate g, then $X(t+1) - X(t) = gX(t)$, and Eq. (12-36) becomes

$$(I - A - gB) X(t) = 0 \qquad (12\text{-}37)$$

This is an equation suspiciously similar to the ones we met in the last section. A growth rate g satisfying Eq. (12-37) will exist if the determinant $|I - A - gB|$ vanishes, and there will typically be as many nonzero gs as there are nonzero rows in the matrix B.

How can these growth rates be characterized? If the determinant of Eq. (12-37) is rewritten as

$$|(1/g) I - B(I - A)^{-1}| = 0 \qquad (12\text{-}38)$$

then the Perron theorem applies, since all elements of $B(I - A)^{-1}$ are nonnegative.

There will be a positive growth rate $\bar{g}$ with a corresponding positive right eigenvector $\bar{X}$ at which steady growth is possible. We seem to have found our way home.

Unfortunately, things are not so simple. The balanced growth $\bar{g}$ corresponds to the *largest* $(1/g)$ solving Eq. (12-38). There are other eigenvalues satisfying this equation also, which may correspond to faster growth in Eq. (12-37) than $\bar{g}$. And with these other eigenvalues will be associated eigenvectors with *negative* components. For empirically plausible A and B matrices, the Leontief dynamic equation simulated forward in time from arbitrary initial outputs can soon produce negative production levels.

Practitioners have responded to this instability inherent in the dynamic model in several ways. One is to focus on characteristics of the steady growth path corresponding to $\bar{g}$, assuming that the economy is managed so as to stay on or near this trajectory in the long run. Some implications of long-term steady growth for the analysis of investment projects are taken up in the following section. Another approach is based on relaxing some of the equalities in the dynamic model into inequalities, to add more flexibility to the system.

An example of the second approach can be developed from the assumption that the capital coefficients b_{ij} are fixed, so that a sector's capacity CAP_i is determined by its available basket of capital goods, without possibility of substitution among them. Then if a vector of competitive imports M is allowed into the accounting, the dynamic model material balances can be written as the following inequalities:

$$X(t) + M(t) = AX(t) + B[CAP(t+1) - CAP(t)] + F(t) \tag{12-39}$$

$$X(t) \leqslant CAP(t) \tag{12-40}$$

$$M^T(t)[CAP(t) - X(t)] = 0 \tag{12-41}$$

In Eq. (12-39), investment demand is related to capacity increments, not output increments as in Eq. (12-36). The second equation says that each sector's production cannot exceed its capacity, and Eq. (12-41) shows that competitive imports into sector i will be positive only when its capacity is fully utilized, $CAP_i(t) - X_i(t) = 0$. Algorithms can easily be designed to solve Eqs. (12-39) through (12-41) for output levels and imports; see the paper by Clark and Taylor in the readings for details. The main practical problem with this sort of system is that it requires a "slack variable" M_i for each sector. For a sector i producing traded goods, M_i is (as above) interpreted as an import. But for a nontraded sector, a positive M_i has to be treated as a shortfall in capacity; if it is "too large," capacity forecasts throughout the system may have to be drastically revised!

Other extensions of the dynamic model through inequalities are possible—for example, the construction of large-scale linear programming planning models. It should be recalled, however, that the need for all these devices in planning follows from a prior decision to use the dynamic model, i.e., to keep track of investment as a source of capital accumulation as well as a component of final demand. Given the difficulty of collection and probable inaccuracy of an empirical B matrix, a dynamic planning model may, in practice, be a luxury that an undermanned planning office in charge of projections could easily forego for the next few years. This will be especially true if the country produces few capital goods. In that case, knowledge about foreign trade restrictions on investment will be far more important than any information that the dynamic input-output system can provide.

12-6 BALANCED GROWTH AND SRAFFA PRICES IN THE DYNAMIC SYSTEM

If the economy *does* have a substantial capital-goods sector, on the other hand, then the dynamic model has planning relevance in the long run. In this section, we work out some of its implications under the assumption that there is balanced growth; i.e., all sectors are expanding at the same rate $[X_i(t+1) - X_i(t)]/X_i(t)$. Balanced growth is an artifice which makes the mathematics of a multisectoral model tractable, but it ignores important aspects of reality, e.g., that, because of Engel's law, the demand for food is going to grow less rapidly than the demand for television sets.

Waiving this difficulty in the interests of making the analysis feasible at all, recall that if there is no exogenous final demand, balanced growth with a positive output vector $\bar{X}$ is possible at a rate $\bar{g}$ where $\bar{g}$ and $\bar{X}$ satisfy Eq. (12-37). There will also be a corresponding set of prices P^{-T} determined by

$$\bar{P}^T(I - A - \bar{g}B) = 0 \tag{12-42}$$

Note that for each sector i this equation can be rewritten as

$$\frac{\sum_{j=1}^{N} \bar{P}_j b_{ji}}{\bar{P}_i - \sum_{j=1}^{N} \bar{P}_j a_{ji}} = \frac{1}{\bar{g}} \tag{12-43}$$

The numerator here is just the value of capital per unit output in the sector at the prices $\bar{P}_j$, while the denominator is value added per unit of X_i. What Eq. (12-43) says is that the ratio of capital to value added is the same for all sectors when it is calculated with the $\bar{P}_j$. We can call these *Sraffa prices* by analogy to Eq. (12-29) of the model Sraffa proposed.

For any output vector X, let its value in Sraffa prices be $X^* = \hat{\bar{P}}X$, where the "hat" over $\bar{P}$ means that its elements are written along the main diagonal of a matrix otherwise equal to 0. Similarly, we can revalue the technology matrices as $A^* = \hat{\bar{P}}A\hat{\bar{P}}^{-1}$ and $B^* = \hat{\bar{P}}B\hat{\bar{P}}^{-1}$.

Now assume that in the real economy there is some final demand vector F growing at a rate h. Then, by direct substitution into Eq. (12-36), one finds that output levels are determined by

$$X(t) = (I - A - hB)^{-1}F(t) \tag{12-44}$$

in which the matrix $(I - A - hB)$ can be inverted as long as h is smaller than $\bar{g}$.

For the economy growing at rate h, we want to figure out its aggregate saving rate and capital-output ratio at Sraffa prices. Let $Z^T = [1, 1, \ldots, 1]$ be the summing vector, and define the savings rate s to be

$$s = \frac{\text{output net of intermediate sales} - \text{consumption}}{\text{output net of intermediate sales}}$$

$$= \frac{Z^T(I - A^*) X^* - Z^T F^*}{Z^T(I - A^*)X^*} = \frac{\bar{P}^T(I - A) X - \bar{P}^T F}{\bar{P}^T(I - A)X} \qquad (12\text{-}45)$$

where X and F come from Eq. (12-44).

Similarly, the aggregate capital-output ratio k will be given by

$$k = \frac{\text{total capital required for output}}{\text{output net of intermediate sales}}$$

$$= \frac{Z^T B^* X^*}{Z^T(I - A^*)X^*} = \frac{\bar{P}^T BX}{\bar{P}^T(I - A)X} = 1/\bar{g} \qquad (12\text{-}46)$$

where the last equality follows from Eq. (12-43).

Finally, along the steady growth path, we will observe

$$Z^T(I - A^*) X^* - Z^T F^* = hZ^T B^* X^*$$

or

$$\bar{P}^T(I - A) X - \bar{P}^T F = h\bar{P}^T BX \qquad (12\text{-}47)$$

so that savings equals investment.

From the foregoing equations, it is easy to show that

$$s = hk = h/\bar{g} \qquad (12\text{-}48)$$

This, of course, is just our old friend the Harrod-Domar equation, showing that the rate of growth is equal to the rate of saving divided by the capital-output ratio. Even in a multisectoral economy, the rate of growth depends ultimately on how much surplus can be devoted to capital formation. The importance of Sraffa prices is that they make the measurement of available surplus possible.

The final question that arises is what sort of technical change of the production coefficients in sector i might increase the growth rate (or reduce required saving for a given growth rate) in the dynamic system. By now the answer should be clear: if the technical advance reduces the ratio on the left side of Eq. (12-43), then the capital-output ratio in sector i will fall and a higher intrinsic growth rate $\bar{g}$ is possible. As in the simpler model of Sec. 12-4, Sraffa prices provide a natural basis for evaluating projects which change technical coefficients as well.

The analysis of this section is due to Leif Johansen, who followed the lead of a number of Eastern European economists in working it out. It can be extended to include consideration of the labor income-consumption linkage as in Sec. 12-3 and can incorporate foreign trade by the device of treating an export of one good as a means to "produce" another through purchases abroad. In all cases, the approach is probably most appropriate to long-range planning in a socialist economy. The under-developed countries are not at that stage yet, but many of their leaders say that is where they want to be.

SELECTED ADDITIONAL READINGS

Adelman, Irma, and Sherman Robinson: *Income Distribution Policies in Developing Countries: A Case Study of Korea*, Stanford University Press, Stanford, Calif., 1977. (Price-sensitive, closed input-output income distribution model.)

Arrow, Kenneth J., and Frank H. Hahn: *General Competitive Analysis*, Holden-Day, San Francisco, 1971. (The definitive work in the field of general equilibrium analysis. Useful reference on the mathematics in this chapter.)

Bacha, Edmar L., Dionisio D. Carneiro, and Lance Taylor: "Sraffa y la Economia Clasica: Relaciones de Equilibrio Fundamentales," *El Trimestre Economico* **44**:53–72, 1977. (Further development of the material in Sec. 12-4.)

Blitzer, Charles R., Peter B. Clark, and Lance Taylor: *Economy-Wide Models and Development Planning*, Oxford University Press, New York and London, 1975. (Many of the chapters are relevant to the material here, especially those by Bruno on investment project analysis, Clark on input-output calculations, and Srinivasan on planning models for foreign trade.)

Bruno, Michael: "The Optimal Selection of Import-Substituting and Export-Promoting Projects," in *Planning the External Sector: Techniques, Problems and Policies*, United Nations, New York, 1967 (ST/TAO/SER. C/91). (A classic paper on its topic; introduces the domestic resource cost criterion.)

Chenery, Hollis B., and Paul G. Clark: *Interindustry Economics*, Wiley, New York, 1959. (Useful, relevant textbook.)

Clark, Peter B., and Lance Taylor: "Dynamic Input-Output Planning with Optimal End Conditions: The Case of Chile," *Economics of Planning*, **11**:10–30, 1971. [Details of the model in Eqs. (12-39) through (12-41).]

Cline, William R.: *Potential Effects of Income Redistribution on Economic Growth: Latin American Cases*, Praeger, New York, 1972. (An early income distribution calculation of the type described in Sec. 12-3.)

India, Government of, Planning Commission: *A Technical Note on the Approach to the Fifth Five-Year Plan of India*, New Delhi, 1973. (Income distribution exercises in an input-output model.)

Johansen, Leif: "The Rate of Growth in Dynamic Input-Output Models: Some Observations along Lines Suggested by O. Lange and A. Brody," in *Jahrbuch der Wirtschaft Osteuropas*, Gunter Olzog Verlag, Munich and Vienna, 1973. (Original presentation of the analysis in Sec. 12-6.)

Kravis, Irving B., and Robert E. Lipsey: "Export Prices and the Transmission of Inflation," *American Economic Review* (Papers and Proceedings), **67**(1):155–163. [Skeptical look at economics of Eq. (12-13).]

Lysy, Frank J., and Lance Taylor: "A Computable General Equilibrium Model for the Functional Income Distribution: Experiments for Brazil, 1959–71," Development Research Center, World Bank, Washington, D.C., 1977. (A price-sensitive closed Leontief model of a highly disaggregated functional income distribution.)

Manne, Alan S.: "Multi-Sectoral Models of Development Planning: A Survey," *Journal of Development Economics*, **1**:43–69, 1974. (Excellent coverage of the field.)

Schwartz, Jacob T.: *Lectures on the Mathematical Method in Analytical Economics*, Gordon and Breach, New York, 1961. (Quizzical presentation of the mathematics of this chapter and other matters by an eminent mathematician.)

Sraffa, Piero: *Production of Commodities by Means of Commodities*, Cambridge University Press, Cambridge, England, 1960. (Elegant verbal analysis of the economics of the model of Sec. 12-4.)

The Case of Chile," *Economics of Planning*, 11:10–30, 1971. [Details of the model in Eq

Srinivasan, T. N., and Jagdish N. Bhagwati: "Shadow Prices for Project Selection in the Presence of Distortions: Effective Rates of Protection and Domestic Resource Costs," *Journal of Political Economy*, **86**:97–116, 1978. (Useful theoretical review of the material.)

Taylor, Lance, and Frank J. Lysy: "Vanishing Income Redistributions: Keynesian Clues about Model Surprises in the Short Run," *Journal of Development Economics* (to appear). (Gives a one-sector condensation of models like those of Adelman and Robinson and Lysy and Taylor cited above and shows in it why their predictions of income distribution shifts in response to policy changes are likely to be small and erratic.)

Watanabe, Tsunehiko, and Shuntaro Shishido: "Planning Applications of the Leontief Model in Japan," in A. Carter, and A. Brody (eds.): *Applications of Input-Output Analysis*, North-Holland, Amsterdam, 1970. [Empirical application of Eq. (12-10).]

THIRTEEN

SHADOW PRICES AND INVESTMENT PROJECT EVALUATION

As already noted, cost-benefit analysis using shadow prices is usually far from the most important element entering the decision about whether an investment project should be undertaken. Nor is it obvious that it should be; shadow prices are based on a particular economic logic which may be largely alien to the political economy (let alone the politics!) of capital accumulation in a poor country. What shadow prices say is that if you run your economy in a Pareto optimal way subject to one or two obvious "distortions" and do not worry too much about income distribution, then certain types of investment look better than others. In a Lewis-style economy, for example, labor-intensive projects are favored; if foreign exchange is short, then export promotion looks good.

Such observations are useful in their place, but they ignore much of the reality of industrial planning—inadequate or downright dishonest technical consultants' reports, short-term considerations about which capital-goods supplier is giving better credits between this year and next, biases resulting from visions of national grandeur or regional growth through big, visibly expensive factory edifices, your political superior's concern about getting as much construction going as possible in an election year (it is always an election year). Even on the first topic, setting the consultants' demand projections right is likely to be much more relevant to an economically rational decision about a project than are the most exquisite of shadow price evaluations.

Despite all these well-known causes for their irrelevance, shadow prices have been the subject of enormous professional interest for the last dozen or more years. One reason, of course, is that they are beautiful analytically, emerging like Venus from the waves of innumerable optimal planning calculations. Probably nine-tenths of the theorists' interest is due to just this—certainly many of them have never looked a real investment project in the face.

196

But even if the esthetics and the politics are discounted, some residual basis for shadow price calculations remains. In a Lewis-style economy, it *does* make sense to try to employ a lot of labor. If planners tend to favor investments of that kind, then maybe some few underemployed workers and their families will be better off. There is really no need for fancy calculus to make the point, but since many economists do not see the evidence in front of their faces until it is seasoned with differential equations and their integrals, perhaps the manipulations are worthwhile. Therefore the purpose of this chapter and also of Appendix G is to lay out the formal logic of shadow price calculation in such a way that those who want to can take it up and apply it to what they see as the big distortions in their own economies.

The discussion begins in Sec. 13-1 with a recitation of the problems regarding choice of technique and other aspects of investment projects that planners actually face. Project analysis as usually applied can deal only with a subset of these— principally, capital-labor substitution and the foreign-exchange costs involved in the project. Its other characteristics—such as the "appropriateness" of its technology or products, economies of scale, rural-urban and regional implications, and so on—are dealt with scarcely at all by the standard methods.

After this introduction, we turn to the problems that project analysis and shadow prices handle relatively well, beginning with capital-labor substitution in a Lewis-style model in Sec. 13-2 (with a parallel, much more formal discussion in Appendix G). How to calculate shadow prices of foreign exchange and how to use them are discussed respectively in Secs. 13-3 and 13-4. Section 13-5 contains a brief sketch of the problems that economies of scale pose for project evaluation, and Sec. 13-6 closes the chapter with a few additional observations about the usefulness of project evaluation techniques in practice.

13-1 THE CHARACTERISTICS OF INVESTMENT PROJECTS

An "investment project" as conceived by economists involves expenditure on a set of capital goods that will be put together (in a factory, road, or dam, for example) and later combined with labor and intermediate inputs to provide an expected stream of

Table 13-1 Characteristics of investment projects and how well project analysis deals with them

Characteristic	Success
Capital-labor substitution	Good
Foreign-exchange content	Good
Increasing returns to scale	Fair
Appropriateness of product and/or technology	Poor
Operating characteristics	Poor
Rural-urban and regional effects	Poor to fair
Income distribution effects	Poor to fair
Linkage effects	Poor
X efficiency	Poor

products. "Project analysis" is based on associating a set of prices with the inputs and outputs of the project and calculating whether the value of outputs (or "benefits") over time exceeds the value of inputs (or "costs"). If so, the project is profitable and presumably should be undertaken. The evaluation can be made with prevailing and expected future market prices (if one can find out what they are) or else with shadow prices specified by planners. The results of these two computations may differ; some of the problems that arise when this occurs are taken up in Sec. 13-6, below.

As pointed out in an illuminating book by Frances Stewart (see the Selected Additional Readings), an investment project has a wide range of characteristics—its technology as embodied in its capital inputs, the exact type of product it produces, whether or not its technology type has increasing returns to scale, how easily its capital goods can be maintained, and so on. A list of such characteristics appears in Table 13-1, along with an informal assessment of how successfully project analysis can decide whether or not they are desirable in given circumstances.

Capital-Labor Substitution

As will become clear in the following sections, project analysis methodology is heavily infected with orthodox economic notions about substitution possibilities and efficiency in production. For precisely this reason, one would expect it to be able to deal fairly effectively with the problem of selecting projects with desirable capital-output and labor-output ratios *if* some possibility of selection exists at all.

At the micro level, it appears that capital-labor substitution possibilities are greater in some lines of output than others. Moreover, when choice of technique exists, it often comes associated with other characteristics of the technology. For example, labor-intensive processes may give rise to products with wide variations in such standards as the thickness of the tin coating on cans, the strength of cement blocks, the weight of a loaf of bread of given size, and so on. Sometimes such product characteristics are important, sometimes not. If not, project evaluations based on shadow prices that favor (say) labor-intensive techniques may be worthwhile undertaking in a poor economy. They can help overcome strong, only partially conscious biases of engineers and bureaucrats toward capital-intensity and large size. How one goes about calculating a rough set of shadow prices for this purpose at the *macro* level is the topic of Sec. 13-2.

Foreign-Exchange Content

Roughly similar observations apply to the intensity of imported inputs (whether capital goods or intermediates) in a project. Using a high shadow price of foreign exchange will penalize projects intensive in imported inputs; it will favor import-substituting and export investments. Whether or not much technical substitutability exists is another question; but if it does, project analysis may help guide choice of technique in the right direction.

Economies of Scale

Many industrial processes enjoy economies of scale or (nearly the same thing) decreasing costs. A cement plant with twice the capacity of a second one, for example, will cost less than twice as much to construct. One physical reason for decreasing costs is the fact that the surface area (and the amount of material) of a vessel increases less rapidly than its volume. Many chemical and metallurgical technologies involve processing and storage of materials in vessels, and construction costs increase less than proportionally to the volume processed and stored. Various other fixed costs may be "spread" over a large production flow in a big plant, with reductions in per-unit costs. The general rule is that total costs have a constant elasticity of about 0.6 or 0.7 with respect to plant size, which marks a substantial economy. A cost curve of this form is sketched in Fig. 13-3, below.

Project analysis techniques deal with economies of scale inadequately if at all. The usual methodology is based on marginal economics, with the project being treated as a small perturbation to a preexisting equilibrium. But as discussed more fully in Sec. 13-5, a project with significant scale economies is anything but marginal; it may have very great effects on the price system and resource allocation. Trying to take these effects into account in deciding whether or not to undertake the project is a difficult business, since it presupposes accurate knowledge about noninfinitesimal economywide responses and a great deal of calculation. Appropriate techniques and approximations for this purpose are discussed in Sec. 13-5, but it should be recognized that they are not always successful. Project analysis deserves a barely passing grade at best in dealing with economies of scale.

Appropriate Products and Operating Characteristics

Most underdeveloped countries import technology. As importers, they have very little control over how well these products and technologies will fit into the local milieu.

For example, a technology which is built into a given investment project imposes certain standards on its products, and these may be entirely too strict for a poor country; food products may be designed to fit (or even require) elaborate packaging, motor vehicles may work better with hard-to-repair radial tires, construction materials may have been made strong enough to support multistory structures even in countries where such buildings are rare. In an analogous manner on the input side, advanced-country techniques often presuppose highly skilled production workers and access to a selection of spare parts and components far wider than a poor economy is likely to offer.

To judge whether or not product and operating characteristics of a project's technology are "appropriate" to a given country is a difficult problem, requiring both value judgments and a good intuitive understanding of both the technology and country concerned. Needless to say, mechanical cost-benefit calculation sheds little light on these project characteristics. Yet they may be among the most important in determining whether an investment will be a failure or success.

Regional and Income Distribution Effects

Investment projects have both immediate and long-run effects on regions and different economic classes. The immediate effects stem from the payment and product flows associated with the project and, in principle, are fairly easy to trace. "Welfare weights" such as a low shadow wage can be used in the formal evaluation to raise the calculated benefits of projects that seem to help certain groups. The selection procedure is tilted to favor "socially desirable" investments by use of the weights.

Such artifices are all right as far as they go, but unfortunately they ignore "second-generation" impacts of the project. For example, suppose that investment in land reclamation generated additional jobs for landless laborers in some region. Such a project would tend to be favored in most "social" cost-benefit evaluations and could be adopted. Suppose, however, that it subsequently increased profit flows of landowners so that they could mechanize agriculture to a much greater extent than previously; the mechanization could throw more people out of work than the number of jobs initially created. Such a secondary impact would be hard to predict and even harder to evaluate in the standard methodology; yet *if* it occurred, it could be the most important result of the project. An intuitive assessment of its likelihood would again be the key to a worthwhile evaluation.

Linkage Effects and X Efficiency

Much the same observation applies to impacts of projects classified under these two headings. The linkage idea was popularized by Albert Hirschman in the development economics literature, though it goes back at least to the eighteenth-century French physiocrats. In Hirschman's terminology, a project putting a new product on the market may create "forward linkages" by encouraging entrepreneurs to set up production processes to use it. For example, investment in the production of chemical products which are intermediate inputs into many commodities is sometimes alleged to create forward linkages. "Backward linkages" are derived demands. If a new factory uses inputs that would otherwise be imported, local entrepreneurs might be stimulated to produce them. The notion of X efficiency (due to Harvey Leibenstein) involves entrepreneurship combined with technology; that is, some types of projects in a certain economy may be operated closer to their technically efficient levels than others. As with linkages, the criteria by which one could forecast whether or not an investment will be operated well are extremely obscure. Their use in formal evaluations is impossible.

To summarize the discussion of this section, any investment project has characteristics that can only be described by many adjectives or in many dimensions. Cost-benefit analysis operates in only a few of these dimensions and is not fully satisfactory even there. Within its limitations, it *can* shed light on some aspects of investment projects, but it scarcely provides a basis for definite decisions. Just how much light it provides depends on the realism of the assumptions underlying shadow price calculations, which is the topic we take up next.

13-2 SHADOW DISCOUNT RATE AND SHADOW WAGE

Most shadow price calculations in a poor economy are based on a streamlined version of the surplus labor model described in Chaps. 10 and 11. The analysis focuses only on the modern or industrial sector, and it is usually assumed that labor is in completely elastic supply at some fixed wage w. As discussed more fully in Chap. 11, this assumption presupposes that the terms of trade between the industrial and agricultural sectors are fixed by international trade or some other intervention, else different demand patterns for the two aggregate products could make their relative price and the wage's purchasing power shift.

The modern-sector material balance equation takes the form

$$X(K,L) = C + I \qquad (13\text{-}1)$$

in which X is the output level depending on employed capital K and labor L; output is used to satisfy demands for consumption goods C and capital formation I. It is usually assumed that modern-sector workers consume only commodities produced there and do not save. If all profit incomes are invested, then consumption is given by

$$C = wL \qquad (13\text{-}2)$$

The rate of growth of the capital stock becomes

$$I = dK/dt = X - wL \qquad (13\text{-}3)$$

In this sort of model, a shadow wage rate can be used to indicate socially desirable levels of employment in the short run (when the capital stock is fixed); together with the wage, the shadow rate of discount guides capital accumulation over time. We begin by discussing the employment problem, under the assumption that at least at the macro level there are capital-labor substitution possibilities that can be described by a neoclassical production function of the kind discussed in Appendix D.

Figure 13-1 illustrates the short-run constraints that planners face. The surplus of production over the consumption level required by Eq. (13-2) is the distance between the production function $X(K, L)$ and the wage bill wL along some vertical line corresponding to the level of employment. Evidently, modern-sector employment cannot be expanded beyond $\bar{L}$, for all output is being consumed at that point and additional production would be infeasible (as long as installed capital stock cannot be "eaten").

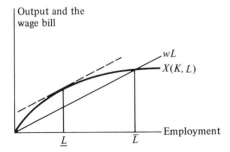

Output and the wage bill

wL

$X(K, L)$

Employment

$\underline{L}$ $\bar{L}$

Figure 13-1 Constraint set in the surplus-labor model.

As employment falls below $\bar{L}$, the investable surplus $X(K, L) - wL$ rises from 0 and finally reaches its maximum at $\underline{L}$, where the slope of the short-run production function equals w (i.e., the marginal product of labor rises to the institutionally fixed wage). A utility-maximizing government would never employ fewer than $\underline{L}$ workers in the modern sector, for this would reduce both total consumption and the investable surplus.

The government will end up employing some number of workers between $\underline{L}$ and $\bar{L}$, depending on the relative valuations it places on investment and consumption in the urban area. If consumption is not valued at all by planners, then they will employ $\underline{L}$ workers and maximize surplus; that is essentially the Galenson-Leibenstein investment criterion, proposed by those authors in the 1950s. The polar alternative of maximizing current consumption at $\bar{L}$ is sometimes associated with "social marginal productivity" theories of shadow pricing which appeared at the same time.[1] In any case, the government is supposed to arrive at its chosen employment point by dictating choice of technique. Alternatively, technique can be affected by employment subsidies to reduce the wage seen by entrepreneurs below w, so that they will increase employment above $\underline{L}$ to drive labor's marginal product down to the level of the subsidized wage. The source of the subsidy is left unspecified; presumably it must come from lump-sum taxes or foreign aid.

The choice of where to end up between $\underline{L}$ and $\bar{L}$ really depends on the relative weights that the government places on investment for the future and workers' consumption now. Presumably, an additional small increment in consumption would generate marginal utility U_C for the lucky person who received it. On the investment side, assume that there is a social valuation p (described in more detail shortly) placed on additional capital formation.

Now suppose that the government is trying to decide whether or not to hire an additional worker in some year t. His consumption will go up (presumably from 0) by the amount of the wage w—the utility benefit in year t will be $U_C(t)w$. If for safety's sake the government applies a pure time discount factor δ for benefits in the future (0.05 seems to be a widely used number) then *current* benefits will be $e^{-\delta t}U_C(t)w$. On the other hand, investable surplus will decrease by the quantity $w - X_L$, that is, the wage the new worker is paid less his marginal product X_L. In value terms, the loss in surplus will be $p(t)(w - X_L)$. At the margin, the government will presumably equate costs and benefits

$$p(t)(w - X_L) = e^{-\delta t}U_C(t)w \qquad (13\text{-}4)$$

for its hiring decision. This criterion was perhaps first suggested by Stephen Marglin. Note that it implies that the current ($t = 0$) value of additional investment in terms of consumption utility, p/U_C, is greater than 1. This is a consequence of hiring workers beyond the employment level $\underline{L}$, where $w = X_L$.

---

[1] Both sets of 1950s theories can be subsumed by the models developed here or in Appendix G. Galenson and Leibenstein set labor's marginal product to the wage to maximize surplus, as in Fig. 13-1. Social marginal productivity theorists (e.g., Chenery and Kahn) recommended equal social valuations on consumption and investment, probably because they thought in terms of something like the Ramsey model of Secs. G-2 and G-3 and ignored the surplus labor restriction of Eq. (13-2).

To interpret p, consider a capitalist or bureaucrat holding a quantity of the single product produced in the modern sector of the economy. Its current value is equal to p. If the person uses this stored product as productive capital for a short time period τ, the return will be equal to $X_K \tau$, where X_K is the marginal product of capital. On the other hand, if the asset is merely held, the incurred interest cost can be measured by the relative change in its price, $[p(t) - p(t+\tau)]/p(t)$. If we assume that costs and benefits are equated and let the time interval τ approach 0, then we get the rule

$$-(dp/dt)/p = -p' = X_K$$

to determine the change in the asset price in a competitive (or "optimally" run) economy in which people weigh gains and losses from manipulating assets over time. If for simplicity we assume that the marginal product X_K stays constant and that the price of capital at some initial time t_0 is $p(t_0)$, then this equation implies that $p(t)$ in the future will be given by

$$p(t) = p(t_0) \exp\left[-X_K(t - t_0)\right] \tag{13-5}$$

where exp stands for the exponential function.

There remains one last definitional matter to be taken care of before we can derive shadow wage and discount rates. This has to do with the rate at which discounted marginal utility decreases over time. If we define $\tilde{U}_C$ as $e^{-\delta t} U_C$ from Eq. (13-4), then

$$i = \tilde{U}'_C = -(jC' + \delta)$$

Here, C' is the rate of growth of consumption: as the consumption level rises, the marginal utility it provides drops off according to an elasticity j which might take a value around 1 or 2. When the pure time discount rate δ is added, one arrives at what is usually called the social rate of discount i. If i stays roughly constant over time, then—by analogy to Eq. (13-5)—one can write future values of $\tilde{U}_C$ as

$$\tilde{U}_C(t) = \tilde{U}_C(t_0) \exp\left[-i(t - t_0)\right] \tag{13-6}$$

where $\tilde{U}_C(t_0)$ is the initial value of $\tilde{U}_C$. With the illustrative values of j and δ mentioned above and a plausible growth rate for consumption, i will be around 0.1 or so—noticeably smaller than the marginal product of capital X_K in Eq. (13-5). On the basis of balance-sheet data or macro considerations as in Chap. 6, X_K might take a value ranging upward from 0.15 or 0.2 in a poor economy.

In the sort of model considered here, an investment project is viewed as a perturbation to a preexisting economic equilibrium. That is, we suppose that the economy is being operated according to the rules of Eqs. (13-1) through (13-5) and then ask what would happen if a new project with employment time flows $\Delta L(t)$ and product time flows $\Delta X(t)$ were to be undertaken.[2] From the allocation rule of Eq. (13-4), the net benefits at any time can be written as

$$B(t) = \tilde{U}_C(t)\, w\Delta L(t) + p(t)[\Delta X(t) - w\Delta L(t)]$$

---

[2] Typically, $\Delta X(t)$ would be negative in the first years of the project, as product is diverted from other uses to be invested; after the investment phase, ΔX would be positive. There would also be variations of ΔL over time, corresponding to the project's construction and operational phases.

in which we recall that $\tilde{U}_C$ stands for $e^{-\delta t}U_C$. Benefits are thus the discounted consumption utility from the employment generated by the project plus the value of the investable surplus at time t.

If the project's expected life is from time t_0 to t_f, then its total benefits are

$$\int_{t_0}^{t_f} B(t)\,dt = \int_{t_0}^{t_f} [\tilde{U}_C w\Delta L + p(\Delta X - w\Delta L)]\,dt \tag{13-7}$$

The project should be undertaken if this integral is positive.

Now we want to put this criterion in more tractable form. Note first that if all terms under the integral are divided by $\tilde{U}_C$ and the definition of Eq. (13-6) is applied, then Eq. (13-7) will be proportional to

$$\int_{t_0}^{t_f} \exp\,[-i(t - t_0)]\,\{(p/\tilde{U}_C)\,\Delta X - [(p/\tilde{U}_C) - 1]\,w\Delta L\}\,dt \tag{13-8}$$

The criterion of Eq. (13-8) is essentially the same as one proposed by the United Nations Industrial Development Organization (UNIDO) in a book actually written by Partha Dasgupta, Stephen Marglin, and Amartya Sen. Note that it has three characteristics:

1. Net current benefits in the expression in braces under the integral in Eq. (13-8) are discounted at the social rate of discount i. We have already noted that this might be expected to take on a value around 0.1 or less.
2. On the other hand, project net output $X(t)$ is valued with a shadow price $p/\tilde{U}_C$, which, from Eq. (13-4), will exceed 1.
3. The shadow wage rate multiplying the project's employment flows is $[(p/\tilde{U}_C) - 1]\,w$, which can either exceed or fall short of the market wage w depending on the magnitude of $p/\tilde{U}_C$. In any case, the price of output is blown up from its market value of unity by a bigger factor than is the wage from its value of w.

The UNIDO rule of Eq. (13-8) was derived by dividing through Eq. (13-7) by marginal utility $\tilde{U}_C$ and applying the corresponding discount factor i. Alternatively, one could divide through by p and apply Eq. (13-5). The resulting criterion is

$$\int_{t_0}^{t_f} \exp\,[-X_K(t - t_0)]\,\{\Delta X - [1 - (\tilde{U}_C/p)]\,w\Delta L\}\,dt \tag{13-9}$$

which was originally proposed by Ian Little and James Mirrlees. According to Eq. (13-9),

1. The discount rate is the marginal product of capital X_K, with a value perhaps ranging between 15 and 30 percent. Discounting takes place at a much steeper rate in the Little-Mirrlees than in the UNIDO criterion.
2. Output is given a shadow valuation of unity, subject to some foreign exchange complications discussed next section.
3. The shadow wage is $[1 - (\tilde{U}_C/p)]\,w$, less than the market wage.

Since both are based on the same surplus labor assumptions, the two decision rules of Eqs. (13-8) and (13-9) are fundamentally the same, differing only in choice of numeraire. The numeraire commodity in the UNIDO rule is consumption in the base period, while investment is chosen by Little and Mirrlees.

The main problems one encounters in trying to apply either rule empirically are (1) valuation of specific commodities and (2) calculation of the ratio $p/\tilde{U}_C$ or its inverse for use in Eq. (13-8) or (13-9). We defer this and similar problems to Appendix G and content ourselves with one last observation. This stems from the fact that when all is said and done, the only things provided by either the Little-Mirrlees or the UNIDO criteria are guesses at a wage rate for unskilled labor and a discount rate that can be used to weigh costs and benefits of an investment project over time. And both these guesses are based on extensive manipulation in a *very* simple model. If the model is empirically inapplicable, then so are the shadow prices that come from it. If a more complicated model were required to summarize the interactions of the industrial sector with the rest of the economy adequately, then its implied shadow price computations would be even more arduous than the ones just described. One of the first lessons a good practitioner of applied economics learns is that long chains of reasoning even in simple models give rise to conclusions that, in practical terms, are very often suspect. The sensible planner will not look upon the results of project evaluations based on shadow prices as clear and unambiguous guides to economic decisions. Too much ratiocination is required to get the prices, and too much common sense may be left out.

13-3 THE SHADOW PRICE OF FOREIGN EXCHANGE

The distinction between goods and services traded (tradable) and nontraded (nontradable) in foreign commerce is key to an analytical approach to many problems in economic development—witness, for example, the devaluation model of Chap. 4. In the context of investment project analysis, it pays to approach this vital dichotomy in two stages. In this section, we take up two different ways of estimating a shadow price of foreign exchange; these have been proposed in a well-defined model with three goods: nontraded, exports, and imports.[3] Then in the following section we discuss how these ideas are applied in a messy real world where, among other things, policy choices about whether a country will in fact pay attention to international commerce in a certain commodity are likely to be quite important.

To look at the analytical basis of foreign-exchange shadow prices, we assume a static economy. This is appropriate to the problem, since hard-to-formalize infant-industry and "learning" phenomena aside, most foreign bottlenecks are not intrinsically dynamic and do not require the optimal growth apparatus used to get shadow discount rates. There are three goods, with material balances given by

$$X_H = C_H \tag{13-10}$$

$$X_E = C_E + E \tag{13-11}$$

[3] The model is due to Rudiger Dornbusch. It elegantly synthesizes an extensive previous literature, summarized, for example, by Bacha and Taylor.

and

$$X_M + M = C_M \tag{13-12}$$

The subscripts are H for the nontraded home good, E for the export good, and M for the import good. Production levels are X_i, consumption levels are C_i, and E and M, respectively, denote volumes of the two commodities that are traded.

We set the price of the home good equal to 1 as the numeraire and assume that prices of the traded goods are determined by the familiar equations

$$P_E = eP_E^* \tag{13-13}$$

and

$$P_M = e(1 + t) P_M^* \tag{13-14}$$

in which world prices are marked by asterisks and there is a tariff t on imports, reflecting the general bias in developing countries to give more protection to import-substituting than to export industries. In the project literature, a variable like e in these equations is usually called the "exchange rate," though this title is overly grand. In the present model, e is no more than a relative price between traded and nontraded goods. We are going to ask how it is affected by the tariff t, and in the answer will lie most proposals for the "shadow price of foreign exchange," or shadow relative price of traded and nontraded goods.

Assume that proceeds from the tariff are distributed back in a lump-sum fashion into personal income, as are capital inflows and foreign aid (initially equal to 0). Then total income Y in the economy is given by

$$Y = X_H + P_E X_E + P_M X_M + etP_M^* M + eF \tag{13-15}$$

where F is exogenous inflow of foreign exchange. Sweeping all Keynesian problems under the rug, assume that income equals expenditure on consumption goods, so that

$$Y = C_H + P_E C_E + P_M C_M \tag{13-16}$$

Eliminating Y between these two equations and some simplification gives

$$D_H = C_H - X_H = e [P_E^* E + F - P_M^* M]$$

where D_H is the excess demand for home goods. The home goods material balance of Eq. (13-10) and the balance of payments

$$P_E^* E + F = P_M^* M \tag{13-17}$$

are alternative conditions for macro equilibrium in the model.

Now assume that volumes traded in the economy depend *only* on own prices (measured relative to the price of home goods):

$$E' = \theta_E P_E' = \theta_E e' \tag{13-18}$$

and

$$M' = \theta_M P_M' = \theta_M \left(e' + \frac{t}{1 + t} t' \right) \tag{13-19}$$

where θ_E (positive) and θ_M (negative) are the relevant elasticities. This special case rules out all cross-price effects, whether in production or in demand for exports and imports, and further implies that all increases in income go for consumption of the home good. For these reasons, most foreign-exchange shadow price calculations have a strong partial equilibrium flavor.

To solve the model under assumptions of Eqs. (13-18) and (13-19), it is simplest to differentiate the balance of payments and insert these two equations. If F is initially 0, one finds that

$$e' = \frac{1}{\theta_E - \theta_M} \left[\theta_M \frac{1}{1+t} t' - \frac{1}{P_M^* M} dF \right] \tag{13-20}$$

Consider first the effect of a tariff change. From Eq. (13-20), the elasticity of the exchange rate e with respect to the import tariff t lies between 0 and -1. The economic reason is that a tariff increase will, with constant e, reduce imports from Eq. (13-19). But then the balance of payments will go into surplus and there will be positive excess demand for home goods. To restore equilibrium, the price of home goods must rise relative to the traded goods or e must fall. The fact that there is adjustment in all markets implies that the elasticity of e with respect to the tariff lies between 0 and -1.

Now suppose that a preexisting tariff is reduced or removed altogether to bring internal relative prices of imports and exports nearer the world price ratio P_M^*/P_E^*. Then e will rise or the price of home goods relative to the traded goods will fall. The downward revision of home goods prices (which should occur when traded goods are valued at world prices) is one proposed method for calculating the shadow price of foreign exchange. The result can be called the *free-trade exchange rate*, e^F. As we will see below, one reading of the Little-Mirrlees project evaluation proposals is to value traded goods at world prices and home goods at a *conversion factor* proportional to $1/e^F$. Naturally, e/e^F is less than 1, or home goods are marked down from their value in terms of world prices at the current exchange rate.

An alternative, utility-based shadow price is preferred by the authors of the UNIDO manual. To derive it, we introduce a social-utility function

$$U = U(C_H, C_E, C_M) = U(X_H, X_E - E, X_M + M) \tag{13-21}$$

which everybody in the economy is supposed to share. If they behave according to the usual utility-maximizing rules, consumers' demand equilibrium will be determined by the equations

$$U_H = \lambda$$

$$U_E = \lambda P_E$$

and

$$U_M = \lambda P_M$$

where subscripts indicate partial derivatives of the utility function and λ is the usual Lagrange multiplier on the budget constraint.

We want to calculate the change in utility resulting from the availability of additional foreign exchange in order to get a measure of welfare generated by the extra resources, e^W. To begin the calculation, observe that

$$dU = U_H dX_H + U_E (dX_E - dE) + U_M (dX_M + dM)$$

$$= \lambda [P_H dX_H + P_E dX_E - P_E dE + P_M dX_M + P_M dM]$$

$$= \lambda [P_M dM - P_E dE]$$

since, if producers in the economy minimize costs, the efficiency condition

$$P_H dX_H + P_E dX_E + P_M dX_M = 0$$

must hold. In familiar terms, this condition simply means that the price hyperplane is tangent to the economy's production possibility surface.

Noting that λ is equal to U_H, we can rescale the welfare gain in terms of the marginal utility of home goods as

$$dV = dU/U_H = P_M dM - P_E dE$$

Differentiation of the balance-of-payments equation [Eq. (13-17)] and substitution into this equation then gives

$$e^W = \frac{dV}{dF} = e \left(1 + t P_M^* \frac{dM}{dF} \right) \tag{13-22}$$

as one representation of the shadow exchange rate e^W. Another can be obtained by noting that with tariff changes equal to 0, $M' = \theta_M e'$ from Eq. (13-19) and an expression for e' in terms of dF comes from Eq. (13-20). Going through the algebra produces

$$e^W = \frac{dV}{dF} = e \left(1 + t \frac{-\theta_M}{\theta_E - \theta_M} \right) \tag{13-23}$$

As with e^F, the shadow exchange rate e^W exceeds the actual rate e by the tariff times the magic ratio $-\theta_M/(\theta_E - \theta_M)$. In this case, however, the interpretation is that imports are socially overpriced because of the tariff. Additional foreign exchange permits imports to expand, even though there is a distortion, because it increases income and expenditure on home goods. To restore equilibrium, the relative price of home goods must rise and imports increase via substitution. The increase in imports per unit of aid is $-\theta_M/(\theta_E - \theta_M)$, and multiplication by the tariff t gives its benefit as perceived by consumers.

Both the free-trade exchange rate e^F and the welfare measure e^W boil down to a weighted average of import tariffs (less export subsidies) added to the current exchange rate, e. In both cases, the "shadow rate" will exceed the current rate if imports are given more protection than exports. Before describing, in the next section, how these shadow prices are applied, it is worthwhile to comment briefly on how the simple calculations described here can be extended in practice.

1. The free-trade rate can easily be extended to an interindustry accounting scheme in which sectors 0 (representing noncompetitive intermediate imports) through T represent traded goods and sectors $T + 1$ through N are nontraded. Then under

restricted trade one has the pricing rules

$$P_i = e(1 + t_i) P_i^* \qquad i = 1, 2, \ldots, T \qquad (13\text{-}24)$$

and

$$P_i = \sum_{j=0}^{T} e(1 + t_j) P_j^* a_{ji} + \sum_{j=T+1}^{N} P_j a_{ji} + w a_{Li} + r a_{Ki} \qquad i = T+1, \ldots, n$$

$$(13\text{-}25)$$

If one adds demand-supply balances for goods and primary inputs in the usual way (see, for example, the Egypt model of Chap. 4), then these cost functions can be solved in a general equilibrium model. Letting tariffs go to 0 provides an estimate of the free-trade exchange rate e^F. One calculation of this type for Chile, by Taylor and Black (see the readings), gave estimates of e^F not far different from those that would result from quick and dirty application of Eq. (13-20). Of course, the detailed calculation provides information about sectoral responses to trade liberalization that would not show up in an aggregate model.

2. Similarly, the calculation of the welfare rate e^W can be extended to many sectors. Or another tack, probably more relevant for policy purposes, would be to ask how much a welfare indicator like real GDP in the Portugal model of Chap. 4 might rise in response to additional foreign exchange. For example, if in Table 4-2 we take constant price GDP as a welfare indicator (call it W), then initially $W = 373.5$ and F, the current account deficit in Eq. (13-17), is 27.9 after accounting for emigrant remittances. The effects of devaluation are $e' = 0.25$, $W' = -0.0369$, and $F' = -0.1864$ assuming the remittances stay constant. Hence the elasticity of GDP with respect to an additional free unit of foreign exchange is 0.198 (= 0.0369/0.1864). The implied derivative, or shadow price of foreign exchange, is $dW/dF = 2.65$. Substitution responses to devaluation might reduce this estimate, but it is clear that free foreign exchange is an extremely valuable resource in Portugal. Investment project analyses should presumably be conducted accordingly.

3. Finally, recall from Chap. 8 that in a two-gap model, the optimal dynamic policy is to build up capital stocks in exporting and import-substituting sectors in the first part of a medium-term plan and then pay foreign debts back slowly thereafter. It is clear intuitively (and demonstrated in the paper by Bruno cited in the readings) that foreign exchange will become relatively scarce during this maneuver or its shadow price will rise. This dynamic consideration should be added to the static models of this section to get a full view of how the shadow relative price of traded and nontraded goods is likely to evolve over time.

13-4 TRADED VERSUS TRADABLE GOODS IN PROJECT EVALUATION

Applying either foreign-exchange shadow price in practice is straightforward. Under UNIDO procedures, for example, the foreign exchange generated by an import-substituting or export investment would be evaluated with the shadow price e^W and counted as a benefit of the project. Its foreign-exchange outlays times e^W would similarly be counted as a cost. Domestic factors, appropriately shadow priced, would of course also enter the final evaluation, which could be expressed in terms of a DRC ratio like Eq. (12-12) with e^W on the left-hand side.

The Little-Mirrlees approach is a bit more complicated. They would take foreign exchange as a numeraire and solve either Eq. (13-20) or its more complicated variant Eqs. (13-24) and (13-25) for a zero-tariff exchange rate e^F. Home goods would then be revalued at (e/e^F) and project analysis proceed. Both the UNIDO and Little-Mirrlees approaches would calculate shadow wages and discount rates according to their respective methodologies described in Sec. 13-2 and Appendix G.

The only question mark about these apparently straightforward recommendations concerns whether or not a tradable good produced at home should be valued in foreign-exchange terms. For example, should steel from the national plant used as a project input be valued at the foreign-exchange cost of a competitive import shipment (times the shadow exchange rate) or at its higher, protected internal price? The standard economic answer to this question, of course, is unequivocal—world prices to any country represent opportunity costs, and it will lose welfare if it does not respect them. Even if a domestic supplier is protected, the second-best solution is still not to penalize the purchaser in project selection by its artificially high costs.[4]

Behind this assertion is, of course, a whole body of economic theory that sanctifies world market decisions. A country *can* choose to accept this theory and its implications; e.g., perhaps Egypt should produce color television sets and not more wheat, because the former activity is more profitable in terms of world relative prices, but then it can also reject it. Egypt could turn its back on the market and opt for autarchy and wheat. There would be a welfare loss involved as measured by GDP valued in world prices, but self-sufficiency and national pride might be worth the cost. The cost could be very high for a country like Egypt, which lacks natural resources and has a small internal market; but in the past large countries like the United States and the Soviet Union, which had enough natural resources to generate exports to pay for essential imports, carried off an autarchic industrialization strategy quite successfully. In their cases, and given their strategy, a reasonable procedure in project evaluation would have been to accept internal prices for inputs produced at home, even if they did exceed import costs. That way, a fully integrated industrial structure could be built up, even if it was (temporarily) inefficient in part.

13-5 ECONOMIES OF SCALE

Part of the efficiencies realized over time in large countries come from their ability to exploit economies of scale in the production of commodities for sale in their large, secured internal markets. Small countries do not have this possibility. In this section, we briefly sketch some of the problems for project evaluation that are created by scale economies, particularly when the size of the plant being considered is large com-

[4] The paper by Srinivasan and Bhagwati gives a formal demonstration.

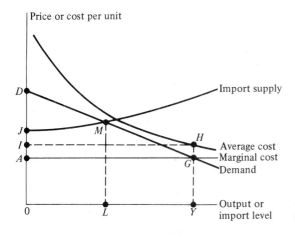

Figure 13-2 Choice between imports and domestic production when there are decreasing costs.

pared to the size of the market. The discussion is based on ideas in the cited survey article by Larry Westphal, which the interested reader should consult.

Figure 13-2 illustrates the main issues in graphical terms. A country is assumed to have the option of either importing a certain commodity with a rising supply curve, as shown, or else producing it under conditions of decreasing average (but constant marginal) costs. Under the usual optimality conditions, if the product is produced at home, its price should be set equal to marginal cost. However, marginal cost always lies below average cost, so in fact production would only take place at a loss. Usually, it is assumed that this would be covered by lump-sum taxes, mainly to avoid cluttering up the discussion with government budget constraints and similar complications.

The operating deficit from production would be the rectangle $AGHI$ in the diagram. The usual principles of project evaluation suggest that if the consumers' surplus at output level G ($= AGD$) exceeds the operating loss, then production is worthwhile. The present problem is made slightly more complicated by the import option, which itself generates a surplus JMD. Simply comparing surpluses, the decision rule boils down to

Import when $JMD > AGD - AGHI$

and produce the commodity at home otherwise.

This sort of decision rule has a number of implications:

1. If it is optimal to import, then costs of the product will be higher than if home production is introduced and demand expands accordingly. However, at the level of demand when the import option is chosen, production costs at home would exceed import costs.
2. As a consequence of the above considerations, the price in the domestic market of the commodity would be substantially different in the import and production situations. The difference would be larger insofar as import and production costs diverge.
3. Selection between the two options is based on economic surplus calculations which can be made only from knowledge of the overall shape of the demand,

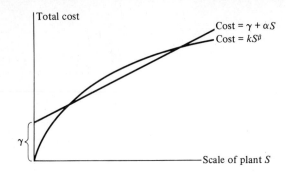

Figure 13-3 Approximations to total cost functions under economies of scale.

import supply, and average cost curves, and not just their local elasticities. Such knowledge is in practice hard to come by.

4. If several projects of this type were being considered, one would in principle have to make calculations of total surplus resulting from all possible combinations of undertaking and not undertaking the projects, since each one could influence resource allocation in a nonmarginal way. If there were N possible projects at any time, $2^N - 1$ such calculations would be required, which could be a very large number.

Under such circumstances, it is perhaps understandable if project evaluators fall back on rules of thumb and partial equilibrium models when they deal with economies of scale. Three are widely used in practice, as follows:

First, if import and export prices and production costs for the commodity in question are not "too far" apart and if a decision has been made to respect world prices in project evaluation, then the problem is not a severe one. Import costs per unit of output give an upper bound on acceptable project costs; if imports could be expected to be cheaper at the level of demand at which the price of the good in question equals marginal cost of home production, then the project is not worth doing. (This is the rule of Fig. 13-2; note that it requires knowledge of the demand curve.) If production costs are less than export receipts per unit of output and if it is really possible to export, then the investment is definitely worthwhile. If costs fall between the import and export (or c.i.f. and f.o.b.) boundaries, then more complicated calculations are required. However, if the bounds lie close together (if transport costs, etc., are low), these additional problems are not likely to arise.

Second, the combinatorial problems mentioned above can sometimes be handled by the technique of "mixed integer programming." The general idea is that total cost of a project can be approximated by a function of the form $\gamma + \alpha S$ shown in Fig. 13-3. If a project of size S is undertaken, then a "fixed charge" of γ has to be paid, plus a marginal cost at rate α, whose total αS depends on the project's size. When the project is *not* undertaken, no costs at all are incurred.

If costs of all projects subject to economies of scale (or the related problem of indivisibilities) are modeled in this way and if all other restrictions on the choice problem are linear, then one could imagine solving separate linear programs for all combina-

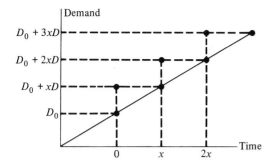

Figure 13-4 Construction cycles for a product subject to economies of scale.

tions of undertaking and not undertaking projects. The solution with lowest overall costs or highest overall surplus would indicate the project combination to be chosen.

In practice, certain integer programming algorithms permit more efficient search procedures than the "complete enumeration" technique just mentioned.[5] Also, depending on the structure of the problem, efficient approximation procedures to "good" (if not optimal) solutions to the combinatorial problem can be devised. For more on this, see the survey article by Westphal.

The third approximate technique was developed from an earlier model of Hollis Chenery by Alan Manne. In its simplest form, it requires the assumptions that the project output is not traded and that its demand goes up as a linear function of time. The situation is shown in Fig. 13-4, in which demand is at level D_0 at time 0 and expands at a rate D per unit of time.

If there are economies of scale in plant construction and other costs are just proportional to the level of output, then it would seem reasonable to build *ahead* of demand growth, i.e., build a large plant now to take advantage of its lower average construction costs and run it at excess capacity for a while until demand catches up. When that happens at some time in the future, a new, large plant could be built again. When the investment decision is viewed from this angle, the appropriate criterion is to choose the plant size that minimizes the discounted cost of an infinite chain of new investments over time.

Suppose that a new plant is to be built every x years. The scale of each would then have to be xD units of output to just keep up with demand. Let the construction cost be $f(xD)$.[6] Let $C(x)$ be total cost over the infinite chain of plants, beginning with a new investment at time 0. A moment's consideration suggests that one can write this

---

[5] Integer programming is the appropriate technique because each project is assigned a variable which takes on a value 1 or 0 depending on whether the investment is or is not undertaken (the fixed charge is or is not paid). Economies of scale and indivisibilities cause problems precisely because one cannot set the integer variables to fractional values. In a more homely example, it is not possible to be half pregnant, and a woman's life is likely to differ greatly depending on which of the two possible states she happens to be in!

[6] In practice, one would usually approximate this cost by the constant elasticity function $k(xD)^\beta$ shown in Fig. 13-3. As already mentioned in Sec. 13-1, the elasticity β would usually take a value near 0.6 or 0.7.

cost function as

$$C(x) = f(xD) + e^{-rx}C(x)$$

that is, the sum of current construction costs plus the same cost stream discounted at rate r back from the time x in the future when another new plant is constructed and another infinite chain is begun. It is easy to solve this equation to get

$$C(x) = f(xD)/(1 - e^{-rx}) \qquad (13\text{-}26)$$

For some specific form of the function $f(xD)$ one can minimize the right-hand side of Eq. (13-26) to get the optimal time phasing of plant construction as a function of the parameters. If the (constant) elasticity of cost with respect to scale is 0.7 and the discount rate r is 10 percent, for example, then the optimal cycle time x turns out to be about 6 years.

This algorithm can be extended to deal with imports, and in more heuristic fashion, to clarify the problem of selecting regional construction cycles for a product like cement that is costly to transport. More importantly, the reasoning that underlies it is often invoked by enthusiasts for large projects to justify their scale. To a point, these people are correct, but it is worth remembering that minimum cost-cycle times in this sort of problem often turn out to be around 5 years (the cited book by Manne gives numerical examples). Sometimes petrochemical and petroleum fanatics in poor countries want to build 10 years or so ahead of reasonable demand growth, "to take advantage of economies of scale." In such circumstances, quantitative refutation of their recommendations on the basis of their own model can be of practical use. Capital is *not* free in poor countries, and one should not spend it needlessly on enormous factories that are not likely to be used in the near future.

13-6 PROJECT ANALYSIS IN PRACTICE

Many of the problems we have discussed illustrate the problem of "control areas," as it is called by Amartya Sen. His point is that investment project analysis is at best an adjunct to an industrialization strategy and has to be tailored to both the grander aims and the limitations of government policy. Formal criteria like those developed here do not take these intangibles into account and have to be interpreted accordingly in use.

To be more concrete, assume that a social cost-benefit analysis based on world prices and appropriate shadow prices for domestic resources shows that a project is "bad" when other indicators—such as market price evaluations, political pressures, access to technology, etc.—suggest that it should be undertaken. Should the project be stopped?

Possibly and possibly not, depending on how important the other factors are considered to be in an essentially nonquantitative assessment. The formal analysis raises doubts about the project which should be weighed. Lacking all the details, one really cannot say more.

The alternative case of interest is where social cost-benefit analysis supports a project while other considerations do not. Again, perhaps the investment should be made, but in this case, unless market prices were to change, it might well require a subsidy. The Finance Minister would be opposed, and even the project evaluator should recognize that industries guaranteed protection by tariff or subsidy rarely perform up to even the modest expectations originally entertained for them. Another intangible necessarily enters the final evaluation.

Other problems such as uncertainty and all the difficulties listed in Sec. 13-1 could be discussed, but enough has been said to show that the formal elegance of social cost-benefit procedures does not completely guarantee their relevance, much less infallibility. They are a partial tool, capable of dealing with some aspects of underdevelopment. There are no panaceas in planning for poor countries. If there were, poverty and misery would have been eradicated long, long ago.

SELECTED ADDITIONAL READINGS

Bacha, Edmar, and Lance Taylor: "Foreign Exchange Shadow Prices: A Critical Review of Current Theories," *Quarterly Journal of Economics*, 85:197–224, 1971. (Detailed though somewhat dated review of the material in Secs. 13-3 and 13-4.)

Bruno, Michael: "Planning Models, Shadow Prices and Project Evaluation," in C. R. Blitzer, P. B. Clark, and L. Taylor (eds.): *Economy-Wide Models and Development Planning*, Oxford University Press, New York and London, 1975. (Synthesis of shadow prices, including exchange-rate dynamics, in a consistent theoretical system.)

Chenery, Hollis B.: "Overcapacity and the Acceleration Principle," *Econometrica*, 20:1–28, 1952. (Initial statement of the interactions of excess capacity and economies of scale analyzed in Sec. 13-5.)

Dornbusch, Rudiger: "Tariffs and Nontraded Goods," *Journal of International Economics*, 4:177–186, 1974. (Neat derivation of foreign-exchange shadow prices in the three-sector model of Sec. 13-3.)

Hirschman, Albert O.: *The Strategy of Economic Development*, Yale University Press, New Haven, 1958. (Chapter 6 introduces the influential linkage ideas discussed in Sec. 13-1 here.)

Leibenstein, Harvey: "X-Efficiency Theory, Conventional Entrepreneurship, and Excess Capacity Creation in LDC's," in Manning Nash (ed.): *Essays on Economic Development and Cultural Change in Honor of Bert F. Hoselitz*, University of Chicago Press, Chicago, 1977. (Restatement and consolidation of much writing on the topic.)

Manne, Alan S. (ed.): *Investments for Capacity Expansion: Size, Location and Time-Phasing*, The M.I.T. Press, Cambridge, Mass., 1967. (Introduces the cost-minimizing algorithm of Sec. 13-5 for building plant capacity ahead of demand under economies of scale.)

Sen, Amartya K.: "Accounting Prices and Control Areas: An Approach to Project Evaluation," *Economic Journal*, 82:486–501, 1972. (Discussion of policy limits to project evaluation procedures by a perceptive theorist.)

Squire, Lyn, and Herman G. Van der Tak: *Economic Analysis of Projects*, The Johns Hopkins Press, Baltimore and London, 1975. (Good cookbook for preparation of standard investment project criteria, written for the World Bank.)

Srinivasan, T. N., and Jagdish N. Bhagwati: "Shadow Prices for Project Selection in the Presence of Distortions: Effective Rates of Protection and Domestic Resource Costs," *Journal of Political Economy*, 86:97–116, 1978. [Discusses solution of formulas like Eqs. (13-24) and (13-25) for second-best shadow prices when trade distortions are present.]

Stewart, Frances: *Technology and Underdevelopment*, Macmillan Press, London, 1977. (Clear and helpful review of the complexities of technological choice, with observations on how they interface with project evaluation.)

Taylor, Lance, and Stephen L. Black: "Practical General Equilibrium Estimation of Resource Pulls under Trade Liberalization," *Journal of International Economics*, 4:37–58, 1974. [General equilibrium numerical solutions of Eqs. (13-24) through (13-25), in log changes, for calculation of exchange-rate responses to tariff change.]

United Nations Industrial Development Organization (UNIDO): *Guidelines for Project Evaluation*, United Nations, New York, 1972 (Sales No: E. 72.II.B.11). (Detailed presentation of the complete set of project criteria summarized in this chapter.)

Westphal, Larry E.: "Planning with Economies of Scale," in C. R. Blitzer, P. B. Clark, and L. Taylor (eds.): *Economy-Wide Models and Development Planning*, Oxford University Press, New York and London, 1975. (Definitive treatment of project-selection difficulties raised by economies of scale—informative reading.)

DERIVATION OF EQ. (4-16)

By inserting Eqs. (4-6) through (4-8) from Table 4-1 into Eq. (4-9) with $T_W = T_Z = G = 0$, we get

$$P_H X_H = \gamma_W Y_W + \gamma_Z Y_Z + P_H I$$

In log-differential form, this becomes

$$P_H X_H (P_H' + X_H') = \gamma_W Y_W Y_W' + \gamma_Z Y_Z Y_Z' + I P_H P_H' \qquad \text{(A-1)}$$

Now note that as e changes, with $v_H = t_0 = 0$, from Eqs. (4-1) and (4-3) the differential of P_H is

$$dP_H = (1 + z) a_{0H} P_0^* de$$

and the log differential becomes

$$P_H' = dP_H / P_H = (1 + z)(1/P_H) a_{0H} P_0^* e (de/e)$$
$$= (1 + z)(1/P_H) a_{0H} P_0 e' \qquad \text{(A-2)}$$

From Eqs. (4-4) and (4-5), with $t_E = \text{REM} = 0$, we also get

$$dY_W = Y_W Y_W' = w a_{LH} X_H X_H' \qquad \text{(A-3)}$$

and

$$dY_Z = Y_Z Y_Z' = z(a_{LH} w + a_{0H} P_0) X_H X_H' + z a_{0H} X_H P_0 e' + P_E X_E e'$$
$$= (1 + z)^{-1} z P_H X_H X_H' + z a_{0H} X_H P_0 e' + P_E X_E e' \qquad \text{(A-4)}$$

noting that $z(a_{LH} w + a_{0H} P_0) = (1 + z)^{-1} z P_H$ from Eq. (4-1), with $v_H = 0$.

Substituting Eqs. (A-2) through (A-4) into Eq. (A-1) and simplifying produces

$$QP_HX_HX'_H = [(1+z)(I-X_H)a_{0H}P_0 + \gamma_Z(za_{0H}X_HP_0 + P_EX_E)]e'$$
$$= (1+z)a_{0H}P_0[(I-X_H) + \gamma_ZX_H]e' \qquad\qquad (A\text{-}5)$$

where Q is defined in Eq. (4-15) and the current account deficit, $P_0a_{0H}X_H - P_EX_E$, is assumed to equal 0 in deriving the second line.

Now observe that with no goverament activity and a 0 current account deficit, the savings-investment identity of Eq. (4-13) takes the form

$$(1 - \gamma_W)Y_W + (1 - \gamma_Z)Y_Z = P_HI$$

and also

$$Y_W + Y_Z = P_HX_H$$

Substituting these two conditions into Eq. (A-5) and simplifying gives

$$X'_H = \frac{(1+z)a_{0H}P_0}{(P_H)^2 X_H Q}(\gamma_Z - \gamma_W)Y_We'$$

which is equivalent to Eq. (4-16).

THE LINEAR EXPENDITURE SYSTEM

As its name indicates, the linear expenditure system (LES) is a complete set of consumer-demand equations linear in total expenditure. In a model like the one set out in Table 4-3, linearity in expenditure is a distinct advantage, permitting solution of the general equilibrium system without computational iterations to determine consumer choice. In this appendix, we develop the algebra of the LES. For practical purposes, its main rival is the "direct addilog" demand system, which is linear in log changes of prices and total expenditure. That system is described in Appendix E.

If we maintain the usual fiction that a group of consumers shares a utility function which each one maximizes subject to the budget constraint, the additional LES hypothesis is that some monotonic transformation of the utility function takes the form

$$U = \sum_{i=1}^{N} m_i \log (C_i - \theta_i)$$

where C_i is the consumption of the ith commodity and m_i and θ_i are parameters of the utility function. Setting up the Lagrangean expression for maximization of U subject to the budget constraint,

$$\sum_{i=1}^{N} P_i C_i = D \qquad \text{(B-1)}$$

we get

$$V = \sum_{i=1}^{N} m_i \log (C_i - \theta_i) + \lambda \left(D - \sum_{i=1}^{N} P_i C_i \right)$$

where λ is a Lagrange multiplier.

The first-order conditions derived by setting $\partial V/\partial C_i = 0$ take the form

$$m_i = \lambda P_i (C_i - \theta_i) \qquad \text{(B-2)}$$

Impose the normalization condition that the sum of the m_i equals 1. Then, from Eq. (B-2), we get

$$1 = \sum_i m_i = \lambda \left(\sum_i P_i C_i - \sum_i P_i \theta_i \right)$$

$$= \lambda(D - F)$$

where D is total expenditure from Eq. (B-1) and F is defined by

$$F = \sum_{i=1}^{N} P_i \theta_i \tag{B-3}$$

Evidently, the Lagrange multiplier is given by $\lambda = 1/(D - F)$. By differentiation, we also find that the elasticity of λ (the "marginal utility of income") with respect to income itself is

$$\beta = \frac{d\lambda}{dD} \frac{D}{\lambda} = -\frac{D}{D - F} \tag{B-4}$$

The elasticity β is sometimes called the Frisch parameter since it was proposed by Ragnar Frisch as a measure of consumer welfare (see the paper cited in the readings). There is some doubt as to whether β can be used for such a purpose, but this need not detain us here. We *will* see shortly that a simple transformation of β is the key to understanding the economics of the LES (or, indeed, any other system of demand equations derived from an "additive" utility index expressed as the sum of identical functions of each consumption level C_i).

To get an explicit formula for demand of commodity i, we substitute for λ in Eq. (B-2) to get

$$C_i = \theta_i + \frac{m_i(D - F)}{P_i} \tag{B-5}$$

This expression can be interpreted if we take θ_i as some absolute minimum level of consumption of commodity i. Then, from Eq. (B-3), F is the total cost of a minimum (or "floor") consumption basket. Any excess of income D over the floor F is spread across the various consumer goods according to the ratios (m_i/P_i). The m_i are "marginal budget shares" which tell how consumers allocate their income above the floor level.

Simple differentiation of Eq. (B-5) shows that the *Engel elasticity* (income elasticity of demand) for commodity i is

$$\eta_i = \frac{\partial C_i}{\partial D} \frac{D}{C_i} = \frac{m_i D}{P_i C_i} \tag{B-6}$$

or

$$m_i = \eta_i \phi_i \tag{B-7}$$

where $\phi_i = P_i C_i / D$, the budget share of commodity i. Equation (B-7) provides an immediate estimate of each m_i on the basis of the Engel elasticity η_i. Note also that the normalization condition on the m_i is equivalent to

$$\sum_{i=1}^{N} \phi_i \eta_i = 1 \tag{B-8}$$

a condition known as *Engel aggregation*. It says that the sum of expenditure elasticities weighted by budget shares must be 1; otherwise, when an increment in income is obtained, either more or less than what has been received will be spent on consuming more goods.

Substituting the demand function of Eq. (B-5) into Eq. (B-6), we get another expression for η_i as follows:

$$\eta_i = \frac{m_i D}{P_i \theta_i + m_i(D - F)}$$

After some manipulation, this can be rewritten as

$$\theta_i = (D/P_i)[\phi_i - m_i(-1/\beta)]$$
$$= (D/P_i)[\phi_i - m_i \sigma^C] \tag{B-9}$$

where we introduce a new parameter

$$\sigma^C = (-1/\beta) = \frac{D - F}{D} \tag{B-10}$$

For the LES, σ^C is called the *supernumerary income ratio*, though it has other interpretations as well. Its label comes from the fact that it is the ratio of the consumer's income excess over the floor to the floor itself. The stylized fact is that σ^C takes a value of about $\frac{1}{2}$ (or the Frisch parameter β takes a value -2) for most consumer groups. From Eq. (B-9), any chosen value of σ^C allows us to determine the LES parameters θ_i if we already have values for the m_i. Such ease in estimation is a godsend to the applied economist.

Another interpretation of σ^C follows from consideration of the impacts of price changes on demand. Differentiation of Eq. (B-5) shows that own- and cross-price demand elasticities are

$$\eta_{ii} = \frac{\partial C_i}{\partial P_i} \frac{P_i}{C_i} = -\eta_i[(P_i \theta_i/D) + \sigma^C] \tag{B-11}$$

and

$$\eta_{ij} = \frac{\partial C_i}{\partial P_j} \frac{P_j}{C_i} = -\eta_i(P_j \theta_j/D) \tag{B-12}$$

In Eq. (B-11), the term $\eta_i(P_i \theta_i/D)$ represents the income effect of a change in the price P_i. It shows that a log change in P_i reduces real income proportionally to $P_i \theta_i/D$, which—multiplied by the income elasticity η_i—gives the proportional reduction in consumption C_i. The term $\sigma^C \eta_i$ measures the substitution effect; as σ^C gets smaller, so do substitution responses in consumer behavior. This interpretation of σ^C as an indicator of the importance of price substitution in demand carries over with other utility functions. Also, an "elasticity of substitution" σ^X will appear in the discussion of production and cost functions in Appendix D. Its interpretation is very similar to that of σ^C here.

Finally, note that the magnitudes of the price elasticities in both Eqs. (B-11) and (B-12) are proportional to the Engel elasticity η_i. The high elasticities for urban goods in the Egypt model are the main reason why food price increases have such a sharp contractionary effect on that sector; most of the real income loss they cause shows up as a drop in demand for "luxury" goods.

Estimation of LES parameters can be illustrated with Egyptian data. Consumer budget surveys provide the basis for the following numbers:

Sector	Rural budget share	Rural Engel elasticity	Urban budget share	Urban Engel elasticity
Imports	0.0094	2.0	0.04	2.0
Rural	0.45	0.5	0.11642	0.2
Urban	0.4656	1.51138	0.55835	1.35059
Food	0.075	0.7	0.28523	0.5

Note that budget shares sum to 1 and, in practice, were hand-adjusted to satisfy the adding-up equations [Eqs. (4-46) through (4-49)] in Table 4-3, where total sectoral consumption levels were given by the input-output accounting. Second, Engel elasticities for urban consumer goods were adjusted to satisfy the aggregation condition of Eq. (B-8).

Marginal budget shares come directly from Eq. (B-7); for example, for import consumption by rural income recipients, $m_{0R} = 0.0188 = (0.0094)(2.0)$. With a value of 0.5 for σ^C, Eq. (B-9) then gives

$$\theta_{0R} = (0.0188/1.0)\left(0.0092 - \frac{0.0188}{2.0}\right) = 0.0$$

Readers should try calculating these parameters for other sectors to make sure they understand the technique. Recall that, in the Egypt model, all consumer prices are 1 except for the price from the food sector, which is 0.5854 because of the subsidy.

SELECTED ADDITIONAL READINGS

Brown, Alan, and Angus Deaton: "Models of Consumer Behavior," *Economic Journal*, 82:1145–1236, 1972. (A thorough and clearly written review of consumer-demand theory, a useful supplement to this appendix and other sections of this book.)

Frisch, Ragnar: "A Complete Scheme for Computing all Direct and Cross Demand Elasticities in a Model with Many Sectors," *Econometrica*, 27:177–196, 1959. [Introduces the parameter called β in Eq. (B-4) and gives a good review of demand theory.]

Lluch, Constantino, Alan A. Powell, and Ross A. Williams: *Patterns in Household Demand and Saving*, Oxford University Press, New York, 1977. (Careful presentation and application of the linear expenditure system and extension to a variety of sources of data. Discusses sensitivity of the parameter we call σ^C to changing levels of per capita income and other variables.)

Sato, Kazuo: "Additive Utility Functions with Double-Log Consumer Demand Functions," *Journal of Political Economy*, 80:102–124, 1972. (Presents evidence on values of the parameters β and σ^C introduced in this appendix.)

Stone, Richard: "Linear Expenditure Systems and Demand Analysis: An Application to the Pattern of British Demand," *Economic Journal*, 64:511–527, 1954. (An original statement and application of the linear expenditure system.)

C

DETAILED SPECIFICATION OF THE CAMBRIDGE AND NEOCLASSICAL GROWTH MODELS FOR BRAZIL

The theme stressed in the first three sections of Chap. 7—that interactions between savings and investment determine inflation rates and income distribution in aggregate models—carries over into applied planning exercises. The major complication is that besides wages and profits, the current fiscal surplus and balance-of-payments deficit act as additional sources of saving and have to be taken into account as well.

In Sec. C-1 of this appendix, a model that can handle all savings sources in the national income and monetary statistics for Brazil is presented and discussed. The two following sections then show how Cambridge and neoclassical closures can be imposed—some of the more unpleasant algebra involved is banished to Appendices D and E. The latter sections of Chap. 7 already describe how Cambridge and neoclassical closures perform in practice—first retrospectively for Brazilian data for the 1960s and then in a forecasting exercise for the 1970s (actually undertaken in 1973).

C-1 THE MODEL FOR BRAZIL

The level form of the Brazil model appears in Table C-1. The first equation, Eq. (C-1), is similar to the simple material balance $PX = PC + PI$ used in Chap. 6 and 7 except that four additional demand categories are included: exports net of competitive imports PE,[1] government purchases for current public consumption PC_G and also for

---

[1] In the Brazilian case, competitive importation is in principle illegal, because of diverse legislation summed up as the "law of similars": products similar to national products are allegedly prohibited. In practice, the laws are not followed rigorously, but in what follows we do, in fact, treat all imports as noncompetitive.

Table C-1 Level form equations for the Brazil model

$$PX = PC_X + PI_X + P\delta_X K_X + PE + PC_G + PI_G \tag{C-1}$$

$$eP_E^* E + eF = eP_0^* M + eP_{0C}^* C_0 + eP_{0K}^*(I_0 + \delta_0 K_0) \tag{C-2}$$

$$\theta_L = w(1 + t_L) \tag{C-3}$$

$$\theta_X = \left(\frac{\rho}{1 - t_K} + \delta_X\right) P \tag{C-4}$$

$$\theta_0 = \left(\frac{\rho}{1 - t_K} + \delta_0\right) P_{0K} \tag{C-5}$$

$$VX = P_0 M + \theta_L L + \theta_X K_X + \theta_0 K_0 \tag{C-6}$$

$$P = (1 + t_V) V \tag{C-7}$$

$$\alpha_M VX = P_0 M \tag{C-8}$$

$$\alpha_L VX = \theta_L L \tag{C-9}$$

$$\alpha_X VX = \theta_X K_X \tag{C-10}$$

$$\alpha_0 VX = \theta_0 K_0 \tag{C-11}$$

$$Y_L = w(L + L_G) \tag{C-12}$$

$$Z = PK_X + P_{0K} K_0 \tag{C-13}$$

$$Y_K = \rho Z + PB \tag{C-14}$$

$$T_L = \xi_L (Y_L)^{S_{TL}} \tag{C-15}$$

$$T_K = \xi_K (Y_K)^{S_{TK}} \tag{C-16}$$

$$R = K_X + K_0 + (H/P) + (B/i) \tag{C-17}$$

$$D = [\gamma_L (Y_L - T_L + Q) + \gamma_K (Y_K - T_K)] \xi_C (R)^{S_{CR}} (i/A)^{S_{Ci}} \tag{C-18}$$

$$\phi_X D = PC_X \tag{C-19}$$

$$\phi_0 D = P_{0C} C_0 \tag{C-20}$$

$$\phi_X + \phi_0 = 1 \tag{C-21}$$

$$I_X + I_G = g_X K_X \tag{C-22}$$

$$I_0 = g_0 K_0 \tag{C-23}$$

$$GE = (1 + t_L) wL_G + PC_G + PB + (P - eP_E^*) E + PI_G + Q \tag{C-24}$$

$$GR = t_V VX + t_L w(L + L_G) + \frac{t_K \rho Z}{1 - t_K} + (P_0 - eP_0^*) M + (P_{0C} - eP_{0C}^*) C_0$$
$$+ (P_{0K} - eP_{0K}^*) (I_0 + \delta_0 K_0) + T_L + T_K \tag{C-25}$$

$$GE - GR = dH/dt + (P/i) (dB/dt) + eF \tag{C-26}$$

$$H = \xi_H P(X)^{S_{HX}} (i)^{S_{Hi}} \tag{C-27}$$

investment PI_G, and depreciation of the stock of capital goods originally produced within the country, $P\delta_X K_X$. This stock will largely be made up of plant and not machinery or equipment (even in a developing country with a moderately active capital-goods industry such as Brazil's) and the corresponding depreciation coefficient δ_X will be relatively small, say 0.02. In Eq. (C-1) this represents *physical* depreciation, but we assume in Eq. (C-4) that δ_X is also the legal depreciation rate used in calculating the user cost of capital. In general, the two concepts need not be the same.

Equation (C-2) is the balance of payments written in domestic prices, i.e., after multiplication of transactions in world prices (indicated by asterisks) by the exchange rate e. Three noncompetitive import categories appear on the right-hand side. The disaggregation reflects Brazil's long history of import substitution, which erected differential trade barriers against complementary imports of intermediates (M), capital goods (I_0), and consumption goods (C_0). The capital inflow term F in Eq. (C-2) is the simplest possible balance-of-payments definition—the "foreign savings gap." Both here and below in the money supply equation, we omit, for simplicity, explicit consideration of exogenous reserve changes, debt service charges, and a host of other financial market complexities. Full treatment of financial flows, although easy to include in a planning framework based on accounting identities in principle, would add much complication to an already messy model; we shunned the additional effort for this reason.

Equations (C-3) through (C-5) give shorthand expressions for the user costs of labor and the two capital goods in the model. Social security taxes t_L blow up wages w to generate total labor cost θ_L, while the depreciation rates δ_X and δ_0 enter the costs θ_X and θ_0 of the two types of capital. Both capital stocks, whether nationally produced (K_X) or originally imported (K_0), are valued in *current* prices P and P_{0K}, so that the terms in parentheses on the right-hand sides of Eqs. (C-4) and (C-5) are decompositions of pure rates of profit (refer back to Sec. 2-1). Competition is supposed to ensure that the after-tax profit rates on the capital stocks are equalized at a single rate ρ. The profit tax rate is t_K.

Using these cost definitions, Eq. (C-6) gives a breakdown of total production cost (including noncompetitive imports, wages, and capital costs) into its components. In the next equation, per-unit costs V are blown up to the market price level through a value-added tax t_V; in Brazil as in other developing countries, such indirect taxes are the largest sources of government revenue. Equations (C-8) through (C-11) define the shares of production inputs in total costs: intermediate imports (α_M), labor (α_L), and domestically produced and imported capital (α_X and α_0).

The next group of equations—Eqs. (C-12) through (C-21)—links factor payments and consumption demands. The first three define labor and capital incomes Y_L and Y_K, with the former including payments to government employees wL_G and the latter including total profits ρZ and also income from government bonds. It is simplest to assume that these are inflation-corrected consuls, each paying the *real* equivalent of 1 cruzeiro per year in base-year prices. Because of the price escalator, total income from bonds is PB, i.e., the stock of bonds multiplied by the price index. [In the absence of "monetary correction" of this form, the price P would not multiply B in Eq. (C-14)]. Interest payments PB show up in the simulations of Chap. 7 as important determinants of government saving in the neoclassical version of the Brazil model.

Equations (C-15) and (C-16) are behavioral—they describe in convenient constant elasticity form the relationship between direct tax revenues T_L and T_K and the corresponding income flows. Here as elsewhere the distinction between capital and labor incomes is supposed to approximate the size distribution of personal income; one expects that the constant ξ_L will be considerably less than ξ_K in a crude representation of a progressive direct tax system.

The next equation, Eq. (C-17), defines total wealth R in base-year prices. Along with the nominal rate of interest deflated by the anticipated rate of inflation, (i/A), this is supposed to have some influence on the *value* of consumption D in Eq. (C-18). As the form of Eq. (C-18) demonstrates, we assume that the elasticities of value consumption with respect to wealth and the "real" interest rate are constant.[2] The other new term in this equation is Q, representing government transfer payments (which go predominantly to recipients of labor incomes or to their families). The next three equations respectively define shares of domestically produced goods and noncompetitive imports in total consumption (ϕ_X and ϕ_0, respectively) and require that these sum to 1.

Equations (C-22) and (C-23) set each type of investment equal to the growth rate of the corresponding capital stock. As in Sec. 7-2, these equations provide a basis for a Cambridge model closure in which g_X and g_0 (or their log changes) are set exogenously, or as functions of historically based expectations, the rate of profit, the rate of interest, planners' preference, or even of animal spirits.

Equations (C-24) through (C-26) give the government accounts. Expenditures GE include government consumption and investment, bond interest payments, the total of subsidies paid to exporters (based on the difference between the domestic price P and the domestic value of export receipts eP_E^*), government transfer payments, and wages and employment taxes for government employees. These taxes are also included in total fiscal receipts GR, along with value added and profits taxes, direct taxes, and tariffs based on the difference between world and domestic prices of imports.[3] Equation (C-26) shows that the difference between government expenditures and receipts is met by the growth of the money supply dH/dt, new bond issues with value given by $(P/i)\,(dB/dt)$, and capital inflows eF, which—in the first round after entry into the country—pass through the Central Bank. The monetary accounting is essentially the same as that in Table 2-2 except that government bond sales to the public become an alternative source of finance for the fiscal cash deficit $GE - GR$. In effect, we assume that Brazilian monetary authorities can undertake open-market operations to control the size of the money base, but such ability is unusual in developing countries.

Finally, the commercial banking system is consolidated with the rest of the economy, so the money base H is also "the" money supply. A rather standard money-demand equation appears as Eq. (C-27) to determine the interest rate i, which feeds back into consumer demand in Eq. (C-18). Real money demand H/P is supposed to be an increasing function of real output X and a decreasing function of the interest rate i, with corresponding elasticities S_{HX} and S_{Hi}. Why such a demand function might be expected to obtain is discussed further in Chap. 9.

---

[2]The nonstandard specification of interest-rate deflation by the anticipated inflation rate A, i/A instead of $i - A$, allows this to be done easily.

[3]Formally, one can set $P_i = e(1 + \tau_i) P_i^*$, where i indexes traded goods and τ_i is an ad valorem tariff. Unchanging tariffs imply that $P_i' = e' + (P_i^*)'$, which can be used to set price changes in the log-change model. In the Cambridge closure for Table C-1, such relationships contain only exogenous variables and are used just for accounting consistency. In the neoclassical closure, e and the P_i are endogenous, so equations relating world and internal prices become active constraints on the solution.

The savings-investment identity in the model of Table C-1 is

$$(Y_L - T_L + Q) + (Y_K - T_K) - D = PI_X + P_{0K}I_0 + (dH/dt) + (P/i)(dB/dt)$$

so that private savings (net of depreciation) equals net capital formation plus that part of the government cash deficit financed from within the country.[4] Another version of the same identity is

$$PI_G + PI_X + P_{0K}I_0 = [(Y_L - T_L + Q) + (Y_K - T_K) - D] + (GR + PI_G - GE) + eF$$

$$(C-28)$$

Here, total net investment (including that of the government) equals the sum of private net savings, the government surplus on current account, and capital inflows. We rely heavily on this equation in interpreting our numerical results below.

C-2 A CAMBRIDGE CLOSURE FOR BRAZIL

Although they are complex algebraically, both closures for the Brazil model can be solved by straightforward numerical techniques. One approach is to transform the Table C-1 equations to their log-change versions, specify exogenous growth rates along the lines of Secs. 7-2 and 7-3, and get predictions of the endogenous log changes. These, in turn, can be used as the starting point for an algorithm like that of Sec. 7-3 to solve the level form of the model in some future year (with predictions of exogenous variables in that year based on growth rates being taken as exact). Three years turns out to be a convenient time period for this sort of calculation, and is used in the empirical analysis.

To solve the Cambridge log-change model, the following exogenous growth rates were chosen:

A. "Naturally exogenous" variables (6): $(P_E^*)'$, $(P_0^*)'$, $(P_{0C}^*)'$, $(P_{0K}^*)'$, ϵ, A
B. Tax and expenditure variables (10): I_G', C_G', P_0', P_{0C}', P_{0K}', t_V', t_L', t_K', Q', L_G'
C. Growth rates determined by stock-flow relationships at the initial time point (4): K_X', K_0', H', B'
D. Parametrically varied growth rates (4): w', $(dH/dt)'$, E', L'
E. Cambridge closure variables (4): g_X', g_0', e', M'

The ambitious (masochistic?) reader who actually turns Table C-1 into its growth-rate equivalent will find that these exogenous log changes lack only one condition to give a closed model. The missing relationship is one to determine the growth rate of the consumption share of national goods ϕ_X'; the growth rate of the import share will then follow from the log-differential version of Eq. (C-21), $\phi_X \phi_X' + \phi_0 \phi_0' = 0$. A sys-

---

[4] Since we omit stock changes from our accounting (in practice including them with consumption, which is estimated as a residual in Brazilian national accounts), they do not put in their usual appearance in the savings-investment balance.

tem of consumer demand functions fitting neatly into growth-rate equations is described in Appendix E, from whence Eq. (E-2) can be used for ϕ'_X.

The explanations above for the rest of the exogenous growth rates are almost sufficient. World prices of traded goods, the residual ϵ, and expected inflation rate A are part of the economic scene and cannot be determined by the macro model (list A). Also, it is reasonable to treat the fiscal variables that the government controls as exogenous (list B). List C includes growth rates of stocks determined by the corresponding flow variables (I_X, I_0, dH/dt, dB/dt) under our assumption that capacities are fully utilized. For purposes of generating solutions, it is convenient to keep growth rates of the money wage, money supply, exports, and employment exogenous (list D). By the log-differential version of the government budget constraint of Eq. (C-26), when fiscal variables and the growth of the money supply are set outside the model, the growth rate of government bond emissions $(dB/dt)'$ has to be determined endogenously.[5]

Finally, the sine qua non of a Cambridge model is determination of savings by investment, so g'_X and g'_0 are exogenous in the growth-rate version (list E). In the balance of payments, the growth rate of the exchange rate e' and capital inflows F' are closely related. As is shown in Appendix D, imposition of cost-equals-marginal-product restrictions in a fully neoclassical specification requires that e' be endogenous, forcing F' to be exogenous. By contrast, in a Cambridge model, e' is only a scaling variable and has to be determined exogenously, with F' endogenous. The last exogenous growth rate, that of noncompetitive imports M', is most conveniently determined by relating it to output growth X' by a constant factor—the elasticity of intermediate imports with respect to output.

To get a level solution of the Cambridge model, it is simplest to iterate on the price level, taking the output forecasts from the log-differential sources of growth Eq. (D-20) in Appendix D as exact. In effect, the price level is varied to generate the amount of forced saving required to ratify real exogenous output and investment forecasts.

Given a guess at the price level P from the growth-rate model, the following iteration will rapidly converge:

1. Using exogenous variables at the end of the forecast period, solve immediately for Y_L, T_L, I_X, and I_0.
2. The end-of-period rate of money emissions $(dH/dt)_T$ is related to the beginning-of-period emissions $(dH/dt)_0$ by the equation

$$(dH/dt)_T = (dH/dt)_0 \exp\left[(dH/dt)'T\right]$$

where exp is the exponential function, $(dH/dt)'$ is the exogenously specified rate of growth of money emissions, and T is the length of the forecast period. Integra-

---

[5] In effect, we permit discrete jumps in the money growth rate, which means that smoothly differentiable stock-flow equations of the form of Eq. (C-22) cannot be used to relate the flow of money emissions dH/dt to the money stock H. This has some implications for computation of a complete new level solution to the model in some future year, discussed below.

tion of this equation gives the end-of-period money *stock* H_T as

$$H_T = \frac{1}{(dH/dt)'} [(dH/dt)_T - (dH/dt)_0] + H_0$$

where H_0 is the initial money stock.

3. With the chosen level of P, now calculate V, Z, i, α_M, α_L, ρ, R, α_X, α_0, Y_K, and T_K, using equations in Table C-1.
4. Next compute consumer expenditure D. Together with P and P_{0C}, this gives estimates of ϕ_X and ϕ_0 from the consumer-demand specification in Appendix E. Consumption levels C_X and C_0 follow.
5. Another estimate of C_X is given by

$$C_X = X - I_X - \delta_X K_X - C_G - I_G - E$$

where all entries on the right side have been calculated previously. If the estimate of C_X from step 4 exceeds this estimate, increase P to generate more forced savings and drive down consumption and iterate back through step 3.
6. When the two estimates of C_X coincide to an acceptable degree of precision (say 0.01 percent), calculate GR, GE, F, and (dB/dt). As a final check, compare both sides of the investment-savings balance of Eq. (C-28). If they are not equal, something is wrong with the computer program.

C-3 A NEOCLASSICAL CLOSURE FOR BRAZIL

To solve the neoclassical model, a similar procedure was followed except that the main iteration in a supply-determined system has to be based on the price-equals-cost identity in production instead of the demand-equals-supply balance for the nationally produced commodity. To get an initial guess at the price level, a model in growth-rate form was used, the same as in the Cambridge closure except that choice-of-technique equations similar to Eqs. (D-15) through (D-18) in Appendix D were also imposed. As it turns out, there are three independent restrictions of this type for the four production inputs, and the growth rate of the exchange rate e' must be endogenous as well (for the reasons why, see Appendix D). Hence, the exogenous variables are the same as those in lists A through D in the previous section plus the rate of growth of the trade gap F'. The four exogenous growth rates in list E for the Cambridge closure have been reduced to one by adding neoclassical production hypotheses to the model.

The steps in solving the level form are

1. Calculate immediately Y_L, T_L and the end-of-period money stock as in the Cambridge version.
2. Pick a value for V from the log-change model or a previous iteration. Then calculate P, X, θ (the cost of a capital aggregate K made up of K_X and K_0), θ_X, θ_0, ρ, P_{0K}, e, P_0, and M. These calculations are based on level forms of CES production functions and the corresponding input-demand equations, as described in Appendix D.

3. Now check if the price-equals-cost identity Eq. (C-6) is satisfied for the chosen value of V. If not, set V equal to the new level of costs calculated from the right side of Eq. (C-6) and return to step 2.
4. After this iteration is complete, calculate Z, i, α_M, α_L, R, α_X, α_0, Y_K, and T_K using equations from Table C-1.
5. Calculate ϕ_X, ϕ_0, C_X, and C_0 as in step 4 of the Cambridge model.
6. Calculate I_X from the material balance Eq. (C-1); I_0 from the balance-of-payments Eq. (C-2); and g_X, g_0, GR, GE, and dB/dt from other equations in Table C-1. Check the savings-investment balance.

D

CONSTANT ELASTICITY OF SUBSTITUTION PRODUCTION FUNCTIONS

In a model where capital and labor are the only factors of production, it is convenient to summarize the response of the labor-output ratio L/X to changes in the real cost of labor w/P with a parameter σ^X, often called the elasticity of substitution:

$$L' - X' = -\sigma^X(w' - P') \tag{D-1}$$

If σ^X is assumed to be constant and this equation is integrated, the result evidently takes the form:

$$L/X = (\beta_L)^{\sigma^X}(w/P)^{-\sigma^X} \tag{D-2}$$

where β_L is a constant of integration.

In a famous article, Arrow, Chenery, Minhas, and Solow (affectionately known as ACMS, or SMAC) pointed out that a labor-demand equation like Eq. (D-2) could be derived from a production function of the form

$$X = [\beta_L L^{-\lambda} + \beta_K K^{-\lambda}]^{-1/\lambda} \tag{D-3}$$

where the exponent λ is equal to $(1 - \sigma^X)/\sigma^X$.

The derivation is straightforward. From Eq. (D-3), the marginal product of labor is

$$\partial X/\partial L = \beta_L (X/L)^{1+\lambda} = w/P \tag{D-4}$$

where the second equality follows from the standard neoclassical hypothesis that under competition the marginal product of a factor equals its real cost. Rearrangement of Eq. (D-4) gives Eq. (D-2). A further interpretation is in terms of the labor share $\alpha_L = wL/PX$:

$$\alpha_L = (\beta_L)^{\sigma^X}(w/P)^{1-\sigma^X} \tag{D-5}$$

which follows from Eq. (D-2) by multiplying both sides by w/P. Note that when σ^X equals 1, the labor share stays constant at the value β_L. In other words, a special case of the *constant elasticity of substitution* (CES) production function of Eq. (D-3) is the *Cobb-Douglas production function*

$$X = a(L)^{\beta_L}(K)^{\beta_K} \tag{D-6}$$

which maintains constant input shares and can be derived as a limit from Eq. (D-3) as σ^X approaches unity or λ approaches 0. In the constant returns Cobb-Douglas form, a is a scaling constant, and $\beta_L + \beta_K = 1$.

Two other special cases are of interest. The first has σ^X approaching infinity or λ approaching -1. From Eq. (D-3), we get

$$X = \beta_L L + \beta_K K \tag{D-7}$$

or the production function is linear. From Eq. (D-4), we find that $w/P = \beta_L$ in this case, and if r is the cost of capital, $r/P = \beta_K$ by analogy. These conditions can be summarized by a *cost function*

$$P = \min (w/\beta_L, r/\beta_K) \tag{D-8}$$

The "min" (or minimum) is taken here since if, say, w exceeded β_L, it would never pay to hire any labor, because its wage would be higher than its productivity.

The other special case follows if the labor-demand Eq. (D-2) and the corresponding equation for capital are substituted into Eq. (D-3) to derive the general version of a *CES cost function*

$$P = [a_L(w)^{1-\sigma^X} + a_K(r)^{1-\sigma^X}]^{1/(1-\sigma^X)} \tag{D-9}$$

where $a_L = (\beta_L)^{\sigma^X}$ and similarly for a_K. Letting σ^X go to 0 here gives

$$P = a_L w + a_K r \tag{D-10}$$

so the cost function is linear. The corresponding production function is

$$X = \min (L/a_L, K/a_K) \tag{D-11}$$

which has *fixed coefficients*; i.e., the amount of labor required to produce X is $a_L X$, and any more employment is otiose. The *isoquants* corresponding to the three special cases are shown in Fig. D-1. Intermediate values of σ^X can be located with reference to the limits 0, 1, and infinity.

The *wage-rental frontiers* measuring trade-offs between r and w for a given P (as isoquants measure trade-offs between K and L for a given X) are of form similar to the curves in Fig. D-1 except that the relationship to σ^X is reversed. For example, when $\sigma^X = 0$, the isoquant is a right angle (as shown in the figure) but the cost function is the straight line represented algebraically by Eq. (D-10). In economic terms, any ratio of input prices is consistent with the fixed input coefficients (or right-angle isoquant) of a *Leontief production function*. Much is made of this coincidence in Chap. 10.

All these linkages between the curvatures of an isoquant for a given value of σ^X and the corresponding wage-rental frontier largely determine the functional income

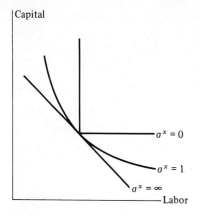

Figure D-1 Isoquants of the CES production function for different values of the elasticity of substitution σ^X.

distribution in a neoclassical world. For example, from Eq. (D-5), the labor share α_L falls with an increase in the real wage w/P when σ^X is greater than 1 and grows when σ^X is less than 1. In the latter case, a low degree of capital-labor substitutability means that when labor cost goes up, it is hard to substitute capital in its place; then labor earnings as a share of the value of output rise.

When the elasticity of substitution σ^X is known, the other parameters underlying the cost function of Eq. (D-9) or the production function of Eq. (D-3) can be derived from factor shares in the base year through equations like Eq. (D-5) and normalization assumptions on w, r, and P. Technical progress can be viewed as an exogenous shift in the coefficients after the base year. For example, if labor becomes more efficient over time, the "effective" labor force is

$$\bar{L}(t) = L(t) \exp{(\epsilon_L t)} \tag{D-12}$$

where $L(t)$ is actual employment at time t and ϵ_L is the rate of labor-augmenting technical progress. Taking technical change into account, the production function (D-3) can be rewritten as

$$X = [\beta_L \bar{L}^{-\lambda} + \beta_K K^{-\lambda}]^{-1/\lambda}$$
$$= [\beta_L \exp{(-\lambda \epsilon_L t)} L^{-\lambda} + \beta_K K^{-\lambda}]^{-1/\lambda} \tag{D-13}$$

where employment is measured in effective units in the first line and actual units in the second. On the basis of the second line, the expression of Eq. (D-5) for the labor share becomes

$$\alpha_L = (\beta_L)^{\sigma^X} \exp{[-\epsilon_L (1 - \sigma^X)t]} (w/P)^{1-\sigma^X} \tag{D-14}$$

so that α_L falls (rises) with labor-augmenting technical progress as the elasticity of substitution is less than (greater than) 1.

For the neoclassical Brazil model, an elaboration of CES production theory was used. Some years after SMAC, Kazuo Sato suggested that it would be convenient to extend the production function of Eq. (D-3) to several levels of aggregation, following an earlier suggestion by Solow. For the Brazil model, two levels were assumed. First, the two capital types K_X and K_0 substitute with each other according to an equation similar in form to Eq. (D-3) to produce a capital aggregate K. The stylized fact (from Sato) is that the corresponding substitution elasticity σ^K ought to have a value around 2. Second, at an upper level, noncompetitive imports M, labor L, and aggregated capital K all substitute with one another at elasticity σ^X in the production of gross output X.[1] Equations describing these trade-offs will now be presented in growth rate form, and the naturally exogenous and endogenous log changes pointed out. The straightforward extension to the level forms actually used in solving the Brazil model is left as an exercise for the reader.

Beginning with costs, note from Table C-1 that if we dispense with useless symbols by ignoring taxes, tariffs, and depreciation, the following expressions for growth rates of input costs result:

Labor (L): w'
Noncompetitive imports (M): e'
National capital (K_X): $\rho' + P'$
Imported capital (K_0): $\rho' + e'$

For either imported input, if tariffs and world prices do not vary, any change in acquisition cost comes from variation in the exchange rate e; the user cost of imported capital is further influenced by the profit rate ρ. Labor costs are measured by the wage w, and the user cost of national capital is ρP when taxes and depreciation are ignored. If the cost of the capital aggregate K is θ, we also have

$$\theta' = (\alpha_X + \alpha_0)^{-1} \left[\alpha_X(\rho' + P') + \alpha_0(\rho' + e')\right]$$
$$= \rho' + (\alpha_X + \alpha_0)^{-1} (\alpha_X P' + \alpha_0 e')$$

This equation is based on the usual principle that summing growth rates of the components of an aggregate weighted by their shares is the way to get the growth rate of the aggregate itself.

These expressions show that all cost growth rates can be expressed in terms of four variables, w', e', P', and ρ'. To see how choice of technique responds, begin by assuming labor-augmenting technical progress at rate ϵ/α_L to get

$$\alpha'_L = (1 - \sigma^X)(w' - P' - \epsilon/\alpha_L) \qquad \text{(D-15)}$$

[Note that the tax rate t_V of Eq. (C-7) is assumed equal to 0, so $P = V$.] Demand for noncompetitive imports is not affected by technical change and takes the simpler form

$$\alpha'_M = (1 - \sigma^X)(e' - P') \qquad \text{(D-16)}$$

Demand for the capital aggregate K can be described similarly except that it must

---

[1] Capital-labor substitution is an ancient article of faith, but economists are often doubtful that imports can substitute for other inputs and thus tend to treat noncompetitive imported intermediates M and output X as proportional. A priori, this may not be realistic; e.g., acceleration of the use of potential hydroelectric capacity in place of increased oil imports is always a possibility. To assume that imports, labor, and capital all substitute with the same elasticity goes well beyond this, but in the absence of contrary evidence the hypothesis is perhaps permissible—if one is neoclassically inclined in the first place.

be broken down into demands for national capital K_X and imported capital K_0. The first step is to note that the neoclassical way of relating the growth rate of the aggregate capital-output ratio to cost changes is

$$K' - X' = -\sigma^X(\theta' - P')$$

Also, if the two types of capital substitute with elasticity σ^K, then the change in the ratio of national capital K_X to the aggregate K is given by

$$K'_X - K' = -\sigma^K(\rho' + P' - \theta')$$

and likewise for imported capital. It is easy to substitute the K' terms out of these equations and put them in factor share form to get

$$\alpha'_X = (1 - \sigma^X)(\theta' - P') + (1 - \sigma^K)(\rho' + P' - \theta') \tag{D-17}$$

and

$$\alpha'_0 = (1 - \sigma^X)(\theta' - P') + (1 - \sigma^K)(\rho' + e' - \theta') \tag{D-18}$$

Now the only remaining task is to analyze which growth rates are naturally endogenous or exogenous in this structure. First, one can show that the four Eqs. (D-15) through (D-18) for factor-share growth rates will satisfy the adding-up condition

$$\alpha_M \alpha'_M + \alpha_L \alpha'_L + \alpha_X \alpha'_X + \alpha_0 \alpha'_0 = 0$$

if the additional restriction

$$P' = \alpha_M e' + \alpha_L w' + \alpha_X(\rho' + P') + \alpha_0(\rho' + e') - \epsilon \tag{D-19}$$

is imposed. Also, from this cost decomposition and the factor-share definitions, it is easy to show that the source-of-growth equation

$$X' = \alpha_M M' + \alpha_L L' + \alpha_X K'_X + \alpha_0 K'_0 + \epsilon \tag{D-20}$$

can be derived as well.[2]

After substitution for θ' and taking into account the definitions of log changes in factor shares ($\alpha'_M = e' + M' - P' - X'$ and so on), we have five independent restrictions on the ten variables X', M', L', K'_X, K'_0, ϵ, P', w', ρ', and e'. Of these, growth rates of employment, and the two types of capital (L', K'_0, and K'_X), the residual (ϵ), and the money wage (w') are exogenous. Growth rates of output (X'), intermediate imports (M'), the price level (P'), and the profit and exchange rates (ρ' and e') thus must be endogenous. A neoclassical production specification puts very rigid restrictions on the selection of exogenous and endogenous variables in general equilibrium.

---

[2]In the level form of the Brazil model, an equivalent statement is that one works *either* with CES production functions $X = f_X(M, L, K; \sigma^X)$ and $K = f_K(K_X, K_0; \sigma^K)$ *or* with the cost functions $V = g_V(P_0, \theta_L, \theta; \sigma^X)$ and $\theta = g_\theta(\theta_X, \theta_0; \sigma^K)$ *and* with input demand equations which are appropriate modifications of Eq. (D-2). Under competitive assumptions, production functions can always be derived from cost functions, and vice versa. See the paper by Diewert in the readings for the proofs.

SELECTED ADDITIONAL READINGS

Arrow, Kenneth J., Hollis B. Chenery, Bagicha S. Minhas, and Robert M. Solow: "Capital Labor Substitution and Economic Efficiency," *Review of Economics and Statistics*, **43**:225–250, 1961. (Original presentation and explication of the CES production function.)

Diewert, W. E.: "An Application of the Shephard Duality Theorem: A Generalized Leontief Production Function," *Journal of Political Economy*, **79**:481–507, 1971. (Gives proofs of the cost-production function duality relationships sketched in this appendix; for the mathematically inclined.)

Sato, Kazuo: "A Two-Level Constant-Elasticity-of-Substitution Production Function," *Review of Economic Studies*, **34**:201–218, 1967. (Original presentation of the two-level production structure used in the Brazil model.)

Solow, Robert M.: "The Production Function and the Theory of Capital," *Review of Economic Studies*, **23**(2): 101–108, 1956. (Explores the implications of "separable" production functions like the two-level CES suggested by Sato.)

E

THE DIRECT ADDILOG CONSUMER DEMAND SYSTEM

As it turns out, consumer demands are also conveniently described in terms of growth rates and an elasticity of substitution. The complete system of demand equations set up in these terms was apparently first developed by Frisch and further interpreted in terms of utility functions by Houthakker and Sato. Here we present the equations relevant for planning models, first in growth-rate and then in level forms.

Suppose total expenditure by a consumer is D. He purchases N commodities (or services) in quantities C_i, and the commodity prices are P_i. Let the share of the ith commodity in his total expenditure be defined as $\phi_i = P_i C_i / D$. Then a plausible decomposition (known as the *Slutsky equation*) for the log change of his consumption of the first good is

$$C_1' = \eta_1 (D' - \phi_1 P_1' - \phi_2 P_2' - \cdots - \phi_N P_N') + \eta_{11} P_1' + \eta_{12} P_2' + \cdots + \eta_{1N} P_N'$$

(E-1)

Here, η_1 is the *Engel* (or *income*) *elasticity* of demand for the first commodity, and the term in parentheses multiplied by η_1 is a natural index of the log change of *real income*, i.e., the growth rate of spending less a weighted average of growth rates of prices. The parameters η_{11} through η_{1N} are called *compensated price elasticities* of demand.[1] They show how consumption C_1 responds to price changes after the change

---

[1] In comparing the results here to those of Appendix B, note that the η_{ij} appearing in Eqs. (B-11) and (B-12) are *uncompensated* elasticities and should be compared to terms like $-\eta_1 \phi_j + \eta_{1j}$ in Eq. (E-1).

in real income is taken into account. For example, if $P_1' > 0$, real income falls and induces a log change in C_1 of the amount $-\eta_1 \phi_1 P_1'$. A further substitution response is given by $\eta_{11} P_1'$. Presumably $\eta_{11} < 0$, so that consumption of good one declines from both *income* and *substitution* effects. If $P_2' > 0$, C_1 will decline from the income effect $(-\eta_1 \phi_2 P_2' < 0)$, but presumably rise from substitution because it becomes cheaper relative to good two $(\eta_{12} P_2' > 0)$.

There are too many parameters for practical use running around in the N equations like Eq. (E-1), so restrictions must be imposed. First, note that the log change in the ith budget share is

$$\phi_i' = (\eta_i - 1) D' + P_i' - \eta_i \left(\sum_{j=1}^{N} \phi_j P_j' \right) + \sum_{j=1}^{N} \eta_{ij} P_j' \tag{E-2}$$

Since weighted log changes in the budget shares must sum to 0,

$$\sum_{j=1}^{N} \phi_j \phi_j' = 0 \tag{E-3}$$

certain restrictions on the elasticities are implied. These are called *Engel aggregation*

$$\sum_{i=1}^{N} \phi_i \eta_i = 1 \tag{E-4}$$

and *Cournot aggregation*

$$\sum_{i=1}^{N} \phi_i \eta_{ij} = 0 \quad j = 1, \ldots, N \tag{E-5}$$

These two sets of conditions can be derived by differentiating the *budget constraint*

$$\sum_{i=1}^{N} P_i C_i = D \tag{E-6}$$

and in effect state that the constraint has to be satisfied both before and after income and price changes. A somewhat similar restriction follows if all prices and income are assumed to increase proportionately, as if 100 new locals (units of currency) were substituted for one old. There should be no change in consumption of the first commodity, or $C_1' = 0$. Since the parenthesis in Eq. (E-1) vanishes by assumption, such insensitivity is assured if the *homogeneity condition*

$$\sum_{j=1}^{N} \eta_{ij} = 0 \tag{E-7}$$

holds.

Homogeneity and Cournot and Engel aggregation almost suffice to determine demand behavior. However, a few more restrictions must still be imposed. A clue is provided by the empirical observation (or stylized fact) that own-price and income elasticities of demand for commodities often seem proportional. A formal statement (slightly modified for algebraic convenience) is

$$\eta_{ii} = -\sigma^C \eta_i (1 - \phi_i \eta_i) \tag{E-8}$$

In words, the compensated own-price elasticity of demand for good i is a fraction σ^C of the income elasticity (after correction for sign) times a fudge factor depending on the budget share and income elasticity of the good. The higher either of these quantities is, the lower is the compensated own-price elasticity of demand (since, in effect, the commodity is more important to the consumer).

From this hypothesis, either Cournot aggregation or the homogeneity condition can be used to derive an expression for cross-price elasticities,

$$\eta_{ij} = -\sigma^C \eta_i \phi_j \eta_j \quad (i \neq j) \tag{E-9}$$

The sensitivity of the ith good to the jth price depends on its own income elasticity and the general price responsiveness of the consumer, $(-\eta_i \sigma^C)$, and also on the budget share and income responsiveness of the other good $(\phi_j \eta_j)$.

If income elasticities are known [subject to budget shares and the condition of Eq. (E-4)], then knowledge of σ^C determines all price responses from Eqs. (E-8) and (E-9). The Slutsky Eq. (E-1) can then be used to predict how consumer demand will respond to income and price changes in the small. For large changes, complete sets of consumer-demand functions must be sought, just as production or cost functions are required on the supply side.

Consumer functions are typically derived by assuming the maximization of some utility function subject to a budget constraint. Once such process was described in Appendix B, to derive the linear expenditure system. Another can be used to derive Eq. (E-1). Suppose that the consumer maximizes the utility function

$$U = \sum_{i=1}^{N} \beta_i (C_i)^{-(1-|\epsilon_i|)/|\epsilon_i|}$$

$$= \sum_{i=1}^{N} \beta_i (C_i)^{(1+\epsilon_i)/\epsilon_i} \tag{E-10}$$

subject to the budget constraint of Eq. (E-6). The parameters β_i are normalizing factors, while the negative constants ϵ_i will be shown to be closely related to the previously introduced η_i, or income elasticities of demand. Observe also the similarity of this utility function to the CES production function of Eq. (D-3). The main difference is that since own-price and income elasticities vary across commodities, one has to work with separate exponents $(1 - |\epsilon_i|)/|\epsilon_i|$ for each good, instead of the single λ in Eq. (D-3).

The first-order conditions for a maximum of Eq. (E-10) subject to Eq. (E-6) take the form

$$\frac{1 + \epsilon_i}{\epsilon_i} \beta_i (C_i)^{1/\epsilon_i} = \mu P_i$$

where μ is a Lagrange multiplier. Multiplication of both sides of this expression by C_i, summation over i, and a bit of manipulation give the following expression for μ:

$$\mu = (1/D) \sum_{i=1}^{N} \frac{1 + \epsilon_i}{\epsilon_i} \beta_i(C_i)^{(1+\epsilon_i)/\epsilon_i}$$

$$= \chi/D$$

Substituting back into the first-order condition finally gives the direct addilog demand equation

$$C_i = \left[\frac{D\beta_i(1 + \epsilon_i)/\epsilon_i}{\chi P_i} \right]^{-\epsilon_i} \tag{E-11}$$

For each C_i, this equation is in closed form *except* for the scaling factor χ. In computational practice, it is easy to vary χ until the budget constraint of Eq. (E-6) is satisfied and thus calculate demands for all goods. However, variability of χ also makes the interpretation of Eq. (E-11) a bit lengthy. First note that if χ stays constant, the own-price and income elasticities of demand for C_i would be ϵ_i and $-\epsilon_i$ respectively. To correct these expressions for variation in χ, one can rewrite Eq. (E-11) in growth-rate form as

$$C_i' = -\epsilon_i(D' - P_i' - \chi') \tag{E-12}$$

or

$$\phi_i' = P_i' + C_i' - D' = -(1 + \epsilon_i)(D' - P_i') + \epsilon_i\chi'$$

The adding-up condition $\Sigma_i \phi_i \phi_i' = 0$ allows one to get an expression for χ', and back substitution into Eq. (E-12) finally gives a log-differential demand function in terms of only income and prices. Lo and behold, it turns out to be the same as the Slutsky equation [Eq. (E-1)] with which we began, with

$$\eta_i = -\epsilon_i/\sigma^C$$

$$\eta_{ii} = \epsilon_i(1 + \phi_i\epsilon_i/\sigma^C) = -\sigma^C\eta_i(1 - \eta_i\phi_i)$$

and

$$\eta_{ij} = \epsilon_i \epsilon_j \phi_j/\sigma^C = -\sigma^C\eta_i\eta_j\phi_j$$

as before.

The substitution indicator σ^C is now revealed as

$$\sigma^C = -\sum_{i=1}^{N} \phi_i\epsilon_i \tag{E-13}$$

or a weighted average of the income terms in the utility function. As the budget shares ϕ_i vary, then so does σ^C, to rescale income and price elasticities so that the normalizing restrictions of Eqs. (E-4), (E-5), and (E-7) will continue to obtain.

The direct addilog system is fairly straightforward to apply in practice, since when one knows the parameters it is easy to vary χ in Eq. (E-11) until the budget constraint holds. With that, all demands are determined. For small changes in D and the P_i, the

Slutsky equation [Eq. (E-1)] is even easier to apply, and the elasticities can be updated using Eq. (E-13).

In the base year, if one knows the income elasticities and budget shares (say from a household expenditure survey), then all other parameters including the ϵ_i can be calculated with a knowledge of σ^C. This can be "estimated" by comparing selected income and own-price elasticities if the latter are known, or by applying the stylized fact that σ^C is usually pretty close to 0.5.

SELECTED ADDITIONAL READINGS

Frisch, Ragnar: "A Complete Scheme for Computing All Direct and Cross Demand Elasticities in a Model with Many Sectors," *Econometrica*, 27:177–196, 1969. (Original statement of much of this appendix.)

Houthakker, Hendrik S.: "Additive Preferences," *Econometrica*, 28:244–257, 1960. [Suggests the use of Eq. (E-10) as a utility function.]

Sato, Kazuo: "Additive Utility Functions for Double-Log Consumer Demand Functions," *Journal of Political Economy*, 80:102–124, 1972. (Extension and description of the Frisch-Houthakker demand equations of this appendix.)

THE LORENZ CURVE

Lorenz curves come in square boxes, with percentage shares of the population measured along the horizontal axis and percentage shares of income on the vertical. A typical specimen appears in Fig. F-1, based on data for quintiles of the size distribution of income. According to the curve, the bottom 20 percent of the population holds 5 percent of total personal income, the bottom 40 percent of the population 15 percent of income, and so on.

One Lorenz curve lying completely below another indicates a more unequal income distribution. The most equal distribution possible is, of course, indicated by the diagonal line in the box, along which X percent of the population holds X percent of the income, for all population fractions X. A widely used measure of income inequality is the *Gini coefficient*, calculated as the ratio of the area between the diagonal line and the Lorenz curve (shaded in Fig. F-1) and the area of the lower triangle. Ob-

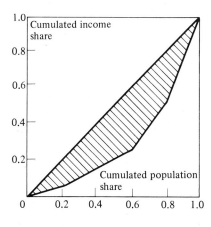

Figure F-1 A Lorenz curve based on quintiles of the income distribution by size.

viously, the Gini can vary between 0 and 1; in practice, countries with relatively egalitarian income distributions might have Gini coefficients ranging around 0.3, while the Gini for an inegalitarian country might be 0.6.

For a more analytical description of the Gini coefficient and other distribution measures, see the book by Sen.

ADDITIONAL READING

Sen, Amartya K.: *On Economic Inequality*, Norton, New York, 1973. (Compact and lucid survey of the measurement and causes of income inequality.)

FORMAL DERIVATIONS OF SHADOW WAGE AND DISCOUNT RATES

The essentials of how to interpret and even calculate shadow wage and discount rates have already been presented in Chap. 13. However, for readers with some interest in theory who want to know (and criticize!) all the assumptions underlying the usual formulas, a more formal and largely self-contained treatment is presented here. Section G-1 gives a heuristic derivation of the optimality conditions that apply when a social welfare index is maximized subject to differential equations describing capital stock accumulation over time. The dual variables arising out of the maximization are naturally interpreted as shadow prices for the evaluation of investment projects, as discussed in Secs. G-2 and G-3 with the neoclassical growth model of Sec. 6-5 as an example. Section G-4 then presents the growth model embodying surplus labor that underlies most project criteria in developing countries and derives the Little-Mirrlees and UNIDO project selection rules discussed in the text of Chap. 13.

G-1 DYNAMIC OPTIMIZATION RULES

In this section we present the rudiments of what is usually called "optimal control theory" in applied mathematics, or "optimal growth analysis" in economics. The book by Bryson and Ho in the Selected Additional Readings is a useful reference on the mathematics (written from an engineering point of view), while Arrow and Kurz and Dorfman talk more about economics.

Suppose that there are N stock (or state) variables X_i in the economy—say different types of capital, total foreign debt, etc. We group these in a column vector X. There are also M flow (or control) variables U_i which influence the accumulation of the stocks according to differential equations such as

$$dX_i/dt = f^i(X_1, X_2, \ldots, X_N; U_1, U_2, \ldots, U_M; t) \qquad \text{(G-1)}$$

Given values of the U vector over time (we suppress the time argument in both state and control variables for simplicity), the entire future "history" of the system is determined so long as we know the levels of the stocks at some initial time t_0:

$$X(t_0) \text{ is given} \qquad \text{(G-2)}$$

A homely example of all this paraphernalia (discussed next section) is the neoclassical one-sector growth model. The amount of capital per head is the state variable, and investment is the single control. When you know the initial amount of capital per head and yearly per capita investment levels (output less consumption per head), you can derive the levels of capital over time from an equation like Eq. (G-1)–specifically Eq. (G-11), below.

Planners are assumed to know a scalar *welfare function* $W(X, U, t)$ which, in economic practice, will often take the form of the discounted utility of consumption per head. If the planning horizon begins at t_0 and ends at some future time t_f (possibly infinity), then they will want to maximize the functional

$$V = \int_{t_0}^{t_f} W(X, U, t)\, dt + \bar{P}^T X(t_f) \qquad \text{(G-3)}$$

The first term in Eq. (G-3) is the integral of "welfare" over the planning period. The second term, written out longhand as

$$\bar{P}_1 X_1(t_f) + \bar{P}_2 X_2(t_f) + \cdots + \bar{P}_N X_N(t_f)$$

is a device for putting values $\bar{P}_i$ on each element $X_i(t_f)$ of the stock vector at the end of the planning horizon. These terminal prices reflect the fact that the economy will need such items as capital stocks even after the plan is completed. In many models, they prevent the state variables from running down to 0 at the end of the plan. In an infinite horizon problem, the inelegant valuation vector $\bar{P}^T$ is usually not required, but then neither is it very convincing to assert that one's plans are valid forever. Practicing builders of computable planning models usually compromise by trying to make their $\bar{P}_i$'s as innocuous as possible. The appendix to the model survey by Taylor summarizes the tricks of the trade.

As in most optimization problems, an effective solution strategy is to adjoin the constraints of Eq. (G-1) to the maximand of Eq. (G-3) with a set of undetermined multipliers $P^T(t)$, which vary over time along with everything else. This procedure gives a new maximand Z:

$$Z = \bar{P}^T X(t_f) + \int_{t_0}^{t_f} \{W(X, U, t) + P^T[F(X, U, t) - dX/dt]\}\, dt \qquad \text{(G-4)}$$

in which $F(X, U, t)$ is the vector-valued function made up of all the f^i from Eq. (G-1), and dX/dt is the vector of time derivatives of each X_i. Inclusion of the constraints within the integral in Eq. (G-4) reflects the dynamic nature of the problem; the constraints of Eq. (G-1) are differential equations, and we want them to hold at each point in time.

To compress the algebra in Eq. (G-4), define something called a *Hamiltonian* as

$$H(X, U, P, t) = W(X, U, t) + P^T F(X, U, t) \tag{G-5}$$

As we will see below, the Hamiltonian usually has an immediate interpretation as a GDP-like current welfare index in economic problems, e.g., the sum of utility from consumption (W) plus the value of capital formation ($P^T F$). Plugging the definition of H into Eq. (G-4) and a bit of sleight of hand gives

$$Z = \bar{P}^T X(t_f) + \int_{t_0}^{t_f} H(X, U, P, t)\, dt - \int_{t_0}^{t_f} P^T (dX/dt)\, dt$$

$$= \bar{P}^T X(t_f) + \int_{t_0}^{t_f} H(X, U, P, t)\, dt - P^T(t_f) X(t_f) + P^T(t_0) X(t_0) + \int_{t_0}^{t_f} (dP^T/dt) X(t)\, dt \tag{G-6}$$

where the second integral after the first equality was integrated by parts to get the last three terms after the second equality.

Now we can go ahead with maximization by setting the total derivative (or "variation") δZ of the maximand equal to 0 as a first order condition. Considering variations δX in the state variables and δU in the controls, we find from Eq. (G-6) that δZ takes the form:

$$\delta Z = [(\bar{P} - P)^T \delta X]_{t=t_f} + [P^T \delta X]_{t=t_0} + \int_{t_0}^{t_f} \left\{ \left[\frac{\partial H}{\partial X} + (dP^T/dt) \right] \delta X + \frac{\partial H}{\partial U} \delta U \right\} dt \tag{G-7}$$

where $(\partial H/\partial X)$ and $(\partial H/\partial U)$ are vectors of derivatives of the Hamiltonian with respect to the N elements of X and M elements of U, by convention written in row form.

To make the variation δZ equal to 0, a number of necessary conditions must be satisfied in Eq. (G-7). First, to make sure that a nonzero variation in the controls δU has no effect, the derivative vector of the Hamiltonian with respect to these flow variables must be 0:

$$\partial H/\partial U_i = 0 \qquad i = 1, 2, \ldots, M \tag{G-8}$$

Second, for a variation δX in the stock variables to leave δZ unchanged, the first bracket within the integral in Eq. (G-7) must vanish, or

$$\partial H/\partial X_i = -dP_i/dt \qquad i = 1, 2, \ldots, N \tag{G-9}$$

Equation (G-9) will, in economic problems, turn out to describe the development of capital-goods prices over time. They are naturally dual to the asset-accumulation Eq. (G-1), as we will see in more detail shortly.

In the rest of Eq. (G-7), note from Eq. (G-2) that the initial levels of the stock variables are given, so the second term on the right-hand side vanishes. To make the first term vanish for arbitrary changes δX at time t_f, we require

$$P_i(t_f) = \bar{P}_i(t_f) \qquad i = 1, 2, \ldots, N \tag{G-10}$$

These equations put terminal conditions on the differential Eq. (G-9) for asset prices, so that these run naturally backward in time [which is what the minus sign in front of dP_i/dt in Eq. (G-9) means as well]. Since the accumulation Eq. (G-1) runs forward from Eq. (G-2), the optimality conditions of Eqs. (G-1), (G-2), (G-8), (G-9), and (G-10) are said by mathematicians to comprise a two-point boundary value problem, the two points being the initial and terminal conditions on the two sets of differential equations.

G-2 OPTIMAL GROWTH IN THE ONE-SECTOR NEOCLASSICAL MODEL

To make economic sense out of all these rather abstract relationships, the best thing is to work through their application to a simple example. We choose one that is extremely well known: the neoclassical growth model of Sec. 6-5.

Recall that the basic assumption in that model is that savings (or output less consumption) determines capital formation:

$$dK/dt = F(K, L) - C$$

in which K is the capital stock, L is employment, and C is total consumption. The production function $F(K, L)$ is assumed to display constant returns to scale and to be well behaved in whatever ways we may require it to be. From the constant-returns assumption, we can "divide through" the capital accumulation equation by L and put everything in per capita terms, as in the following slightly modified version of Eq. (6-25):

$$dk/dt = f(k) - c - nk \tag{G-11}$$

Here, k is the capital-labor ratio ($k = K/L$), and $f(k)$ is output per capita $[(f = F/L = F(K/L, 1)$ from the constant-returns property]. Consumption per head is c ($c = C/L$), and the rate of population and employment growth is exogenously specified to be n. In keeping with Eq. (G-2), the initial capital stock per worker, $k(t_0)$, is given.

We suppose that the planners' welfare functional takes the form

$$V = \int_{t_0}^{t_f} \exp(-\delta t) L(t) U[C(t)/L(t)] \; dt + \bar{p}k(t_f)$$

The integrand here is some utility function U based on consumption per capita at time t, weighted by the total population then expected to be alive. (This formulation is supposed to prevent more numerous future generations from being deprived of their rightful share of the per capita consumption pie.) We discount this weighted utility index at a rate δ in order to take into account planners' myopia, uncertainty, etc. At the end of the planning period, there is a valuation $\bar{p}$ placed on the per capita capital stock willed to subsequent generations. With the population growing at rate n, we can transform the integral above to get

$$V = L(t_0) \int_{t_0}^{t_f} \exp(-\lambda t) U[c(t)] \, dt + \bar{p}k(t_f) \tag{G-12}$$

where $\lambda = \delta - n$. For simplicity, $L(t_0)$ is hereafter normalized to equal 1. The planner overseeing the optimal growth of a given economy is thus assumed to maximize Eq. (G-12) subject to Eq. (G-11) and the initial value $k(t_0)$. Now we turn to the details of the solution.

In the nomenclature of Sec. G-1, k is the state variable in the optimal growth problem and c is the control. The Hamiltonian is

$$H = \exp(-\lambda t) U(c) + p[f(k) - c - nk]$$
$$= \exp(-\lambda t) \{U(c) + q[f(k) - c - nk]\} \tag{G-13}$$

in which $q(t)$ is defined as $\exp(\lambda t)p(t)$, the current value of the capital shadow price at time t. This current asset price is introduced to make interpretation of the Hamiltonian easier, since the term in curly brackets in the second line of Eq. (G-13) is clearly a welfare-based index of the level of economic activity at time t. The $U(c)$ term measures total utility from consumption per head, while the second term evaluates the growth in capital stock per head from Eq. (G-11) at its asset value q. The Hamiltonian comes very close to being GDP per capita except that it includes *total* utility from consumption instead of its market value (or marginal utility, on consumption theory grounds) and values capital formation at the shadow price q. The fact that a cunningly specified optimization problem will mimic market valuations so closely is one of the reasons why optimal planning models appeal to neoclassicals.

Such esthetic judgments aside, it is easy to get optimality conditions like Eqs. (G-8) and (G-9) from Eq. (G-13). The first is

$$dU/dc = \exp(\lambda t)p = q \tag{G-14}$$

and the second is

$$df/dk - n = -p' = -(q' - \lambda) \tag{G-15}$$

in which p' means $(dp/dt)/p$, as usual.

The first of these conditions asserts that, on the optimal growth path, the marginal utility from consumption per head should equal the shadow price of the single good in the system. Such an equality is to be expected from consumption theory, but it will turn out to be violated when we take up optimal growth in a Lewis-style economy in Sec. G-4. In Eq. (G-15), the marginal product of capital df/dk is set equal to the utility discount rate δ (equals $\lambda + n$) less the *change* in the capital asset price q. One could imagine this sort of equality arising when a person is deciding whether to invest resources productively or to save them for an instant. In the first case there would be a production return df/dk; and in the second, there would be a bank return δ less any fall in the current value of the assets from one instant to the next. Arbitrage between these two opportunities could be assumed to provide an equality like Eq. (G-15). Again, optimization is supposed to mimic the market, or vice versa.

We can get another characterization of the optimal growth path by defining the quantity $-j$ as the absolute value of the elasticity of the *marginal* utility of consumption (the elasticity of dU/dc with respect to c). This definition arises quite naturally if the planners' utility function conveniently takes the familiar form of Eq. (E-10) in Appendix E.

$$U(c) = \begin{cases} \dfrac{c^{1-j}}{1-j} & j \neq 1 \\ \\ \log(c) & j = 1 \end{cases} \tag{G-16}$$

In this case, the elasticity of marginal utility is the constant $-j$, with j required to be nonnegative.

Using j, one can rewrite Eq. (G-14) in the following form:

$$(dU/dc)' = -jc' = q' \qquad \text{from Eq. (G-14)}$$

$$= -(df/dk - n) + \lambda \qquad \text{from Eq. (G-15)}$$

$$= -(df/dk - \delta) \qquad \text{from the definition of } \lambda$$

In slightly rearranged form, the last equality is

$$jc' + \delta = df/dk = \partial X/\partial K \tag{G-17}$$

On the left side here, $jc' + \delta$ is just the rate at which the planners' measure of utility from per capita consumption $\exp(-\delta t)U(c)$ falls off as c grows at rate c'. The right side shows the increment in output from diversion of resources to use as capital in production.[1] On the margin, Eq. (G-17) asserts that the utility loss (sometimes called *the social rate of discount*) and the production gain (the *marginal product of capital*) should be equal. Once again, in the Lewis model we will see that this convenient identity between two plausible rates of discount does not apply.

Before we turn to investment project analysis per se, one final bit of interpretation of the neoclassical optimal growth model is in order. To begin, rewrite Eq. (G-17) in the slightly modified form

$$dc/dt = (-c/j)(\delta - df/dk) \tag{G-18}$$

which we can christen the *Ramsey rule* in honor of the Cambridge philosopher-economist Frank Ramsey, who first proposed optimal growth models in a famous article in 1928.

In the Ramsey rule for optimal consumption over time, we have the time derivative of consumption dc/dt depending on the capital stock variable k. In Eq. (G-11), dk/dt depends on c. Given this joint determination of dc/dt and dk/dt, it is illuminating to discuss their evolution over time in terms of a *phase diagram* such as the one appearing in Fig. G-1. Here the vertical line at k^* represents Eq. (G-18), with k^* being the value of k at which df/dk equals δ. When k exceeds k^*, Eq. (G-18) shows that c is falling (and vice versa when k^* exceeds k), as shown by the small arrows on the graph. Similarly, the curved line corresponds to the condition $f(k) - nk - c = 0$,

---

[1] The reader should verify $df/dk = d(X/L)/d(K/L) = \partial X/\partial K$, as asserted in Eq. (G-17).

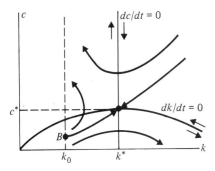

Figure G-1 Phase diagram for the simple optimal growth model.

which—from Eq. (G-11)—assures that dk/dt is 0. For combinations of c and k above this line, dk/dt is negative (and vice versa for combinations below the line), again as shown by the small arrows.

The large arrows show how c and k move over time, starting from given initial conditions. For example, if the initial capital stock is k_0, then only the path starting from the initial (k_0, c) combination B converges to the stationary combination of capital and consumption (k^*, c^*). This combination represents the balanced growth path in our maximization problem.

Thus, the model demonstrates a turnpike property characteristic of all optimal growth problems. There is only one initial (k, c) combination which leads through the differential Eqs. (G-11) and (G-18) to a stationary balanced growth solution. All other paths (as shown by the large arrows in Fig. G-1) diverge in some way. However, one can show that throughout "most" of their evolution, even the divergent paths stay arbitrarily close to the turnpike path beginning from B. Naturally, the same comments apply to a model in which one works with initial combinations of k and the asset price q (or p) instead of k and c.

The planning implication of this is that often the first years of the plan produced by an optimizing model will *not* depend on how terminal conditions are specified, which is reassuring, since we do not know how to specify the terminal value of capital $\bar{p}$ very well in any case. The other planning use of these models lies in the discount rates for capital and other shadow prices they produce. For the neoclassical model, this is the topic we take up next.

G-3 SHADOW PRICING IN THE NEOCLASSICAL GROWTH MODEL

At the level of abstraction of optimal growth models, investment projects are best viewed as perturbations of a precalculated optimal solution. For example, suppose that we have solved the model of last section, finding thereby time paths of capital, consumption, etc., which are "optimal," at least in terms of the planners' preference function specified in (G-12). Now suppose that after the model is solved, a specific investment project becomes possible. Its effects on capital accumulation can be described by some function $h(t)$, which must be added to Eq. (G-11) to give a new

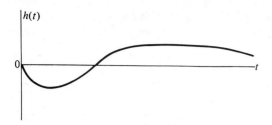

Figure G-2 Possible time shape of net benefits from an investment project $h(t)$.

accumulation equation

$$dk/dt = f(k) - c - nk + h(t) \qquad \text{(G-19)}$$

Usually, the function $h(t)$ might be expected to have the time shape illustrated in Fig. G-2. It is negative (using up capital) during the first part of the project's lifetime. Thereafter, it gives a positive level of product for some years. The basic question in project analysis is whether or not we should undertake this investment.

In the framework of the growth model, we could obviously answer this question by maximizing Eq. (G-12)—first with respect to Eq. (G-11), then with respect to Eq. (G-19)—and checking which problem gives the higher value of the maximand V. If this occurs when Eq. (G-19) is the equation describing capital accumulation, then the project should be undertaken.

A simpler method of project analysis is implicit in the fact that, to a first-order approximation, the change in V resulting from the project is given by

$$\delta V = \int_{t_0}^{t_f} p(t)h(t)\, dt \qquad \text{(G-20)}$$

where $p(t)$ is the shadow price of capital introduced in the last section. The evolution of p over time is described by the differential Eq. (G-15), which in slightly rewritten form is

$$dp/dt = -p(f_k - n) \qquad \text{(G-21)}$$

in which f_k is shorthand for the marginal product of capital df/dk. This equation is linear in p, and we can immediately write down its solution as

$$p(t) = p(t_0) \exp\left[-\int_{t_0}^{t} (f_k - n)\, d\tau \right] \qquad \text{(G-22)}$$

in which $p(t_0)$ is the initial value of p, and τ is a dummy variable of integration. Factoring out $p(t_0)$ as an inessential constant, we can insert Eq. (G-22) into Eq. (G-20) and express the acceptance criterion for the investment project ($\delta V > 0$) as

$$\int_{t_0}^{t_f} h(t) \exp\left[-\int_{t_0}^{t} (f_k - n)\, d\tau \right] dt > 0 \qquad \text{(G-23)}$$

But this condition amounts to no more than discounting the investment project's flow of product $h(t)$ with the marginal product of capital f_k (minus a correction for the fact that the whole model is expressed in per capita terms). This can be seen more clearly if we assume that the marginal product stays constant at some value $\bar{f}_k$. In this case, Eq. (G-23) reduces to

$$\int_{t_0}^{t_f} h(t) \exp\left[-(\bar{f}_k - n)(t - t_0)\right] dt$$

the present value at rate $(\bar{f}_k - n)$ of $h(t)$. As long as this present value is positive, then the project is worth doing. [Of course, in the general case the marginal product of capital will change over time, so that the more complicated formula of Eq. (G-23) must be used to calculate present value; but the principle remains the same.]

Finally, note from the Ramsey rule, Eq. (G-17), that it does not really matter whether we use the utility-based rate of discount $jc' + \delta$ or the marginal product of capital f_k to figure the present value of $h(t)$ in Eq. (G-23); both discount rates in the neoclassical model are the same. Now we take up optimal growth in a Lewis-style model, in which the two rates are not identical. The difference has given rise to a vast amount of sterile controversy, as we will see shortly.

G-4 SHADOW PRICING IN LABOR-SURPLUS ECONOMIES

By far the most widely used methodology for calculating shadow prices in developing countries is based on the Lewis labor-surplus model discussed in Chaps. 10 and 11. In the simplest version, the modern sector is the focus of all attention. The subsistence sector enters only insofar as it furnishes labor at a fixed real wage w, and no heed is paid to the welfare of the people who do not get modern-sector jobs at all.

Accounting relationships based only on the modern sector are very simple. There is some output level X, produced by employed labor L and capital K. It is used for investment I and consumption C:

$$X(K, L) = C + I \tag{G-24}$$

The essential surplus-labor assumption is that modern-sector consumption comes only from labor payments at a *fixed* wage w,

$$C = wL \tag{G-25}$$

Capitalists and/or the government as profit recipients are supposed to invest all the income they receive. As in the Ramsey problem of secs. G-2 and G-3, planners want to maximize total welfare V generated by modern-sector consumption over time.

$$V = \int_{t_0}^{t_f} U(C) \, dt \tag{G-26}$$

subject to Eqs. (G-24) and (G-25). No welfare valuation is placed on whatever crumbs people in the subsistence sector generate for themselves or otherwise receive. Also, a utility discount factor $\exp(-\delta t)$ is omitted from the integrand in Eq. (G-26) to save algebra. Figure 13-1 has already been used to illustrate the nature of the constraints that planners face in this economy. These can be stated formally if we let m stand for the labor-capital ratio L/K. Assuming constant returns to scale, the production function can be expressed as

$$X = x(m) K$$

and the restrictions of Fig. 13-1 become

$$\underline{m} \leqslant m \leqslant \overline{m} \qquad \text{(G-27)}$$

where

$$\left. \frac{dx}{dm} \right]_{m = \underline{m}} = w$$

and

$$x(\overline{m}) = w\overline{m}$$

Consumption in this new specification is given by

$$C = wmK$$

and investment is

$$dK/dt = [x(m) - wm] K \qquad \text{(G-28)}$$

Substituting from the above consumption relationship into Eq. (G-26), we can restate the planners' problem as the maximization of

$$\int_{t_0}^{t_f} U(wmK)\, dt \qquad \text{(G-29)}$$

subject to Eqs. (G-27) and (G-28).

Proceeding in the usual fashion, set up this problem's Hamiltonian as

$$H = U(wmK) + p[x(m) - wm] K \qquad \text{(G-30)}$$

where p is the asset price of capital. The first-order condition for maximization of H subject to Eq. (G-27) can be written as

$$\frac{\partial H}{\partial m} \begin{cases} \geqslant 0 \text{ when } m = \overline{m} \\ = 0 \text{ when } \underline{m} < m < \overline{m} \\ \leqslant 0 \text{ when } m = \underline{m} \end{cases} \qquad \text{(G-31)}$$

as one can easily see by realizing that the derivative of H must be positive for a maximum when m is constrained from above and negative when m is constrained from below.

The explicit expression for the partial derivative in Eq. (G-31) is

$$\frac{\partial H}{\partial m} = \frac{dU}{d(wmK)}\, wK + p \left(\frac{dx}{dm} - w \right) K \qquad \text{(G-32)}$$

Using the expression, we can easily show that m must lie between the extreme points $\underline{m}$ and $\overline{m}$ in an infinite horizon plan. Suppose first that $m = \underline{m}$, then—by the definition of m given in connection with Eq. (G-27)—the second term in Eq. (G-32) must vanish. Then Eq. (G-31) requires that the first term be nonpositive, i.e., the derivative of the utility function must not be greater than 0. As long as we rule out satiation in consumption (a reasonable provision in a poor economy—or even a rich one) this cannot occur, and m must exceed $\underline{m}$. As long as *any* utility value is attached to current consumption by modern-sector workers, the Galenson-Leibenstein point will not be chosen.

In an infinite horizon, it is clearly suboptimal for the economy to remain with $m = \overline{m}$, because no investment takes place and the utility integral must finally diverge to minus infinity as long as the integrand takes the form of Eq. (G-16) with $j > 1$. Under the same assumptions, capital accumulation at a finite rate will lead to a convergent integral in the welfare functional Eq. (G-29), since the function in Eq. (G-16) is bounded from above by 0 when $j > 1$. On the other hand, if m does equal $\overline{m}$, then the second term in the Hamiltonian Eq. (G-30) vanishes and $\partial H/\partial m$ exceeds 0, as it should from Eq. (G-31) for equilibrium at $m = \overline{m}$. The economy will never grow beyond the maximum consumption point once it reaches it; hence it is suboptimal ever to go there in the first place.

From these heuristics, we conclude that $\partial H/\partial m$ must equal 0 as the necessary condition for an internal maximum in Eq. (G-31), or

$$p[w - dx/dm] = w(dU/dC) \qquad \text{(G-33)}$$

This condition can be called the *Marglin rule*, after the economist who perhaps first proposed it. The left side of the equation is the loss in physical investable surplus $(w - dx/dm)$ which results when an additional worker is hired in the modern sector, valued at the investment shadow price p. The right side is the marginal consumption utility that new workers enjoy, i.e., they consume all their wages w, and the social marginal utility of this consumption is dU/dC. At an optimum, these gains and losses must be equalized, and this is what the equation says. Also note that the marginal utility of consumption is less than the asset price p; or, for a given asset price, consumption is higher (marginal utility is lower) than it would be in a neoclassical optimal equilibrium like that described by Eq. (G-14). In effect, the condition of Eq. (G-33) suggests that workers' consumption should be subsidized so that the marginal utility it generates falls below its cost in terms of foregone investment p. Equivalently, in Fig. 13-1 employment is subsidized so that it rises above the wage-equals-marginal-product point $\underline{L}$. Either of these statements explains why a shadow wage differing from the subsistence wage w is necessary in the surplus-labor model.

Before we go into calculation of the shadow wage, it is useful to pursue the implications briefly of the other optimality condition $\partial H/\partial K = -dp/dt$. For the surplus-labor model, this takes the form

$-dp/dt = U_C wm + p[x(m) - wm]$ where $U_C = dU/dC$

$= p(w - x_m) m + p[x(m) - wm]$ from Eq. (G-33), where $x_m = dx/dm$

$= p[x(m) - x_m m]$

$= p(\partial X/\partial K)$ from constant returns to scale in the production function

As in Eq. (G-15) without the population-growth correction term n, the rate of decrease of the capital asset price $(-p')$ is just equal to the marginal product of capital $\partial X/\partial K$.

Suppose that this marginal product X_K stays fairly constant over time. Then the above differential equation can be solved in the form

$$p(T) = p(t) \exp \left[-X_K (T - t)\right] \qquad (\text{G-34})$$

for $T > t$. Similarly, if we let i stand for the social rate of discount $jc' + \delta$ introduced in Eq. (G-17), with $\delta = 0$ for convenience in the current problem, and if further assume it to be approximately constant, then the relationship

$$U_C(T) = U_C(t) \exp \left[-i(T - t)\right] \qquad (\text{G-35})$$

must also hold.

An investment project in this model amounts to increasing the labor-capital ratio by an amount Δm in order to get an increment Δx in output per unit of capital. Following Eq. (G-33), there is a utility benefit $U_C w \Delta m$ associated with increased consumption from the employment increase, while the value of investable surplus increases by $p(\Delta x - w \Delta m)$. The total benefit over the planning horizon is

$$B = \int_{t_0}^{t_f} \left[U_C w \Delta m + p(\Delta x - w \Delta m)\right] dt \qquad (\text{G-36})$$

This can be rewritten as

$$B = \int_{t_0}^{t_f} U_C(t) \left\{ \frac{p(t)}{U_C(t)} \Delta x(t) - \left[\frac{p(t)}{U_C(t)} - 1\right] w \Delta m(t) \right\} dt$$

$$= U_C(t_0) \int_{t_0}^{t_f} \exp \left[-i(t - t_0)\right] \left[\frac{p}{U_C} \Delta x - \left(\frac{p}{U_C} - 1\right) w \Delta m \right] dt \qquad (\text{G-37})$$

where the second line follows from application of Eq. (G-35).

The criterion of Eq. (G-37) is essentially the same as one proposed by the United Nations Industrial Development Organization (UNIDO) in a book written by Partha Dasgupta, Stephen Marglin, and Amartya Sen. Note that it has three characteristics:

1. Net current benefits [in the bracketed expression in the second line of Eq. (G-37)] are discounted at the social rate of discount $i = jc' + \delta$. Since in practice j might, in a planners' utility function, take a value between 1 and 2,[2] c' might be a few percent per year, and δ might be 5 percent, i could take on a value of 0.1 or less. By comparison with profit rates routinely observed in underdeveloped countries, this discount rate looks low.

2. On the other hand, project outputs and capital inputs in the early years are valued at p/U_C, which, from Eq. (G-33), will exceed 1.

---

[2] If j is 2, marginal utility from consumption is 4 times as high for one person than for another with an income twice as large. If j is 1, marginal utility of the first person is twice as high; and if j is 0, there is no difference. Planners are supposed to pick a value of j on the basis of their own or their political superior's introspection.

3. The shadow wage rate will be $[(p/U_C) - 1]w$, which can either exceed or fall short of the market wage w depending on the magnitude of p/U_C. In any case, the price of output is blown up from its market value of unity by a bigger factor than is the wage from its value of w.

The criterion of Eq. (G-37) was derived by dividing through Eq. (G-36) by U_C and applying the discounting formula of Eq. (G-35). Alternatively, one could divide through by p and apply Eq. (G-34). The result is

$$B = p(t_0) \int_{t_0}^{t_f} \exp\left[-X_K(t - t_0)\right] \left[\Delta x - \left(1 - \frac{U_C}{p}\right) w \Delta m\right] dt \qquad \text{(G-38)}$$

a criterion proposed by Ian Little and James Mirrlees.[3] Here,

1. The discount rate is the marginal product of capital X_K. Presumably, its value can be ascertained by computing average rates of return implicit in recent government investment projects, looking at profit rates reported by corporations in reports filed with the income tax or regulatory authorities, or from macroeconomic considerations of the type discussed in Chaps. 6 and 7. A value between 15 and 30 percent might be reasonable for X_K. Discounting takes place at a much steeper rate in the Little-Mirrlees than in the UNIDO criterion.
2. Output is given a shadow valuation of unity, subject to some foreign exchange complications discussed in Chap. 13.
3. The shadow wage is $[1 - (U_C/p)]w$, less than the market wage.

Since both are based on the same surplus-labor assumptions, the two decision rules of Eqs. (G-37) and (G-38) are fundamentally the same, differing only in choice of numeraire. The numeraire commodity in the UNIDO rule is consumption in the base period, while investment is chosen by Little and Mirrlees.

The main problems one encounters in trying to apply either rule empirically are valuation of specific commodities, and calculation of the ratio p/U_C or its inverse for use in Eq. (G-37) or (G-38). The problem of commodity prices is tied in with whatever assumptions one makes about foreign-trade prices and is discussed in Chaps. 12 and 13.

About all we know from surplus-labor considerations is that, from Eq. (G-33),

---

[3] Actually, Little and Mirrlees work with a somewhat more complicated version of the surplus-labor problem, assuming that all workers in agriculture receive an average income a and have a lower agricultural marginal product y_m. They also maximize a welfare function based on both rural and urban consumption. Their version of the Marglin rule, Eq. (G-33), is

$$p(w - x_m) = U(c) - U(a) + U_a(a - y_m)$$

where c is the urban consumption level per head and U_a is the marginal utility from consumption in the rural sector. As before, the investment cost of moving a new worker from agriculture to industry appears on the left of this expression. The right side shows that the worker gains an amount of utility $[U(c) - U(a)]$ from additional consumption in the urban sector while also "leaving behind" an amount of new consumption $(a - y_m)$ in the rural sector. Those remaining derive additional marginal utility from this consumption increment, as measured by the factor U_a. All this is perhaps empirically more relevant than Eq. (G-33) but it is the same analytically.

p/U_C should exceed 1. One way to figure out its value would be to estimate an "optimal" marginal product of labor x_m and compare it to the market wage w. If the production function has constant returns to scale, it is easy to show that

$$x_m = \frac{dx}{dm} = \frac{d(X/K)}{d(L/K)} = \frac{X}{L} \left(1 - \frac{K}{X} X_K\right) \qquad \text{(G-39)}$$

If one knows output, employment, and the capital-output ratio in the modern sector, then a guess at the optimal marginal product of capital will give an estimate of x_m. Knowledge of the current modern-sector wage w and Eq. (G-33) then suffice to get p/U_C.

Alternatively, Eqs. (G-34) and (G-35) can be combined to give

$$(p/U_C)' = i - X_K < 0 \qquad \text{(G-40)}$$

This equation shows that p/U_C will fall over time, so long as the marginal product of capital X_K exceeds the social rate of discount i. If at some time T in the future the labor surplus disappears and (p/U_C) equals 1, then we can use this as an end condition in Eq. (G-40) to find values for the ratio at preceding times t,

$$\frac{p(t)}{U_C(t)} = \exp\left[(X_K - i)(T - t)\right], \quad t < T \qquad \text{(G-41)}$$

This is a fairly crude approximation, but something similar is required in any empirical application of the UNIDO criterion or the Little-Mirrlees variant. [One small advantage of the Little-Mirrlees rule is that the elusive ratio p/U_C shows up only in the shadow wage and not in the output shadow price, as in Eq. (G-37). However, if one undertakes a thorough sensitivity analysis of project choice with respect to this ratio, the advantage is more apparent than real.]

Finally, remember that all this long discussion quite critically depends on Lewis-type assumptions; in terms of Fig. 11-2, the labor-supply curve to the modern sector has got to look like S_I. If, for example, the labor-supply elasticity developed in Chap. 11 is large or negative, as in supply curve S_{II} of the figure, then the whole story changes. It is intuitively clear that, in the negative elasticity case, the shadow wage should far *exceed* the market wage, even with the Little-Mirrlees choice of numeraire! This sort of result shows the extreme dependence of shadow price estimates on the estimator's assessment of the stylized facts about the economy which is allegedly being modeled. Beyond noting this fact, a book like this one can provide very little additional guidance about this matter except to recommend skepticism about the shadow price estimates that any economist or institution, no matter how famous or influential, may actually produce.

SELECTED ADDITIONAL READINGS

Arrow, Kenneth J., and Mordecai Kurz: *Public Investment, The Rate of Return, and Optimal Fiscal Policy*, The Johns Hopkins Press, Baltimore and London, 1970. (Clear presentation of optimal growth theory; application to project evaluation in the one-sector neoclassical and other models.)

Bryson, Arthur E., Jr., and Yu-Chi Ho: *Applied Optimal Control*, Blaisdell Publishing Co., Waltham, Mass., 1969. (Intuitive presentation of optimal control theory, with mostly engineering applications.)

Chenery, Hollis B.: "The Application of Investment Criteria," *Quarterly Journal of Economics*, 67:76-96, 1953. (Early presentation of "social marginal product"—essentially Ramsey model—investment criteria for underdeveloped countries.)

Dorfman, Robert: "An Economic Interpretation of Optimal Control Theory," *American Economic Review*, 59:817-831, 1969. (Clear interpretation of optimal growth in the Ramsey model.)

Galenson, Walter, and Harvey Leibenstein: "Investment Criteria, Productivity, and Economic Development," *Quarterly Journal of Economics*, 69:343-379, 1955. (This article proposes the project selection rules discussed in Sec. G-4.)

Kahn, Alfred E.: "Investment Criteria in Development Programs," *Quarterly Journal of Economics*, 65:38-61, 1951. (Suggests social marginal-product project criteria.)

Little, Ian M. D., and James A. Mirrlees: *Project Appraisal and Planning for Development Planning*, Basic Books, New York, 1974. (Most recent statement of the set of project evaluation criteria originally proposed by the authors in the late 1960s.)

Marglin, Stephen A.: *Value and Price in the Labor Surplus Economy*, Oxford University Press, New York and London, 1976. (Belatedly published version of a mid-1960s manuscript that strongly influenced thinking about the project criteria discussed in Sec. G-4. Clear presentation of the material.)

Ramsey, Frank P.: "A Mathematical Theory of Savings," *Economic Journal*, 38:543-559, 1928. (First statement of the optimal growth problem discussed in Sec. G-2.)

Taylor, Lance: "Theoretical Foundations and Technical Implications," in C. R. Blitzer, P. B. Clark, and L. Taylor (eds.): *Economy-Wide Models and Development Planning*, Oxford University Press, New York and London, 1975. (The appendix to this paper summarizes the standard ways of setting terminal conditions in dynamic optimizing planning models.)

INDEXES

NAME INDEX

Abel, Andrew B., 66
ACMS (*see* Arrow, K. J.)
Adelman, Irma, 186*n*., 194
Ahluwalia, Isher, J., 173, 175
Ahluwalia, Montek S., 150*n*., 161
Arrow, Kenneth J., 97, 187*n*., 194, 232, 237, 245, 258
Atkinson, Anthony B., 95, 96

Bacha, Edmar L., 106*n*., 109*n*., 118, 150, 155, 162, 185, 194, 205*n*., 215
Bardhan, Pranab K., 167*n*., 173, 175
Beleza, Luis M. C. P., 66
Bell, Clive, 164, 167*n*., 175
Bhagwati, Jagdish, 120, 126, 127, 175, 182*n*., 195, 210*n*., 215
Black, Stephen L., 209, 215
Blitzer, Charles R., 28, 47, 178, 194, 215, 259
Bowles, Samuel, 161
Brody, A., 195
Brown, Alan, 222

Bruno, Michael, 93, 96, 123, 126, 129, 140, 182*n*., 194, 209, 215
Bryson, Arthur E., Jr., 245, 259
Bukharin, N. I., 173
Burger, Albert E., 28

Cardoso, Eliana A., 99*n*., 106, 118, 136, 137, 139-141
Cardoso, Teodora, *30*
Carneiro, Dionisio, 185, 194
Carter, A., 195
Cauas, Jorge, 133, 141
Cavallo, D. F., 129, 141
Chakravarty, Sukhamoy, 120, 126
Chenery, Hollis B., 48, 123, 126, 127, 161, 178, 194, 202*n*., 213, 215, 232, 237, 259
Chichilnisky, Graciela, 164, 170, 175
Clark, Paul G., 48, 178, 194
Clark, Peter B., 28, 47, 178, 191, 194, 215, 259

SUBJECT INDEX